for 29/02

MASS EXODUS

Mass Exodus

Catholic Disaffiliation in Britain and America since Vatican II

STEPHEN BULLIVANT

OXFORD
UNIVERSITY PRESS

OXFORD

UNIVERSITY PRESS

Great Clarendon Street, Oxford, OX2 6DP,
United Kingdom

Oxford University Press is a department of the University of Oxford.
It furthers the University's objective of excellence in research, scholarship,
and education by publishing worldwide. Oxford is a registered trade mark of
Oxford University Press in the UK and in certain other countries

Published in the United States of America by Oxford University Press
198 Madison Avenue, New York, NY 10016, United States of America

British Library Cataloguing in Publication Data
Data available

Library of Congress Control Number: 2018965164

ISBN 978–0–19–883794–7

Printed and bound by
CPI Group (UK) Ltd, Croydon, CR0 4YY

Links to third party websites are provided by Oxford in good faith and
for information only. Oxford disclaims any responsibility for the materials
contained in any third party website referenced in this work.

For Francis Benedict Bullivant,
the bravest baby in the world

Acknowledgements

Researching and writing a book like this makes one incur all manner of debts, personal and professional. Over the past five or so years, discussions with a large number of colleagues, friends, and/or students have helped to refine my ideas. These include—in no particular order—Dr Jacob Phillips, Victoria Seed, Fernanda Mee, Susan Longhurst, Hannah Vaughan-Spruce, Tim Kinnear, Julie Mersey, Marc Barnes, Fr David Poecking, Revd Dr Greg Murphy OP, Dr Maria Power, Mgr Andrew Burnham, Dr Damian Thompson, Greg Daly, Dr Brendan Ryan, Dan Hitchens, Luke Coppen, Gavan Ryan, Andrew Tucker, Caroline Farrow, Fr Robin Farrow, Jordan Summers Young, Paul Summers Young, Prof. Philip Booth, Prof. John Charmley, Prof. Francis Campbell, Revd Dr Ashley Beck, Prof. Peter Tyler, Dr Jon Lanman, Dr Hugh Turpin, Dr April Manalang, Dr Ben Clements, Dr Lois Lee, Dr Miguel Farias, Fr Ian O'Shea, Mgr John Walsh, Mgr Richard Madders, Br Shaun Bailham OP, Dr Brett Salkeld, Dr Catherine Pakaluk, William Johnstone, and Dr Joseph Shaw. I am especially grateful to Dr David McLoughlin for the wonderful vignette of post-war Catholic Birmingham quoted in Chapter 4.

A number of kind and constructively critical souls deigned to read and comment on various draft chapters: Revd Dr Stephen Morgan, Fr David Palmer, Dr Shaun Blanchard, Luke Arredondo, Fr Hugh Somerville-Knapman OSB, Dr Christopher Altieri, and Dcn Tom Gornick. These, along with OUP's anonymous peer reviewers, have made this a vastly better book than it could otherwise have been.

Marc Barnes did some sterling Research Assistant-ing towards gathering the data included in the Appendix. Maura McKeegan Barnes did a brilliant job in whipping the final manuscript—along with my various Britishisms, slang terms, and (she says) egregious slurs against Peter, Paul, and Mary—into submittable shape.

At Oxford University Press, Tom Perridge and Karen Raith have been the excellent and indulgent editors I have come to expect.

Several of the main ideas in *Mass Exodus*, and the odd bit of its phrasing, have been previously road-tested on the readers of various periodicals, including *Catechetical Leader, Pastoral Review, America,* the *Tablet,* and—above all—the *Catholic Herald.*

Most of all, though, I wish to express my deepest love and gratitude to my wife Joanna, daughters Grace and Alice, and baby son Francis: the best and most lovable family a man could ask for. Thank you for letting daddy write another of his 'boring, boring, boring' books.

Contents

List of Figures

List of Tables

1

Looking Foolish

On 11 October 1962, Pope John XXIII formally opened the Second Vatican Council. Its avowed purpose was, he told the thousands assembled in St Peter's Basilica, to 'really succeed in bringing men, families and nations to the appreciation of supernatural values'. While this would require some 'timely changes' to 'keep up to date with the changing conditions of this modern world, and of modern living', John declared that the Church must 'never for an instant lose sight of that sacred patrimony of truth inherited from the Fathers' (John XXIII 1962). Though not oblivious to the crises threatening humanity 'at the threshold of a new age' (John XXIII 1961), the future saint's optimism was both palpable and—as it soon proved—contagious: 'For with the opening of this Council a new day is dawning on the Church, bathing her in radiant splendour' (John XXIII 1962).

Vatican II ran until December 1965, outliving its convoker by two and a half years. With a serious claim to being 'the biggest meeting in the history of the world' (O'Malley 2006: 10), it is not surprising that the Council's teachings, spread across sixteen documents and broaching a huge range of topics, defy easy summary. That said, among the more prominent themes is undoubtedly that of the *laity*: that is, those baptized Catholics who are neither clergy nor belong to religious orders;[1] the overwhelming majority of the faithful, without

---

[1] This is the classic, shorthand definition, and the one used by the Council itself: 'The term laity is here understood to mean all the faithful except those in holy orders and those in the state of religious life specially approved by the Church' (*Lumen Gentium* 30). While it is generally agreed that defining the laity principally by what they are *not* is unsatisfactory (e.g., Lakeland 2004: 10–13; Ratzinger [1966] 2009: 89–90), it is admittedly a struggle to find a better, positive description that is so clear and succinct.

whom 'the Church would look foolish', as Newman famously quipped.[2]

The prominence Vatican II accorded to the laity is striking, especially in light of prior councils' reticence on the subject. It declares, for instance, that 'the laity, dedicated to Christ and anointed by the Holy Spirit, are marvellously called and wonderfully prepared so that ever more abundant fruits of the Spirit may be produced in them' (*Lumen Gentium* 34). As befits those called to 'consecrate the world itself to God' (*Lumen Gentium* 34), and possessing their *own* 'apostolate of evangelization and sanctification' (*Apostolicam Actuositatem* 6), the laity are thus 'not only bound to penetrate the world with a Christian spirit, but are also called to be witnesses to Christ in all things in the midst of human society' (*Gaudium et Spes* 43). This stirring vision of the laity has been enthusiastically received among commentators. To cite only recent examples, it is described as 'a central and crucial element of the legacy of the council' (Lakeland 2004: 81), 'one of its groundbreaking achievements' (Hunt 2015: 55), and as ushering in an 'age of the laity' (Hagstrom 2010: 78). It was only at the Second Vatican Council, we are often told, that the laity finally and fully *came of age* (Hagstrom 2010: 12–13).

*   *   *

It is now over fifty years since the close of Vatican II. According to recently published British data, nearly half of all born-and-raised Catholics no longer consider themselves to be Catholic; the vast majority of these—almost two out of every five British cradle Catholics—claim to have 'no religion'. These leavers *from* Catholicism outnumber converts *to* Catholicism by a ratio of ten to one. Furthermore, among those who do still identify as Catholic to pollsters, somewhat fewer than one in three attend church on a weekly basis—roughly the same proportion as attend 'never or practically never' (Bullivant 2016a). Meanwhile in the USA, much-publicized reports suggest that two in every five born-and-raised Catholics no longer identify as such; around half of these—i.e., one-in-five

---

[2] Contrary to how this story is often recounted, Newman specifically states that his original remark, to Bishop Ullathorne's question 'Who are the Laity?', was '*not* those words' ([1859–61] 1969: 141). Happily, his *Diary* entry for 22 May 1859 allowed him to record for posterity what he evidently *wished* he had said.

of all cradle Catholics—are now religious 'nones'. Stateside, there is roughly one convert for every seven who leave (Pew Research Center 2015a).

Towards the end of his detailed and nuanced study of 'the collapse of Boston's Catholic culture', the journalist Philip Lawler observes:

> Today, former Catholics constitute the largest religious bloc in the Boston area. Some of these ex-Catholics have joined other religious bodies. Others take no interest in religious affairs. Still others think of themselves as Catholic, but they neither practice their faith nor honour its teachings. In the opening years of the twenty-first century, practising Catholics are once again a small minority in Boston [. . .]. (2008: 247)

Boston, once America's archetypal Catholic town, may be a special case. But it is not *that* special. Leading American sociologist Michael Hout notes, 'More than ever, people raised Catholic are leaving; most drop out of organized religion altogether' (2016: 1). In the view of the Fordham historian Patrick Hornbeck: 'deconversion—the process of moving from identification and active engagement with Roman Catholicism to disaffiliation and disengagement—is one of the most theologically significant phenomena in contemporary American Roman Catholic life' (2011: 1).

The same is true not only of Britain, but of a good number of other nations too, and on several continents. This fact has been acknowledged for at least forty years by the highest levels of the Catholic hierarchy. As early as 1975, Paul VI could observe that 'Today there is a very large number of baptized people who for the most part have not formally renounced their Baptism but who are entirely indifferent to it and not living in accordance with it' (*Evangelii Nuntiandi* 56). In 1990, Pope John Paul II reiterated these concerns: 'Entire groups of the baptized have lost a living sense of the faith, or even no longer consider themselves members of the Church, and live a life far removed from Christ and his Gospel' (*Redemptoris Missio* 33). And much more recently, Pope Francis observed in 2013 that '[We cannot] overlook the fact that in recent decades there has been a breakdown in the way Catholics pass down the Christian faith to the young. It is undeniable that many people feel disillusioned and no longer identify with the Catholic tradition' (*Evangelii Gaudium* 70).

At least in certain areas, it would seem that the postconciliar laity have not so much 'come of age', as that they have packed up, moved out of the family home, and rarely—if ever—call.

DISAFFILIATES AND DISAFFILIATION

This is a book about two things. The first is a group of *people*; a very large and diffuse group, comprising men and women, young and old, and all manner of races and ethnicities. The second is a *process*, or perhaps better a *pattern* or *trajectory*; it too is a decidedly diverse phenomenon, involving historical, social, cultural, religious, psychological, and no doubt a great many other sorts of elements. The people I will be calling, primarily, *disaffiliates*. The process or pattern I will be calling *disaffiliation*.

At a basic level, the phrase 'Catholic disaffiliate' can be defined quite easily. It is simply *somebody who would once have considered themselves to be a (Roman) Catholic,[3] but who now no longer does*. This obviously includes those who converted to Catholicism in adulthood, just as much as it does those who were born into, and thus brought up within, Catholic families. For certain practical reasons, especially sheer numbers and the limits of the datasets we will be

---

[3] The qualifier 'Roman' is used in this definition to exclude members of churches who describe themselves as Catholic, but who are not in communion with the Pope (for example, Anglo-Catholics or Old Catholics). It is *not* intended to limit the scope of our inquiries only to Catholics of the Latin Rite. While in practice the vast majority of the disaffiliates discussed herein will undoubtedly be Latin Rite Catholics, members of the Eastern Catholic Churches in communion with Rome (e.g., the Melkite Greek Catholic Church, the Ukrainian Catholic Church, the Syro-Malabar Catholic Church) are equally 'eligible', as too are any and all members of, say, the various Anglican Ordinariates within the Latin Church. In fact, since those administering major national surveys and censuses do not (understandably enough) care about such ecclesiological details, it will almost certainly be the case that some of these types of Catholics appear 'anonymously' in the statistics which will form the focus of Chapter 2.

Due to immigration over a long of period of time, there are in fact significant numbers of Eastern Catholics in both Britain and the USA, the main geographical foci of this study. Though only briefly mentioned directly in these pages, there is a great deal of interesting future research to be done on how the overall dynamics of Catholic disaffiliation apply (or not) in these individual communities. At present, what little (largely anecdotal) evidence there is, is decidedly mixed. On the one hand, Britain's Syro-Malabar community, totalling an estimated 40,000, appears to be doing rather well for itself: well enough to have been newly granted its own Eparchy (only the third to be erected outside the traditional homeland of Kerala, India). On the other, though, witness this informed estimate concerning the fortunes of America's Eastern Catholics as a whole:

> Eastern Catholics are notoriously bad at numbers- and record-keeping, and their small size often means that larger surveys [...] fail to pick them up because they are statistically insignificant. Trying to get a sense of current demographics is thus a fraught business, but what records we have clearly indicate massive decline. (DeVille 2017: 246 n. 76)

using, it is these latter 'cradle' Catholics who will be our main topic of concern. Also obviously, our definition includes both those who now identify with a different Christian or other religious tradition, and those who now identify as having no religious affiliation whatsoever: we shall term these two types 'switchers' and 'leavers' respectively.

More will be said about the various conceptual issues surrounding affiliation and identity later on in this chapter. Here, it is worth stressing that the definition I am adopting relies on a substantially subjective understanding of disaffiliate: that is, it depends on whether individuals *consider themselves* to have been, but no longer to be, a Catholic. This will be most evident when we survey a wealth of statistical data in Chapter 2. There, a disaffiliate will be simply defined as someone answering 'Catholic' when asked their religion of upbringing, but *something other than Catholic* when asked their current religious affiliation.

According to the formal teaching of the Catholic Church, our disaffiliates remain part of it—and always will—by virtue of their baptism, whether they like it or not. 'Baptism incorporates us *into the Church*', and moreover 'seals the Christian with the indelible spiritual mark (*character*) of his belonging to Christ. No sin can erase this mark, even if sin prevents Baptism from bearing the fruits of salvation' (*Catechism* 1267, 1272). This theological fact does not, of course, obviate the empirical one that 'millions of individuals *do* describe themselves as "former", "ex-", "post-" or "recovering" Catholics' (Beaudoin and Hornbeck 2013: 35). (Incidentally, those with a penchant for the niceties of canon law may find much to interest them in footnote 4; others, probably not.[4]) Chapters 2 and 3 of this book will

---

[4] On three occasions, the original version of the 1983 Code of Canon Law cites the possibility of a baptized Catholic having made what it calls an *actus formalis defectionis ab Ecclesia catholica*, that is, 'a formal act of defection from the Catholic Church'. All of these occur in the context of marriage, for example: 'A marriage between two persons, one of whom has been baptized in the Catholic Church or received into it and has not defected from it by a formal act and the other of whom is not baptized, is invalid' (Can. 1086 §1; see also cans 1117, 1124). The Code offers no further clue as to what such an act might entail. Having 'for quite some time [received] a considerable number of [...] questions and requests for clarification', the Pontifical Council for Legislative Texts (PCLJ) eventually released a statement setting out 'the requirements or juridical formalities that would be necessary so that such an action would constitute a true "formal act" of defection' (2006). While the specific, convoluted procedure need not be recounted here, its fulfilment would authorize a local bishop to have explicit mention of the occurrence of a '*defectio ab Ecclesia catholica actu formali*' to be formally added against that person's name in a baptismal register. Broadly similar

present a detailed, quantitative and qualitative, portrait of *Catholic disaffiliates.*

'Catholic disaffiliation', meanwhile, has two main senses herein. In the first sense, it is simply the cognate noun that goes with disaffiliate, such that when I refer to a country's 'disaffiliation rate' I simply mean the percentage of disaffiliates among those who were born and raised as Catholics. Likewise, if I refer to 'the phenomenon of disaffiliation', I mean simply the phenomenon of there being people who are disaffiliates. In the second more specific sense, though, it refers to the *process(es)* whereby those born-and-raised have *come to be* disaffiliates. This can refer to an *individual's* path to disaffiliation, or in more generalized terms, to the shared trajectories of whole groups of people. This will occupy Chapters 4–7 of this book, where I will attempt to construct a plausible, though selective, history of disaffiliation, exploring how and why it happened when it did, beginning in the immediate preconciliar period and ending in the present day. Admittedly, the slight ambivalence between the generic and

procedures, albeit using less Latin, are available in some other religious denominations, as for instance in the national Lutheran Churches of several Scandinavian countries (Niemalä 2007; Lüchau and Andersen 2012) and the Church of Jesus Christ of the Latter Day Saints.

Critically, however, the PCLJ's statement is at pains to emphasize that, in a Catholic context, such an act is a purely 'juridical-administrative' one, and *in no way* confers a 'true separation from the constitutive elements of the life of the Church'. Hence: 'It remains clear, in any event, that the sacramental bond of belonging to the Body of Christ that is the Church, conferred by the baptismal character, is an ontological and permanent bond which is not lost by reason of any act or fact of defection.' To put it mildly, this created a very strange state of affairs (cf. Hornbeck 2013: 269 n. 35)—essentially, a *Hotel California*-esque situation whereby 'You can check out anytime you like, but you can never leave'.

Three years later, Pope Benedict XVI then issued a decree simply deleting the relevant passages from the 1983 Code, unsurprisingly citing 'numerous pastoral problems' (2009a) thrown up by the wording. As was made clear in a commentary by Cardinal Coccopalmerio, the Prefect of the PCLJ, one of these problems had to do with the fact that in certain central European countries, people pay a civil 'worship tax' which accrues to their respective denominations unless they specifically opt out (2010). Naturally, it was this financial opting out that the PCLJ had meant by its reference to a 'juridical-administrative act' in 2006, somewhat euphemistically glossed with 'the removal of one's name from a Church membership registry maintained by the government in order to produce certain civil consequences'. While intended for a specific purpose—and, as has been noted, explicitly not conceived as *actually* removing a person from the Church—it is hardly surprising that some disaffected Catholics sought to exploit this canonical possibility to have themselves formally removed from the Church, even if only 'symbolically'. Since 2009 this possibility now, of course, no longer exists.

particular sense of disaffiliation is here a little unfortunate. It would certainly be helpful if there were a word like *disaffiliatization* that one could use to distinguish the sense of a process or pattern. But there isn't, and there are already enough obscure pieces of jargon in this work without inventing yet more. The ambiguity will have to remain. I trust my readers to be sufficiently insightful and attentive to understand which I mean on the odd occasion when misinterpretation might feasibly make some genuine difference.

Also regarding terminology, certain minefields must be navigated when describing people in a specific way. This is especially so with a sensitive subject like this where, with some justification, people can feel unfairly judged by certain labels, which they do not typically use of themselves. Within the modest but growing sociological literature in this area, a number of terms to describe our 'disaffiliates' have currency (see Streib et al. 2009; Hammer and Cragun 2011; Wright et al. 2011). Some have, at least to certain ears, an undeniably pejorative flavour: defector, apostate, drop out, deserter. Understandably, these have now generally fallen out of favour. Several others have been suggested in their place—exiter, deconvert, disidentifier, disaffiliate—though none has yet become standard. Disaffiliate is the primary term chosen here. It is intended simply as a shorthand, and hopefully not pejorative-sounding, way of saying: *somebody who would once have considered themselves to be a (Roman) Catholic, but who now no longer does*. Other specific bits of terminology will be adopted, or occasionally coined, in due course, but these will be explained as we go.

While we are on the subject of drawing distinctions, it is worth noting that discussions of disaffiliation often form but one part of general inquiries into a much wider 'Catholic crisis' (e.g., McInerny 1998; Greeley 2004a; Steinfels 2003; Lawler 2008; Shaw 2013). This is typically taken to encompass a number of other phenomena evident in the decades after the Council: significant numbers of clergy and religious leaving their vocations, and severe declines in the number of those wanting to replace them; crises of identity among Catholic charitable and educational institutions; demonstrable gaps between Church teaching and what the majority of lay Catholics believe or do, including on a very broad range of topics relating to sexuality; the abuse crisis, including all the manifold tragic causes and effects that form a part of it; and rather more besides. While several of these will feature, in some cases very heavily, in what follows, none is a direct object of study or comment here. My interest in them *here* is solely insofar as they do, or don't, help shed light on the phenomenon of disaffiliation.

That said, the phenomenon of Catholic disaffiliation is indeed being hypothesized here as part of the far broader and better-documented phenomenon of *lapsation*: that is, of Catholics falling away (or 'lapsing') from normative levels of Catholic practice or belief, while—typically, at least—retaining some sense of 'belonging'.[5] In a great many countries, lapsation has long been recognized as a dominant feature of the Catholic landscape: official Church materials, for example, speak of there being 'approximately four million' lapsed Catholics in England and Wales alone (CBCEW 2015). Viewed against this backdrop, disaffiliation becomes evident as a kind of extreme case of lapsation. To some degree, this is a matter of common sense. Large numbers of cradle Catholics never pray or attend Mass, and indeed no longer believe in God, yet still regard themselves to be 'Catholic' at least to the extent of saying as much to those conducting sociological surveys. However, it is far less common to find Mass-attending, Natural Family Planning-practising cradle Catholics who now tick the 'no religion' box. That is to say, while one often finds

---

[5] It will not have escaped some readers' notice that 'lapsed' is as susceptible to criticisms of being negative, and indeed 'of reflecting inherent bias in favor of religion' (Cragun and Hammer 2011: 150), as are terms like 'apostate' and 'defector' (see also Hornbeck 2011: 8–9; Casson 2014: 8). For this reason a wealth of apparently less judgemental-sounding terms, such as 'non-practising', 'non-churchgoing', 'inactive', or even 'resting' have been suggested in various quarters, though none has yet been widely adopted. Without denying all this, it remains true that lapsation is both the traditional phraseology within the sociology of religion, and retains a wide currency within the Catholic community itself—*including*, critically, among large numbers of those who seem happy enough to describe themselves as being 'lapsed'. Hence 'lapsed' will appear throughout this book, used more-or-less interchangeably with some of the newer synonyms like 'inactive' and 'non-practising'.

A little tangentially, though testifying to the importance and continuing salience of 'lapsed' as a category *within* Catholicism, it may be instructive to quote the following passage from Terry Eagleton's memoir *The Gatekeeper*:

Even in those pious days [i.e., Salford in north-west England in the 1940s and 1950s], being a lapsed Catholic was almost acceptable; it was rather like being a country rather than a city member of a club, still on the books but less in evidence around the joint. 'Lapsed Catholic' was a convenient label for ensuring that you never actually left the Church; it simply shifted you from one ontological category to another, rather like resigning your peerage but staying on in politics. In any case, it put you in some remarkably distinguished company. (2002: 9–10)

some sense of 'belonging' without belief and practice, one almost never finds significant levels of belief and practice without some sense of belonging. Among the more intricate and interesting topics broached in this study will be the interplay between the lapsed in general, and their specific (and rapidly growing) disaffiliate subset.

GEOGRAPHICAL FOCUS

For reasons soon to be explained, Britain and the USA are the twin foci of this study. While comparisons with other countries will occasionally be drawn, they are not the true objects of this research. Yet before so restricting our attention, some appreciation of the cross-national breadth, scale, and diversity of Catholic disaffiliation is in order. Quite apart from being interesting in its own right, this wider perspective will highlight how Britain and the USA are simply two possible case studies. Conclusions drawn on the basis of these may have wider import and application, but equally they may well not.

In this regard, consider the data presented in Figure 1.1, derived from the 2008 wave of the International Social Survey Programme (ISSP). The selection of countries is admittedly haphazard. Of the forty-four countries in the ISSP, these are the twenty-nine with sufficiently large Catholic populations to register over a hundred respondents who were brought up as one. Nevertheless, the data are indeed suggestive.

Let us begin with those countries with relatively high levels of disaffiliation: say, where over 20 per cent of cradle Catholics now claim either a different religious affiliation, or none at all. Twelve countries fit this description, drawn from five separate continents: Africa (South Africa, Kenya), North America (USA), South America (Uruguay), Oceania (Australia and New Zealand), and Europe (Britain, France, Belgium, Netherlands, Switzerland, and Spain from the west, plus post-communist Czech Republic). While in most countries the majority of disaffiliates now claim 'no religion', this is not so in three: South Africa, Kenya, and the USA. It is perhaps also worth noting how well-represented Anglophone countries are on the list. Significant rates of disaffiliation are not, however, common to all countries. Among the eleven countries with the lowest disaffiliation rates—say, less than 10 per cent—there is again a good range of continental

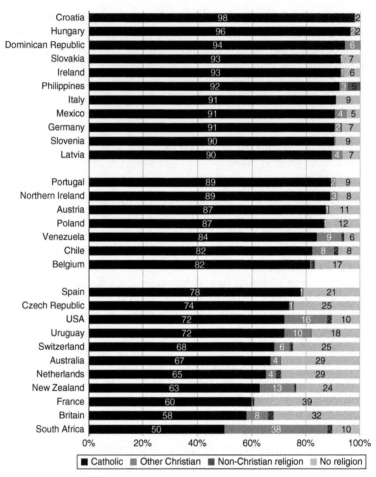

Figure 1.1. Current religious affiliation of cradle Catholics in selected countries (2008)

Source: ISSP (2008; weighted data)

representation: Africa (Tanzania), Asia (Philippines), Latin America (Mexico, Dominican Republic), and Europe (also with western— Ireland, Italy, Germany—and post-communist—Croatia, Hungary, Slovakia, Slovenia—representatives).

One graph, using fairly old data from an odd range of countries, should not be freighted with too much significance. Nevertheless, it can at least be said that disaffiliation is by no means universal or inevitable. This fact is well-illustrated by the presence of adjacent countries (i.e., ones where, all other things being equal, one might expect to see similarities based on shared geography, history, socio-economics, etc.) in both our highest and lowest lists. But that important caveat aside, it is abundantly clear that disaffiliation is a significant trend within contemporary Catholicism, *and a global one*. It is not, as it is often assumed to be, simply a 'local' concern for a fairly narrow band of western European countries, plus a handful of others in the Anglosphere. Disaffiliation is demonstrably a large and non-localized issue for the Catholic Church.

Why, then, the decision to limit the scope of our investigations to just two countries? And why Britain and the USA in particular?

Probably the most important reasons are straightforwardly practical. Above all, there is the simple constraint that this monograph seeks to present a systematic exploration of Catholic disaffiliates and Catholic disaffiliation over the fifty-or-so years since the Second Vatican Council. Almost of necessity, this exploration will be part theological, part sociological, and part historical. The kind of detail required to do all these things well, and to present them in a manner that is sufficiently attractive to be worth the while of both a publisher and some readers, impose necessary limits. While a single case study could have been achieved more easily and more thoroughly, I felt that some measure of cross-cultural comparison would greatly enrich the whole. The possibility of three case studies was also considered (e.g., adding either Ireland, Canada, or Australia to the two already here), but rejected so as not to dilute the depth of analysis.

Britain and the USA are places I know quite well, including their specific Catholic cultures. I have lived in Britain all my life, and have been a Catholic there since 2008.[6] While I have no pretence of being an American 'insider', it is a country I am fortunate enough to have travelled widely in, and to visit often. I also have many American friends and colleagues, helpfully including leading scholars of both Catholicism and nonreligiosity.

The choice of Britain and the USA may be rationalized on deeper grounds also. On the one hand, the two have much in common: both

---

[6] Callum Brown, noting the personal commitments of certain sociologists of religion, remarks: 'There may be no flaw in this, though a "declaration of interests" may sometimes be helpful' (2012: 5). This is good advice. My own views on a wide range of religious and moral topics are discoverable via Google. The extent to which these may colour or taint my scholarship is a matter for others to judge.

are western economic and geopolitical 'powers' (albeit not equally so), possess a common language, enjoy a great deal of cultural overlap, and have a somewhat parallel history over our period of interest (including some episodes of special interest here, such as the Second World War, the Baby Boom, a rollercoaster 1960s, the Cold War and its ultimate thaw, and major acts of Islamist terrorism in the early twenty-first century). On the other hand, sociologists of religion have long viewed the countries as contrasting extremes, with Britain emblematic of 'Godless Europe' (Weigel 2005; Jenkins 2007: 26–54), and the USA as essentially still justifying Alexis de Tocqueville's impression that 'there remains here a greater foundation of Christianity than in any other country in the world' ([1831] 1996: 57). Accordingly, there is significant argument over which of the two constitutes the *exception* to expected patterns, and why (e.g., Davie 2002; Greeley 2004b: 197–214). Yet as already noted, both countries have relatively high levels of Catholic disaffiliates. This generates an interesting question: how can such different socio-religious contexts generate broadly similar effects; why is disaffiliation such a significant feature of the Catholic landscape in what are ordinarily considered to be among the most and the least religious of developed nations? This conundrum could itself justify this book's specific choice of foci. In attempting to solve it, we will note other curious coincidences in the recent religious pasts of Britain and America (Bullivant 2010), and indeed question whether they are quite such opposites as they are so often taken to be (cf. Bruce 2011: 157–76; Voas and Chaves 2016).

POST CONCILIUM, ERGO PROPTER CONCILIUM?

The beginning of this chapter deliberately framed the central issues surrounding Catholic disaffiliation in a certain way: one implying, though not *quite* stating, some clear connection between the Second Vatican Council and large numbers of cradle Catholics becoming sufficiently estranged from the Church as no longer to consider themselves a part of it. One of the primary purposes of this monograph is to investigate whether, how, and to what extent that implication is true—at least, in Britain and the USA. Is the *since Vatican II* of the book's title a mere indicator of chronology, narrowing my investigation to an arbitrary half-century-or-so period? If so, then

I might just as well have subtitled it, say, *Catholic Disaffiliation since Dylan Went Electric*. Or does it instead signify a causal link, or more likely a great web of them: direct and indirect, intended and accidental? If that is so, then *since Vatican II* ought really to be understood as meaning *because of Vatican II*. Of course, causality is notoriously difficult to prove within the realms of human social life and history. Nevertheless, these are the precisely the kinds of judgements—supported by the best available evidence, but even then, tentatively and with an openness to future correction—which it will be necessary to make in the course of a study such as this.

This is not the place to embark upon an extensive literature review: we shall be meeting and engaging with *quite enough* existing scholarship and opinion in the following pages as it is. Nonetheless, it is worth observing that Catholic commentators, at least, typically divide into three broad tendencies.[7]

The first lays the blame—and blame it indeed is—squarely at the door of Vatican II, whether directly or indirectly. Even a cursory acquaintance with the relevant data presents a compelling, *prima facie* case in its favour. As we have seen, the Council devoted a great and unprecedented deal of attention to laypeople, and many of its most striking reforms were explicitly designed with them upmost in mind. Since it is certainly true that 'the Council *wanted* something to happen' (O'Malley 2006: 33), it requires no great deductive leap to ascribe what *did* then happen, even if quite contrary to what the Council Fathers had hoped would be the result, to Vatican II itself. Graph lines charting severe declines first in practice, then later in belief and self-identification, in the years and decades after the Council make the case for the prosecution very strong indeed.

That said, ascribing contemporary Catholic disaffiliation wholly or largely to Vatican II does not necessarily tell us a great deal. There is a range of things which the phrase 'Vatican II' might, and in practice often does, include. What does it mean to say that Vatican II is (or isn't) to blame (or thank) for something? Presumably, one does not mean the sheer fact *that* there was such-and-such a gathering with such-and-such a name. Rather, what is normally meant is one or more of (i) some specific aspect(s) of the Council's teaching, or (ii) the

---

[7] The following paragraphs seek to capture certain *general tendencies* within the existing scholarship, rather than to give well-rounded and nuanced accounts of individual writers' own positions.

way in which that teaching was understood or implemented, and/or (iii) some particular thing that some combination of this teaching/understanding/implementation either gave rise to, or failed to give rise to, *whether intentionally or not*. We will meet many particular examples in the pages to come, but we may note here that these distinct levels are often difficult to separate in practice. The liturgical reforms—many people's prime suspect—are, as we shall see in Chapter 5, a case in point.

While commentators in my second camp don't necessarily deny the lapsation/disaffiliation problem, they tend not to dwell on it when discussing the Council's reception and legacy.[8] When it is broached, however, the emphasis tends to be on how the conciliar 'age of the laity' has been somehow thwarted. This comes in two main versions. The first tends to indict supposedly conservative tendencies or figures within the Church itself for having either applied brakes to the Council's far-reaching reforms, or even actively betrayed them. While there is no shortage of contenders here, perhaps the chief culprit is Pope Paul VI, with his reaffirmation of the prohibition on artificial means of contraception in 1968—a date soon enough after the Council to offer a serious counter-interpretation for some of the 'decline and fall' statistics otherwise attributed to Vatican II. The fallout surrounding *Humanae Vitae* is a vast and fascinating topic in its own right and, like the liturgical reforms, will be treated as such in Chapter 5. Here though, let us quote the influential assessment of Andrew Greeley, writing in 1985:

> To deny that the abruptly begun and abruptly ended decline in Catholic religious practice is the result of a violent reaction to the birth control encyclical is to fly in the face of research evidence of such quality and persuasiveness that on any other matter there would be almost no room for doubt. (1985: 57)

Several things are worth noting here. Firstly, the fact that a well-documented decline in Mass attendance since the 1960s is regarded as having been only a *temporary* drop, hence 'there does not appear to be any long-term tendency towards decline' (Greeley 1985: 72).

---

[8] Incidentally, it is remarkable just how many books and articles about either the Council as a whole, or even on its engagement with the laity specifically, essentially ignore the kinds of sociological evidence with which we shall be so preoccupied herein.

Secondly, that blame for this is apportioned exclusively to *Humanae Vitae*, with no responsibility for any negative pastoral phenomena accorded to the Council or its implementation. Indeed, as Greeley writes elsewhere in the book: 'virtually no one has left the Catholic Church in the wake of the changes since the Second Vatican Council beyond that which would have been expected [from earlier trends]' (Greeley 1985: 50) and 'There is nothing in the empirical data available to us to suggest that the generation of Catholics who have grown up since the Second Vatican Council are any less loyal, any less committed, any less devout than their predecessors' (Greeley 1985: 173). Greeley's later views on these subjects will be discussed in due course.

The third main tendency is, like the second, also a form of 'frustration thesis'. This one, however, focuses less on factors internal to the Church (curial intransigence, reactionary popes, or whatever) as it does on wider social and cultural pressures. Pointedly looking beyond the 'Catholic bubble', this approach recognizes that problems with non-practice, disaffiliation, and much else besides are not just present in other Christian denominations, but are frequently far more openly talked and worried about (Schultz and Schultz 2014; White 2014). Furthermore, there is some evidence to show that these issues were already beginning well before the 1960s, both inside and outside Catholicism. Only the Catholic Church held a major ecumenical Council in the mid-1960s, and was one of very few denominations still affirming the traditional Christian teaching on contraception. Hence it is short-sighted to assume that the greater part of the pastoral crisis is due to one, or both, of those things alone (Douthat 2018: 27–8). The French theologian, and later cardinal, Yves Congar put this general observation well in 1984:

> I do not believe that the present crisis is the fruit of Vatican II. On the one hand, much of the disturbing facts we see today were on their way already in the 1950s, sometimes already in the 1930s. Vatican II has been followed by a socio-cultural mutation whose amplitude, radicality, rapidity, and global character have no equivalent in any other period in history. The Council felt this mutation, but it did not know every aspect nor its violence.   (Quoted in Faggioli 2012a: 80)

This basic approach—essentially, that declines in Catholic practice and affiliation have occurred *despite* Vatican II, and assuredly not *because* of it, due to an unprecedentedly challenging socio-religious climate—receives considerable support from historians and sociologists of religion with no special interest in Catholicism. The scholarship surrounding 'secularization' is admittedly a vast, ever-growing, and controverted field. However, I consider myself in very good, mainstream sociological company in stating that, *at a minimum*, the general populations of much of western Europe, North America, and Australasia are demonstrably less religious than in the past, as measured by the standard indicators of identification, belief, and practice (see Bruce 2011; Brown 2012). Albeit with some local variations, this holds true across virtually all mainstream Christian denominations (see King-Hele 2010). Quite *when* and *how* this all began is a matter of some debate, and almost certainly differs from place to place. Yet there is a strong current of thinking that assigns a special place to the 'long' 1960s, either as an actual starting point, or as the decade in which earlier-initiated processes suddenly and decisively bore fruit. In the words of the social historian Callum Brown:

> In unprecedented numbers, the British people since the 1960s have stopped going to church, have allowed their church membership to lapse, have stopped marrying in church and have neglected to baptise their children. [...] The cycle of inter-generational renewal of Christian affiliation, a cycle which had for so many centuries tied the people however closely or loosely to the churches and to Christian moral benchmarks, was permanently disrupted in the 'swinging sixties'. Since then, a formerly religious people have entirely forsaken organised Christianity in a sudden plunge into a truly secular condition.
>
> (2001: 1)

Britain is undoubtedly a striking, though hardly unique, case. While nothing like a collapse on this scale has occurred in the USA, neither is it so immune as has previously been thought. The American 1960s, of course, were even more disruptive than the British ones. And if the USA has not yet witnessed 'European' levels of decline (and might never), American religiosity is no longer looking quite as buoyant as it once did. This is a point to which we shall return in Chapter 7.

This wider vista of across-the-board religious decline complicates the Catholic picture in important ways. In common with every other 'community composed of men' (*Gaudium et Spes* 1), the Catholic Church does not exist within a social or cultural vacuum. Neither, therefore, did the Second Vatican Council occur within one. Quite the opposite, in fact: the 1960s were a tumultuous time for all sorts of reasons. Hence even without the upheavals wrought by Vatican II and

Humanae Vitae, it seems inconceivable that Catholic pastoral life would have been entirely unaffected. And if the experiences of practically every other Christian community are any kind of guide, then practice, belief, and affiliation would almost certainly have suffered to some degree, and perhaps a very serious one, anyway. All of this makes interrogating the specific connections between Vatican II and the kinds of disaffiliation rates cited earlier all the trickier. Indeed, suppose one wanted to perform an experiment whereby certain changes were introduced to the life and practice of a religious group, in order to gauge the relative impact, positive or negative, of such changes. To do this, one would pick a time and place in which as many other surrounding factors as possible stayed the same. Western Europe or North America during the 'Turbulent Sixties' (Ahlstrom and Hall 2004: 1079) is, to put it mildly, a far cry from so-called 'laboratory conditions'. Among leading scholars charting and/or explaining societal secularization, few devote much attention at all to Vatican II or any other Catholic-specific matters: while such denomination-specific matters might add a bit of 'local colour' to the precise patterns of decline, they are considered epiphenomenal to the general trends.

The paragraphs above sketch three basic positions vis-à-vis Vatican II and contemporary disaffiliation. The first attributes the current situation overwhelmingly to the Council, whether directly (i.e., to its specific intentions and/or formal teachings) or indirectly (i.e., to the manifold ways in which those intentions/teachings were received and put into practice).[9] The second attributes it not to the Council and its implementation, but rather to a more-or-less deliberate thwarting of the Council's vision—if not, much more loosely, its *spirit*—by forces

---

[9] It need hardly be said that there is scope for a significant diversity of diagnoses within this category, not least because it elides the theologically fundamental distinction between the 'letter' of the Council, and its 'reception' afterwards. The classic expression of this comes from the 1985 Synod of Bishops: 'In truth, there certainly have [. . .] been shadows in the post-council period, in part due to an incomplete understanding and application of the Council, in part to other causes. However, in no way can it be affirmed that everything which took place after the Council was caused by the Council' (quoted in Faggioli 2012a: 12). This critical distinction will, however, receive due recognition in later chapters. It is also worth noting here, though, that while the Synod is correct in affirming (with Greeley) that not everything *post Concilium* is necessarily *propter Concilium*, it is indeed possible for the Council to have been a (or even *the*) cause of things which it did not intend. After all, there is a reason why scholars of Vatican II are fond of pointing out that 'There is such a thing as the law of unintended consequences!' (Komonchak 2012: 167).

within the Church itself, with the promulgation of *Humanae Vitae* in 1968 often depicted as an early, and catastrophic, harbinger of things to come. The third regards the pastoral strategies emanating from the Council to have effectively been neutered by wider social and cultural forces, such as have taken their toll on so many other Christian groups in the postconciliar half-decade or so: whatsoever good or ill *might* have flowed from Vatican II in this area, is comparatively irrelevant when compared to the external pulls of secularization. Each of these three has its defenders; we shall be meeting a good number of them. The tendencies are, moreover, not so mutually exclusive as they might at first appear. It is, for example, perfectly possible that one large slice of the disaffiliation pie is attributable to the conciliar renewal itself, another to the fact that the reforms did not go nearly far enough, and a third to some mixture or another of modernization, pluralization, and increasing 'existential security'—to cite just three popular contenders for what causes secularization—that have equally eroded, say, levels of Anglican/Episcopalian practice and self-identification. Catholic disaffiliation is, as shall be quantified in the next chapter, a pretty big pie. Other combinations are also possible. For instance, the Council *might* actually have had a hugely positive and lasting effect on engaging and keeping the laity, resulting in significantly lower disaffiliation than the Church would otherwise have suffered under the ravages of late-modern, western secularization.

Again to quote Andrew Greeley: 'That a change has occurred since the end of the Vatican Council does not mean that the council has caused the change' (1985: 15). That was true in the mid-1980s and, as a matter of elementary logic and common sense, it remains true today. But equally, if an event of such magnitude in the life of the Church as the Second Vatican Council *hasn't* played some major role—positive or negative, direct or indirect, intended or accidental—then that would itself be an astonishing fact, and one well worth discovering. What is more, it would require considerable argument and explanation in its own right.

RELIGIOUS IDENTITIES

Before explaining the structure of *Mass Exodus*, one further background issue requires attention. Throughout this investigation, our central analytic category is one of *identity*: 'a multi-dimensional classification or mapping of the human world and our places in it, as individuals and as members of collectivities' (Jenkins 2008: 5). The very notion of a 'Catholic disaffiliate' depends upon both the reality of a specific type of religious identity (i.e., 'Catholic'), and there being something significant about people changing it. But what precisely is a person doing when they describe themselves, either internally or to others, as 'a Catholic'? And what does it mean for someone to have regarded him or herself as a Catholic *in the past*, but now to do so no longer? Further, do self-designations such as 'none' or 'ex-Catholic' signify simply the absence of a particular identity, or can and do they function as substantive identities in themselves?

While different perspectives on these questions will emerge, implicitly and explicitly, over the course of the book, it is necessary to make some preliminary observations here. The first is simply that *real-life* religious identities, of all types, are rarely sharply or straightforwardly defined. If religious identification is, at base, 'a personal cognitive attachment to a religious group or tradition' (Sherkat 2014: 31), one must therefore be sensitive to 'the complex and messy relationships between [. . .] different aspects and forms of religion which make up the "fuzzy frontiers" of religious identity' (Gregg and Scholefield 2015: 10). Statistics presented in Chapter 2, showing that a large proportion of self-identifying Catholics do not attend church on any regular basis, and sometimes do not even believe in a God with any great conviction, let alone any more specific doctrines that appear in the *Catechism*, should thus not come as any great surprise.

This leads to the second point: that there are a large number of reasons why people might count themselves as 'belonging' to a religious tradition, not all of which map easily onto that tradition's own 'ideal'. The kind of rich, qualitative work needed to tease out the varieties of what 'being Catholic' can mean (it will, of course, mean very different things to different people) has, to the best of my knowledge, not yet been carried out. Some hints might, however, be gleaned from recent research into *Christian* identity more generally. The British-based anthropologist Abby Day's 2011 book *Believing in Belonging*, for instance, draws on her own detailed fieldwork in a northern English town. Among much else of interest here, Day asked those who had identified as 'Christian' on the 2001 Census what, exactly, they had meant by doing so. She reports:

> Half of my informers who answered 'Christian' were either agnostics or atheists, who either overtly disavowed religion or at least never

20 *Mass Exodus*

incorporated religion, Christianity, God, or Jesus into their own discussions. They were [...] functionally godless and ontologically anthropocentric. (2011: 71–2)

Later, referring to her sample as a whole, she adds:

When I asked [my respondents] why they had ticked the 'Christian' box, a common explanation was because they had been baptized, or had attended Church of England services when they were younger, or had otherwise been 'brought up' Christian. To be Christian, for them, did not include participating in liturgy or ritual, or engaging with Christian principles such as faith in God, the resurrection, or the life of Jesus. It was an ascribed identity from which they could not apparently disassociate themselves. (2011: 180)

It would be tempting to regard this kind of 'nominal' or 'notional' Christian belonging as meaningless. However, as Day rightly points out, that 'Many people without faith in God, Jesus, or Christian doctrine self-identify as "Christian" in certain social contexts' (2011: 174) is itself a social fact of some significance. She adds: 'nominalism is far from an insignificant, empty category but a social, performative act, bringing into being a specific kind of Christian identity' (2011: 174). Similar things might be said of other identities which will feature heavily in later pages. Hence whereas earlier scholarship tended to dismiss 'none', 'no religion', and 'nonreligious' as merely residual, catch-all labels, artificially created by survey researchers (Vernon 1968; Pasquale 2007), newer studies have emphasized that these can be meaningful, substantive self-descriptions which are adopted 'proactively' (Lee 2015). The same is perhaps true of labels such as 'former Catholic', 'ex-Catholic', or 'recovering Catholic'—i.e., not simply statements of the absence of a former religious identity, but self-classifications that are felt to be *presently* meaningful to those claiming them. American sociologist Helen Ebaugh's foundational work on *Becoming an 'Ex'* is especially important here. Drawing on her own 'role exit' from being a nun in the early 1970s, as well as the experiences of many others kinds of 'ex-', she points out:

The phenomenon of becoming an ex is sociologically and psychologically intriguing since it implies that interaction is based not on current role definitions but more important, past identities that somehow linger on and define how people see and present themselves in their present identities. [...] What characterises the ex is the fact that new identity incorporates vestiges and residuals of the previous role. To be an ex-member of a group is essentially different from being a non-member in that non-members have never been part of the group.   (1988: xii, 4)

These observations are pertinent, given the traditional strength of 'tribal', 'customary', or 'cultural' Catholic belonging (Hornsby-Smith 1987, 1991; Demerath 2000). This is especially significant here, given that 'what is often viewed as "identity"—the individual's act of freely identifying with some external object—is always more widely constructed' (Day and Lee 2014: 346). Most obviously, it will be important to bear in mind throughout this study that *being* a Catholic will mean different things to different people—just as, of course, will *no longer being* one. For some individuals, the process of disaffiliation might involve a quite dramatic shift from high levels of belief, practice, and a sense of belonging, to a definite and self-consciously chosen disavowal of all this, accompanied by the clear adoption of another, equally committed-to religious or nonreligious identity. In others, however, it may involve a vague feeling of being 'technically' or 'officially' Catholic due to having been baptized as one, but which is rarely actualized beyond ticking the requisite box on surveys, gradually drifting towards an even vaguer feeling of not being very much at all, and so no longer even ticking the box. Naturally, these are just two examples across a wide spectrum of possibilities. No doubt for many people religious identity is a much more ambivalent affair: perhaps there is, for example, a sense in which they do, and a sense in which they don't, feel like they (still) have a particular religious affiliation. Ebaugh refers here to 'role residual [as] the continued identity an individual holds with aspects of a previous role'. She adds: 'We can think about role residual as "hangover identity," that is, as aspects of self-identity that remain with an individual from a prior role even after exiting' (1988: 173–4). This perspective helps make sense of the well-documented variability of responses to surveys' religious identity questions, depending on the precise wording or other, seemingly incidental factors (cf. Hackett 2014).[10] As we shall

---

[10] A classic example here is the UK Census 'What is your religion?' question, which in both years it has been administered (2001 and 2011) yielded far higher proportions of self-identifying Christians than, say, the BSA did with its 'Do you regard yourself as belonging to any particular religion?' question. Assuming that the BSA samples are representative of the British population, more or less the only logical explanation is

see in Chapter 3, there is strong evidence that sizeable numbers of people may answer the *same* question differently at different times, without any other discernible shift in their stance vis-à-vis religion (see Lim et al. 2010; Hout 2017).

Both the fuzziness and fluidity of religious identity undoubtedly pose interpretive problems in a study such as this. It is freely admitted that tick-box survey responses—which will feature quite heavily in Chapter 2 especially—are a decidedly blunt tool with which to explore either the extent or significance of Catholic disaffiliation. Blunt tools do, however, have their place. They will allow us to hew out the statistical contours of British and American disaffiliation, onto which more sensitive and nuanced instruments, including those drawn from qualitative sociology and social history, may then be put to work.

OVERALL STRUCTURE

This chapter is a form of disjointed overture to the rest of the book—introducing themes to be worked out, more fully and satisfactorily, in the pages ahead. These include the definition, nature, extent, and geographical variability of the phenomenon of Catholic disaffiliation; the relative roles of the Second Vatican Council (broadly conceived), other intra-Catholic factors, and/or wider socio-religious trends in bringing this fact about; and various issues we need to be mindful about when handling so rich, complex, and potentially fragile a thing as (non)religious identity. The following six chapters will seek to make progress on all these fronts, and indeed on several more, in what will hopefully feel like a coherent, well-rounded, and systematic manner.

The central six chapters of this book can be divided into two main 'movements'. The first—Chapters 2 and 3—presents an up-to-date portrait of contemporary Catholic disaffiliates, using survey data from Britain and the USA. Chapter 2 offers new analyses of recent data from large-scale, nationally representative datasets: the British

that a significant number of people who answered 'No religion' to the BSA's wording contrarily answered 'Christian' to the Census' (for possible reasons why, see Voas and Bruce 2004; Day 2011; Hackett 2014: 402–4; Voas 2015: 12–13).

Social Attitudes survey, and the General Social Survey. These will be used to investigate the general questions of *When?* and *Who?*. In answer to the former, we will seek to chart lapsation and disaffiliation over time, paying particular attention to the critical matter of *when* it all began. Meanwhile, in answer to the second question of *Who?*, we will give a general portrait of the Catholic disaffiliate population(s), with special attention given to certain key demographic and religious variables. This will allow us to see, in broad terms, what *types* of Americans and Britons are most likely to have ceased to practise, and/or affiliate, as Catholics. Chapter 3 then turns from 'big picture' quantitative sociology, to qualitative studies of personal narratives of lapsation/disaffiliation. Chief among these will be a small number of dedicated studies, commissioned by the US bishops (1979–80) and three individual dioceses: Trenton, New Jersey (2011), and Spring-field, Illinois (2012–13) in the United States; and Portsmouth (2015) in Britain. Among much else, such sources will remind us of the rich and diverse individual experiences 'underneath' the numbers and graph lines of Chapter 2.

From this foundation, the next four chapters together offer a (necessarily selective) history of Catholic disaffiliation. While the primary focus here is on the last fifty-or-so years (i.e., the 'since Vatican II' of our title), for reasons that will become clear in Chapter 2, it is necessary to begin our story rather earlier. Chapter 4 will thus cover the immediate preconciliar period, especially from the time following the Second World War. Chapter 5 interrogates the 'Catholic sixties' (Massa 2010), with obvious interests in the Council itself, its immediate aftermath, and the remarkable controversy surrounding *Humanae Vitae*. Chapter 6 charts the (uneasy) settling down of the Church over the 1970s and 1980s. Chapter 7 then brings us up more-or-less to the present, with particular attention afforded to the sexual abuse crises, the New Atheism, and the so-called 'rise of the nones'. A major theme throughout will be the importance of cumulative, generational effects.

Chapters 4–7 are *not*, I must stress, intended as a general history of British and American Catholicism during this period. This is an area that is already, and indeed ever-increasingly, well-served. It is rather a very specific and selective history, concerning itself *only* with those events or patterns that (as I see it) are germane to understanding our chosen topic. It is, moreover, a kind of topical history that will not always follow a single narrative thread, and which will occasionally divagate into sociological or theological commentary where relevant. This will be particularly the case in two chapters. Chapter 4 will introduce and explain three critical ideas from the social sciences: plausibility structures, social network theory, and Credibility Enhancing Displays. These theoretical principles will then serve to guide and structure much of our subsequent investigations. In Chapter 5, a decent grounding in both the Council's liturgical teachings in *Sacrosanctum Concilium*, and Paul VI's sexual teaching in *Humanae Vitae*, are prerequisites for assessing either one's impact (or not) on lapsation and disaffiliation.

Finally, a short (but not sweet) Epilogue will recapitulate the main points of my overall argument, revisit a number of issues flagged up in this first chapter, and answer directly the question of the Council's role in, and thus responsibility for, our eponymous *Mass Exodus*.

Before embarking on all this, I might note here that a self-consciously interdisciplinary work such as this both is and needs must be, drawing together the findings and theories of sociologists, anthropologists, theologians, and historians, risks a great deal. Most obviously, there is the real possibility that each set of specialists will find their *own* discipline engaged here with superficial brevity, while coverage of others' disciplines seems both exhaustive and exhausting. (To mitigate this, I have tried to keep some of the more technical, discipline-specific discussions in the footnotes. Readers enchanted by this chapter's footnotery digressions on canon law may, therefore, be less entranced by the following chapters' disquisitions on social survey methodology, and vice versa.) It will probably not be possible to please all of my readers all of the time. But I will try my best not to alienate any of them too disastrously. Certainly, this book does not presume to be the last word on disaffiliation in *any* of the fields on which it trespasses. I will be quite content if it inspires other scholars to take up the subject for themselves, and really show me how it ought to be done.

2

The Demographics of Disaffiliation

The focus in this chapter is on what can be learned from large-scale, nationally representative surveys. Such sources are critical when apprehending so diffuse and hidden a constituency as interests us here. Were we instead studying practising Catholics, then we might turn up at Mass on Sundays, in order to count and interview them. But disaffiliates, and the lapsed in general, do not typically congregate *en masse*. Nor do appreciable numbers sign up for dedicated societies, mailing lists, or Facebook groups. Only by surveying sizeable cross-sections of the population as a whole, and then identifying one's subsample out of this much larger body—assuming, of course, that the requisite questions are asked—can one gain any reliable sense of either the extent or general characteristics of the lapsed/disaffiliate subpopulation. One can also index this information against all sorts of other items in the overall set of data. If the original survey is done right, with sufficient numbers and rigorous sampling and weighting procedures, then one can gain a solid foundation on which to layer thicker, though less easily extrapolable, kinds of data.

Accordingly, this chapter is based around original analyses of data from two such national survey programmes: the British Social Attitudes survey (hereafter BSA), and the General Social Survey (hereafter GSS). The BSA conducts face-to-face interviews with around three thousand adults annually, accompanied by a follow-up written survey, with the sample selected from across England, Wales, and Scotland.[1] Waves have run each year since 1983, except in 1988 and 1992. Those invited to participate are contacted by post twice in advance of an interviewer's visit. Likewise, each GSS wave comprises

---

[1] Only the most northerly (and sparsely populated) reaches of Scotland are excluded on grounds of prohibitive cost (NatCen Social Research 2015: 7).

Table 2.1. Comparison of primary survey questions used for identifying Catholic disaffiliates

	Question wording	
	Religious upbringing	Current religious affiliation
General Social Survey (USA)	*In what religion were you raised?*	*What is your religious preference? It is Protestant, Catholic, Jewish, some other religion, or no religion?*
British Social Attitudes	*In what religion, if any, were you brought up?*	*Do you regard yourself as belonging to a particular religion? If yes, which?*
CATHOLIC DISAFFILIATE =	'Catholic'	**Any answer other than 'Catholic'**

Sources: The General Social Survey (GSS) is a project of the independent research organization NORC at the University of Chicago, with principal funding from the National Science Foundation. British Social Attitudes (BSA) is run by NatCen Social Research and is made possible by funding received from a variety of charitable and governmental sources each year.

face-to-face interviews with between two and three thousand US adults, sampled from across the nation. The GSS survey ran near-annually between 1972 and 1994, and then every two years to the present. Response rates for both the BSA and GSS are high, typically around 50 per cent.[2] In both cases, the raw data are then weighted according to key demographic indicators (e.g., region, age, and sex).[3]

As noted in the previous chapter, how questions are phrased in these kinds of surveys is important. Table 2.1 shows the precise wording of the two questions used to define our disaffiliates in the GSS and BSA. Naturally, it would be preferable if both surveys worded their questions in the same way: as it stands, we are not

[2] These are notably higher than those normally achieved by polls employing less labour-intensive means of data collection. This is potentially significant since the worth of polls/surveys relies on the promise of reliable extrapolation from samples to wider populations. But even with the best sampling methods, one can only extrapolate from those who actually respond. The possibility lingers, therefore, that the kinds of people who respond to pollsters' requests might, *ipso facto*, be non-representative of the population as a whole (Singer 2006; Wuthnow 2015: 155–62). While the *risk* of so-called 'nonresponse bias' is an issue for all survey research, it is obviously magnified when, say, nine out of every ten people in a sample either cannot be contacted or refuse to participate (i.e., a response rate of 10%, as is increasingly common for phone- or internet-based opinion polls).

[3] For full technical details of sampling, weighting, and other methodological issues regarding the BSA and GSS respectively, see NatCen Social Research 2015 and Smith et al. 2015: 2932–51.

quite comparing like with like. These differences are not, however, critical—a fact supported by comparison with data from the International Social Survey Programme[4]—and thus do not undercut the meaningfulness of the comparison.

Most of the analyses below use combined data from the years 2012 through 2016 inclusive. At the time of writing, these are the most recent waves—five of the annual BSA; three of the biannual GSS—to have been released. Pooling data from consecutive waves enables us to draw on larger samples: 2376 cradle Catholics in the BSA, and 2526 in the GSS. This is especially useful when one is interested in subgroups within subgroups (e.g., 'cradle Catholics who now affiliate as something other than Catholic'). Basing one's figures on a mean of five years' data also protects against a single anomalous year unduly distorting the overall picture. Of course, there is a balance to be struck between increasing sample size and losing contemporaneity. By the time this book is published, 2012 data should hopefully still *feel* more-or-less current in a way that 2002 data would not. Neatly, 2012 naturally carries a certain symbolism in these pages, marking fifty years on from the start of the Second Vatican Council.

Contemporaneity is not everything. Indeed, a signal advantage of our datasets lies precisely in their longevity. The GSS gives us over forty years' worth of data; the BSA over thirty. These let us reach back to within a decade or two of the critical period in and around the Council. Being able to track how responses to the same questions have or haven't changed over this time will be a key weapon in our statistical arsenal.

Finally, before we move on to exploring the data themselves, it is worth noting that these are not the *only* such sources which are useful and interesting to us. In addition to the original analyses presented in

---

[4] In Britain and the USA, the ISSP 'piggybacks' on the BSA and GSS. Respondents therefore answer the usual GSS/BSA questions in a face-to-face interview, and also answer questions for that year's ISSP module by a self-completion questionnaire. This means that in 2008, participants in the GSS and BSA were asked about their religious upbringing *twice*: once using the usual (and different) wordings of those surveys, and a second time with *both* using the ISSP's wording ('What religion, if any, were you raised in? Was it Protestant, Catholic, Jewish, some other religion, or no religion?'). In both countries, the two ways of asking yielded near-exact figures reporting a Catholic upbringing; in each, differences were less than one percentage point. Though further analysis is possible, the above presents a reasonable *prima facie* case for parity between the BSA and ISSP, the GSS and ISSP, and thus (albeit indirectly) between the BSA and GSS, when it comes to the wording of at least the upbringing question.

this chapter, comparisons will be made to the published findings from other highly regarded surveys. Chief among these is the Pew Research Forum's Religious Landscape Survey (hereafter RLS), whose two waves in 2007 and 2014 each included over 35,000 responses from a cross-section of American adults.

RETENTION AND DISAFFILIATION

Figure 2.1 shows the current religious affiliation of cradle Catholics in Britain and the USA, subdivided into four categories: (i) those who still identify as Catholic; and those who no longer do, but now identify as belonging to (ii) a different (i.e., non-Catholic) Christian grouping; (iii) a non-Christian religion; or (iv) no religion.

Retainees—i.e., those brought up Catholic whom the Church has retained into adulthood—form the largest group in each country. These 'still-Catholics' account for two out of every three American cradle Catholics (66 per cent), and a little over half of all British ones (56 per cent); an appreciable, though by no means huge, difference.

The other three categories (ii–iv), of course, make up our *disaffiliates*. Thus 44 per cent of all British cradle Catholics, and 34 per cent of all American ones, now no longer identify as Catholic. These are serious

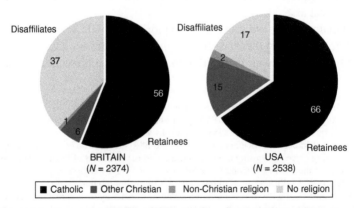

Figure 2.1. Current religious affiliation of cradle Catholics in Britain and the USA

Source: BSA and GSS (2012–16; weighted data)

proportions. (Note that the RLS suggests an even higher disaffiliation rate for US Catholicism, at 41 per cent; Pew Research Center 2015a: 39.) Some striking comparisons emerge within the disaffiliate category. In Britain, the overwhelming majority, accounting for nearly two-in-five of all cradle Catholics, now identify as having no religion at all. In America, meanwhile, nones account for fewer than one-in-five. Even in the USA, however, this is the most numerous of our three types of disaffiliate: more US cradle Catholics now identify with no religion (17 per cent) than with a non-Catholic Christian affiliation (15 per cent). These differences *among* the disaffiliate subgroups are the most notable when comparing Britain and America. This can be usefully put like so: the proportion of British cradle Catholics who now identify with no religion—we might call them *Catholic nonverts*—is over twice that of their American counterparts; while the proportion of American cradle Catholics who now identify with a different Christian label—that is, *Catholic switchers*—is almost three times that of their British ones. Meanwhile, although leaving the Catholicism of one's upbringing for a non-Christian religion seems to be twice as common in the USA as it is in Britain, in both countries the overall proportions are very small: 2 per cent versus 1 per cent. This latter phenomenon, without denying its intrinsic interest, will accordingly receive little direct attention in the pages to come.

Percentages, of course, are all very well. But what do these numbers mean in terms of real people? Correlating GSS 2012–16 data with the US Census Bureau's estimate of a 2016 adult population of 249.5 million, gives us 86.8 million cradle Catholics (i.e., 34.8 per cent of the total). Based on the proportions given above, this results in *29.5 million* disaffiliates, of whom 14.8 million now have no religion, 13 million affirm a different Christian label, and 1.7 million belong to a non-Christian religion (NB: even small proportions add up considerably when dealing with large populations). Doing the same thing for Britain brings 7.2 million cradle Catholics, or 14.4 per cent from a total 2016 adult population of 50.3 million. This yields *3.2 million* disaffiliates, of whom 2.7 million are nones, 0.4 million are another kind of Christian, and a little under 0.1 million are members of a different religion.[5]

---

[5] 2016 estimates of the adult (i.e., 18+) population are taken from data publicly available on the websites of the US Census Bureau (http://www.census.gov/topics/population.html) and the Office for National Statistics (http://ons.gov.uk/ons/taxonomy/index.html?nscl=Population).

These 29.5 and 3.2 million disaffiliates are not, of course, evenly spread out across their respective countries: national averages are often built out of significant regional variation. Table 2.2, which breaks down our American statistics into nine (admittedly rather large) geographical areas, is a good example here.

Retention levels range from the low-70s at the upper end, to the mid-50s at the lowest. This means that a born-and-raised Catholic

Table 2.2. Current religious affiliation of cradle Catholics within different US regions

Region	Current affiliation (%)			
	Catholic	Other Christian	Non-Christian religion	No religion
West South Central (Arkansas, Louisiana, Oklahoma, Texas)	72	16	0	12
East South Central (Alabama, Kentucky, Mississippi, Tennessee)	72	18	2	8
Middle Atlantic (New Jersey, New York, Pennsylvania)	70	10	1	18
New England (Connecticut, Maine, Massachusetts, New Hampshire, Rhode Island, Vermont)	69	13	3	15
Pacific (Alaska, California, Hawaii, Oregon, Washington)	67	11	2	20
East North Central (Illinois, Indiana, Michigan, Ohio, Wisconsin)	66	16	2	16
West North Central (Iowa, Kansas, Minnesota, Missouri, Nebraska, N. Dakota, S. Dakota)	63	16	4	18
South Atlantic (Delaware, District of Columbia, Florida, Georgia, Maryland, N. Carolina, S. Carolina, Virginia, W. Virginia)	59	21	2	18
Mountain (Arizona, Colorado, Idaho, Montana, Nevada, New Mexico, Utah, Wyoming)	54	19	5	22
USA TOTAL	66	15	2	17

Source: GSS (2012–16; weighted data).

living in West or East South Central has a likelihood of retaining their identity into adulthood almost twenty percentage points higher than one living in Mountain. Or to put it another way, out of every twenty cradle Catholics in the former two regions, some fourteen still identify as such; in the latter, it is around eleven. While that may not sound like a huge difference, when applied to populations in the hundreds of thousands or even millions, those three-in-every-twenty add up considerably.

Once again, there is variability within the disaffiliate categories too. The proportion 'switching' from Catholicism to another religious affiliation, whether Christian or non-Christian, outnumber nonverts in all but two areas: Pacific and Middle Atlantic. The latter is particularly striking here, especially when considered together with East South Central. The two regions share near-identical levels of both retention and joining a non-Christian religion, but while Middle Atlantic cradle Catholics are now twice as likely to affirm no religion than to have adopted another Christian denomination (18 per cent vs. 10 per cent), in East South Central these two percentages are almost exactly reversed (8 per cent vs. 18 per cent).

Students of American religion, indeed of America itself, will not be surprised by such regionality (see Newport 2012: 143–67). Nor will they struggle to moot *possible* explanations for the variegation. For just as the physical geography of the United States is diverse, so too is its human geography. It should then be expected that area-specific historical, cultural, political, demographic, economic, ethnic, and socio-religious realities would impact upon Catholic pastoral life. For instance, the relatively strong retention rate in West South Central is plausibly due to its inclusion of Texas, with its large numbers of Latinos, famously *sui generis* religious culture (Wuthnow 2014), and high levels of religiosity across the board (a feature it shares with the other, though far less populous, states in its region). Equally intuitive is the fact that greater numbers of disaffiliates in the largely rural East South Central—with Tennessee, Alabama, and Mississippi routinely cited among the USA's 'most religious' states (Gallup 2016)—prefer another Christian identity over no religion, but this is reversed in the cosmopolitan Middle Atlantic, comprising New Jersey, New York, and Pennsylvania. Three-quarters of the states in the Mountain region, which has the lowest Catholic retention rate and the highest proportion of Catholic nonverts, have themselves a higher-than-average overall proportion of nones (Pew Research Center 2015a: 145); the exceptions being Utah, which has lots of Mormons, and New Mexico, with a very high proportion of Latinos. Lastly, the Pacific region—noteworthy for a near-average Catholic retention rate, but a high proportion of Catholic nonverts—is an interesting example of how competing trends might play out across a region. Closer examination reveals that it includes *both* three states commonly identified as general hotbeds of none-ness—i.e., Alaska, Washington, and Oregon (Pew Research Center 2015a: 145; Killen and Shibley 2004)—*and* California, a populous state whose Catholics include large numbers of Latinos and other immigrants, most of whom believe, practise, and affiliate at rather higher levels than the American Catholic average. It is not too great a stretch to suggest that these factors, undoubtedly alongside a great many more, counteract each other.

As they stand, the above surmises are little more than informed speculation—and there is not space in a book like this to delve much more deeply into matters of *regional* specificity (at least, not in any systematic way: much local detail, ranging from detailed case studies to cursory vignettes, will of course contribute towards the whole). Nevertheless, it is worth noting the intuitive plausibility of ascribing differences in retention/disaffiliation patterns to wider socio-cultural realities. If this is reasonable enough *across different places but at the same time*, then perhaps the same would be true *across different times but in the same place*. Exploring this latter possibility will, in fact, be a major theme of Chapters 4–7.

The point made above about variation *within* particular regions is made even plainer in our data from Britain: the whole area of which would fit comfortably within most, if not all, of our US regions. Indeed, the entire United Kingdom—i.e., Britain *plus* Northern Ireland—is, as per the CIA's winning description, 'twice the size of Pennsylvania; slightly smaller than Oregon' (Central Intelligence Agency 2016).

These close confines, as is clear from Table 2.3, nevertheless contain considerable variance. Whereas the highest and lowest proportions of retainees in the USA deviate by 18 percentage points (72 per cent to 54 per cent), in Britain it is 21 (66 per cent to 45 per cent). Retention is strongest in the North East and North West of England (both of which, the latter especially, have a relatively high proportion of Catholics; see Bullivant 2016b: 7). At the lower end, two regions—South East (excluding London) and the East Midlands—have retention levels below 50 per cent: that is to say, among those currently

Table 2.3. Current religious affiliation of cradle Catholics within different British regions

Region	Current affiliation (%)			
	Catholic	Other Christian	Non-Christian religion	No religion
North East	66	4	1	29
North West	60	5	1	34
Outer London	59	7	1	34
Eastern	59	7	0	35
West Midlands	58	6	1	34
Scotland	56	3	0	40
Inner London	56	5	3	37
Wales	53	0	2	45
Yorkshire/Humberside	52	3	0	45
South West	50	9	1	40
South East	49	9	1	41
East Midlands	45	5	2	48
BRITAIN TOTAL	56	5	1	38

Source: BSA (2012–16; weighted data).

living there, having been brought up Catholic is a stronger predictor for regarding oneself to be a *non*-Catholic adult than a Catholic one. This is not necessarily a reflection of Catholic upbringings *in* the South East or East Midlands: it could simply be that certain sorts of people—upwardly mobile young people, say—gravitate to these regions from elsewhere in Britain. Or perhaps these regions tend to be less attractive, for all sorts of possible reasons, to immigrants from strongly Catholic countries. This point applies the other way too, of course.

While the *overall* British retention rate is somewhat lower than in the USA, there is nonetheless significant overlap in terms of regional rates. Thus the lower half of the American table and the upper half of the British table span roughly the same range: the mid-60s down to the mid-50s. This point is worth emphasizing given the last chapter's hopes for the fruitfulness of our transatlantic comparisons, and indeed on the growing suspicions that 'secular Britain' and 'religious America' might not be such contrasts as they used to be.

Clear differences do, however, emerge when we look at the three disaffiliate categories. In every single British region, 'no religion' is the winner among all those who no longer regard themselves as Catholics: even in South East and South West, where the differences are closest, nonverts outstrip switchers by a ratio of four-to-one. In the region with the strongest retention, religious nones now account for three out of every ten cradle Catholics. In the region with the weakest retention, it rises to five-in-ten. (By contrast, the US regions with the highest proportion of Catholic nonverts—Pacific and Mountain—register around two-in-ten.) Switching shows a great deal of regional variance too: those adopting a different Christian affiliation account for around one-in-ten cradle Catholics in the South West and East, whereas in Wales the BSA's researchers didn't encounter a single one.[6] The proportion of those affirming a non-Christian affiliation, meanwhile, varies between 0 per cent and 3 per cent, in broad parity with the US levels.

HOW DO CATHOLICS COMPARE?

As noted in Chapter 1, rising lapsation and disaffiliation over the past several decades are far from a Catholic-only concern. Despite a singular focus on Catholic disaffiliation, this wider context is of critical importance to our current investigation. Not least, it strongly suggests that Catholic disaffiliation might have causes and influences—even if, as shall be argued in due course, only partial ones—independent from purely Catholic concerns. After all, none of the west's other major Christian communities vernacularized its liturgy, or relaxed its Friday fasting obligations, or upheld the traditional Christian teaching against artificial contraception—all major parts of the Catholic-specific story, as we shall see in Chapter 5—within the watershed period of the 1960s. What is more, they permit us to view our Catholic data in proper perspective. In a book focusing so unremittingly on the relative weakness of Catholic retention when compared with the past, it will be salutary to explore in some detail its relative *strength* when compared with other denominations.[7]

---

[6] Obviously, this does not mean that there are no such people in the whole of Wales. However, it does testify to their relative paucity: there are too few of them, that is, to reliably show up in a sample like this, even with five years' worth of pooled data.

[7] The table presents the most common types of Christian denominational affiliation. In some cases, a single category is made up of several independent church organizations—as, for example, with various Baptist and Methodist groups listed separately in the GSS. A person raised as a Missouri Synod Lutheran, but who now

Table 2.4. Current religious affiliation of those raised in selected denominations in the USA and Britain

Raised as...		Current affiliation (%)			
		Same as raised	(Other) Christian	Non-Christian religion	No religion
USA	Catholic	66	15	2	17
	Baptist	60	23	2	15
	No(n) denominational	52	27	1	19
	Lutheran	52	28	2	18
	Episcopalian	51	27	2	20
	Methodist	48	33	1	18
	Presbyterian	47	32	4	17
BRITAIN	Catholic	56	5	1	38
	No(n) denominational	53	3	1	43
	Anglican/Episcopalian	52	7	1	41
	Presbyterian/Church of Scotland	47	9	1	43
	Methodist	32	23	1	44
	Baptist	27	36	0	37

Source: GSS and BSA (2012–16; weighted data).

A cursory glance at Table 2.4 makes this point rather well. In both countries, Catholicism in fact has the *highest* rate of retention among the main Christian groupings. While America's Catholic Church has lost a third of those brought up in it, its Presbyterian, Methodist, Episcopalian, Lutheran, and 'No(n) denominational' counterparts have each lost half. In Britain, the Catholic retention rate is over one and a half times the Methodist one, and more than double the Baptists'.

identifies with the Evangelical Lutheran Church in America, is counted as a Lutheran retainee.

An interpretive difficulty is raised by what is described here (following Steensland et al. 2000) as the 'No(n) denominational' category. This comprises those in both the BSA and GSS who give their religious affiliation as 'Christian' without any further qualification. This category is evidently an awkward one—especially when presented, as it is here, as a quasi-denomination in its own right. For example, there are strong grounds for thinking that it includes *both* those with only a relatively weak sense of Christian belonging (i.e., they have no specific attachment to any Christian community, but still identify as Christian, perhaps for cultural or national reasons), *and* often highly committed members of avowedly 'non-denominational' churches. For these reasons, due caution must therefore be taken in construing this category as a coherent grouping akin to Catholics, Methodists, and Baptists.

Without downplaying the scale of Catholic disaffiliation—an odd move in a book of this title, in any case—the Church's success in this sphere should not be ignored. The Catholic retention rates represent genuine, if meagre, 'winnings' in what is, as other denominations can testify, very much of a losing game. This point is worth emphasizing, not least since it is sometimes obscured in both academic and media reporting on American religious change. For example, when 'Protestant' is used as a generic category alongside 'Catholic', then the very large quantity of switching *between* Protestant denominations simply disappears from the data. The same effect occurs, albeit to lesser extent, when distinct denominations are divided up into subgroupings like Mainline, Evangelical, or Black Protestant (Steensland et al. 2000): those switching *within* each category go unrecorded (see, e.g., Pew Research Center 2015a: 13). That is not to say that collecting Protestant groups together in these ways for analysis is always illegitimate; for many purposes, it makes perfect sense. Nevertheless, depending on what one is measuring and why, it has—as here—the potential to mislead (Center for Applied Research in the Apostolate 2008: 2–3). For instance, it is clear from Table 2.3 that the *proportion* of cradle Catholics who become adult nones is similar to most other denominations. However, since around one-in-three Americans was brought up Catholic (compared to, in second place, fewer than one-in-five who were brought up Baptist), cradle Catholics account for a headline-grabbingly large number of nones. Hence, as the Pew researchers put it:

> While the ranks of the unaffiliated [i.e., nones] have grown the most due to changes in religious affiliation, the Catholic Church has lost the most members in the same process; this is the case even though Catholicism's retention rate of childhood members [. . .] is comparable with or better than the retention rates of other religious groups.
>
> (Pew Research Center 2009: 21)

One final interesting thing revealed by our comparisons, international and interdenominational alike, is the apparent predilection of former Catholics for choosing no religion over a different religious affiliation. This is most clearly marked in the American data. Here, 50 per cent of all Catholic disaffiliates now identify as nones. Among the other listed denominations, however, the corresponding figure lies between 31 per cent (Lutheran) and 37 per cent (Presbyterian). Furthermore, Catholicism is the only group with a higher proportion of nonverts than switchers to a different Christian identity. In the

British data, meanwhile, we see a much stronger preference for nonversion over switching: 83 per cent of all Catholic disaffiliates now identify as none. In Britain, however, this general pattern is apparent in other denominations too (though note the striking exceptions of cradle Methodists and, especially, Baptists).

Tentatively, one might hypothesize that there is some connection between this effect, and the comparatively high Catholic retention discussed above: i.e., that Catholic identity is sufficiently strong to both 'keep' a higher proportion of those brought up within it, and for a higher proportion of those who *do* end up leaving to, in effect, 'accept no substitutes'. On this theory, Catholicism acts as a kind of 'default' religious identity, which is thus more likely either to be retained (even if nominally), or to be cast off altogether.[8] In this vein, consider Garry Wills' oft-quoted remark: 'We "born Catholics," even when we leave or lose our own church, rarely feel at home in any other' (1972: 15). This is not the only possible explanation of Catholic disaffiliation's specific texture. One might equally conjecture that being raised Catholic is just more likely to put a person off Christianity for good than is, say, being raised Baptist or Episcopalian. (Incidentally, this suggestion is not *necessarily* as facetious as it might seem. At the time of writing, 'recovering Catholic' turns up over 40,000 hits on Google, 'recovering Episcopalian' less than 500, and 'recovering Baptist' approaching 200. Even 'recovering Evangelical' and 'recovering fundamentalist' get fewer than 4000 and 8000 respectively.) Naturally, the statistics alone cannot adjudicate. There is more to be said on these topics in the chapters to come.

Contrast the above with some analogous statistics relating to the obverse of disaffiliation: *conversion*. Table 2.5 essentially flips the previous one. It breaks down people's current religious affiliation by the religious affiliation in which they were brought up. If Table 2.4 demonstrated the relative *strength* of Catholic retention when compared to other major denominations, we see now its relative *weakness* in attracting new people into the fold. In both countries, over nine out of ten current Catholics were raised as such. This means, *ipso facto*, that fewer than one in ten is a convert. In Britain, this proportion places Catholicism (again, interestingly enough) shoulder-to-shoulder

---

[8] Feasibly, this kind of 'default' explanation might also account for why, in the British data, Anglicanism and Presbyterianism—as the national, Established religions of England and Scotland respectively—exhibit somewhat similar patterns of disaffiliation.

Table 2.5. Religious upbringing of those who currently identify with selected denominations in the USA and Britain; plus, disaffiliate ratios

	Current affiliation	Raised as ... (%)				
		Same as current	(Other) Christian	Non-Christian religion	No religion	*Disaffiliates per convert*
USA	Catholic	93	6	0	2	*7*
	Baptist	76	20	0	4	*2*
	Presbyterian	67	33	0	1	*2*
	Methodist	65	29	1	5	*2*
	Episcopalian	63	32	1	4	*2*
	Lutheran	63	33	0	3	*2*
	No(n) denominational	35	56	1	8	*0.5*
BRITAIN	Presbyterian	94	6	0	0	*17*
	Catholic	93	6	0	1	*10*
	Anglican/ Episcopalian	92	6	0	2	*10*
	Methodist	80	19	1	1	*8*
	No(n) denominational	75	21	0	4	*3*
	Baptist	59	39	0	3	*4*

Source: GSS and BSA (2012–16; weighted data).

with the Anglicans and Presbyterians. In America, Catholicism ranks dead last among the denominations, significantly behind the penultimate Baptists. Though again, given the extent of American Catholicism, even a relatively small proportion adds up to a large number of actual people: perhaps 4.3 million Catholic converts, accounting for around one in every sixty American adults.[9] Without denying the impressiveness of such big numbers, or the impact such converts have on the life of the American Church,[10] it is nonetheless critical to view them within their proper context.

A thorough discussion of such conversion statistics is a subject for a different book. Worth remarking on here, though, are the high proportions of converts among many of the Protestant denominations. These, coupled with the high proportions of Protestant disaffiliates adopting another Christian affiliation we saw in Table 2.4,

[9] This estimate uses the same US Census Bureau figures used above, alongside a GSS 2012–16 estimate of 24.6% of the US adult population identifying as Catholic.

[10] Tellingly perhaps, those joining Catholicism have received even less recent sociological attention than have those leaving it. For some very welcome, trend-bucking exceptions, see: Gray 2014; and Yamane 2014.

testify to the much-reported phenomenon of denominational switching. Note also, across almost all denominations, the typically very low proportions of current affiliates who were brought up in either a non-Christian religious tradition, or no religion. Once again, Catholics are among the worst-performers here—one in fifty in the USA; one in a hundred in Britain—though nobody fishes magnificently well in these waters. Theoretically, it would be possible for every Christian group to report high rates of conversion (due to a significant minority switching between denominations), while overall Christian numbers continue to decline (due to large numbers of born-and-raised Christians becoming nones, and only small numbers of people converting from a non-Christian background).

This latter point is made plain in the final, right-most column of Table 2.5, under the heading 'Disaffiliates per convert'. This is based upon the absolute numbers of each denomination's leavers and joiners present in our datasets. This is arguably the most revealing set of figures in the whole chapter. They show that for each single American who has entered the Catholic Church at the Easter Vigil, there are *seven* people who feel sufficiently estranged from the Catholicism of their upbringing to now no longer describe themselves as such. This ratio, closely corroborated by RLS data (Pew Research Center 2015a: 35), is far and away the highest—i.e., worst—ratio of any of our American Christian groupings.

This ratio is yet direr among British Catholics. Especially in England, the idea of the 'Catholic convert' holds a strong resonance (Hornsby-Smith 1987: 23–4). From the nineteenth century onwards, many of the Church's most prominent members have been converts: Newman and Manning, Chesterton and Greene, Widdecombe and Blair. In addition, much media attention has been given to disaffected Anglicans joining the Church over the past two decades. Despite this, Table 2.5 shows that current conversions *to* Catholicism are dwarfed, by a ratio of one to ten, by disaffiliations away *from* it.

RELIGIOUS PRACTICE, SEX, AGE

As discussed in Chapter 1, disaffiliation is conceived here as an extreme case of the wider phenomenon of lapsation. As such, as we delve more deeply into our statistics, it may be salutary to add a further division to our four basic categories: a distinction between Catholic retainees who attend Mass on a regular basis, and those who do not. The rationale for this split is based on two assumptions. Firstly, that *practice* is the most significant indicator of religiosity (Bruce 1996: 34; Smith 2018: 20–76). Praying, attending services, reading scriptures, attending discussion groups at places of worship, or doing all manner of other things—everything from eating (or not eating) certain things on certain days, to discerning when and if to have children (and if not, *how* not to)—*because* of one's professed religious identity and beliefs actually takes up time, effort, and oftentimes expense. Ticking boxes on surveys is cheap; second collections are not. Secondly, there are good reasons to suppose that low/non-practising affiliates are, or often can be, a transitional group between regular practisers and at least the nonvert type of disaffiliate (Voas 2009). Of course, it is not impossible that someone might instantly go from being a weekly-Mass-attending Catholic to regarding him or herself to be a none. Indeed, dramatic *de*conversions are just as possible as are dramatic conversions (Bullivant 2008). But both common sense and, more importantly, a good deal of evidence (see Chapter 3) suggest that this is far from the normal pattern.

In the following analyses, therefore, we will distinguish between *regular practisers*, who say they attend church on at least a monthly basis, and *low/non-practisers*, who say that they attend less frequently than that (up to and including 'never'). Naturally, there is an arbitrary element to this. Quite apart from the much-discussed vagaries of self-reported measures of religious practice,[11] the boundary between 'regular' and 'low/non' attendance is not always clear cut. Furthermore, each of our two categories masks a significant degree of internal

---

[11] There exists a formidable body of research questioning the reliability of such measures, based on comparisons with both actual attendance counts and evidence from time-use surveys, some of it Catholic-specific (Hadaway et al. 1993; Chaves and Cavendish 1994). Serious over-reporting has, however, been most clearly demonstrated in the USA; evidence for the effect in Britain and the rest of Europe is substantially weaker (Brenner 2012). It is worth noting, however, that even in the USA, this effect has been most studied in terms of claims of *weekly* attendance: e.g., people who actually make it most weeks still think of themselves as being weekly attenders. It is plausible, therefore, that by combining several categories into a more generic 'monthly or more' category, we are here able to subvert at least some of this effect (i.e., it doesn't matter if three-in-every-four-Sundays attenders claim to be weekly attenders, since both frequencies fall happily within 'monthly or more'). Even so, due caution should be observed, especially when making direct comparisons between British and US data.

difference. At one end, daily Mass-goers are grouped together with those who turn up roughly thirty times less often. Whereas, at the other end, those who make it fairly often, perhaps one Sunday in four or five, sit alongside those who never once darken the parish door (or know where it is). Nevertheless, lines must be drawn somewhere. Adding further categories would only serve to make the analysis more convoluted and opaque. While 'monthly or more' is broad, it captures a genuine regularity of habit that is itself significant. And while, especially with a focus on Catholicism, one could certainly make a strong case for 'weekly or more' being the more meaningful measure of 'regular' practice, this would produce a 'low/non-practisers' category that would be both very large (incorporating the great majority of all retainees), and encompass a vastly broader and more incoherent range—everyone from the 'nevers' to the most scrupulously honest weekly attender who can remember 'that one time' when they missed a Sunday—than does the one we are in fact using. (In Chapter 6, statistics focusing on weekly Mass attendance *will* be presented and discussed.)

Figure 2.2 demonstrates a clear gender divide. This applies to the overall proportions of retainees (37 per cent female vs. 30 per cent

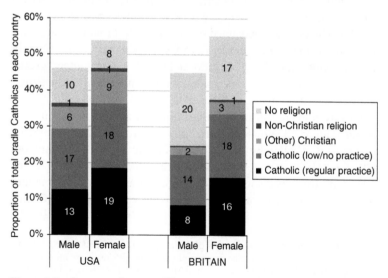

Figure 2.2. Current religious affiliation/practice of cradle Catholics in the USA and Britain, by sex

Source: GSS and BSA (2012–16; weighted data)

male in the USA; 34 per cent female vs. 22 per cent male in Britain), and among the retainees, to levels of practice. In both countries, women divide up more or less equally into regular and low/non-practisers, whereas among men, the low/nons outnumber the regulars. In general terms, these confirm the overwhelming testimony of other studies regarding the positive correlation between womanhood and religiosity, and moreover of the preponderance of men among religious nones (Trzebiatowska and Bruce 2012: 1–23; Pew Research Center 2012a). Not only are women in both countries noticeably less likely to disaffiliate, but those who do, are more likely than men to adopt a different Christian or religious identity.

Yet those headline trends, while important, ought not to mislead us. Compared to cradle Catholic men, cradle Catholic women are indeed more likely to retain a Catholic self-identity, and among those who do, to be relatively more practising. But that does not prevent there being a large proportion of cradle Catholic women who do neither. In fact, Figure 2.2 throws up an intriguing statistic: despite what has just (and truly) been said, *women nevertheless make up half of all Catholic disaffiliates*. Of the 35 per cent of American born-and-raised Catholics who now identify as something else, 17 per cent are male and 18 per cent are female. In Britain, the disaffiliated share is 44 per cent, divided near-equally between women and men. How can this be? The puzzle is explained by the simple fact that there are, or at least appear to be, more cradle-Catholic women than cradle-Catholic men in both countries. This ratio of 11 to 9 is, intriguingly, greater than the rate at which women slightly outnumber men in the British and American populations as a whole.[12]

Our fivefold classification may fruitfully be applied to the question of age. Figure 2.3 shows the variations in current affiliation/practice of cradle Catholics by respondents' decade of birth. Within our GSS 2012–16 sample, 60 per cent of those born between 1925 and 1934 (and thus aged somewhere between 78 and 91 at the time they were surveyed) are once-a-month-or-more practising Catholics.

---

[12] This curious fact admits of several possible explanations, two of which I consider plausible enough to float here. The first hypothesis is that girls really are more likely to be raised religiously than boys (cf. Voas and McAndrew 2012). Perhaps, for instance, Irish grannies are disproportionately likely to take an interest in the religious upbringing of girls than boys: a vestigial example of Brown's 'discourse of pious femininity' (2001: 180) in action. The second is that women may be more inclined than men to interpret an ambiguous upbringing (one that was neither particularly religious nor conspicuously non-religious) as having been 'religious' rather than not.

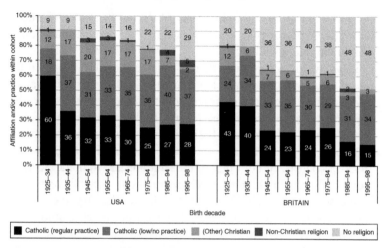

Figure 2.3. Current religious affiliation/practice of cradle Catholics in the USA and Britain, by decade of birth

Source: GSS and BSA (2012–16; weighted data)

Meanwhile, in our BSA 2012–16 sample, 48 per cent of those born between 1994 and 1998 (i.e., aged 18–22 when interviewed) now affirm no religion. I give those two examples, not to draw any direct comparison between them, but simply to explain what the graph is actually showing, using the most easily findable—i.e., very bottom left, and topmost right—and also, coincidentally, the largest and most obvious individual data points.

There are a great many things that could be said about Figure 2.3, and its import. But here we might confine ourselves to just two highlights.

Firstly, in general terms, disaffiliation rates tend to increase as one moves from the oldest to the youngest age categories. Within the disaffiliates, moreover, the proportion of nonverts also grows fairly steadily. In neither case nor country, are these trends perfectly smooth: the overall disaffiliation rates of the two youngest US cohorts, for instance, are somewhat more robust than one might predict.[13] Countering this, note the strikingly high proportions of nonverts in these

---

[13] Some caution is, however, warranted here. It is possible, for example, that a significant proportion of these have *not yet* disaffiliated (see Center for Applied Research in the Apostolate 2008: 6–7). This interpretation might gain some credence from the relatively high rates of low/non-practisers (if, as hypothesized, this functions for many as a transitional state towards becoming a none).

categories (a feature of the youngest British cohorts also), and with it, the waning popularity of the long-established American tradition of denominational switching.

Secondly, in each country there is a single, very clear drop in the rate of regular practisers (and less dramatically, the rate of retainees as a whole) from one specific decadal cohort to the next. However, this happens at *different* times in each place. In America, this shift occurs between those born between 1925 and 1934 and those born between 1935 and 1944. In Britain, it occurs between the 1935–44 and 1945–54 cohorts. In both places, the shift appears to mark a certain 'point of no return'. Moderate, relative rallies do occur thereafter (in both cases, interestingly, there is a two-decade rise after the original two-decade low), but neither retention itself, nor practice among the retainees, ever return to anything close to the 'pre-Fall' levels.

This appearance of a definitive and dramatic downturn can be shown in still sharper relief. While Figure 2.3 only includes responses collected in the 2012–16 waves of the GSS and BSA, we do of course have access to the full range of years that the relevant questions were asked—since 1972 and 1991 respectively—in each survey programme. Pooling these allows us sufficient numbers of cradle Catholics (over 10,000 in each country) to plot *overall* retention levels, not by decade, but by individual *year* of birth.[14]

As one would expect from a year-on-year breakdown, there is a good deal of fluctuation in Figure 2.4's data. Nevertheless, the overarching linear trends, signified by dotted lines, in both countries are clear. The proportion of cradle Catholics from each birth year who still identified as Catholic when they responded to the survey declines over time. Furthermore, over the six decades from 1920 to 1980 the rate of decline has been slightly sharper in America than in Britain. That is to say, retention rates of those born in the 1920s are around 15 percentage points higher in America than in Britain. By the time one gets to those born in the late 1970s, the American retention rate has declined by around 25 percentage points, and the British by about 20, to reach the 10 percentage point difference we have seen throughout

---

[14] Only those aged 30 or over at the time of being interviewed have been included here, due to data suggesting—as alluded to briefly in the previous footnote—that a significant degree of disaffiliation occurs in the late teens and twenties (cf. McClendon and Hackett 2014). The full range of birth years has also been curtailed, due to low numbers at the very low and very high end of the range.

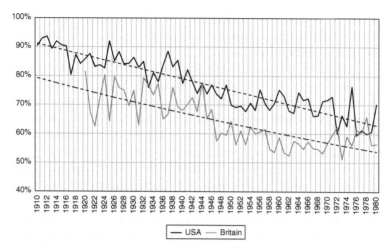

Figure 2.4. Overall rate of retention of cradle Catholics in the USA and Britain, by year of birth

Source: GSS (1973–2016; weighted data) and BSA (1991–2016; weighted data)

this chapter. Of course, what the graph doesn't tell us is *when* those disaffiliated actually did so, or perhaps better, when that (typically long) process began—just that people born different birth years have different likelihoods of being disaffiliated by the time they were interviewed. In light of this book's title, it is worth noting that all respondents were interviewed 'since Vatican II'.

On the question of 'points of no return', note what occurs in the British data in the mid-1940s. Taken together, 1945 and 1946 seem to mark a clear watershed. Compared to the retention rates of the years immediately prior, they mark a relatively low point, with only three years in the previous twenty recording equal or lower levels. However, in the thirty-odd years which follow them, *no* year's retention rate is higher, and only a couple (i.e., 1950, 1972) really come close. Furthermore, the mean retention rate from 1920–44 is 72 per cent, whereas from 1947–80 it is just 58 per cent; a drop of fourteen percentage points. As a slight aside—foreshadowing topics broached more fully in Chapter 4—we might note this 1945/6 watershed is striking in light of wider literature on British secularization. Much of this focuses on the immediate post-war Boomer generation who, of course, began coming of age in the early- to mid-1960s (Bruce and Glendinning 2010; Field 2015: 1–15). Religiously speaking, something certainly 'happened' in connection with Britons born from 1945 onwards. Quite *what* is, to a major degree, one of the largest questions hanging over this whole book.

Our American data tell a somewhat different story. There is not such an obvious watershed moment. One could, however, argue for a transitional period, from roughly 1943 to 1949, where retention rates fluctuate between the mid- to high-70s. In the three decades prior, all but three years record retention rates in the 80s or even higher. After 1943–9, not only are the 80s never reached again, but even the mid-70s become ever rarer exceptions to the general rule. There are, moreover, two specific troughs: those born between 1950 and 1955 (and thus coming of age in the late 1960s and early 1970s), with retention holding steady around the 70 per cent mark, and then with those born from 1972 onwards, whose retention levels, albeit with some striking exceptions, are not far from the 'British range' of high-50s to low-60s. Note that Figure 2.4 specifically excludes those who responded to the survey before the age of 30, to allow for fairer comparisons across each year. That a high proportion of so-called 'millennials'—roughly speaking, those born from 1980 onwards—identify with 'no religion' is, however, no secret (Pew Research Center 2015b: 20–5).

On this reading of the US data, we must still contend with a significant post-war, downward trend in retention, and therefore with an upward trend in disaffiliation. Certainly, the downturn was less sharp there than in Britain; as we have noted, the 'transitional phase' there was much briefer, beginning later, and ending earlier, than in America. Why this might be the case is, once again, a topic to be explored in Chapter 4.

ETHNICITY AND IMMIGRATION

Earlier on, while discussing regional differences, we touched briefly on the question of ethnicity. Specifically, the relatively high retention rates in some areas of the USA were ascribed, in part, to a significant Latino presence. This raises two critical topics for discussions of Catholic identity and practice in Britain or America (or anywhere): race/ethnicity, and immigration. Strictly speaking, these are separate issues. Since in practice they overlap a great deal, we will treat them here interrelatedly.

To a great extent, the history of Catholicism in both our countries is one of immigration. The specifically Irish contribution to the Church in Britain, over several waves from the mid-nineteenth century onwards, is widely acknowledged; Italians, Poles, Spaniards, Ukrainians, Lithuanians, Vietnamese, Keralan Indians, Filipinos, and many others, have all also made their mark. Further, from the Spanish settlement of Florida in the sixteenth century and Jamestown's 'secret Catholics' (LaFrance 2015) in the seventeenth, followed by constant waves of Catholics, first primarily from the Old World of Europe (see O'Toole 2008: 94–144), and then increasingly from the New Worlds of East and West, the American Church is indeed well-described as a 'communion of immigrants' (Fisher 2007).[15]

This process is, of course, as much a present reality as it is a historical one. Just as in the past, today's immigrants do not simply bring with them an abstract Catholicity; rather, their Catholicism comes as (often a large) part of an ethnic identity and culture, and thus carries with it specific customs, festivals, devotions, favoured saints, musical styles, worship preferences, even (in the case of members of the Eastern Catholic Churches) its own liturgy and hierarchy. Since, initially at least, immigrants tend both to live among their own—hence Edinburgh's Little Ireland or Miami's Little Havana—and to feel it important and comforting to preserve aspects of 'back home', this has clear implications for Catholic identity and practice. This is most noticeable where levels of religiosity are already higher in the country of origin than in the new locale. Whether Mexicans in El Paso, Italians in Glamorgan, Vietnamese in San Jose, or Lithuanians in Coatbridge, they cannot but raise the religious average if present in sufficient numbers.

What effect does all of this have on disaffiliation in particular? At this point, unfortunately, our British data are of little direct help. The BSA asks little about immigration-related subjects directly. Nor is its 'race and ethnicity' question (of interest in itself, but also potentially a proxy for immigration) much help to us: there is only a single 'White' category, which means we can't specially seek out, say, Poles, Italians, or Irish. While breakdowns *are* possible for a small number of other racial or ethnic groups, they are not present in sufficient numbers for

---

[15] Vivid confirmation of this is impressed upon visitors to the National Shrine of the Immaculate Conception in Washington, DC, through a series of stunning statues and chapels dedicated to the 'Our Lady of . . .' most beloved of a particular people. Our Lady of Walsingham is, I noticed, sadly absent.

the kinds of analyses we are doing here to be performed with any confidence. That said, there is reasonable evidence suggesting that cradle-Catholic members of ethnic minorities are significantly more practising than cradle-Catholic Whites (Bullivant 2016b: 20), which, given the presumption of a link between lapsation and disaffiliation, is certainly worth knowing. Using 2016 European Social Survey data for the whole UK, we may also note that 21 per cent of current Catholics are foreign-born, compared to 8 per cent of the adult population at large (Bullivant 2018a). The biggest groups of Catholic immigrants come from Poland (9 per cent), Ireland (6 per cent), and the Philippines (3 per cent). These hints aside, however, the rest of this subsection will focus on US data.

In addition to our standard affiliation categories, Table 2.6 also breaks down the overall retainee share into regular (i.e., monthly-or-more) and low/non practisers, as per Figures 2.2 and 2.3. As there, this enables us further to identify patterns within Catholic affiliation. Here we have three categories, corresponding to the three most numerous race/ethnicity options among American cradle Catholics: White, Hispanic,[16] and Black/African American. For reference, these

Table 2.6. Current religious affiliation/practice of American cradle Catholics from selected (self-identified) racial/ethnic backgrounds

Race/ethnicity	Current affiliation (%)			
	Catholic [regular + low/no practice]	(Other) Christian	Non-Christian religion	No religion
White	65 [29 + 36]	15	2	18
Hispanic	76 [41 + 36]	12	1	10
Black/African American	51 [31 + 20]	24	0	25

Source: GSS (2012–16; weighted data).

[16] An important caveat must be raised here regarding the labels 'Hispanic' (as used by the GSS, following the US Census Bureau's current convention) and 'Latino' (as generally used in this book, except where commenting directly on sources using something different, as here). In the first place, neither 'Hispanic' nor 'Latino' are, strictly speaking, racial designators, despite being often used in this way as self-designations. In fact, the persistent use of them as such is what eventually prompted

respectively account for 77 per cent, 12 per cent, and 5 per cent of all born-and-raised Catholics. The roughly dozen other groupings, who make up the remaining 6 per cent, don't show up in the GSS data in sufficient numbers for inclusion here. However, a Pew Research Center study of Asian Americans revealed a retention rate of 72 per cent among cradle Catholics, with 13 per cent now claiming a Protestant affiliation, and 5 per cent religiously unaffiliated (2012b: 57). Filipino- and Vietnamese-Americans are the largest Asian groups in the Catholic population. Though accounting for a small percentage of the total, their absolute numbers are nevertheless significant. I estimate that around 2.5 million Filipino-Americans and 0.6 million Vietnamese-Americans, of all ages, currently identify as Catholic.[17]

Each of these labels includes, or rather obscures, a great span of diversity. Hispanic is a case in point—and one of particular, and ever growing, salience to American Catholic demographics (Wuthnow 2007: 197–201). It is worth noting that while such generic labels are undoubtedly useful, 'When it comes to describing their identity, most Hispanics prefer their family's country of origin over pan-ethnic terms' (Pew Hispanic Center 2012: 3). This is significant. Historians of nineteenth-century Catholic America are fond of delineating the differences, interplay, and (often enough) rivalries between communities hailing from diverse *European* national backgrounds. The same undoubtedly applies today with those of Cuban, Mexican, Venezuelan, Salvadoran, or Dominican descent. As Timothy Matovina points out, referring to the alternative catch-all label of 'Latino' (and the same applies to Hispanic too):

> It is difficult to make simple generalizations about Latinos. Although 'Latino Catholics' may be a convenient term to distinguish those with

the Census Bureau to include 'Hispanic' as an option within a new, combined 'race and ethnicity question'. Accordingly, it's perfectly possible to be—and to regard oneself—as both White *and* Hispanic/Latino, or indeed Black *and* Hispanic/Latino. Indeed, according to Pew data, 31% of American Latinos regard their primary racial identity as White, and 3% as Black (Pew Hispanic Center 2012: 3). Hence even more so than usual with racial/ethnic identities, the categories used here should not be regarded as wholly clear cut: they reflect how respondents choose to characterize their race/ethnicity background from a set menu of options, and where two or more such options are given, they reflect the first one mentioned.

[17] Based on the US Census Bureau's 2016 American Community Survey figures of 3.9 million and 2.1 million for the Filipino and Vietnamese populations, and Pew's 2012 findings of 65% and 30% Catholic affiliation for each group (Pew Research Center 2012b: 16).

ancestral or personal origins in the Spanish-speaking world from U.S.
Catholics with ties to the majority culture or other ethnic and racial
groups, the idea of a generic Latino Catholic is no more useful than that
of a generic African, Asian, European, or Native American Catholic.

(2011: ix)

This fact, in turn, impacts upon the 'regionality' of patterns of belief,
practice, and affiliation. There is no reason to suppose, and lots of good
reasons *not* to suppose, that (say) a 30 per cent Latino/Hispanic share of
a particular area's Catholic population, made up as it will be of a
complex mix of ethno-national communities each with its own specific
history and texture, 'amounts to the same thing' as a similarly sized
Hispanic/Latino population elsewhere. This much is clear even from
successful efforts at forging a 'pan-Latino solidarity' out of groups from
multiple national backgrounds, as at the *Misión Católica Nuestra
Señora de las Américas* in Doraville, Georgia, on the north-eastern
outskirts of Atlanta. There, as with the Latino population as a whole,
those of a Mexican background form by far the largest contingent. But
alongside a richly Mexican-inflected devotional and cultural life, the
Misión also serves as a hub for the Feast days cherished by the Peruvian,
Honduran, Dominican, Ecuadorian, and other national communities
from across the Atlanta Metro area (Marquardt 2005). Incidentally, the
retention of distinctively national religious identities, at least among
first- and (far less so) second-generation immigrants, is taken even
further among Filipino-Americans. At least in areas with a significant
concentration of Filipino Catholics, it is often the distinctive culture of
one's native region, or indeed hometown, that takes precedence.
Aprilfaye Manalang's absorbing research among the large Filipino
community in the Hampton Roads area of Virginia, for example,
highlights the importance of such regionalism in fostering both
religious and civic identity (2013: 51–94).

Even understood as averages made up of a wide variety of contributing groups, the differential retention rates of Whites, Hispanics,
and Blacks in Table 2.6 are striking. Three in every four Hispanic
cradle Catholics still identifies as Catholic, and over half of these say
they attend church at least monthly (cf. Pew Research Center 2014).
By contrast, only two-thirds of White born-and-raised Catholics still
regard themselves as such, with the less-than-monthly attenders
predominating among them. (In point of fact, though, Whites and
Hispanics produce the same *proportion* of low/non-practisers: slightly
over a third in both cases.) In both cases, those who do disaffiliate

divide more or less evenly between switchers to a different religious identity and nones.

The Black/African American figures, with only half having retained a Catholic identity, are more striking still. Meanwhile, no religion and other Christian denominations account for a quarter apiece. This may seem to be at odds with traditional assumptions, and indeed a good deal of evidence, as to the comparative strength of African-American religiosity (e.g., Masci 2018). However, a good proportion of 'Black religious distinctiveness' arises from a confluence of demographic, socio-economic, and regional factors (Hunt and Hunt 2001). For example, a majority of Blacks live in the South where, as noted above, levels of religious belief and practice are typically robust. The correlation between economic deprivation and religiosity is naturally also a factor in a nation where 22 per cent of Blacks live in poverty, compared to 19 per cent of Hispanics, and only 6 per cent of non-Hispanic Whites (US Census Bureau 2017). Given the particular history of Black Catholics in America, it would not be surprising if this so-called 'minority within a minority'—albeit one amounting to perhaps three million people, and with more members than several large and historic Black Protestant denominations (Cressler 2017: 5)—were to have a distinctive social, economic, and geographical profile, and thus a distinctive religious one too. As things stand, despite Black Catholics' low overall retention rate, the proportion of regularly practising Catholics is very similar to that of Whites. Black cradle Catholics, it would appear, are less likely than are White ones simply to lapse while remaining nominally Catholic. Rather, they tend either to switch to a different Christian identity, or to renounce religious identity altogether. This apparent propensity of Black cradle Catholics for nonversion is, incidentally, noteworthy: in general, African-Americans have the lowest proportion of nones of all America's main ethnic groups, though this is steadily growing (Jones and Cox 2017: 33).

Let us turn now to immigration. This is currently, as it ever has been, a major contributor to American Catholic life. A quarter of cradle Catholics say that they were not born in the USA. Two-fifths have at least one foreign-born parent; one-in-three have two. As one would expect there are significant differences here across ethnic groups. The foreign-born account for 66 per cent of Filipinos, 60 per cent of Hispanics, and 23 per cent of Black/African Americans. Even among White cradle Catholics, the proportion is still fairly high at around 17 per cent. And in fact, there are more foreign-born Whites (albeit itself a broad category) among adult US cradle Catholics than there are from all other ethnicities put together.[18]

In an attempt to gauge the correlation of identity/practice with different immigration profiles, Table 2.7 presents four categories: (i) Natives (themselves, both parents, and all four grandparents born in the USA); (ii) Third Generation immigrants (all four grandparents born outside of the USA, but both parents and themselves US-born); (iii) Second Generation immigrants (themselves US-born, but both parents and all grandparents foreign-born); and (iv) First Generation immigrants (neither themselves, parents, nor any grandparents born in the USA).[19]

Our data demonstrate a clear correlation between 'nativeness' and disaffiliation. Within the Native group itself, only three-in-five still identify as Catholic, with a clear skew towards the low/non practising end. By contrast, three-quarters of both First and Second Generations have retained their Catholic identity, with regular practice the norm. Third Generations, meanwhile, are something of a halfway house between Natives and First/Seconds. The parity between First and Second Generation immigrants is surprising. One might have expected that being born in the USA *oneself*, or not, would be a decisive factor. But the big difference, it would seem, is between having *parents* who are US-born, as do the Natives and Thirds, and *parents* who are foreign-born, as do the Seconds and Firsts. Compared to this, whether or not oneself is US-born seems not to matter.

This is a highly suggestive finding. In recent years, an impressive body of research has established the critical nature of parental religiosity as a predictor of their children's religiosity as adults (e.g., Bader and Desmond 2006; Storm and Voas 2012; Bengtson et al. 2013; Brañas-Garza et al. 2013). Crockett and Voas' analyses of successive waves of the British Household Panel Survey, for example, demonstrate that where both parents practise monthly or more, the likelihood of their young adult children (i.e., 16–29) doing likewise is around one-in-two; where only one does, it is around one-in-five; and where neither does, one-in-forty. Affiliation, moreover, is only somewhat more resilient.

---

[18] All statistics in this paragraph are based on weighted GSS 2012–16 data.

[19] Obviously, this breakdown represents a fair degree of tidying: those with only one parent born in the USA, or, say, three grandparents foreign-born have been excluded in the interests of clarity.

Table 2.7. Current religious affiliation/practice of American cradle Catholics with different immigrant profiles

	Born in USA?			Current affiliation (%)			
	Self	No. of parents	No. of grandparents	Catholic [regular + low/no practice]	(Other) Christian	Non-Christian religion	No religion
Native	Y	2	4	58 [25 + 33]	17	2	22
Third Generation	Y	2	0	68 [34 + 34]	10	8	14
Second Generation	Y	0	0	78 [42 + 36]	9	1	12
First Generation	N	0	0	75 [43 + 32]	14	0	10

Source: GSS (2012–16; weighted data).

Where both parents affirm a religious identity (i.e., something other than 'no religion' or 'don't know'), one-in-two young adult children also do; where only one does, it is just under one-in-three; where neither does, one-in-ten (Crockett and Voas 2006: 577–8). While such numbers are not exactly encouraging for the churches, they nevertheless testify to the *difference* that familial religiosity during one's upbringing makes to adult outcomes (albeit, as noted previously, in a difficult climate to begin with for religious transmission).

That the more strongly religious families *tend* to produce more strongly religious children, who in turn *tend* to become the more strongly religious adults, is not in itself a surprising finding. After all, one would expect levels of religiosity in childhood and adolescence to have notable continuity with adult levels. Needless to say, it is normally one's parents who are the decisive influence here (even if direct influence begins to wane as time goes on): whether and how often a child goes to church (and which!), religious habits in the home (celebrations, grace before meals, bedtime prayers), religious schooling or catechesis, permission to participate in church-related activities (and willingness to pay and/or drive), are all under parental control.

While fairly obvious when stated like this, what it should perhaps do is shift our perspective when looking at the kinds of patterns-over-time delineated in, say, Table 2.7. If the immigrant status of a person's parents is, *prima facie*, a key factor in their affiliation and/or practice as an adult, then might not parental influence manifest in other ways also? Thus if we are interested in why, say, retention rates among Baby Boomers are suddenly and significantly lower than for those born in earlier years, then we surely need to think carefully about how their *parents* might have brought them up differently, and why. Rather than ask only 'what happened to the Baby Boomers to make them less religious?', we must also ask 'what happened to the Baby Boomers' parents to make them produce less religious children?' Accordingly, this 'parental perspective' will be a recurrent theme throughout Chapters 4–7.

CONCLUSION

The quantitative evidence presented above lays out a skeletal account of Catholic disaffiliation in Britain and the USA. Most important here are (a) the sheer size of the phenomenon as a whole, and (b) the diversity within our generic category of 'Catholic disaffiliation' (i.e., coming to adopt 'no religion' is a rather different affair to joining a megachurch, or indeed a mosque). More specifically, we have focused here on a number of specific areas: regional and denominational comparisons, shifts over time, and breakdowns according to sex, age, racial/ethnic, and immigration profiles. Along the way, we have noted some major differences between Britain and the USA. These are, of course, significant. But so too—and perhaps more so—are the many similarities.

A large number of the findings presented in this chapter will end up being referred back to in the chapters to come. Perhaps most important will be the changing historical patterns to disaffiliation identified in Figure 2.4. These dynamics undergird the structuring of the historical chapters, 4 to 7. Also significant targets for further discussion (and, to some degree, attempted explanation) are the gendered nature of lapsation and disaffiliation, the varied impacts of immigration, and, although no systematic account here will be possible, vagaries of geography within each country. It is worth noting too, of course, that very few of the topics we have focused on can be understood in isolation. The point has been made explicitly with regard to regionality, where mention was made of immigration levels, as well as of wider religious culture (including, of course, what's going on in other denominations). But it applies more generally too.

Critical as these kinds of big-picture statistical overviews are, they can only ever take us so far. These are the bare bones, giving necessary shape and structure to the more nuanced layers which will soon flesh out the whole. Accordingly, we turn now to consider a body of qualitative research attempting to discover the reasons *why* significant numbers of Catholics either lapse or disaffiliate entirely.

3

Why They Say They Leave

The obvious way to discover why and how Catholics lapse or disaffiliate is, of course, simply to ask them. This chapter's main aim, therefore, is to present and discuss the findings from the small number of studies that have done precisely that. These will principally be: Dean Hoge's nearly 200 interviews with so-called 'dropouts' in 1979 (Hoge et al. 1981); a late 2011 survey of 'nearly 300 non-churchgoing Catholics' both within, and commissioned by, the Diocese of Trenton, New Jersey (Byron and Zech 2012); the Diocese of Springfield, Illinois' online survey of over 500 'inactive, lapsed and drifting parishioners' in late 2012 and early 2013 (Hardy et al. 2014); and, from Britain, the Diocese of Portsmouth's online survey of around 260 'inactive Catholics', for which I served as principal investigator in late 2015 (Bullivant et al. 2019).[1] In all cases, the primary focus is on lapsation in general, rather than disaffiliation specifically. That is not, of course, in itself a problem. As argued previously, the 'lapsation milieu' is a critical context for understanding disaffiliation itself. Furthermore, several of the studies do indeed touch on affiliation and identity directly. This is most clearly the case with the Portsmouth study.

The use of telephone or face-to-face interviews, or detailed mail or online surveys, allow plenty of scope for digging deeply into a range of key questions at the heart of this monograph. For who can better tell

---

[1] While these four studies are the most directly relevant here, and as such will be our main sources, it is worth noting some wider qualitative work on lapsed or disaffiliated Catholics. These include a major study commissioned by the Australian Bishops' Conference (Dixon et al. 2007), as well as some broader studies of religious lapsation, which include either British or American Catholics in their sample (e.g., Richter and Francis 1998; Francis and Richter 2007; Streib et al. 2009; Zuckerman 2011).

us how, when, and why Catholics come no longer to practise, or what having a Catholic identity—and indeed, having had one, but discarded it—*means*, than such people themselves, and in their own words? Critically, such methods allow us to move far beyond the 'tick-box talk' of large-scale surveys, to at least the outskirts of 'how people describe themselves in real talk' (Day and Lee 2014: 346).

All this is true enough, and much will be made of such evidence both here and in the chapters to come. Matters are not so absolutely straightforward, however. For example, one need not be so cynical as TV's Dr House—'Everybody lies!'—to note that the narratives people present, to themselves as much as to other people, do not necessarily tell the full story. This could take several forms. Someone might, say, overemphasize the role that a particular point of principle really played in his or her particular journey (e.g., 'I realized I couldn't possibly belong to an institution that prohibits X'), over more significant yet prosaic factors (e.g., in the busyness of work and family life, attending Mass gradually slipping down, then eventually off, the 'to do' list, until after a long period of non-practice realizing that he or she hasn't 'felt' Catholic in many years). Equally, a person might not appreciate that moving away from family and the *Cheers*-like parish 'where everybody knows your name, and they're always glad you came' played a vastly stronger role in undermining their Catholic practice, belief, and identity (in that order) than did the more intellectual aspects of their time grappling with physics or philosophy at university. In neither case, of course, would the moral or intellectual factors be irrelevant. Far from it; our wholly hypothetical examples *really do* disagree with the Church about X, and *really did* struggle to understand how Y could be true if Z is (which it is). However, they are neither the only, nor the most, significant influences.

Issues of sampling and representativeness must also be borne in mind (cf. Hoge et al. 1981: 81–2; Richter and Francis 1998: 170). For good practical reasons, the kinds of sampling methods undergirding the last chapter's quantitative data are simply not possible in this realm. Instead, researchers must find ways of actively targeting members of a desired group. Non-practising Catholics tend not to congregate together. Hence the only means by which some of them can be contacted—often via friends or family members who do practise— near-certainly skew the sample in certain directions. Furthermore, even when they have heard about it, one would also expect certain sorts of 'eligible' people to be more likely than others actually to take the trouble to respond. This applies especially to those with a specific story to tell or complaint to make (as opposed to those for whom the shift from practice to non-practice, or from 'Catholic' to 'none', simply happened without it really being given a thought, either then or since). Certain types of people from certain backgrounds also might feel more comfortable talking to strangers, or filling out long web surveys.

Needless to say, concerns such as these are not specific to our topic: not only are they endemic to qualitative research, but practitioners are well aware of them, and have various means of mitigating them so far as is possible. It must also be stated, forcefully, that a survey or interview sample *needn't* be fully representative in order to yield a huge amount of rich and significant data. Thus a survey might, for whatever reasons, recruit a greater proportion of middle-class women in their fifties and sixties than would be typical among Catholic disaffiliates as a whole. Such respondents might well not 'speak for', say, the large proportion of young working-class men who are more-or-less absent from the sample. But it needn't stop them from being broadly representative of *some* types of people with the same or similar socio-demographic profiles. The mere fact that findings from a certain sample can't be generalized to the whole, does not entail that they cannot legitimately be generalized to a part (and perhaps a very large part) of it. That is to say, so long as we are aware of the limits of our samples, and exercise due caution when generalizing or extrapolating from them, we stand to gain a very great deal indeed.

AMERICAN 'DROPOUTS' OF THE LATE 1970s

That significant numbers of cradle Catholics in America (as else-where) were no longer practising their faith was no secret by the 1970s and early 1980s. Disaffiliation or 'dealignment' was also a recognized, if not yet fretted-about, phenomenon (e.g., Greeley 1985: 50–2). In the late 1970s, the American Bishops' Committee on Evangelization commissioned a non-Catholic sociologist, Dean Hoge, to lead a major study of 'religious change among Catholics' in late 1979 and early 1980. This ultimately involved hundreds of detailed telephone interviews across seven different dioceses (see Hoge et al. 1981: 4–8).

As the resulting book's title—*Converts, Dropouts, Returnees*—indicates, the project's remit was rather broader than the specific element that shall be our focus here.

The term 'dropout', while memorable, is by no means the preferred term within *Mass Exodus*. Nevertheless, since it features so prominently in Hoge's pioneering study, where it is defined in quite specific terms, it shall be retained in this section. By Hoge's definition, a dropout is a baptized Catholic 'who has changed from active to inactive status within the past three years'. 'Active' status is defined by having attended Mass at least twice in the previous year, aside from weddings, funerals, Christmas, and Easter; 'inactive' accordingly refers to someone who attends less often than this, including not at all (Hoge et al. 1981: 5). The overarching purpose of the study was to explore *recent* changes within the Catholic community. Hence, in order to count for the purposes of the survey, Hoge's dropouts were required to have moved from activity to inactivity within the past three years. Given our overarching interest in disaffiliation, it is important to note that:

> These definitions do not include whether a person considers himself or herself a Catholic, or whether the person has certain beliefs or personal practices. The definitions are solely a matter of actual involvement in Catholic church life. (Hoge et al. 1981: 5–6)

Note also the low threshold Hoge's methodology specifies for being active or not (far lower, for example, than the 'at least monthly' watershed adopted in our last chapter to divide 'regular practisers' from 'low/non practisers').

> The level of involvement deemed adequate for being active is minimal. [...] In fact, the definition of active sounded too minimal to a number of people we interviewed. Some persons told us they were inactive, but when they became aware of the definition we were using in the study, they said, 'Well, by that definition I guess I'm an active Catholic!' and they chuckled. (Hoge et al. 1981: 6)

Before discussing the findings themselves, the study highlights a number of other interesting things. It cites, for example, intriguing Gallup data charting the falling levels of weekly Catholic church attendance between 1955 and 1978 (Hoge et al. 1981: 24). This affected the 18–29 age group most sharply: from levels in the low 70 per cents (!) up to 1960, to around 55 per cent by 1970, and down to around 38 per cent or so by the end of the 1970s. Significantly, this decline began to register *before* the end of Vatican II. (In fact, it first shows up in the data for 1964, perhaps not coincidentally when the first wave of Baby Boomers were entering the 18–29 age bracket.) Among the two older age groups, 30–49 and 50+, clear signs of decline are only apparent from 1969 onwards. Also worth noting, Hoge and colleagues estimated that 'about 35% of those dropping out did so by age 20, and 54% did so by age 25' (Hoge et al. 1981: 84).

Simplifying a great deal of rich detail here—the final report synthesizes findings from 182 interviews—*Converts, Dropouts, Returnees* identifies five distinct groupings of dropouts. The first group are labelled the *family-tension dropouts* who 'drop out because they are in rebellion against family pressure' (Hoge et al. 1981: 97–105).[2] For obvious reasons, this type was most prevalent among the younger interviewees. It could take one of two main forms. At the more moderate end, these are Catholic young adults who, despite years of family attendance, catechesis, and sacramental preparation, nevertheless feel little personal attachment to Catholicism.

> As they grow older, they feel no motivation to go to church, and as soon as family pressure is off, they drop out. Parents do not strongly object, since they have defined their duty as exposing their child adequately to the faith and tradition, and if the child wants to walk away from it, it is the child's business.

In the second and sharper form, the situation is far less peaceable on either side, playing out within 'a general rebellion by the youth against their families and all their families stand for'. In these cases, although specific criticisms were (often emotionally) levelled against Catholicism—'that the church is full of hypocrites, that it is unbearably boring, and that the priests are always asking for money'—the researchers interpreted these to be 'not explanations for their behavior; they are rationalizations'. Central to the researchers' characterization of *both* kinds of family-tension dropouts, 'is that they drop out of church life for reasons other than church life'. Perhaps this is so with the latter group, whose rejection of church attendance is caught up within a much broader pushing away from their family's norms.

---

[2] For neatness' sake, each précis of one of the five types will be accompanied by a single reference to the short span of pages from which all quotations in that paragraph have been taken.

I am not so convinced, however, that this is accurate of the former, more moderate sort. At a bare minimum, these would seem to be cradle Catholics who, despite a high level of religious input through most of their lives up to this point, 'for various reasons have never internalized or "owned" their faith'. The fact that 'church life' holds so few attractions for such people—even at so minimum a level as attending Mass twice in twelve months, not including Christmas and Easter—is scarcely irrelevant to the fact of their dropping out, even if additional factors are in play.

In fact, there is clear overlap here between this category and Hoge et al.'s second, and indeed largest, type, the *weary dropouts*: 'What defines this type is that, for some reason, these persons had no motivation for Mass attendance and thus stopped going' (Hoge et al. 1981: 105–11). With this very diverse grouping, the most interesting question is what triggered their dropping out at some specific time. That is to say, 'why didn't they stop earlier, if they lacked motivation to go?' (cf. Richter and Francis 1998: 22–3). As it turns out, the proximate causes tended to be variedly prosaic: children growing up and leaving home, removing the motivation to go to church oneself; new job, longer hours, less spare time; separation or divorce from partners who had been the main pushers of church attendance; recent experience of an unpleasant conflict with a priest or with others in the parish. Some of these people, the researchers remark, are perhaps better described as 'bored dropouts' than as 'weary' ones. What all have in common is the lack of a strong, intrinsic motivation for attending church.

> In short, something had happened to remove an earlier extrinsic motivation, and no intrinsic motivation remained. Or an unhappy incident or ongoing struggle had overpowered their weak intrinsic motivation.

As with the previous category, specific criticisms of the Church, its teachings, and practices, *are* often enunciated along the way. However, in the researchers' own words, 'The extent to which these criticisms motivated them to drop out is not clear, but we suspect that in most cases they were not the main motivation.'

The third group, *lifestyle dropouts*, were those whose 'present attitudes and lifestyles', especially in matters of sexual and relationship matters, 'were in conflict with the church at this point, and when faced with the choice of changing lifestyles or dropping out of the church, they left the church' (Hoge et al. 1981: 112–16). Most specifically, 'their unhappiness was caused by the rules governing birth control, the church's stand on divorce and remarriage, and the changes since Vatican II'.[3] Interestingly, lifestyle dropouts as a group tended not to differ significantly from many of those in Hoge et al.'s other categories on these points—that is, dropouts tended generally to think that the Church was misguided on such sexual matters. For the 'lifestylers', however, such disagreements were not purely theoretical. In several cases, they had resulted in specific points of conflict with a priest.

> Indications are that the conflicts had more to do with church authority and law than with personal differences. Lifestyle dropouts were sometimes angry at the church and at the priests when the priests refused their requests—sacramental remarriage after divorce, approval for artificial birth control, approval for premarital cohabitation, and so on.

The fourth and smallest category are those whose practice had lapsed due to not having felt supported by their Catholic communities during an hour, or much longer, of need (Hoge et al. 1981: 116–24). Hoge's team dub these *spiritual-need dropouts*, and note that they are both overwhelmingly women (some four-fifths of their sample), and also include a higher-than-average proportion of Blacks and Hispanics.

> The spiritual-need dropouts left in a time of spiritual need or personal crisis when they felt that they could not go to church for help. [. . .] All of them told of personal problems or recent experiences that deeply troubled them.

These could take a wide range of forms: bereavement, divorce, 'situations of marital crisis, menopause, or long-term recurring emotional problems'. Significantly, a good proportion of these people had already become practising members of other denominations or religious groups. Others, the researchers comment, 'are ripe for outconversion, since their predispositions for change are strong, and when facilitating persons appear, they will join other groups'.

---

[3] It is unclear to what 'the changes since Vatican II' refers here. It seems unlikely that a consonance with the concerns of the *antichange dropouts*, discussed below, is implied. Feasibly, the *re-emphasis* of the traditional prohibition of artificial birth control in 1968's encyclical *Humanae Vitae* (see Chapter 5) is meant, though this can scarcely be regarded as a 'change'. On balance, perhaps what is meant here is the fact that, at a time of many *other* changes, the teaching on birth control wasn't among them.

The final group are the *antichange dropouts*: those leaving in protest, or perhaps frustrated resignation, at one or more of 'the changes' in Catholic life occurring in the wake of the Second Vatican Council (Hoge et al. 1981: 124–9). Though small in number,[4] their existence in the sample at all is itself noteworthy. Given the fact that the study's data-collection period was 1979–80, and included as dropouts only those who had done so within the past three years, one might not expect there to be any such people still left. In fact, the 'long tail' of the turbulence engendered by the Council, and its implementations, will be a major topic in our Chapter 6. Hoge et al.'s comment on this, though, is worth recording here:

> When we designed the Study of Religious Change, we preferred to exclude those persons who dropped out of the church during the late 1960s and 1970s—when change was the fastest—so we limited the study to those who dropped out within the past three years. However, we got some antichange dropouts anyway, partly because many parishes have been making changes in style and program, even up to the present.

Perhaps not surprisingly, antichange as a primary motivation was limited in the sample to the older dropouts (the youngest grouping, aged 22 or below, would have been 10 at most by the Council's close). Indeed, the average of dropping out was 40 among antichangers, the oldest of the categories' by some margin. Intriguingly, however, this group tended not to have been particularly strongly active prior to their lessening of practice; many were 'persons whose church commitment in the past decade was superficial'. Still, they nevertheless expressed some strong views:

> The Mass was clearly the focal point of their feelings. Typically, they found the new liturgy too social, too modern, and not serene or quiet enough. Many disliked the new musical forms, such as folk music. A second theme was dissatisfaction with the priests or nuns: they were too socially oriented, too buddy-buddy, or, in the case of nuns, they should dress like they used to.

No apologies are made here for dwelling in such descriptive detail on *Converts, Dropouts, Returnees*' fivefold typology of recently lapsed

---

[4] Seven per cent of the sample are categorized as having dropped out primarily for antichange reasons, the same proportion as for spiritual-need ones. In the sample as a whole though, 19% of older dropouts, and 3% of younger, are recorded as having 'Objections to changes in Mass or other recent changes' (Hoge et al. 1981: 86).

Catholics of the late 1970s and very-early 1980s. As well as being *the* seminal study in this area, it offers an invaluable, and now-unrepeatable, insight into Catholic lapsation during a critical period. The three other studies we'll be focusing on, meanwhile, were all undertaken within the past half-decade. In itself, this is not a bad thing, given our overarching focus on understanding *contemporary* disaffiliates and disaffiliation. But how we *got* to the contemporary situation is a major part of that. And, of course, a good proportion of today's lapsed or disaffiliated Catholics would themselves have first 'dropped out' in the 1970s and 1980s.

Two further things are worth noting. First, there is the simple fact that Hoge et al.'s five types (family-tension, weary, lifestyle, spiritual-need, and antichange) will, if perhaps in different proportions and with different specific concerns, be recognizable in our 2010s samples. While the terminology used to describe them may be different, we shall meet all of these, in some cases many times, again. Second though, it must be stated that, in many cases, lapsed and disaffiliated individuals avoid easy or straightforward categorization. Hoge et al.'s categories are attempts at sorting out, logically and usefully, 182 real-live interviewees, all with a complex mix of influences and motivations (cf. Hoge et al. 1981: 86–7), into some semblance of order. So far as it goes, they succeed. But one can always cut the same piece of cloth in different ways. A person whom one researcher might count as, say, a family-tension dropout, might just as plausibly be a spiritual-need one in another's eyes. This is not a criticism of the Hoge study per se. It is simply an observation concerning the 'complex and messy' (Gregg and Scholefield 2015: 10) nature of real-life religiosity. We have made it before in this study, and we will have cause to make it again.

TRENTON, NEW JERSEY

It is no secret that increasing numbers of baptized Catholics in the United States never or rarely attend Sunday Mass. In the late fall of 2011, we asked some of them a simple question: Why?

(Byron and Zech 2012: 17)

Thus begins William J. Byron and Charles Zech's write-up in *America* of their research on 'non-churchgoing Catholics' in the Diocese of Trenton, comprising four counties in central New Jersey.[5] Trenton itself, the State capital, has a strong industrial and Catholic heritage, a good proportion of it Irish-tinged. In terms of the Census Bureau's divisions used in Chapter 2's geographical breakdowns, New Jersey comes within the Middle Atlantic. This whole area has a relatively strong retention rate at 70 per cent. Among those who have disaffiliated, however, approaching two-thirds are now nones.

Concerned by the fact that 'only 25 percent of our Catholic population were attending Mass on a regular basis' (quoted in Fliteau 2012), Trenton's new bishop David O'Connell wanted to know why. The resulting study was—to the best of my knowledge—the first such officially-commissioned study in America since Hoge's. Furthermore, Byron and Zech's precise questionnaire schedule formed the basis, with modifications, for the Springfield and Portsmouth surveys to be discussed anon. In Byron and Zech's case, respondents were found by trying to reach 'registered parishioners who no longer practise [...] by placing articles in the secular and diocesan press, posting notices in parish bulletins and asking pastors for contact information'. Those willing to participate received a short schedule of generally open-ended questions, either by email or post, in English or Spanish. Respondents in the sample ranged from the ages of 16 to 90, with 53 the average. Respondents overwhelmingly identified as White/Caucasian (95 per cent), and approaching two-thirds (63 per cent) were women (Byron and Zech 2012: 17).

Among several interesting findings, Byron and Zech report that an 'overwhelming majority' of respondents felt separated not just from their particular parish but from the Church itself, though a quarter volunteered that they still considered 'themselves to be Catholic'.[6]

---

[5] The full findings were submitted directly to the bishop, with the original intention being for a version of the report to be publicly released: i.e., 'when [Bishop O'Connell] goes public with our report' (Byron and Zech 2012: 18). This has, however, yet to occur. In a personal communication, however, Prof. Byron has confirmed that the *America* article is nonetheless 'fairly comprehensive' (personal email, 27 April 2012), and is thus sufficient for our purposes here.

[6] In fact, the survey didn't ask any direct question as to whether respondents still considered themselves Catholic or not. This reported finding presumably, then, refers to people making a point of stating that they do still think of themselves in this way. It doesn't necessarily imply, of course, that everyone who didn't specifically say so *doesn't*. That is to say, a natural reading of the *America* article might suggest that 75% of those participating are disaffiliates. Such an inference is, however, probably unwarranted.

While respondents were asked directly whether their leaving was the result of a 'conscious decision', the researchers report 'a fair amount of ambivalence' in the answers given. That said, only '[r]elatively few indicated that they simply "drifted away"'. Noteworthy too—and largely echoed in the Portsmouth study—is the fact that:

> Respondents clearly welcomed the opportunity to express their opinions [. . . and] to post their views somehow "on the record," with an assurance that they will be heard [. . .]. Considering that these responses come, by definition, from a disaffected group, it is noteworthy that their tone is overwhelmingly positive and that the respondents appreciated the opportunity to express themselves.
>
> (Byron and Zech 2012: 18, 23)

As expected, the specific reasons given for leaving were mixed. Naturally, 'The scandal surrounding the sexual abuse of minors by clergy was mentioned often'. Moreover, 'Several respondents noted that they were victims of sexual abuse by clergy'. (This topic, a major one in the Springfield and Portsmouth studies too, is the most obvious difference from the Hoge study. The abuse crisis, in all its complexity, will naturally loom large later in the book.) A number of complaints cluster around frustrations with parochial life and worship: 'There were many complaints about the quality of homilies as well as about poor music at Mass', and several respondents resented repeated requests for money. Pastors, more-over, were not universally loved: 'Words like "arrogant," "distant," "aloof " and "insensitive" appeared often enough', though this was certainly not so in all cases. More generally, the disappointed feelings of alienation reported by one respondent are worth reproducing here:

> I did not experience community in the sense that I knew people just from going to church. The ones I knew, I knew them outside of church. No one misses the fact that we stopped going. No one has called from the parish, even though we were regular attendees and envelope users [i.e., supported the parish financially]!

Given the summary nature of the *America* piece, it is not always clear what are the actual *reasons* for people leaving, and what are ancillary factors or accompanying dissatisfactions with no direct causal role in the exiting process. However they are to be categorized, doctrinal issues unsurprisingly loomed large. One respondent's list of 'the church's view on gays, same-sex marriage, women as priests and priests not marrying, to name a few' evidently sum up a general trend. And indeed, as the researchers themselves summarize: 'Not surprisingly, the church's refusal to ordain women, to allow priests to marry, to recognize same-sex marriage and to admit divorced and remarried persons to reception of the Eucharist surfaced, as did contraception' (Byron and Zech 2012: 23). In at least some cases these were not simply abstract disagreements, but had had concrete effects:

> Mention was made, however, of bad experiences in the confessional; refusals by parish staff to permit eulogies at funerals; denial of the privilege of being a godparent at a relative's baptism; verbal, emotional and physical abuse in Catholic elementary school; denial of permission for a religiously mixed marriage in the parish church. In one case the parish priest 'refused to go to the cemetery to bury my 9-year-old son because it was not a Catholic cemetery.'

Interestingly, as a final aside before we move on to the Springfield study, it is perhaps worth noting here that, unlike with Hoge et al.'s 'lifestyle dropouts', none of the concrete conflicts flagged up explicitly concern cohabitation or the use of birth control.[7] This is perhaps not, one might venture, because such activities are no longer practised. More likely, it is because they are sufficiently accepted, even if thanks to an unspoken policy of 'don't ask, don't tell', that they are no longer the battle grounds they once were in the 1970s.

SPRINGFIELD, ILLINOIS

Springfield, one of the State's five Catholic dioceses, covers the southern central area of Illinois. Though the capital, Springfield itself is only Illinois' sixth largest city with a little over 100,000 residents (Chicago, the largest by far, has approaching three million). The diocese is primarily rural, and its economy accordingly agriculture-centric. In terms of region, the diocese sits towards the south-west

---

[7] Though 'bad experiences in the confessional' might cover, literally enough, a multitude of sins.

corner of East North Central. This closely mirrors the overall US pattern: a retention rate of 66 per cent, a different Christian identity and no religion accounting for 16 per cent apiece, and 2 per cent having joined a non-Christian religion. How representative Springfield is *within* East North Central is difficult to judge. Nevertheless, having data from a predominantly rural, Midwestern diocese offers a pleasing complement to Trenton.

As there, the impetus appears to have come from the bishop, Thomas Paprocki, who then approached faculty at Springfield-based Benedictine University 'about developing a strategy for studying why some individuals were no longer attending Mass and, in some cases, why people were leaving the Catholic Church altogether' (Hardy et al. 2014: 5). This resulted in a significantly expanded version of the Trenton questionnaire, administered as a web survey in late 2012 and early 2013, targeting 'self-identified inactive, lapsed, or drifting Catholics' based within the diocese. Word was spread through a range of means, including both the local Catholic and secular press. This resulted in a little over 500 respondents, almost 60 per cent of whom were men (which, in contrast to the Trenton sample, is a reasonable reflection of the gender bias in lapsing as a whole). Age-wise, fully 45 per cent of respondents were in the 50–64 bracket. Though this percentage is almost certainly disproportionately high (implying significant under-recruitment among younger cohorts), one would nevertheless expect a strong showing here, given Baby Boomers' comparatively high rates of lapsation and disaffiliation. For purposes of comparison, the researchers also developed a second survey, aimed at practising Catholics. Aside from the odd comment, these will not really be discussed in our brief summary here. Full results from both surveys were published in September 2014, under the title *Joy and Grievance in an American Diocese*.

Summarizing their findings, the Benedictine team observed that 'when asked to explain why they stopped attending Mass regularly, Church doctrine was included in more responses than any other reason' (Hardy et al. 2014: 18). Moreover, when offered a list of eight 'specific Catholic doctrines', six were cited by over half of all respondents as a factor for their having left: birth control, fertility treatments, homosexuality, women as priests, marital status of priests, and divorce/remarriage. In addition, the other two suggested doctrines, abortion and 'The Bible', were cited by a third and a quarter of all respondents. While the survey question itself is not perfect,[8] it is clear that a good proportion of inactive Catholics in Illinois' central plains, as indeed elsewhere, are markedly out of both step and sympathy with significant Church teachings. Quotations from three of those surveyed give a good flavour:

> I do not approve of the [Church's] stance on many issues. Abortion, gays, women as priests, and several others.
>
> My daughter came out to me as gay, and I went through a divorce after 28 years of marriage. The Church doesn't want either one of us.
>
> We were both devout Catholics who tried to have children with no luck. We decided to go with in-vitro fertilization and the result is 3 awesome boys through 2 pregnancies. The Catholic Church rails against that.
>
> (Hardy et al. 2014: 17)

Worth particular mention here is the fact that, in the latter two cases, these are yet again not merely theoretical quibbles: they are points at which Church teaching touches, painfully, the most sensitive areas of marriage and family life. Such doctrines are *taken personally*. This pattern is common to all the studies discussed in this chapter. Interestingly, significant proportions of active Catholics are *also* troubled by the same sorts of moral teachings (see Hardy et al. 2014: 7, 42–6), though for these people they have evidently not led to their leaving. This might feasibly be because, in the latter cases, these doctrinal qualms are either less strongly held, or they are more effectively outweighed by other factors (such as, say, feeling a strong sense of parish community; something cited by a majority of Springfield actives, see Hardy et al. 2014: 34). Not surprisingly, there are also strong reasons for thinking that the lapsed and disaffiliated disproportionately include those for whom Church teachings have been

---

[8] For example, what it means to include 'The Bible' on such a list of 'specific Catholic doctrines', I have no idea. I don't imagine that many of the respondents were much the wiser either. Other items on the list potentially present problems of interpretation too. The Church's actual teachings on 'fertility treatments' (which encompass a wide variety of things—e.g., natural fertility awareness, NaPro Technology—which the Catholic Church not only does not prohibit, but actively promotes), 'homosexuality', or 'divorce/remarriage' are, of course, complex and nuanced. Nevertheless, as a rough way of gauging the influence of different *areas* of Church teaching on lapsation and disaffiliation, this kind of measure does indeed have value, especially when supplemented (as here, as well as in the Portsmouth study) with adequate scope for respondents to elaborate.

'brought home' in a real way. For instance, the Springfield inactive sample includes around double the number of divorcees than does the active one, for instance.

Relatedly, a good number of those citing 'bad experiences' with a priest or other parish representative relate to personal family issues: e.g., a deacon's refusal to bless an ill, non-Catholic spouse, or priests pointing out the irregular nature of a couple's living arrangements (Hardy et al. 2014: 24). Of course, one only has one side of the story in these reports. Feasibly, what might have felt like being 'insulted and embarrassed [. . .] in front of my family due to my marriage status' might, from the priest's perspective, have been a gentle, tactful, and pastorally sensitive *attempt* at 'accompany[ing] with attention and care' a person showing 'signs of a wounded and troubled love' (Francis, *Amoris Laetitia*, 291). But again, given the personal and sensitive nature of these topics, such paths are difficult—and in many cases, perhaps, impossible—to tread without causing offence.

More briefly, several more points of contact with our other studies emerge. Scandals, most especially vis-à-vis sexual abuse and conse-quent cover-up, unsurprisingly also loom large: 'too many HYPO-CRITES and LIARS and PERVERTS' as one respondent emphatically observes. Further, 30 per cent of inactive Springfielders 'indicated they are uncomfortable with the feeling of community in their con-gregation'. As one put it, closely echoing one of our above quoted Trentonians: 'I'm still seeking a church with a sense of community, friendliness. I joke with my friends that I've gone to a church for 7 years and no one has ever spoken to me' (Hardy et al. 2014: 23). For another: 'My parish was a cold place. You could walk in on Sunday, go to Mass and walk out without speaking to another soul. I longed for fellowship' (Hardy et al. 2014: 27). These were not, of course, the only parochial problems to surface. Political agendas perceived as being pushed from the pulpit managed to turn off Democrats and Republicans alike (Hardy et al. 2014: 23–4). And the Mass itself, inevitably, was not always to everyone's taste—though again for different, and likely mutually exclusive, reasons. Those desiring that 'EVERYTHING [be] more upbeat, passionate, and energetic' likely have different liturgical predilections from those wanting a 'Spirit-led rejuvenation' to be brought about 'through silence'. And neither, perhaps, would have much in common with those—the heirs of Hoge's antichangers?—wanting 'the Mass to be more traditional in presentation' (Hardy et al. 2014: 25–6).

PORTSMOUTH, ENGLAND

In 2013, England and Wales' diocese of Portsmouth—covering Hampshire, parts of Berkshire and Oxfordshire, and the Isle of Wight in southern England, plus the Channel Islands—announced a major curial restructuring. This came at the instigation of its new bishop, Philip Egan, who had been consecrated six months earlier. A major pillar of this new set-up was a Vicariate of Evangelisation, responsible for, among other things, a Department for the New Evangelisation. This, in turn, included both a Social Research Unit and a Marginalised and Inactive Catholics team, dedicated to studying 'trends in religious practice and the causes of lapsation or non-practice within the Catholic community' (Portsmouth Catholic Diocese 2017).

When in June 2015 I had the idea to replicate the kinds of research done in Trenton and Springfield, I accordingly approached Portsmouth. They immediately accepted. Since this would also be administered as a web survey, it made sense to replicate (with permission) a fair proportion of the Springfield team's design, which had itself drawn from the Trenton study.[9] However, several changes were made. Most importantly, the Portsmouth survey gave participants free range to narrate their own story, in their own words: 'Was there a time in your life when you attended Mass on a more regular basis [than just specified]? Please explain what has changed between then and now. *Feel free to give as much detail as you would like.*' While in later items more specific issues were probed directly, having so open a question early in the survey allowed respondents to frame their journeys of lapsation/disaffiliation howsoever they chose, without being nudged to do so in terms of set tropes or categories. A second novel feature was a dedicated set of questions probing issues of identity.

While the diocese itself sits, more or less squarely, in the centre of the southern English coast (though reaching up north as far as Oxford), it counts as 'South East' in our regional breakdown. Since

---

[9] The methodology was further informed by consideration of the survey design used for the 'Varieties of Deconversion in Roman Catholicism' project of two Fordham scholars, Patrick Hornbeck and Thomas Beaudoin. While full findings of this project have yet to be released (hence not being included in this chapter), both authors have published several insightful pieces on American Catholic disaffiliation (see Bibliography).

the British regions are much smaller than American ones, and a British diocese typically takes up a much greater proportion of its region,[10] we may be quite confident of our data providing a reasonable guide to disaffiliation in Portsmouth. The South East's overall retention rate, at 49 per cent, places it near the bottom of the ranking. As elsewhere in Britain, the great majority of disaffiliates—41 per cent of all cradle Catholics—now identify with no religion. However, a much higher-than-average proportion here now affirm some other Christian affiliation: 9 per cent of all South East cradle Catholics, compared to a national average of 5 per cent.

The survey was live from the beginning of October until the end of December 2015. Word was spread via social media, local radio stations, parish newsletters, and the national Catholic media, that Bishop Egan 'would love to hear to hear from' baptized Catholics who, for whatever reason, no longer attended Mass on a regular basis if at all. In order to be eligible, participants needed (i) to be over 18; (ii) to have either been baptized a Catholic, or formally converted to it; (iii) to live, have lived, and/or have close family connections with the Diocese of Portsmouth; and (iv) to no longer be regularly practising the Catholic faith, for whatever reason. In all, 256 valid responses were received. Three-fifths of these were from women which, given Chapter 2's statistical investigations in this area, strongly suggests that men were under-recruited (a common problem for survey researchers; see Smith 2008). The age range was broad, with at least one respondent born in each year from 1936 to 1997, although a majority were aged between the low-30s and the mid-50s. These responses together amounted to hundreds of thousands of words, which were analysed by a joint team from St Mary's University and Portsmouth Diocese. Our full description and analysis, reproducing a great deal of our participants' own words, may be found in the short book: *Why Catholics Leave, What They Miss, and How They Might Return* (Bullivant et al. 2019).

Among much else, the study lends support to understanding lapsation as often being prepared by a slow build-up of qualms or

---

[10] For example, Springfield is just one among twenty-eight dioceses covering the East North Central states of Illinois, Indiana, Michigan, Ohio, and Wisconsin. Portsmouth, meanwhile, is one of only five dioceses in the South East region of England, and one of only three (with Southwark and Arundel & Brighton) that fall wholly or mostly within it.

dissatisfactions. A specific incident or perhaps life-event then triggers either a sudden stop in Mass attendance, or else a conscious recognition that one has *already* stopped attending with any regularity (and is quite comfortable with this new status quo). For example, a significant number of our respondents cited reaching an age when they were no longer 'forced' to go to Mass with their parents, and/or leaving the family home for work or university, as the 'watershed moment'. For some, this moment was long looked forward to, and effected a more-or-less instant ceasing of religious practice. For others, however, this was not a conscious decision at all: despite the best of intentions, Mass-going simply, and slowly, slipped. The following two quotations demonstrate each of these basic patterns:

Once I was no longer 'required' to attend Mass at the request of my parents—at age 18—I stopped going. I had stopped believing by age 14.
(Male, 32)

Once I moved out of the family home I stopped attending. My lifestyle and daily routine had changed and attending Mass fell down my priority list until it seemed to filter out completely. This was not a conscious decision but a slowly realized side effect of a lifestyle change.
(Female, 25)

Importantly, in neither case can it be said that 'removal of parental pressure' or 'leaving home' is the sole reason for their ceasing to practise, even if these are what one might call the proximate causes. Most clearly, in the former case, his having ceased believing some years prior made a major (and perhaps primary) contribution—as presumably, though he does not mention it directly here, did the following four years of attending under sufferance. (If so, he was by no means alone in the sample.) Other, auxiliary factors are also implicit in our second example. For her, like several others in our sample, losing a habit of church attendance was not done deliberately. However, in order for 'Mass to fall down my priority list', presumably she did not feel any great intrinsic compulsion to go over and above the force of ingrained habit—a habit easy enough to continue when living at home, but just as easily shed having flown the nest. In essence, this is the same complexity identified earlier regarding the overlaps between Hoge's 'family-change' and 'weary' dropouts. Related to this, the Portsmouth study evidences an interesting, and hitherto largely overlooked, phenomenon: *parents* ceasing to practise once their young-adult children do. This could happen for several reasons, but by and large the common factor is that once the felt obligation of 'going to Mass as a family' disappears, they too discover they have little motivation to go simply for their own benefit. In the words of one 47-year-old woman:

> Once [my children] started at their Catholic secondary school I gave them the option of whether they wanted to attend Mass, which they declined. I stopped going again because the homily was dull, never relevant, and read from a piece of paper with no substance to it.

As one might expect, many of the same themes identified in the American studies recur here—albeit, perhaps, in varying proportions (although given the sampling methods, and their limits, it is impossible to state definitively if these differences are real or only apparent). Most notably, the range of issues relating to sexual or physical abuse at the hands of clergy or religious, and/or how this was dealt with by the Church authorities, do not seem to be *quite* so prominent in our Portsmouth responses as they were in Trenton and Springfield. Though that is not to say that it wasn't a major theme in a good number of testimonies here too. This was especially so, understandably, for the relatively few who had themselves suffered personally. Also deeply affected were those who, while not themselves the victims, had come to learn of these horrendous crimes being carried out in parishes known to them, or most devastatingly, by people they had known and admired. Two comments, both attesting to the centrality of priest and parish to Catholic life, and the difficulty therefore of dissociating horrific revelations concerning one or both from one's wider Catholicity, may stand for several similar ones. The first comes from a 58-year-old woman:

> I used to go and take our children regularly. However, like many people I have felt betrayed by the (not only Catholic) Church's attitude to the seemingly countless acts of abuse, especially since the parish priest of X was convicted [. . .] It made me feel very uncomfortable going into the church and thinking of all the children he had baptized and given sacraments to, and it made me wonder if any of the past priests were abusers too. [This is especially painful since] I was baptized in this same church. I received first Communion, Confirmation and was married there 37 years ago. My parents' funerals were held there.

And, in the words of a 69-year-old man:

> I discovered several awful truths about things that had happened in our small parish [. . .] A priest that we were all very in awe of, and who we

trusted with our children, committed suicide whilst awaiting trial for his sexual abuse with other children, our son's friend and several others [...] How could anyone knowing all that carry on going to Mass and not stand up and shout about it? [...] The result of all this is that our lives are spoilt as we had lots of good friends through going to Mass and now they are all rather distant. Also we had a faith which has gone, and it affects our lives, present and future.

Other, already discussed factors which likewise feature strongly in the Portsmouth sample are the Church's teachings on certain moral and doctrinal matters, especially those relating to marriage, family, and sexual ethics. For the most part, these only *directly* influenced lapsation where they were not simply abstract disagreements, but rather deeply *personal* ones. That is, when they touched on the individual circumstances of the respondents or people very close to them. Such is obviously the case, for instance, with homosexuality. While around half of all respondents affirmed, when prompted, that Church teachings in this area had had some effect on their distancing from the Church, this typically came out as an explicit theme only for those participants who were themselves homosexual, or had close family members who were.

The same is true of life and fertility issues: for those who had had abortions, or who had tried IVF treatments when struggling with childlessness, these were major issues. For those who *hadn't*, even where they signalled disagreement with Church teaching on these matters, these topics rarely came up in their own accounts of why they left. Interestingly, and in broad agreement with the Trenton study, birth control was not often raised spontaneously by respondents when recounting their own lapsation stories, even though it is clear from elsewhere in the survey that a large majority of respondents indeed disagree with Church teaching in this area. As in Trenton, this is perhaps due to the large majority of the sample coming of age post-*Humanae Vitae*, and thus at a time when disregard for the Church's teaching on this point was simply the status quo, and occasioned no great crises of faith as it had for Hoge et al.'s 'dropouts' over thirty years earlier.

Divorce-and-remarriage featured prominently in the Portsmouth sample, with several respondents expressing a keen sense of hurt and injustice. While some respondents were aware of the existence of an annulment process, few felt this was a path that, in their own situations, they either were qualified, or desired, to explore. For one woman, the trauma of the annulment process was itself the immediate cause of both her and her children's ceasing to practise:

> It made me feel as if I had been judged and excluded. [...] The process is secretive and takes ages. [...] I stopped going to church because I can't reconcile the talk about compassion and family with the [lack of support for] families with real responses when relationships are under stress. My oldest child now sees herself as Buddhist in principle and my second refused to do Confirmation and told me she will never marry in the Catholic Church because of my experience.

Others simply felt confused and frustrated at having received conflicting advice from different 'authorities'. In one such case, a remarried man had been told by his parish priest that he *could* receive communion. His new wife, and their young son, both began attending, and were received together at the Easter Vigil: 'a wonderful time'. Several years on, a new parish priest announced (correctly) that those in his marital situation *may not* receive communion. As a result: 'I felt that clearly I do not have a place within the Church and should not attend Mass. The consequence is that neither does my wife or young son who, aged nine, should have some religious connection to the Church, or at least a church.'

Most of those raising doctrinal and moral issues did so with the desire, however forlorn, that the Church should 'update' its teachings and/or their application. They felt, as we put it in the report:

> that the Church should bring its formal teachings more into line with the ethical and cultural norms prevalent in Britain today. For many of our respondents, the Church's views on, say, homosexual relationships, or contraception, or marriage, or 'women-in-general', are simply 'behind the times', 'backward', 'outdated'.

This should come as no surprise. After all, these are common enough views among practising Catholics, whom one might reasonably expect to feel greater affinity with the official line, let alone non-practising ones. Nevertheless, it must be stressed that not all our respondents fit this mould. In fact, they break it. Like others before it, our survey uncovered a notable 'minority report'—drawn from all ages—of those wanting the Catholic Church to stand firmer in defending traditional teachings. Thus for one 56-year-old man: '[The] Church is too liberal, too man-centred, not God-centred; too "touchy feely", not orthodox.' And in the words of one 33-year-old woman:

My concern is the increasing liberalization of Catholicism that takes it away from the strength provided by the beautiful traditions and culture. [. . .] It is watering down its teachings to please people in the short term and thereby losing what is special and true about the faith, and thus less able to sustain people spiritually in the longer term. This may seem like a small issue, but it has truly broken the hearts of thousands of ordinary people who are expected to forget or dismiss the teachings they were brought up with and adapt to new ideas. This is not Catholicism.

While relatively few had reached adulthood either before or during Vatican II, for several of those who had, it precipitated a long period of turbulence and trauma. For one 64-year-old woman:

From the late 70s, I attended Mass less and less until about 1990. I was of the generation where I was a teenager during Vatican II. I found the early seventies a difficult time as everything was up in the air. It was a time where my faith, in the Church at least, started to die away [. . .] There was an attitude, by priests and others, that people like myself needed to 'get with the spirit of the times' and that we weren't following the will of the church if we objected to whatever idea they decided to do (removing altar rails, moving the altar, changing the music, stopping Latin, stopping devotions, reducing access to confessions etc.). Lots of stuff like this happened before I stopped going. It felt like an ongoing stripping of identity—well, it really was. It was dismissive and patronising to many in the congregation and we had little say [. . .] I think the Church changed, I didn't.

For another, who was a religious sister at the time of the Council:

The changes that were pushed on us by leadership teams in the wake of Vatican II in our Orders were painful and distressing. Thousands of us left feeling that our sense of calling and vocation had been attacked and gutted by a liberal revision and takeover. I have felt lost ever since I left, but I knew I couldn't stay in that environment. The Church leadership offered us little to no acknowledgement for the trouble they had inflicted on us or for the work we had done or that was being lost. The Church, in its madness, has driven away plenty. The self-deception, to a large extent, still goes on.

Having ultimately left her congregation, after twelve years in vows, she says: 'I [still] regard myself as Catholic, but have since made the Orthodox Church my spiritual home.'

This summary really only scratches the surface of the full report. Before moving on to focus on the specific issue of identity, two further contributors to lapsation from the Portsmouth study ought at least to be mentioned, however briefly.

The first relates to a perceived lack of community within Catholic parishes, noted by many respondents.[11] Several reported that, despite having attended and/or been actively involved in their parishes for many years, when they had then been away from Mass for a period of time (e.g., because of illness, or family troubles, or a crisis of faith) no one got in touch to see how they were. Whatever the reasons for this—those acquainted with British cultural norms might hypothesize social awkwardness or reticence about 'being thought to be poking their noses in' as a contributing factor here—the upshot was the feeling that nobody noticed, or cared, whether they were there or not.

The second issue is dissatisfaction with certain aspects, or perhaps 'styles', of parish liturgy. As already noted with the Springfield sample— and as seen above with regard to doctrinal/moral issues (with which, albeit with notable exceptions, there are clear correlations)—this could be highly polarized. For every respondent who found Mass to be too staid or dreary, who wished for a more 'up-to-date', charismatically 'Spirit-filled' worship experience, and for whom (perceived) 'recent changes in the Church—moving back to more traditional outlooks and practices—have felt very alienating', there is another who is thoroughly sick of parish liturgies that have become 'all-singing, all-dancing productions', 'like a primary school assembly [where] it is impossible to connect to God', and even—from someone born in the early 1990s, it should be said—'hippy Masses straight out of 1972'. Evidently, one cannot please all of the People of God, all of the time.

ONCE CATHOLIC, ALWAYS CATHOLIC?

One area where the Portsmouth study differed from its forebears was in directly probing issues of identity and affiliation. Respondents were asked 'Would you say that you now regard yourself to be Catholic?

---

[11] This view was not uniform, however. A significant number of other respondents said that 'the sense of community' was one of the main things they *missed* about going to church.

(E.g., when asked about your religious affiliation on forms or sur-veys)', and given the options of 'yes', 'no', and 'sometimes, but not at others'. Those answering 'no' or 'sometimes' were then offered a standard tick-box list of denominational and religious identities, plus a write-in 'Other' option. Finally, all respondents were invited: 'If you would like to add any further comments about how you view your religious affiliation and/or identity, please feel free to do so here.'

Half of the sample (126; 49 per cent) simply answered 'yes', while the other half divided near equally between 'no' (68; 27 per cent) and 'sometimes' (62; 24 per cent). Among the straightforward disaffiliates (i.e., the nos), approaching half now identified as 'No religion', with a further handful using 'Other' to specify 'agnostic' or 'atheist'. 'Church of England/Anglican' and non-specific 'Christian – no denomination' were the next most popular, with each garnering roughly one in six. Among the sometime disaffiliates, however, the pattern was rather different. Here, 'No religion' was chosen only by a quarter, while half claimed the non-specific 'Christian' label.

Even at this basic level, these findings are intriguing. Most evi-dently, they testify to the very real shades of grey in real-life religious identities: that is, to 'the complex and messy relationships [. . .] which make up the "fuzzy frontiers" of religious identity' (Gregg and Scholefield 2015: 10), as was quoted in Chapter 1. That is clearly the case with those sometimes identifying as Catholic, but sometimes not. Often, theirs is an ambivalence born from there being certain, irreversible facts about their background and history that 'make them' Catholic, alongside the recognition that their current beliefs, prac-tices, and attitudes are *de facto* non-Catholic—indeed, often simply non-religious—ones. A few examples here will suffice:

I was raised as a Catholic, so I guess technically that is my religious background, but I don't feel I am a religious person so I think 'No religion' is more accurate for my current status.   (Male, 35)

I feel an underlying connection to the Catholic Church, but am no longer a practising Catholic. I sometimes see myself as a believer, and at other times not. I disagree with several of the Church's doctrines.

(Female, 19)

Raised in a Catholic household and still hold Christian values however do not feel an affiliation to the Church in particular in my day-to-day life. [I] occasionally attend church for special occasions or with family.

(Male, 23)

Given such people's conflictedness, it is understandable if, when prompted to pick an identity on a tick-box survey, which one they opt for may vary according to several factors. Feasibly, these could take many forms: the nuances of the questions' wording or position, for example, or the time of year (e.g., proximity to Christmas or Easter), or perhaps simply on what has been happening in that person's life or the wider world. A little flippantly, one might think of such people as 'Schrödinger's Catholics'. That is to say, they might equally well, and with good reasons, identify either as being Catholic or as something else (most often 'No religion' or simply 'Christian'), but it is only when prompted that they opt for one or the other. There are strong grounds for thinking that, for many people, this 'sometimes Catholic, sometimes not' identity is an intermediate stage on the way to outright disaffiliation. Indeed, it is quite feasible to imagine that, for the relatively young respondents quoted above, the influences that upbringing and family religiosity still hold over their sense of self might well weaken over time.

The general phenomenon of 'sometimes X, sometimes not X' is not, as it happens, exclusive to British Catholics. In 2010, three American researchers—Chaeyoon Lim, Carol Ann MacGregor, and Robert D. Putnam—published an important article, analysing changes in religious affiliation using panel survey data (i.e., where questions are put to the same set of respondents in successive waves, allowing differences in *individuals'* responses to be tracked over time). The researchers observed that while the *overall* proportion of religious nones remained fairly consistent over time, underneath this stability was a significant amount of identity switching among the respondents themselves: i.e., a good number of people who in the first wave identified as having no religion, now identified with one, and vice versa. Typically, however, this flipping of identities was not associated with any other notable changes in religiosity. Accordingly, the researchers hypothesize that such people are what they term *liminal nones* (or *liminars*):

> [W]e argue that many religious nones are actually liminal somethings, who still hold a weak sense of attachment to a religious tradition and thus may identify with the tradition sometimes, if not always. [...] Liminars, in our view, are individuals betwixt and between the religious and the secular but they are not necessarily on the path to being one or the other. They stand halfway in and halfway out of a certain religious

identity. [. . .] Because of the liminal nature of their religious identity, they may identify with a certain religious group at one point, but claim no religious preference at another, although their overall religious involvements change little.   (Lim et al. 2010: 597–8)

These 'liminal somethings' are precisely the kinds of people quoted above from the Portsmouth survey. Pleasingly, the use of qualitative methods here allows the hypothesized individuals inferred from quantitative survey data, to now be fleshed out as real, three-dimensional people. Subsequent research, using other US datasets, both supports the existence of these liminars, and indicates that they make up a quite significant portion of the American population—perhaps as much as 20 per cent (see Hout 2017). Here too there is a suggestion that 'liminality' might often function as an intermediate stage, as people migrate gradually from one religious identity to the lack of one.

However, it is not only the 'sometimes' who demonstrate the complexity of religious identity/ies. Those answering either a straight yes or no to 'Would you say that you now regard yourself to be Catholic?' also both give a range of justifications for their answers, and recognize the various types of factor contributing to their answer. Take, for example, two nuanced accounts from young disaffiliates, both of whom gave write-in responses for their current identities ('Agnostic' in the first; 'More spiritual than joined to an organised religion' in the second):

I feel that I never chose to be a part of Christianity, I was baptized when I was just a month old; I had zero say or choice in the matter. Now that I feel old enough and mature enough to have my own opinion I don't claim to be Catholic. Even if technically I am as I'm baptized.
(Male, 19)

I always speak of being raised as a Catholic, with the choice at 16 to continue going to Church. Being Catholic is still part of my identity because I was raised as Catholic. But I consciously no longer affiliate myself as Catholic.   (Female, 21)

Even here, with those no longer identifying as Catholic, we find reference to various types of belonging, whether welcomed or not. For the former, 'technically' being Catholic, and indeed being 'a part of Christianity', is something acknowledged but resented. For the latter, having been 'raised' such means that 'being Catholic' remains a constituent 'part of my identity', despite no longer 'consciously affiliat[ing] myself' that way. One is again reminded here of Ebaugh's discussion of 'role residual' (i.e., 'those aspects of self-identity that remain with an individual from a prior role even after exiting'). Unsurprisingly, this phenomenon is most prevalent when the previous identity was an important one, and therefore deeply ingrained (1988: 173–8). In this regard, we should remember that the above respondents necessarily felt connected enough to Catholicism to take part in a survey addressed to non-practising Catholics. Such feelings may well not be typical of disaffiliates in general.

Among those still identifying as Catholic, despite not practising, this was glossed in various ways. At the most unequivocal end, comes this comment from a 65-year-old woman: 'I AM A COMMITTED ROMAN CATHOLIC, just not attending Mass/Sacraments at this time. I VERY PROUDLY TELL PEOPLE "I AM A ROMAN CATH-OLIC" too!' Other respondents were rather more circumspect, commonly qualifying their Catholicity in some way. Compare the following: 'Being a Catholic is part of my cultural identity. Even if I never go to Mass again I will always consider myself a Catholic' (Female, 52); 'My Catholic upbringing is simply part of my personal history' (Male, 64); and 'I regard myself as a Catholic in terms of upbringing and as a guiding principle rather than a structure that feeds into my day to day living' (Female, 62). Instructively, these are not a million miles away from the rationales offered by those who *don't* now identify as Catholic, as quoted in the previous paragraph. That is to say, these forms of ongoing attachment (i.e., cultural, upbringing, personal history) are evidently weighted differently by different people. For some, the givenness of this identity is regarded as overriding: the question is not whether they are Catholics—this is simply taken as a fact, whether they want to be or not—but whether they still desire to be *practising* Catholics. For others, while the givenness of baptism or upbringing may still be acknowledged, that is not, in itself, sufficient to determine identity. On that note, it may not be coincidental that, of the responses quoted in this section, the latter position is more clearly evident among young participants. For these, perhaps, the fact that a Catholic culture and upbringing imposes itself less strongly on their senses of self is due to the Catholic cultures in which they were brought up being less strong than for previous generations. This, too, is a point to which we shall return.

CONCLUSION

This concludes the first part of the book. This has had two main aims: (i) to explore a number of fundamental conceptual and contextual issues regarding Catholic disaffiliation; and (ii) to give as rounded a sociological portrait of contemporary British and American disaffiliates as existing data allow. In this third chapter, we have answered (ii) in terms of the evidence provided in four qualitatively rich survey studies undertaken in America and Britain. While the explicit focus of each was on low- or non-practising Catholics, this is both an important constituent feature of disaffiliation (after all, very few people who consider themselves to be ex-Catholics still fulfil their Sunday obligation[12]), and often—as we have now seen in some detail—a decisive, if rarely instantaneous, step along a road ultimately leading to it.

As remarked upon several times, even where there is a single, identifiable 'trigger' for lapsation, this often is able to *be* a trigger only because of a number of other, interacting factors. Take, for instance, the commonly cited reason for stopping Mass-going of moving to university, and either gradually getting out of the habit of going, or else stopping immediately since one is no longer 'forced'. On either mode, leaving home might be the efficient cause, but it wouldn't and couldn't be so if the young people in question significantly enjoyed, felt spiritually uplifted by, and/or regarded themselves beholden to the Church's strictures on Sunday 'as the primordial holy day of obligation' (*Code of Canon Law*, 1246 §1; 1247).

As we have also seen, the losing (or, in fewer cases, actively shedding) of one's Catholic identity is typically a gradual process, and one marked by ambivalence and ambiguity. To be sure, this oughtn't to surprise us, given the primarily subjective nature of affiliation or disaffiliation adopted in this book. That is to say, we are not dealing here with a formal administrative process, whereby a person revokes (or has revoked) their Church membership. The point at which a person no longer *feels* like 'a Catholic', at least to the degree of ticking a box on a (hypothetical) survey, is, obviously enough, a fairly amorphous one to be trying to pin down. And as discussed in the

---

[12] It is not, of course, an impossibility. For example, such could be precisely the situation of a parent who goes along to Mass solely for the benefit of his or her spouse and children.

case of 'liminals' above, for many such people there is no clearly defined watershed moment. All that said, it is often the case in social research that the most important and interesting realities—and more-over, shifts from one reality to another—are precisely the most difficult to apprehend in a fixed and unarguable way. The cluster of themes and trends picked out in such a term as 'emerging adulthood' (Arnett 2000), for example, while real enough, do not necessarily map precisely onto a precisely-defined time span, beginning on one's 18th birthday and ending on the eve of one's 26th.[13] Likewise, a 'Catholic identity', and the (often gradual) fading of it, is a difficult thing to pinpoint with precision. This is so not simply for researchers, but as the above testimonies affirm, for the people in question. Nevertheless, this sense of identity, however hard to define, is clearly often something felt to be significant. This is worth bearing in mind as we turn now from individuals, to the much broader canvases of social and religious history. It is time to consider, not just how isolated individuals with their idiosyncratic personal histories, but rather how large swathes of them—millions, in fact—came to lose their Catholic identities, and in the restricted period of just a few decades.

---

[13] Likewise, I dare say 'twentieth-century political history' has a number of coher-ent characteristics which distinguish it from its nineteenth- or twenty-first-century analogues. However, it would be a pedantically bold textbook that begins its story on 1 January 1900 and ends it on 31 December 1999. Far more likely, it would adopt some symbolic bookends: the start of the First World War (1914) until the fall of the Berlin Wall (1989), perhaps, or from the death of Queen Victoria (1901) until 9/11 (2001).

4

The Night Before

On 5 June 1933, the foundation stone for the Metropolitan Cathedral of Christ the King in Liverpool, north-west England, was solemnly blessed and lain. Designed by Edwin Lutyens, the final structure, prophesied for completion around seventy years hence, would be colossal. Replete with fifty-three altars—the High Altar was to be literally so, looming some 4 metres above the floor of the Nave—it would house a congregation 10,000-strong. Its overall size would both near-equal St Peter's in Rome, and dwarf the Anglican Cathedral being constructed a half-mile away (Glancey 2007; Metropolitan Cathedral 2016). Such was the project's ambition that even G. K. Chesterton's remarks on this 'erection of a great cathedral for a great city', comparing the 'expansion and exaltation of great building . . . or the lifting of great domes pointing their way to destiny' to the 'expansion and exaltation' of Christianity itself ([1933] 1990: 451–3), must have sounded rather more subdued than hyperbolic.

On 14 May 1967, Pentecost, a Catholic Cathedral for Liverpool was finally consecrated. Yet this one was strikingly different, in almost every way, from that embarked upon thirty-four years earlier. Designed by Frederick Gibberd, whose other projects in this period included two power stations and Terminals 1–3 at Heathrow Airport, this 'Cathedral in Our Time' (British Pathé 1967) was built from concrete rather than Maltese marble. Its conical shape, resembling a circus big top (hence its affectionate nicknames 'Paddy's Wigwam' and the 'Mersey Funnel'), encloses a large, light, circular space. This was because, in Gibberd's own words, 'three thousand people had got to be as close as possible to the central altar' (British Pathé 1967).

This dramatic change of plan, from what was begun in the 1930s to what was completed in the 1960s, was initially motivated by cost considerations. By the early 1950s, in the austere atmosphere of

post-war Britain, spiralling projected costs had already caused
Lutyens' full vision to be abandoned. After abortive plans for a
scaled-back version faltered, Gibberd's design finally won out in a
competition held in 1959. But finances alone hardly explain the
startlingly 'new language' (British Pathé 1967) with which the Archdiocese of Liverpool chose to express itself. 'Who, at first glance,
would suppose that this building could possibly be a cathedral?', a
contemporary newsreel pointedly asked (British Pathé 1966). In fact,
Gibberd's plans, responding to the design competition's detailed
brief, self-consciously reflected several liturgical, aesthetic, and cultural currents already well underway by the late 1950s: a pre-
emptively bold instance of what would soon become known, not
always kindly, as '*post*-Vatican II' church architecture (see Walker
2002; Doorly 2007; Proctor 2014).

Arguably, the ultimate design of Liverpool Metropolitan Cathedral
was presciently 'post-Vatican II' in other ways too. As has been noted,
whereas Lutyens' original was designed for 10,000 Mass-goers,
Gibberd's aimed to fit less than a third of that (and in fact, this was
itself scaled back to just 2,200). Even before the Council, even in so
staunchly Catholic a city as Liverpool, triumphal talk of 'expansion
and exaltation' seems rather to have dampened down. Perhaps, as we
shall see, this was with good reason.

THE POST-WAR BOOM

In both Britain and America, the decade-and-a-half following the
Second World War has typically been viewed as an era of Christian
vitality, with Catholics taking (more than) their fair share of the
spoils. It is not hard to see why.

Against the backdrop of a 'larger postwar revival of American
Christianity, [. . .] a kind of Indian summer for orthodox belief'
(Douthat 2012: 180), one can certainly see the 1950s as Catholicism's
breakout decade. As Cold War tensions were rising, the Church could
boast unimpeachable credentials in what the Jesuit-educated Senator
Joseph McCarthy stirringly described in 1950 as the 'final, all-out
battle between Communistic atheism and Christianity' (quoted in
Marty 1996: 335). It was Catholic 'hyperpatriotism' (Shaw 2013:
91) that spearheaded the campaign to have 'under God' added to
the Pledge of Allegiance in 1954. A decade earlier, a stream of hit

Catholic-inspired movies—*Going My Way* (1944), *The Song of Bernadette* (1944), *The Bells of St. Mary's* (1945)—acclimatized Americans of all backgrounds to seeing attractive, Fatherly role models on screen. No doubt this helped prepare them to welcome Bishop Fulton J. Sheen, clad in full episcopal garb, into their living rooms on Tuesday evenings throughout much of the 1950s. His original television series, the Emmy-winning *Life is Worth Living*, regularly attracted audiences in their millions (see Smith 1997). More important than all this, in dioceses across the land the tried-and-true Catholic pastoral machine seemed to be ticking along nicely: big families filling pews and schools, producing plenty of vocations, in turn creating the priests and sisters necessary to staff the growing numbers of churches and schools (see Lawler 2008: 2–3). And so it went on, seemingly *in saecula saeculorum*.

In general terms, the immediate post-war years had a markedly different, and more austere, feel in Britain than in America. In the former, the mid-1950s finally saw the end of meat rationing; in the latter, they marked the advent of the All-You-Can-Eat buffet. In religious terms, however, the similarities arguably outweighed the differences. Callum Brown, for instance, has famously characterized the period between 1945 and 1958 as a 'return to piety', featuring 'the greatest church growth that Britain had experienced since the mid-nineteenth century' (2001: 170). While subsequent scholarship has questioned or qualified some of these claims (Field 2015: 1–15), the general contention that, at the very least, British religiosity in the 1950s was far more robust than it would be again, is difficult to contradict.

The Catholic case certainly bears this out. When the Irish-American priest Fr Patrick Peyton toured England in 1952, the estimated one million Catholics who attended his open-air 'Family Rosary Crusade' rallies must surely have felt that theirs was a denomination on the up and up (see Harris 2013a: 130–4). And it was, at least for the time being. Catholic baptisms accounted for just under 10 per cent of all live births in England and Wales in 1945; by the early 1960s, it was 16 per cent. Priestly vocations and Catholic marriages both rose steadily in this period, as too did the numbers of adult converts. In 1959, some 16,000 were received into the Church, up from under 10,000 in 1945 (Latin Mass Society 2013).[1]

---

[1] These figures are based primarily on those published in the annual *Catholic Directory*. A note of caution, however. Since at least the 1940s, questions have consistently been raised as to the reliability of the *Directory*'s statistics, reliant as

Large numbers of immigrants certainly helped fuel impressive Catholic growth in this period (Field 2015: 27–9). These were above all Irish, but also included Poles, Ukrainians, and Lithuanians under the post-war European Voluntary Worker scheme, and many others besides, often forming significant local pockets (cf. Harris 2013a: 35). Even so, British Catholicism was not just doing, but was seen to be doing, rather well. For some years later, even a non-Catholic could be heard to prophesy—at the time not wholly implausibly, however false it would turn out to be—that 'with the birth rate and conversions it seems to me that we'll all be Catholics in thirty or forty years' time!' (quoted in Scott 1967: 1).

Here is not the place for a transatlantic social history of preconciliar Catholicism. Our interest in these 'bigger pictures' is only insofar as they help to shed light on postconciliar disaffiliation. But of course, such topics *do* shed such light, albeit indirectly. If levels of Catholic practice and identity from the late 1940s to the early 1960s were considerably higher than they would ever be again, it is worth our considering (i) why that might have been, and (ii) what then changed, and why so seemingly suddenly. Furthermore, Mornings After tend not to come out of nowhere. Nights Before usually play a rather significant causal role. For example, Chapter 2 already observed that cradle Catholics brought up within these boom years show distinctive patterns of disaffiliation as adults. Might, as with the Liverpool Metropolitan Cathedral, the times have been a-changin' even before the Council came along?

Thinking social-scientifically, two major facets of post-war Catholic life, both firmly established in Britain and America (even if with a good deal of local variation), stand out. These are (i) the close-knit community life of Catholic parishes, and (ii) the richly elaborate devotional life that these fostered. Often, and with good reason, these two elements are lumped together; certainly, in real life, they were closely intertwined. Here, though, I wish to consider them separately. This is because each contributed something distinctive to the fostering of Catholic belief, practice, and identity. Three quite different theoretical ideas, *plausibility structures* and *social network theory* in the case of parishes, and *Credibility Enhancing Displays*

---

they are on the diligence (and honesty) of individual parish priests. That said, the general tenor of these trends survives closer scrutiny (e.g., Field 2015: 26–9).

vis-à-vis devotional life, will be drawn upon to illustrate this. These will be explained as we go.

PAROCHIAL CONCERNS

In the decades preceding Vatican II, the parish was the centre of both religious *and* social life for Catholics. This is most true of the inner cities—Glasgow or Boston, Salford or Chicago—with large, working-class Catholic populations, many with strong ethnic identities. These are the paradigmatic examples. As such, they will be most heavily leaned upon here for fleshing out the general, theoretical argument. But the essential hallmarks apply much more widely. Rural and semi-rural parishes, from the villages surrounding my native Preston, to the insular prairie towns epitomized by Garrison Keillor's fictionalized Lake Wobegon, are as far a cry from Edinburgh's Cowgate or New York's Little Italy as they are from each other. But a good proportion of the preconciliar 'Catholic experience' would, *mutatis mutandis*, most likely be common to all.

In this period, and for some decades before, the parish was indeed 'the center of people's lives, it ordered their universe' (Dolan 2002: 130). In fact, in certain American cities, it was common for Catholics to identify themselves as coming not from specific neighbourhoods, but from specific parish communities: 'We're from St Anthony's', or whatever. So ingrained was this convention that, in some urban centres, even estate agents' adverts would follow it (McGreevy 1996: 21–2). The boundaries of these territories would be familiar to all: you would *know* which side of the street made you a denizen of St Bridget's rather than St Pat's.

A 'Parishes in Philadelphia and Environs' map, drawn up around 1949, conveys a vivid sense of just how densely-packed all this could be (see Figure 4.1). Concentrating solely on the more-or-less downtown area of the City itself (i.e., Philadelphia County), I count ninety-seven separate parish territories. This is in a total area of just 143 square miles, slightly smaller than the Isle of Wight. Astonishingly, the map identifies a further *fifty-one* Catholic churches or chapels within this modest expanse, most identified with a particular constituency. These include Italian (13), German (9), Polish (9),

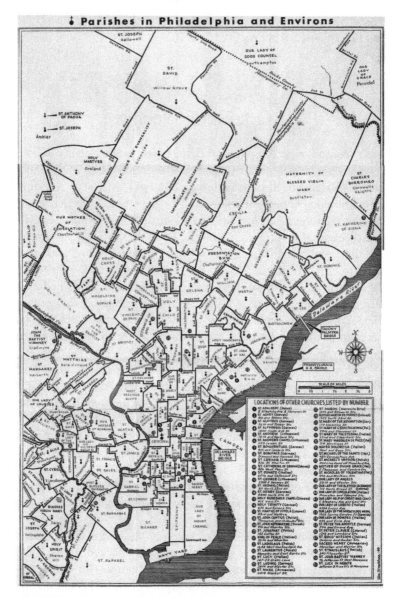

Figure 4.1. Parishes in Philadelphia and Environs (1949)
Source: Catholic Historical Research Center of the Archdiocese of Philadelphia

Lithuanian (4), Slovak (2), Colored (4),[2] Spanish (1), Hungarian (1), Armenian (1), Maronite (1), and Chinese (1). This pattern of 'two overlapping grids of parishes, one based on geography (called "territorial" parishes), the other on language or ethnicity ("national" parishes)' was a familiar, and by this time long-established, one across the North East and Midwest (O'Toole 2008: 102).[3] The Polish-Americans of Milwaukee, Wisconsin, whose statement-making Basilica of St Josaphat dominates the city's southern approach, could boast seventeen national parishes in the early twentieth century (Gibson Mikoś 2012: 66). Meanwhile, O'Toole cites the example of St Bridget's parish in Bridgeport, Chicago. Established in 1850, between 1868 and 1910 it spawned a further ten parishes—three territorial, and seven national—'all within walking distance of one another in the square mile that was Bridgeport' (O'Toole 2008: 102–3).

The same tight packing of parishes was also common in Britain, as may be demonstrated from 1950s diocesan maps (collected in Gandy 1993). For instance, within a three-mile radius of the famous Liver Birds lay forty-one parishes of the Archdiocese of Liverpool, and—on the opposite bank of the River Mersey—a further ten in the Diocese of Shrewsbury. Discounting the area in the river itself, this equates to around two parishes per square mile. In Glasgow, within a three-mile radius of St Andrew's Cathedral, I similarly count around forty parishes. Broadly comparable (and even, in areas of London, greater) densities of churches occur in several industrial cities, such as Leeds, Newcastle, and Manchester. One obvious difference to the US picture, however, is a lack of intermeshing territorial with national parishes. This was so for several reasons. Primarily, large concentrations of

---

[2] The creation of churches specifically for black Catholics has its roots in the nineteenth century. The first such canonical parish was erected in New Orleans in 1895 (Alberts 1998: 192–271), though mission churches—such as New York's Church of St Benedict the Moor—had existed prior to this. The twentieth-century history of these churches, to which we shall return in Chapter 6, may be found in McGreevy 1996 and Cressler 2017.

[3] For reasons largely beyond the scope of this chapter, this 'model' went out of fashion after the Council, with national parishes often encouraged either to convert into, or be integrated into existing, territorial parishes. This general trend was not, however, a uniform one (see Stump 1986). Interestingly, since the 1980s the same basic idea has undergone something of a renaissance, with almost 200 newly established 'personal' (i.e., extra-territorial) parishes across the USA, catering to an array of 'niche' groups. While some of these are ethnic/national (e.g., Vietnamese, Hispanic), others cater to charismatics, Latin Mass-devotees, former Episcopalians, and so on (Bruce 2017).

immigrants from a specific country or region (Ireland, as ever, excepted) were not so common in Britain. Yet even where viable local 'pockets' of, say, Lithuanians *were* present in Glasgow and Lanarkshire in the early twentieth century, local hierarchies often preferred for these to fit within existing parish structures. Though happy enough to permit them a dedicated chaplain from their home-land, diocesan authorities drew the line at letting them have a parish or church of their own (see O'Donnell 1998). Partial exceptions did exist, mind. The 1950s maps of the Archdiocese of Westminster list French, Italian, Polish, Lithuanian, German, and Ukrainian churches all within walking distance of each other in central London (Gandy 1993: 8). These tended to be either 'chaplaincies', and/or churches in the care of a particular religious order from the country in question, rather than canonical parishes on the American model.[4] The most significant examples of these were, and indeed still are, the commu-nities under the care of the Polish Catholic Mission in England and Wales. Originally founded in 1894, it played a key role in supporting Polish servicemen during the Second World War and especially afterwards when a quarter of a million veterans and their families were permitted to build new lives in Britain (Polish Catholic Mission 2005). In 1948, the Scottish and Polish hierarchies agreed to set up an analogous Polish Catholic Mission of Scotland, with a similar purpose (Stachura 1999: 120–7). Admittedly, for most practical purposes, these chaplaincy churches (or often communities 'nesting' within other, diocesan churches) functioned as parishes. Nevertheless, these remain very much exceptions to the overall trends of British parish organization.

This dense urban geography involved not just the churches them-selves, but presbyteries, schools, and social spaces—including, in Britain, 'parish clubs': essentially small pubs run by the parish and for the parish—as well. As the priest-sociologist Anthony Archer once put it, referring to just such 'city immigrant parishes' in the north-east of England: 'They lived, were schooled, worked, found their friends and recreation in the same area and with the same people' (1986: 87). All of this had serious practical ramifications.

---

[4] One exception here is the Ukrainian Catholic Church which, as with several other Eastern Catholic Churches in Britain, is an autonomous Church in communion with Rome, and hence establishes its own canonical parishes independently of the normal (i.e., Latin rite) system.

Especially given how close together they could be, a person could scarcely step onto the street without encountering fellow parishioners. Bumping into one's local priests and nuns would also have been a common, and perhaps daily, occurrence. Missing Mass would, moreover, be *noticed*.

And not just Mass. Commentators from both sides of the Atlantic point to the rich array of events, clubs, societies, sodalities, and associations which surrounded parish life (e.g., Scott 1967: 51; O'Toole 2008: 148–57; Harris 2013a: 36). These could take all manner of forms. Some, of course, had an *explicitly* religious or devotional remit (discussed below), but many did not. Parish dances, bazaars, picnics, and plays were regular social fixtures. A parish's young folk might also join the Catholic Scouts or Catholic Girl Guides. Their fathers, who as Catholics were denied entry to the Freemasons or Rotarians or Shriners, could gain similar fraternal camaraderie and mutual advancement in the Knights of Columbus, if American, or the Catenians, if British (see Harris 2013b). All in all, as Dolan comments referring specifically to America, though the same could equally be said of Britain:

> [T]he parish permeated the neighborhood with a religious quality that was uniquely Catholic. Together with its many social, educational, religious, and recreational organizations it created a Catholic milieu in which the faith of the people would develop and flourish. (2002: 131)

The popularity of Catholic sports teams is a case in point. This was particularly true at the local level, through participation in parish or school competitions. One gets a sense of their competitiveness from the *New York Times*' reporting of the city's Catholic Youth Organization cheerleading finals in 1960—a subject felt of be sufficient interest to its millions-strong readership to warrant a full page. With sixty school and parish teams competing, and watched by '3,500 fiercely partisan spectators in Fordham University's gymnasium', the stakes were high. So too were the emotions. According to the *Times*' article subheading: '1,000 girls cheer, then have a cry' (Robertson 1960). In some British cities, these passions could also be channelled through professional sports, through supporting those outfits founded, and/or traditionally supported, by previous generations of one's co-religionists. The Scottish football teams Celtic and Hibernian, for instance, proudly proclaim the Irish origins of Glaswegian and Edinburgensian Catholics. Manchester United, for similar reasons, has a long history as Ireland's 'English club'. For many supporters, therefore, one's Catholicism was not simply a Sunday morning affair, but a Saturday afternoon one too.

'IT IS IMPOSSIBLE TO BELIEVE ON OUR OWN'

The tight social, cultural, and religious matrices we have been describing are important in light of two complementary strands of sociological theory. The first, social network theory, has come to prominence in recent decades, inspired by growing interest in networks among mathematicians and physicists (Barabási 2002; Christakis and Fowler 2009). In very basic terms, the social network perspective is an attempt to study not merely the individuals that make up social groups, but also the complex systems of connections, relationships, and interactions—of all kinds, and of varying intensities—that exist between them. The effectiveness of a football team, for example, depends not just on the cumulative total of the isolated abilities of each individual player, but on the complex ways in which these players interact—and, moreover, in how this dynamic network of players interacts, in even more complex ways, with an opposing set. In the same way, it is argued, all manner of social groups can only be understood by studying the 'tissue' of their *sociality*: that is, the ways in which they are linked, and interact, with each other. Put in these terms, of course, then there is nothing so very novel about this: anthropologists, ethnographers, and social psychologists have always aimed at producing such thick descriptions of social groups. The impetus behind formal social network theory, however, has come from devising new methods of codifying and quantifying connections and interactions, new statistical models for exploring them, and critically, the ready availability of technology able to store, analyse, and graphically represent these new kinds of data. For our purposes, we need not delve too deeply into the full intricacies here. However, there is a small but steadily growing body of literature applying social network analysis and theory to religious groups— from mapping the transmission of texts within the early Church (Smith 2017), to Islamist radicalization strategies on Instagram (Badawy and Ferrera 2018)—several aspects of which will be discussed throughout the book.

One major insight of social network theory, for example, is the effect of 'density' (or 'clustering') within groups. In basic terms, this is the extent to which members have meaningful ties to lots of other members. A social circle in which one's friends are all friends *with each other* has very different dynamics to one consisting simply of a series of one-on-one relationships. In religious terms, studies have shown that congregations where (loosely speaking) 'everyone knows everyone else' have higher levels of commitment and identity. Furthermore, individuals with only few and weak ties within a given congregation—i.e., they know few other people, and even then only slightly—are far more susceptible to leaving.

> Research has found that [members of a group] are more likely to conform when they are embedded in dense networks rather than sparse ones. One reason is that dense networks make it easier for groups to monitor the behavior of their members and prevent them from engaging in deviant behavior. [...] And because people who are embedded in dense networks are probably more likely to possess ties they are reluctant to lose (i.e., strong ties) than are those embedded in sparse networks, social conformity tends to be more common in the former than in the latter. (Everton 2018: 128)

An analysis of data from the mid-1980s Notre Dame Study of Catholic Parish Life found that: 'the overall social integration of parishioners within their parishes [...] appears to be the most critical factor for increasing commitment and involvement among rank-and-file parishioners' (Welch 1993: 327; see also Cavendish et al. 1998). If so, then the Catholic parish system's success during the first half of the twentieth century in fostering high levels of commitment makes a great deal of sense. As we have seen, these were precisely examples of densely-clustered social networks. One could scarcely fail to be on close terms with a great many of one's fellow Sunday worshippers, for they were also one's neighbours, co-workers, fellow Rosary Crusaders, Children of Mary, or Catenians, the parents of your children's schoolmates, and—not infrequently—actual relatives. The vast majority of these 'significant others' would also be 'significant others' to each other. One was unlikely to have as many close ties with people from outside the parish, and even most of these would likely also be Catholics. This is, *nota bene*, a very far cry from the types of parish community reported in Chapter 3—e.g., 'I have gone to a church for 7 years and no one has ever spoken to me'; 'You could walk in on Sunday, go to Mass and walk out without speaking to another soul'.

An emphasis on the specifically social supports of religious commitment also plays a major role in our second theoretical lens: Peter Berger and Thomas Luckmann's classic concept of 'plausibility structures' ([1966] 1971). In essence, the term is a shorthand way of describing the complex social and cultural architectures which shape and support specific worldviews:

> Worlds are socially constructed and socially maintained. Their continuing reality [...] depends upon *specific* social processes, namely those processes that ongoingly reconstruct and maintain the particular worlds in question. [...] Thus each world requires a social 'base' for its continuing existence as a world that is real to actual human beings. This 'base' may be called its plausibility structure.   (Berger [1967] 1990: 45)

Consider, for example, a situation in which all one's friends, family, and co-workers subscribe to a specific, shared set of core political views. The newspapers and magazines—at least, the only ones you read—all do so too. These same principles, which undergird the political processes, are taught in schools. National heroes are considered heroic precisely because of their contributions either to framing the doctrines in the first place, or to dying in support of them. National holidays, likewise, mark events—the writing or signing of specific documents; victories or tragedies along the way—regarded as significant landmarks along the way of creating, upholding, and defending 'our way of life'.

In such a situation, the specific set of political views is likely, for the great mass of the people, to be taken wholly for granted. So much so, that its essential correctness and indeed naturalness is perhaps never consciously questioned or doubted. Furthermore, the vast majority of doubts or questions that might arise are probably dismissed or shrugged off well before they risk encountering the scorn, or ridicule, of others. Of course, even in such more-or-less complete plausibility structures, there are always radicals and mavericks, who for various reasons resist envelopment into this common social consensus. However:

> These exceptions are always interesting, but they do not falsify the sociological generalization that human beliefs and values depend upon specific plausibility structures. In other words, this generalization is probabilistic—but the probability is very high indeed.   (Berger 1980: 19)

Obviously, the kind of pure examples imagined above are extreme cases. Few real societies would fit the bill exactly, though approximations of one sort or another—Victorian England, perhaps, or Cold War Russia or America—come, if qualifiedly, to mind. But the same general processes of 'social consensus and social control' (Berger 1980: 48) apply, albeit with varying degrees of precarity, at much lower levels too. To give a fairly uncontroversial example, it is much easier to be a doctrinaire socialist or libertarian when all your closest friends, go-to news sources, and favourite blogs reinforce that stance. Critically, these not only function as an effective plausibility structure for confirming *you* in these views. By being your friends' friend, by enthusiastically consuming, sharing, and retweeting those news stories, and by commenting supportively on the blogs, you are yourself part of the plausibility structure *for others*. Naturally, in densely connected networks this effect is all the stronger: each member's witness is reinforced by everyone else's, plus each likely have fewer close ties with people who disagree.

According to this line of thinking, religious worldviews and identities are not immune from requiring 'specific plausibility structures, that is, the specific social base[s] and social processes required for [their] maintenance' (Berger and Luckmann [1966] 1971: 174). In fact, as much of Berger's own work shows, they offer much scope for seeing how the general theory might work in practice. This is particularly so with regard to the serious problem posed by pluralism. Worldviews are strongest when they can be taken for granted: when 'all the important social processes within [a society] serve to confirm and reconfirm the reality of this world' (Berger [1967] 1990: 48).

As others have pointed out before me (e.g., Shaw 2013: 6, 194–7), the tight-knit parish structures of the 1940s and 1950s are exemplars of Bergerian plausibility structures. Despite living in majority-Protestant countries, many British and American Catholics lived out their lives in robustly Catholic worlds. This was the product of both accident and design. It was the former, most obviously, insofar as immigrant workers tended to flock together. That, in the late nineteenth and early twentieth centuries, waves of Irish Catholics had congregated in the industrial towns of Britain and America was not, whatever their new neighbours might have muttered, an entryist Papist plot. Furthermore, the lack of welcome they received—the infamous 'No Irish need apply' tags on American job adverts (Fried 2016), or 'No Irish, No Blacks, No Dogs' outside English pubs (see

Lydon et al. 1994)—was not something that was actively sought, though it naturally served to galvanize community identity.

Yet Catholics themselves were far from passive in the creation of their 'subculture[s] of separateness' (Corrin 2013: 12). The setting up of expansive, and indeed expensive, networks of Catholic schools, vocational colleges, and (in the USA) universities was a major priority. Catholic hospitals, hospices, adoption agencies, trade unions, life insurance providers (a major *raison d'être* of the Knights of Columbus, founded in 1882) were all established. So too were a wealth of newspapers and periodicals, catering to different levels of readership, but all offering a distinctly 'Catholic take' on current affairs. Several of these boasted huge circulations right up into our period: 300,000 copies per week for Britain's the *Universe* in the mid-1950s; just under a million for *Our Sunday Visitor* in 1961 (Harris 2013a: 18; White 2007: 393).

Such subculturation was never total, and nor was it ever intended to be: 'There was indeed a Catholic wall of separation [. . .] but it was a low wall and it had many holes in it; it was a wall you could jump over or crawl through without too much difficulty' (Carlin 2005: 109). Even while retaining a clear sense of religious and/or national identity, it would be a grave mistake to think that this was at the exclusion of both feeling, and wanting to feel, a part of their host towns, cities, states, and countries. As Russell Shaw comments of American Catholics, they 'listened to the same radio shows, went to the same movies, and rooted for the same teams as everybody else' (2013: 72). The same was broadly true in Britain except, as noted above, in certain places for the 'teams' part. Furthermore, working-class Italian- and Irish-American Catholics, like their Anglo-Irish counterparts, fought and died in the two World Wars for their (or their parents' or grandparents') adopted homelands in just the same numbers as their 'non-hyphenated' countrymen.

Nevertheless, the 'Catholic difference' was real (Sewell 2001: 1–8). This social and cultural setting-apart, implicit—and indeed often explicit—within their elaborate network of 'institutional carriers' of a distinct Catholic identity and worldview, drilled right down into the private, everyday living and thinking of ordinary Catholics. Derek Worlock, Archbishop of Liverpool in the aftermath of Vatican II, reminisces here about his upbringing in 1930s London:

> I was brought up not to enter a Protestant building, let alone take an active part in what took place there. Even to be present at the funeral or

wedding of a non-Catholic relation required ecclesiastical permission and due care not to give the impression of taking part in the recitation of Protestant prayers or in hymn singing. Fish on Fridays was as important as not falling into the trap of adding 'for thine is the Kingdom' etc., to the 'Our Father' and 'who', not 'which', was a public protestation of faith.

(Quoted in Longley 2000: 28; see also Rockett 2001: 148–9)

In the kinds of close neighbourhoods we have been describing, 'lapsing' from regular Mass attendance could be a source of serious stigma. The fact that one's absence would be noticed, and then thoroughly discussed throughout the parish's full weekly social calendar, surely incentivized getting out of bed on a Sunday morning. (Note, again, the point made above about densely connected networks reinforcing social conformity.) Similarly, marrying a non-Catholic, should one ever manage to meet one in a setting conducive for romance to blossom, while hardly unknown, was not encouraged.

'The awfulness of everything before Vatican II (and the wonderfulness of everything after, and because of, it)' is, with only a little artistic licence, a well-worn cliché from both popular and academic writing. Indeed, as a colleague once put it, 'It is a commonplace to present Vatican II as some kind of liberation from a dark age of thinking, and almost compulsory to back the argument up with a garish anecdote' (Towey 2009: 207). According to this supersessionist trope—a socio-cultural analogue to the 'hermeneutic of rupture'— the 1940s and 1950s are depicted as the insularly dysfunctional darkest hour giving way to a new dawn. It is traditional here to decry the bunker mentality of post-war-but-preconciliar Catholics, aloofly imprisoning themselves within an 'authoritarian and paternalistic' (Corrin 2013: 9) fortress Church. No doubt there is some truth to this: the charge of a 'self-imposed ghetto mentality' was one made, at least in some quarters, at the time itself (Ellis 1956: 57). Moreover, the haste with which the bastions would, all too soon, be razed is perhaps best explained by a pent-up, collective claustrophobia. Nevertheless, in the excitable afterglow of the Council, a clear-eyed appreciation of what was being left behind was, perhaps unavoidably, obscured.

During his 2008 trip to the USA, Pope Benedict was asked to comment on the '"certain quiet attrition" by which Catholics are abandoning the practice of the faith, sometimes by an explicit decision, but often by distancing themselves quietly and gradually from attendance at Mass and identification with the Church'—that is to say, on precisely the phenomenon of lapsation and disaffiliation with which this book is concerned. He began his brief reply by noting:

> Certainly, much of this has to do with the passing away of a religious culture, sometimes disparagingly referred to as a 'ghetto', which reinforced participation and identification with the Church.   (2008)

Knowingly or not, the Pope Emeritus captures here precisely what Berger and Luckmann are getting at. Fundamentally the same idea also finds expression in Pope Francis' first—and/or Pope Benedict's last[5]—encyclical *Lumen Fidei*: 'It is impossible to believe on our own. [...] We can respond in the singular—"I believe"—only because we are part of a greater fellowship, only because we also say "We believe"' (39).

It is necessary to recognize here that social, cultural, and religious plurality is an established feature of modern societies, and has brought with it a great many benefits, both to society in general, and to religions' own self-understandings. The opening sentences of Vatican II's Decree on the Relation of the Church to Non-Christian Religions, for example, speak very positively here:

> In our time, when day by day mankind is being drawn closer together, and the ties between different peoples are becoming stronger [... the Church] in her task of promoting unity and love among men [...] considers what men have in common and what draws them to fellowship.   (*Nostra Aetate* 1)

Nevertheless, even while celebrating such a tolerant and welcoming attitude towards others, one need not lose sight of the importance of social plausibility structures for maintaining and transmitting a given faith. The sheer presence of different worldviews side-by-side—*even if not in open competition with each other*—serves to weaken the taken-for-granted plausibility of each one of them. For Berger, it is modernity's role as 'a great relativizing caldron' (1980: 9) that makes it one of the key drivers of secularization. He is by no means alone in

---

[5] As Francis writes in the introduction, at the time of Benedict's resignation in early 2013, 'He himself had almost completed a first draft of an encyclical on faith. For this I am deeply grateful to him, and as his brother in Christ I have taken up his fine work and added a few contributions of my own' (7). While one cannot be sure that the above lines were part of the original draft, it must be said that they have a certain 'Benedictine ring'.

this view. According to a recent work by Steve Bruce, Britain's leading sociologist of religion:

Ideas are most convincing when they are universally shared. If everyone shares the same beliefs, they are not beliefs; they are just how the world is. Any worldview is most powerful, not when it is supported by aggressive propaganda but when it is so much taken for granted that it does not require such promotion. The elaboration of alternatives provides a profound challenge. (2011: 37)

Note that these are general principles, with wide applications: neither Berger nor Bruce is thinking specifically of Catholics of the immediate post-war period. And in fact, the classic, textbook examples of this social 'deep architecture' in action, undergirding religious conviction and identity, typically come from much smaller sect-like churches or new religious movements (see Thompson 2005: 11–19). While the extreme cases of a Jonestown or Waco—tiny 'bunker' communities, sealed off from the outside world—might come to mind here, a far better and more benign parallel would be to a group like the Amish. Numbering around 300,000—around two-thirds live in the states of Ohio, Pennsylvania, Indiana, and New York—the Amish clearly demonstrate the possibility of maintaining a highly distinctive Christian subculture within the heart of contemporary American society.

Moreover, the Amish are not simply 'clinging on', but are rapidly growing. This is largely down to the classic combination of a high birth rate, and very high retention rates, averaging at around 85 per cent across the different groups (Nolt 2016: 4–6). In fact, there is good evidence that retention rates are highest, perhaps up to 95 per cent, among the strictest Amish communities (Kraybill 1994b). Sustaining this is by no means easy: 'the church is in a constant struggle with the forces of worldliness, hoping to avert absorption into mainstream cultural values', and this 'struggle to be a separate people is translated into many areas of life—dress, transportation, marriage to outsiders, the use of mass media, membership in public organizations, and public officeholding, to name a few' (Kraybill 1994a: 6). All this adds up (to revert briefly to our Bergerian jargon) to a huge commitment to plausibility structure construction in the pursuit of religious 'world-maintenance'. That said, it is worth pointing out that Amish communities are not walled off from the outside world.

The Amish are a separate people, to be sure, but they are not as socially and technologically isolated as we often imagine. Instead, they interact with the wider world by bargaining with modernity. The Amish participate in modern life on their own terms. [. . .] In many places today Amish women are more likely to be found behind Walmart or Target shopping carts than around an old-fashioned quilting frame.

(Nolt 2016: 2, 7)

While the Amish are a special case, the general principles here apply to a wide range of successful religious groups. For reasons to be explained, another example, *ostensibly* very different to both Amish districts and Catholic parishes, will feature in Chapter 6: Evangelical megachurches.

CREDS AND *QUARANT'ORE*

Thinking about religious subcultures and communities in these terms is an admittedly well-worn path, though it is nonetheless relevant or illuminating for that. The general theory exposited above will undergird, explicitly and implicitly, much that will follow in the rest of the book. It is not, however, the only key item of social-scientific theorizing that will guide our discussion. Nor, given the particular contours of Catholic life, practice, and history in our chosen times and places, is it necessarily the most important.

In 2009, the American psychologist Joe Henrich proposed a hypothesis about what he calls 'Credibility Enhancing Displays', or CREDs for short (2009). The basic premise is simplicity itself: that human beings are significantly more likely to adopt a belief, if those proposing it to them are seen to live out 'costly' implications of it. Such 'costs' may include such things as time, effort, social standing, money, and health. For instance, a policy proposal urging all-in-this-together, belt-tightening austerity rings truer from politicians who will themselves feel the pinch. Conversely, my mother never could take our family dentist's strictures on avoiding sugar totally seriously once she had spotted him enjoying a coke and a doughnut in a café.

The evolutionary rationale Henrich proposes for this is interesting: the key idea is that, as human beings evolved language, they acquired, along with all its manifold benefits, a greater capacity to be deceived, and indeed exploited, by others. Henrich himself gives a simple illustration: if there are two types of berries, one nutritious and one toxic, it might be in my interests to persuade others to eat the toxic ones, leaving more of the nutritious ones for me. Without language, I probably have to eat some myself, or at least pretend to do so, in the hope you might copy. With language, however, I can tell you to eat the toxic ones, remarking how delicious and wholesome they are, etc. (2009: 246–7). According to Henrich, human beings have developed 'a kind of cultural immune system' to mitigate such possibilities for exploitation: a bias towards believing things only when, and to the extent that, the proposer's own *actions* are consistent with what is claimed. Someone who goes on and on about the deliciousness of a type of berry, but is never seen actually eating one, is unlikely to be believed. Someone who eats them all the time—i.e., is regularly seen to perform the relevant CREDs—is a far better propagator of the opinion:

> The CRED hypothesis suggests that we learn beliefs from others to the extent that these beliefs are backed up by credible displays. When someone behaves in a way that is credible and consistent with their beliefs [...] their associated beliefs become more plausible and more likely to be acquired by observers. Their actions underwrite their words.
> (Willard et al. 2016: 225)

Catholic readers may, of course, be more familiar with Pope Paul VI's statement of the same basic idea: 'Modern man listens more willingly to witnesses than to teachers, and if he does listen to teachers, it is because they are witnesses' (*Evangelii Nuntiandi* 41).

English is littered with folksy clichés affirming the central tenets of the CRED hypothesis: 'walk the walk, don't just talk the talk', 'practise what you preach', 'put your money where your mouth is', 'put up or shut up', 'talk is cheap'. It is a staple of love songs in all genres, from 'Show Me' in *My Fair Lady* to 'More Than Words' by Xtreme, and from the folksong 'Scarborough Fair' to Meat Loaf's 'I Would Do Anything For Love (But I Won't Do That)'. For that matter, The Proclaimers' promise 'to be the man who walks a thousand miles to fall down at your door', and Beyoncé's observation that 'if you liked it, then you should have put a ring on it', both properly concern 'behaviors that a cultural model would not perform if they did not believe what they said they did' (Langston et al., forthcoming). A considerable body of experimental data supports this general principle. Young children, for example, are far more likely to eat something from a stranger presented as food, if the stranger eats some first. They also have far fewer difficulties in believing in certain types of intangible entities as germs, where there is an elaborate set of corroborating practices built around them (the ritual of washing one's hands before eating, throwing food away if it's been on the floor, etc.), than they have in believing in things they have merely been *told* about, such as unicorns or mermaids (Lanman 2012: 52).

The importance of CREDs exposure to the acquisition and trans-mission of religious beliefs—and along with them, identity and accompanying practice—is potentially very significant. Henrich points, among other things, to the emphasis placed on heroic indi-viduals (i.e., saints) as models to be held up to believers; to the well-documented significance of martyrdoms (an extreme case of a CRED) for strengthening and spreading religions; and to the tendency of religious leaders to undertake certain supererogatory vows (not least poverty, chastity, and obedience). All of these, he argues, are examples of 'costly displays', enhancing the credibility of the doctrines espoused, and thus rendering them more likely to convince.

Two things are worth clarifying here, however. First, the promin-ence of terms like 'display' and 'performance' are apt to mislead, suggesting as they do a calculated ploy to persuade. But CREDs are not typically done *in order to* sway other people. If they were, then the downfalls of being predisposed to them would likely outweigh the benefits. After all, the entire (hypothesized) rationale for a CREDs-based cultural-learning bias is that it makes it harder to be manipu-lated. Rather, the whole point is that people who practise what they preach ordinarily do so because they are convinced that what they preach is true, and not simply because they want to persuade other people of it (even if they want to do that also!). The blood of the martyrs may indeed be the seed of the Church, but that is not the reason *why* martyrs go bravely to their pyres. Second, no one is suggesting here that the presence of CREDs *guarantees* the adoption of the beliefs which they support. We all know people who 'have the courage of their convictions', and admire them for that, even if we do not find the convictions themselves plausible. Rather, the suggestion is that the presence of CREDs counts in a proposition's favour, even if not decisively, and that, in their absence, certain beliefs (especially ones not immediately verifiable) are a very hard sell indeed.

Plausibly, such 'a CREDs bias' (Lanman and Buhrmester 2017: 4) would be most efficacious when exposure occurs over a sustained period, among those who are already significant role models (family, friends, peers), and at particularly formative stages of a person's life. Childhood and adolescence would, then, be the obvious contenders. This chimes very well with the significant body of research, discussed in Chapter 2, affirming a clear correlation between a person's family religious practice while growing up, and his or her religiosity as an adult. To reiterate, 'the single most important measurable factor determining the religious and spiritual lives of teenagers and young adults is the religious faith, commitments, and practices of their parents' (Smith et al. 2014: 27). Or more pithily, 'the best predictor of anyone's religious involvement is how they were raised' (Storm and Voas 2012: 131). Still more intriguingly, there is specific evidence that consistency between parents' attitudes and actions—i.e., where they *both* emphasize the importance of religion *and* practise regularly, rather than simply talk a good game but never attend, or else lay no great stress on religion throughout the week despite going through the motions each Sunday—is a particularly efficacious combination (Bader and Desmond 2006). CREDs are not, it is true, the only theorized mechanism for how and why this occurs (see Atran and Henrich 2010); and even if the theory is broadly correct, it need not be the sole contributor. Nevertheless, while Henrich's CREDs hypothesis is still young, there is a growing corpus of empirical studies which seem to support it.

Applied to the specific history of twentieth-century Catholicism, the adoption of a CREDs-eye view is, to say the least, highly suggestive. This is so for several reasons. Most obvious are the profusion and popularity of devotional practices in the century's early decades (Dolan 2002: 169). The huge numbers of British Catholics attending Fr Peyton's Family Rosary Crusade rallies in 1952 was noted above. This Irish-born televangelist 'Rosary Priest'—a Catholic analogue, indeed rival, to Billy Graham (Harris and Spence 2007)—had an even bigger following in the USA, as indeed he did throughout much of the world.[6] Yet for all Peyton's razamatazzy deployment 'of all the modern means of persuasion and indoctrination that were

---

[6] Given the mention above of American Catholics' 'hyper-patriotism' in this era, it is worth noting Fr Peyton's oft-expressed conviction that (as he put it in a 1946 radio address) 'The rosary is the offensive weapon that will destroy Communism—the great evil that strives to destroy the faith'. Many others agreed, including the CIA, who accordingly funded the Family Rosary Crusade's mission throughout Latin America in the early 1960s (Gribble 2003).

available to him' (Turnham 2015: 144) at such set piece events, the Crusade's true purpose was to promote the daily recitation of the rosary within ordinary homes; 'the family that prays together, stays together' being a phrase Peyton did much to popularize. The English and Welsh bishops full-throatedly concurred, having themselves launched a nationwide Mission in 1949, the 'earnest hope' of which was to 'leave Catholic families reinvigorated' and that 'every Catholic family will re-establish once more the grand Catholic custom of family prayer, in particular of the family rosary' (quoted in Rockett 2001: 150). By its nature, the true uptake of these and other efforts is difficult to gauge. However, in her detailed study of the history of England's Diocese of Middlesbrough, Margaret Turnham estimates that in the run-up to Peyton's rosary rallies in the cities of Hull, Scarborough, York, and Middlesbrough, some seventeen thousand (!) volunteers were involved in publicizing it door-to-door. Furthermore, 'In total 54,586 pledges [i.e., regularly to pray the rosary together as a family] were received, a total of about sixty percent of the eligible Catholic population' (Turnham 2012: 277). While one need not suppose that all those pledging, no doubt with the best of intentions, actually persevered, there is plenty of evidence—not least in the grown-up recollections of bored children[7]—that 'the family rosary' was a common daily practice on both sides of the Atlantic (see Werner-Leggett 2012: 186–7; Harris 2013a: 135–6).

Football stadia and family homes were not, of course, the only venues for rosary praying. Rosary sodalities and circles were popular features of parish life: O'Toole cites one regular Tuesday-night group in Boston for whom any attendance lower than 400 was regarded as a disappointing turnout (2008: 148). Nor was the rosary, while pre-eminent, the only devotion to which large numbers of ordinary Catholics might dedicate serious amounts of time, effort, and occasionally expense: Adoration, the Stations of the Cross, novenas, First

---

[7] See the novelist David Lodge's comment, recalling his youth in suburban London of the 1930s and 1940s:

> The Rosary is the most mind-numbing of all Catholic devotions, consisting in the repetition of multiple "decades" of prayers [...] While reciting these prayers, silently or aloud with others, you were supposed to meditate on one of the "Mysteries" of the Faith to which each decade was dedicated [...] But the repetitious droning of the prayers, and the disconnection between their words and the theme of each decade, made focused thought impossible.
>
> (2015: chap. 4; see also Geiringer 2016: 75–6)

Fridays, First Saturdays, Corpus Christi processions, pilgrimages. While many of these also revolved around Mary, a great many focused on other saints. Some of these were called upon for topical reasons: St Anthony of Padua (lost objects), St Jude (lost causes), or St Joseph (fatherhood or, presumably having proven his mettle in finding an adequate roof over the Holy Family's heads in Bethlehem, house-hunting).

Others, with St Patrick being the most famous, were especially dear to particular ethnic or regional groups. In Scotland, thousands of pilgrims flocked to the unlikely destination of Carfin, a mining village to the north-east of Motherwell. Begun in the 1920s, with a replica of the Grotto at Lourdes built by local Catholic miners, by our period it had gradually accumulated other shrines and statues dedicated to a range of devotions or saints, 'present[ing] a whole compendium of influences on Catholic Scotland' (Williamson 2016: 106). Alongside those of more-or-less universal appeal in this period—St Thérèse of Lisieux, Our Lady of Fátima, St Maria Goretti—several were particularly directed towards, and indeed funded by, certain ethnic groups, including the native Scots and Irish, as well as the significant Lithuanian, Polish, and Italian communities (see Williamson 2016: 103–23; Harris 2015a). Such impulses were even stronger in America, where dominant local concentrations of Catholic immigrants from specific backgrounds were much more common than—the Irish excepted—in Britain. This produced a rich ecology of local devotions and customs inherited, albeit often with significant modifications, from the 'old country'. The Feast of St Joseph, patron saint of Sicily, was thus a day for prayers, processions, and *zeppole*-laden feasting in the Little Italies of New York, Chicago, Philadelphia and elsewhere. It is also why (as I once wondered aloud while driving from Oklahoma City to Okemah) there should be a National Shrine of the Infant Jesus of Prague in the middle of the Sooner State. Prague, Oklahoma, was settled by Czech immigrants in the late nineteenth century. The shrine was built in 1949, at the parish Church of St Wenceslaus, patron saint of Bohemia.

For our purposes here, we may simply note that such 'rampant' (Fortin 2002: 232) devotionalism equates to huge amounts of time, thought, effort, and expense. This is especially true when one considers that funding for all the shrines and statuary, plus a great deal else besides, was normally donated or raised by ordinary Catholics themselves. If the CREDs hypothesis is even half-way right, this must have exerted a significant cumulative influence over those living, and especially *brought up*, in such environments. The sheer amount and seriousness of religious practice underwrite the credibility, and therefore both the communicability and 'stickability', of the religious convictions upon which they are based—and without which, critically, they make little sense. The once-popular *Quarant'Ore* devotion is a case in point. Its centrepiece, a forty-hour silent vigil before the Blessed Sacrament, requires volunteers to take on hour-or-more shifts throughout the two nights—an honour typically borne by the hardy men of the parish. However they themselves might have felt about it, it certainly made an impression on their children. Witness, for example, the testimony of a friend of mine, born in the early 1950s to Irish immigrants living in Birmingham:

> Dad worked in Dunlop's, a tire factory, doing very heavy manual work in shifts. It was the Forty Hours, and the Parish Priest asked the men of the parish to sign up for watching through the night. Dad signed up and I asked if I could do it with him. I was about 9 years old. We were on the early morning watch, about 2am. I felt very grown up getting out of bed and dressed and walking with my Dad to the church I was baptised in and where I would later be ordained, where my brother would be married, and where both my parents would be buried from.

> When we arrived the body of the church was in muted lighting but the Sanctuary was full of flowers and candles with the Blessed Sacrament high over the altar which was still east facing. Two other men quietly acknowledged us with a nod of the head and left us to watch. We both had our favourite prayer books, my Father's very well thumbed and full of memory cards, and we both had our rosaries. We knelt side by side throughout the hour. I think as a child I thought of it as standing guard to protect the sacrament. But we were both used to prayer and the time passed quickly enough. Then two other working men came, nodded to us, and we got up did a double genuflection and left as quietly as we came, contentedly walking silently home in the dark. Then a cup of tea and to bed with Dad getting up very soon to catch the bus for Dunlop's and me a little later to go and serve the early Mass at the local convent, before the young Sisters went out to the schools and hospitals where most of them worked.

As this vivid recollection amply testifies, his kneeling father 'guarding' the Sacrament in an unheated church for an hour in the dead of night, before an early start to work a long shift of heavy labour— obvious examples of 'behaviors that a cultural model would not perform if they did not believe what they said they did' (Langston et al., forthcoming)—remains a powerful and cherished memory to this day, over fifty years later. The importance of it being particularly his *father* is also worth highlighting. Much literature on 1940s and 1950s religiosity rightly emphasizes the dominant role of women, and mothers especially, as carriers of piety (Brown 2001, 2011). Within our own consideration of Catholic contexts, we have accordingly seen much stress placed on the family, home, and domesticity—symbolized by the popular ritual of the 'Enthronement of the Sacred Heart in the Home' (Harris 2013a: 69–75; Chinnici 2004: 60–3)—as the front line for religious transmission and formation. Against this background, it would not be surprising if specifically masculine expressions of piety, precisely because they are less everyday, might make a special impression. This fits with the growing body of research noting the disproportionately paternal influence over their children's own adult religiosity (Baker-Sperry 2001; Bengtson et al. 2013: 76–9).

Before moving on, it is worth noting that devotions focusing on Jesus, Mary, and the saints, might perhaps have had a doubly-reinforcing effect from a CREDs perspective. After all, their objects are themselves exemplars of practising what they preached. Meditating upon the Sorrowful Mysteries of the Rosary, or spiritually journeying to Calvary along the Stations of the Cross, is precisely to impress upon one's mind Christ's following the costly implications, 'even unto death' (Matthew 26:38), of his avowed mission. The prominence given to saints, and to martyrs especially, arguably has a similar effect. To quote once again from our CREDs theorists:

> The classical example [of a CRED] for religion would be the pairing of verbal statements about beliefs in life after death and the actions of martyrdom. Martyrdom is powerful as a transmitter of the faith because it shows that—if nothing else—the martyr must have unreservedly held the belief he or she verbally expressed. (Willard et al. 2016: 225–6)

BLACK BOXES AND GOLDEN ARCHES

The rococo richness of devotional life in our period ought not to distract from less colourful aspects of, at the time, perfectly ordinary

Catholic practice. I shall briefly confine my attention to just two here, each of which will be picked up again in later chapters.

Writing in 1950, Bishop Beck of Brentwood, covering eastern London and Essex, mentions with pride the 'patient, prayerful queues—a Catholic characteristic long before the queue habit become part of our national life—waiting in the quiet shadows outside the confessional on a Saturday evening' (quoted in Rockett 2001: 156). This had been standard practice since the early century, following Pope Pius X's repeated urging 'that the faithful should be invited to the sacred banquet as often as possible, even daily' (*Sacra Tridentina*, 1905). Frequent communion demanded frequent confession, on pain of spiritual death. As the 1958 *Penny Catechism* pointedly quoted in answering 'Is it a great sin to receive Holy Communion in mortal sin?': 'he who eats and drinks unworthily [...] eats and drinks judgement to himself' (#243; quoting 1 Corinthians 11:29). The 1941 *Baltimore Catechism*, the *Penny*'s American cousin, is equally blunt: 'He who knowingly receives Holy Communion in mortal sin [...] commits a grave sin of sacrilege' (#368). True, this stricture only applied to those in a state of *mortal* sin, defined in both as 'a grievous offense against' God (*Penny*, #121; *Baltimore*, #66). But who could dare presume not to be? Certainly, the overall tenor of neither *Catechism* encourages giving oneself the benefit of the doubt: indeed, both warn starkly against the sin of 'presumption' (*Penny*, #326; *Baltimore*, #208). Hence the high demand for weekly confession, prior to weekly communion, and with as little time as practically possible between one and the other. Given the high volumes of penitents, several hours therefore needed to be set aside on a Saturday afternoon and evening, if not also on Sunday morning, to accommodate them all.

This custom had two salient effects. The first, adopting our CREDs-eye view, is simply that is *yet another* example of serious time and effort being expended because of, and thus witnessing to, certain religious convictions. Queuing up, perhaps for a decent length of time, in order to confess one's many failures in thought, word, and deed; being duly assigned a number of additional penances (typically prayers); in order to return to church the next morning, with the intention of joining *another* queue, to receive a small piece of wafer . . . such laborious practices only really make sense if you—or at the very least, the community of which one is, and hope to remain, seen as a member in good standing—genuinely believe in the web of

Catholic doctrines which underlie these practices. And if you *do* believe them, of course, then all of this is but a very small price to pay. Paradoxically enough, given the anonymous, behind-closed-doors nature of private confession, note how *public* an act all this is. Those long, silent queues are a very open expression of mutual witnessing.

Second, to return to our other leitmotiv of plausibility structures, it is worth stressing just how effective frequent confession surely was for internalizing both these beliefs and moreover the wider worldview in which they—to paraphrase Acts 17:18—live, move, and have their being. Making a 'good confession' required a rigorous self-audit of one's thoughts, actions, and indeed inactions ('sins of omission') in the light of 'the commandments of God and of the Church, and the particular duties of [one's] state of life, and by asking [oneself] how [one] may have sinned with regard to them' (*Baltimore*, #387). For those desiring to understand in what precisely these 'commandments of God and of the Church' consisted, the *Baltimore Catechism* helpfully devoted 116 articles to their explication, and the pithier *Penny* 80. Helpfully, a wide array of schematic 'Examinations of Conscience' were available to aid would-be penitents. These too, however, were by no means undemanding. Typically, these could range from several pages of highly specific questions, densely packed in tiny fonts (e.g., Callan and McHugh [1960] 2016: 21–4), to a 'mere' several dozen questions of much wider scope, like so:

> Have you spent your time, especially on Sundays or other holidays, not in sluggishly lying in bed, or in any sort of idle entertainment, but in reading, praying, or other pious exercises; and taken care that those under your charge have done the like, and not wanted the instructions necessary for their condition, nor time for prayer, or to prepare for the sacraments? (Laudate Dominum 1957: 31)

This could not but inculcate a feeling of constant vigilance—if not, as many memoirs from the period have it, anxiety—throughout the week. Of course, that does not mean that nobody ever sinned. But when they had, they *knew* that they had: mindfulness of the doctrines of the Church thus imbued every aspect of day-to-day living (O'Toole 2008: 181–5). In the terminology that would soon become fashionable, truly this was a sacrament that fostered full, conscious, and active participation.

Another example of Catholicism infusing one's ordinary, daily doings was the tradition of abstaining from meat on Fridays (and heavily limiting it—confined to just one meal a day—during Lent, Sundays excepted). Of course, traditions and rules are one thing; their rigorous observance in ordinary Catholic parishes, very often another. In this case, we have pleasingly neat verification that this was indeed so, at least in Montfort Heights, an overwhelmingly Catholic neighbourhood of north-eastern Cincinnati, Ohio.

In 1960, Lou Groen, the area's first McDonald's franchisee, was fretting over his accounts. While business was okay enough on most days, the dismal hamburger trade on Fridays and throughout Lent was killing his new venture. This was, demonstrably, far from a custom more observed in the breach than the observance. The dietary scruples of Catholics—not excluding Groen himself—were punishing his bottom line. In desperation, Groen set about developing a battered fish sandwich, to rival those sold by competing restaurant chains. Pitching it to Head Office in 1961, the idea was met with reluctance. A test-run on Good Friday, 1962, proved the concept however. Following some modification—the original version was made with halibut, for instance—it joined McDonald's then famously short menu in 1964, under the same Irish-tinged name it bears today: 'Filet-O-Fish' (see Smith 2013).

This vignette testifies to the strength of ordinary Catholics' commitment to the Church's norms on abstinence and fasting: theirs was a faith that could move, if not mountains, then at least multinationals.[8] This practice, while significant enough in itself—a paradigmatic example of a CRED—possessed a powerful symbolic role as a cultural marker. As Fr Leonard Feeney, a Jesuit who wrote regularly for *America*, commented before the War: 'To thousands of our fellow Americans we Catholics are known merely as the people who eat fish on Friday', and remarks wryly on 'the constant danger we are in of giving scandal to those outside our Faith, should we neglect to do what they would think it absurd for us to do, even if we did it' (1934: 3, 6).[9] Though writing in New England in the early 1930s, Feeney's observation would not have gone amiss in old England some twenty or thirty years later. Indeed, the cultural memory of a 'chippy tea'—i.e., dinner from a fish and chip takeaway; Divine Providence having mercifully spared British Catholics from having to resort to

---

[8] Or rather, soon-to-be multinationals. Its first non-US store opened in Canada in 1967.

[9] On aspects of Feeney's later life, see Bullivant 2012a: 47–8.

the Filet-O-Fish—remains deeply and nostalgically ingrained to this day, especially in the historically-Catholic North West.

True, eating fish and chips is rather more of a pleasure than a penance. As abstinence goes, it scarcely counts as a great feat of asceticism. (Though note that, from 1955, Catholics were also obliged to fast for at least three hours before receiving communion, itself a substantial relaxation of the earlier 'from midnight' rule.) Nevertheless, the underlying purpose of avoiding meat on certain days for religious reasons—'we are Catholics, and this is just what we do, and have always done; eating meat on Fridays is a sin'—is important. As an action 'that a person would be unlikely to engage in unless they truly believed their expressed conviction' (Willard et al. 2016: 225), it is therefore a CRED underscoring the importance of Catholic identity, the reality of sin, and the importance of avoiding it. That is, one must admit, quite a side-order to get with one's chippy tea.

BRITAIN: 'THE LOST AND STRAYED'

In successive May 1964 issues, the *Tablet* published two long articles under the banner 'Why Do Catholics Lapse?'. The author points out that official church statistics for England and Wales, collected in the annual *Catholic Directory* but ultimately based on parish priests' returns to their own bishops, estimate the total Catholic population at around 3.8 million. Of these, around 2.1 million are at Mass on any given Sunday: a difference of some 1.7 million. Moreover, rather robuster estimates, 'based upon the relationship between infant baptisms and total live births in the years of birth of the present population, and allowing for conversions, immigration, deaths, and emigration', suggest that the real number of baptized Catholics is more like 5.75 million. Assuming that the Mass counts are broadly accurate—after all, it is easier to count those who are there, than those who aren't, but ought to be—then that amounts to some 3.65 million 'missing' Catholics (Roberts 1964: 517).

Regardless of the precise numbers involved, it is evident that lapsation was already a significant phenomenon by the early 1960s, and had been for some time. Indeed, Scottish sociologists' estimates that fewer than half of Glaswegian Catholics were at Mass on a given Sunday had already begun appearing in the mid-1950s (MacMillan

1955; Cavanagh 1959). This admittedly strikes a rather different, dissonant note to those we have been outlining above. It is, however, by no means the only one.

Confining our attention to Britain for the moment, several indicators from the post-war-but-preconciliar period suggest that, however large the number of Catholics in church, there was a large and quietly growing number who weren't, but (from the Church's perspective, if not their own) should have been. In the 1940s, for instance, it was widely felt that 'Wartime disruption and its social and moral effects [had] led many Catholics to become lax in their religious obligations and caused some to turn away from the faith' (Hagerty 2013: 466; see also Rockett 2001: 141–2). Recognizing this, the Catholic Missionary Society, founded in 1910 to convert non-Catholics, began turning its attentions to lapsed Catholics. This new direction, novel enough to pique *Time*'s interest—'British Roman Catholics are [. . .] making an intensive drive for the lost and strayed' (1949)—was initially pioneered under the leadership of Fr John Heenan, who took over in 1947 but left to become Bishop of Leeds in 1951 (Hagerty 2013). Neatly enough, it was Heenan, who was made Archbishop of Liverpool in 1957, who commissioned the opinion-dividing Metropolitan Cathedral discussed at the opening of this chapter.

Similarly, when Fr Derek Worlock—another future Archbishop of Liverpool (1976–96)—was appointed parish priest of Stepney, East London in 1964, the previous incumbent warned him 'to have no illusion about the East End, that it was no longer a reputable part of the Catholic life of the diocese' (quoted in Longley 2000: 189). Worlock himself estimated that, at the start of his own tenure, 'We had about 7,000 parishioners with a Mass attendance of under 1,000' (Longley 2000: 193; see Scott 1967: 189). So-called 'leakage' among the large numbers of recent Irish immigrants in big cities was also an issue of widespread concern (see, in great detail, Delaney 2007: 160–9). It was, moreover, a touchy subject. In 1960, a highly critical report on the Church's failures in integrating Irish immigrants was suppressed at the heavy insistence of the Hierarchy (in the person of Worlock, wearing his other biretta as the Cardinal's Private Secretary). The author of the report, statistician Anthony Spencer, later wryly remarked that he at least 'escaped extradition to Dublin, and a hanging on a gibbet outside the cathedral' (2008: 2). The report *was* eventually published, albeit over fifty years too late to be of anything other than historical use ([1960] 2012).

The above three paragraphs are, *prima facie*, difficult to square with the much rosier view of British Catholic pastoral life painted in earlier sections of this chapter. 'Alternative facts' have acquired a bad press recently, but they are necessary here if we are adequately to grasp what was going on in the decades preceding Vatican II. Two considerations, in particular, are worth bearing in mind.

The first is simply a matter of perspective. Levels of lapsation which, in the 1940s and 1950s, were causes of serious concern, can look from the present vantage, sixty or seventy years further down that same road, to be unimaginably aspirational. According to Enda Delaney, 'A report on the Irish in Birmingham prepared in 1955 concluded that "the number who miss Mass, *though still a minority*, is truly alarming"' (2007: 169; my emphasis). Meanwhile, recent BSA data shows that a considerable majority of English and Welsh cradle Catholics—59.6 per cent—do not merely 'miss Mass', but 'never or practically never' attend church services of any kind, except for weddings, baptisms, or funerals (Bullivant 2016b: 14). Likewise, the alarm-ringing 1964 *Tablet* article quoted above estimates a 3.65 million shortfall from the total baptized Catholic population to the number at Mass on a typical Sunday. In 2014, the *Catholic Directory*'s figures showed an average Sunday attendance for England and Wales at 850,000 (Spencer 2014). Based on my own figure, using BSA data alongside official population statistics, of 6.2 million cradle Catholics at this time (Bullivant 2016b: 8)—only 0.45 million higher than the 1964 estimate—that amounts to a missing 5.35 million.

This difference of perspective is quite clear from the 1957 Youth Research Council Survey of Young People's Religion and Lifestyles. This truly remarkable dataset, that has only recently become publicly available (McAndrew 2016a, 2016b), contains almost 6000 responses from English 18- to 24-year-olds.[10] For our purposes here, it contains 932 responses from Catholics born between 1933 and 1939, mostly from London, but with good representation from elsewhere, including 205 from Liverpool, 128 from Manchester, and 75 from Birmingham. Of these, 25 per cent said that they attended Mass weekly, and a further 43 per cent monthly. Twenty per cent said that they never attended Mass at all. Against recent figures suggesting that 14 per cent of Catholic 18- to 24-year-olds say they attend weekly, a further

---

[10] The data given in this paragraph are from my own analyses, with the weight 'psweight' (McAndrew 2016a: 21) applied.

5 per cent monthly, and fully 44 per cent 'never or practically never' (Bullivant 2016b: 15), then 1957's young adults look positively fervent. But that was very far from how such figures were viewed at the time.

The second, more substantial explanation is that the kind of dominant Catholic subcultures we have been detailing—and with them (as argued at length) the plausibility structures so integral to instilling and maintaining strong Catholic identities, beliefs, and practices—were, during these very decades, already in the process of disappearing. This point, so critical to understanding all else that follows over the course of the next three chapters, requires some elaboration.

Recall Chapter 2's demonstration of a clear watershed in levels of adult affiliation and practice between cradle Catholics born prior to or during the Second World War, and those born from 1945 onwards. For example, as was shown in Figure 2.3, among those born between 1935 and 1944, 44 per cent are now still regularly practising (i.e., monthly or more) Catholics, while 28 per cent have disaffiliated in one way or another (with 23 per cent now affirming no religion). Yet of those born between 1945 and 1954, only 28 per cent are now regular practisers, and fully 45 per cent are disaffiliates (38 per cent with no religion). The year-by-year data, moreover, revealed the birth years of 1945 and 1946 to mark a real 'point of no return' (see Figure 2.4). Given the significance of one's upbringing to adult religiosity, as discussed previously, this implies a likelihood that the Baby Boomers were, in general, raised differently to those born even a few years earlier. Of course, even if so, upbringing need not be the only significant factor: in the following chapters we shall explore several others. Nevertheless, if we are after the *root* causes of Boomer lapsation and disaffiliation, then it makes sense first to look to their parents. How and why might they have raised their children differently from how they themselves had been raised?

The obvious factor here is the social upheaval of the Second World War (Bruce and Glendinning 2010; Bruce 2011: 71–4). Suddenly, the young Catholic men from one of our close-knit parishes found themselves not only far from the habits of home, but—by design, born from tragic experience[11]—divided up into different services and

---

[11] In the early stages of the First World War, the formation of 'Pals Regiments', recruiting volunteers from the same town or local area, was actively encouraged in order to instil solidarity and camaraderie. While they no doubt accomplished this, it

regiments, and sent off to live and fight alongside otherwise-similar young men from different social, religious, and ethnic backgrounds. Meanwhile, the parish's young, childless women typically went off to do war work themselves, whether in factories, on the land, or in the services. Very often this too involved leaving home, and living among and befriending other young women from different backgrounds. For both sexes, whatever other hardships wartime brought, it permitted a great deal of unchaperoned social and romantic opportunities, far beyond those afforded by the largely parish-centric social calendar back home (Summerfield and Crockett 1992). It is not hard to imagine how, especially given the formative lifestage of the people, these experiences might have had a significant, if subtle, influence effect on these soon-to-be agents of the Baby Boom.

For a start, a significant proportion did indeed find spouses from outside of the pool of eligible bachelor(ette)s back home. True, interest has tended to focus on the prevalence of relationships which crossed national or racial, rather than religious, divides (e.g., Webster 2013). But the fact that tens of thousands of British women were willing to marry Americans or Canadians and follow them home, shows that British young adults' romantic horizons were extending far beyond 'the next parish over'. It also, of course, implies a willingness—and perhaps even a desire—in many young adults, by now well used to living away from home, to settle a good distance from the extended families and neighbourhoods in which they were brought up. We might note here two well-substantiated findings from social network analysis: a generally 'negative correlation between geographic mobility and religious commitment', and the propensity for changes in one's kith-and-kin circles—through marriage and/or settling in a different region, say—to increase the odds that one might adopt a different religion (Everton 2018: sections 4.3, 3.2; Sherkat 2014: 72–87).

There is strong evidence for so-called 'mixed marriages' between Catholics and non-Catholics becoming both more common and more acceptable, with each presumably reinforcing the other, in the

---

also meant that the young men of a given place could be wiped out at a single stroke. At the Battle of the Somme, for instance, the 'Accrington Pals' (named after one of the small cluster of East Lancashire towns—each with significant Catholic populations— from which its soldiers were drawn) lost 235 men, with a further 350 injured, within the first half hour. Because of this and similar tragedies, the Pals strategy was quickly abandoned.

immediate post-war years (Hornsby-Smith 1987: 90–102; Hornsby-Smith et al. 1987). Among the 18- to 24-year-old Catholics in the 1957 Youth Research Council survey, born too late to have been part of the war effort themselves, only 62 per cent of the 159 who were married were so to a fellow Catholic (and some of these may well have converted in order to marry though, evidently enough, this was not required). Figures for weddings conducted in Catholic churches show that in 1958, 30 per cent involved a non-Catholic spouse. By 1972, the proportion had risen to 47 per cent (Spencer 1975: 100). And of course, these do not include any marriages involving Catholics not performed in a Catholic Church, the vast majority of which would be mixed or otherwise 'irregular'.

There is a persuasive body of research showing that the children of religiously mixed marriages tend to grow up less religious than those from religiously homogamous ones (see Bengtson et al. 2013: 113–29; Muttarak and Testa 2015). Reasons for this are not hard to imagine. Parents may decide not to go 'all in' with any particular religious or denominational upbringing, allowing their children to 'make up their own minds'. Even where a decision is made to bring the children up fully in one tradition, and the other parent is fully supportive, they may still only receive a half-dose of parental influence, as indeed they will of grandparental and other extended-family influence (Bengtson et al. 2013: 99–112). Anecdotal evidence, at least, bears this out. Hence according to a 1959 *Tablet* article on 'Religion in Glasgow': 'The Catholic who has lapsed through mixed marriage, with a whole family subsequently lost to the Faith, is all too common, in the experience of all priests' (Cavanagh 1959: 428). In fact, the growing prevalence and normalization of religious intermarriage, from the end of the Second World War onwards, has been hypothesized as a significant factor in the secularization not just of the Catholic community, but of British society as a whole (Voas 2003; Bruce 2011: 73).

Even among the majority who did end up settling down with another Catholic, whether from their own locale or elsewhere, other factors were likely influential on how they raised their ensuing children. For a start, wartime experience and other means of exposure to non-Catholics often softened the sharpest edges of 'us and them' contrasts between Catholics and Protestants. Even if the broad generalizations about 'Proddies', imbibed in childhood, were still held to be true, exceptions might of course be allowed in the case of one's own former comrades-in-arms or fellow Land Girls—or, for that matter, of one's new brothers or sisters-in-law. And the same, of course, was true vice versa. Admittedly, this did not apply uniformly across the whole of Britain: serious sectarian strife showed little sign of abating in areas of Scotland, for example, and was moreover fuelled by the new waves of Irish immigration.[12] Nevertheless, and despite the intrinsic merits of better ecumenical relationships and a general lessening of religious antagonisms, an inevitable by-product was that from the 1950s onwards, increasingly 'denominational allegiances were not always strongly held, nor were strenuous efforts made by parents to pass them on to their children' (Field 2015: 99).

Allied to this were various structural changes in British society, motivated by a need to rebuild bombed-out cities, the influx of immigrants, and the pitter-patter, very soon to be a stampede, of tiny feet. Various 'slum clearance' projects had already begun in the 1920s and 1930s. But these were soon expanded in the post-war decades into large-scale, planned migrations of the urban working classes to new public housing developments: concrete tower blocks ringing major conurbations, sprawling suburban council estates, and various 'New Towns' built—a tad optimistically—for Jetsons-style modern living (see Kynaston 2007: 160–70). In England alone, local authorities built 1.5 *million* new dwellings between 1945 and 1964, with over half of these categorized as suburban houses (Clapson 1998: 42–3). Such schemes, affecting millions of Britons, could not but have a serious impact upon Catholic life, especially given that many of the areas most affected included those with high Catholic populations such as Glasgow, Liverpool, Birmingham, and the East End of London (Boyce 1999; Paice 2008; Werner-Leggett 2012: 46–60). Furthermore, given the 'sense of a new national community and of

---

[12] It is tempting to understand, say, the entrenched enmity between groups of Glasgow Rangers and Celtic supporters as simply footballing and ethnic rivalries, only 'historically' bound up with religion. However, this is hard honestly to do, when a Polish goalkeeper making the Sign of the Cross—an unremarkable and unremarked-upon thing for Catholic footballers to do anywhere else—can still be widely perceived as an act of 'incitement' (Bradley 2015).

On a lighter note, it gives me great pleasure to pass on an anecdote I once heard in an Oxford Senior Common Room:

On a visit to Glasgow once, I saw that someone had scrawled "Fuck the Pope" on the side of a building. Underneath, however, someone else had written "Fuck the Moderator of the General Assembly of the Church of Scotland". Which was particularly amusing, since the then-Moderator was a former colleague and friend of mine...

social mixing' (Clapson 1998: 39), it was designedly not a case of existing neighbours being transplanted wholesale into new neighbourhoods. Rather, existing communities were broken up, with their members being reassigned to build new communities—of all kinds, parishes included—afresh. In the eyes of some city planners, this golden opportunity to dismantle the Catholic 'ghettos' was welcomed, if not openly admitted.[13]

All of this took time, and the full effects of urban dispersal were still underway until well into the 1960s and beyond. As such, throughout the 1940s and 1950s, the kinds of paradigmatic Catholic worlds described earlier were at once experiencing something like their heyday—constantly 'topped up', of course, by large numbers of new migrants—and in the process of passing away forever. It is also true, and of particular relevance here, that the young post-war couples were disproportionately likely to settle down into the new suburban communities earlier in the period: after all, they were the ones in most urgent need of a new place to live. Large numbers of Baby Boom children, therefore, grew up in very different environments from those in which their parents were raised. In the suburbs, council estates, and New Towns, it was not always a given that there *was* a local Catholic church, at least to begin with. The building of a Catholic school was often the first priority of the newly formed (or expanded) parishes: since the 1944 Butler Act—another key plank of the 'post-war settlement'—a large proportion of the Catholic schools system became a semi-autonomous part of the state education sector, co-funded by both government and the Church. In the meantime, various makeshift arrangements were made, with school halls, converted scout huts, or even garages standing in. Given a national need to ration in-demand building materials in the immediate post-war period, moreover, it was far easier to get planning permission for schools than for churches. Restrictions were only eased in the mid-1950s, whereupon British dioceses set about building perhaps a thousand new churches over the next twenty years (Proctor 2014: 3–4). By this time, the concrete-inflected 'new language' of church architecture, mirroring the 'architectural Esperanto' for which the

---

[13] For instance, Vince Cable recalls that William Gray, Chairman of the Scottish Special Housing Association from 1966 to 1972, 'once told me that his greatest achievement was to have used slum clearance and council rehousing to break up the old Catholic and Protestant ghettos' (2009: chap. 6).

New Towns have themselves been criticized (Christopher 2015: 218), produced liturgical and sacramental environments also very, and indeed determinedly, different from those of previous generations. We will have much more to say on this topic in the following chapter.

This is not to say that the parish was no longer often a major part of the young Baby Boomers' and their parents' lives. There is a great deal of evidence to suggest that it was: not least in the fact that the building up of the new parishes' infrastructure was very much a community effort, and one taken much pride in. And indeed, recollections by those brought up in the growing middle-class communities, often recall their family's involvement (e.g., Beckett 2010: 22–3). Neverthe-less, even while parishes remained important, they no longer held a default monopoly over parishioners' time and social life. Families might still choose to associate primarily with other Catholics, and for decades might still regard not being Catholic as a point in some-one's disfavour, even if not an irredeemable one: 'My Mother, and her mother as well, were always saying things like "He's not a Catholic *but he's a very good man*"', as one late-Boomer brought up on the outskirts of Reading recalls (Thompson 2015). But this keeping to one's own was now a *choice* made in a world of other social possibil-ities (Berger 1980: 27–8). Steadily growing affluence was a factor here too. By 1960, 79 per cent of British adults owned a television, and by 1966, 53 per cent owned a car (Kynaston 2014: 102–3; Clapson 1998: 48). Simply put, there were suddenly other things one might do on a Sunday instead of Mass in the morning, followed by Benediction in the evening. And indeed, as 1962's 17 million regular viewers of *Coronation Street*—a soap opera set on the kind of northern terraced street a large proportion of Catholics either still lived on, or recently had—could testify, there were other things to do on a Wednesday night than trudge out to pray the rosary in a converted scout hut.

All of this, and much more—including the advent of the Welfare State, reducing *in extremis* reliance on the social capital of their own parish communities, and indeed on (often religious) charities— marked a remarkable phase of social change in post-war British life. But while their parents and grandparents may well, as Prime Minister Harold Macmillan famously put it in 1959, 'have never had it so good', for the Boomers themselves such newfound freedoms and opportunities could mostly be taken for granted. Though I would not dream of stereotyping an entire generation—there were, after all, over eight million babies born in Britain from 1945 to 1954 (the 'Early

Boomers')[14]—I have fewer scruples about quoting one of their own. According to the 1945-born Francis Beckett, raised in suburban London's outer reaches among 'decent, pious, lower middle-class fifties folk' (Beckett 2010: 22):

> In place of the great ideals of the [post-war] Attlee government, the baby boomers idealised youth and modernity. They created a society where the ultimate good lay in being new, and young, and modern, and new, especially new. [...] The young rather despised the past, a small faraway country of which they knew little. Things were done differently there. [...] The stage was set for a generation that had the instinctive radicalism of the young, the freedom to express it that had been denied to its predecessors—and nothing in particular to do with it.
>
> (Beckett 2010: xv, 64, 29)

They were also a generation who, having benefited from the Butler Act's expansion of secondary education, then had the option of a fully funded higher education, at a rapidly growing choice of institutions, thanks to legislation enacted in the early 1960s (Anderson 2016). For many bright young Catholics from working and lower middle-class backgrounds, they were the first in their families even to imagine attending university (see Hornsby-Smith 2010: 50; Corrin 2013: 56–60; Williamson 2016: 10).

This achievement, while a source of undoubted pride for their parents, could nevertheless drive a further wedge between the generations. In fact, a major storyline begun in the very first episode of *Coronation Street* revolved around tensions between university graduate Ken Barlow—technically a pre-Boomer, having been born in 1939—and his postman father, appalled at his son's new 'snooty' airs and 'high-and-mighty pals' (Independent Television [1960] 2015). Three years away from the habits of home meant other things too: exposure to new ideas, beliefs, lifestyles; living and identifying with likeminded people from a range of religious backgrounds and none (on the latter, see Brown 2012: 64), with an increased likelihood of meeting a non-Catholic future spouse; and—naturally—the likelihood of a middle-class career and lifestyle carrying one still further from one's home neighbourhood, this time for good.

---

[14] This figure is taken from the live birth statistics published by the Office for National Statistics and National Records for Scotland.

As already noted in Chapter 3, the 'young adulthood/starting university' transition is now a widely recognized trigger for lapsation. Here is where that tradition began. Already by the mid-1960s, a great many students were said to arrive at university either already lapsed, or just about to begin being so (Scott 1967: 173). With those who stayed, meanwhile, their growing education and self-assurance began to impact upon the relationship between priests and people. It was evident even to outsiders that 'As the mass of the people advance educationally, socially, economically, so the dependence of Catholics upon their priest diminishes' (Scott 1967: 63; Corrin 2013: 57).

Crucially, it was this bumper generation of young British Catholics who came of age as seemingly everything—or rather, everything *but one*—in the Church was in the process of changing.

AMERICA: 'ON THE BRINK'

On the face of it, the post-war decades played out rather differently in the USA. The transition from war to peacetime was, for obvious reasons, less abrupt than in Europe. With neither rationing nor bomb-ravaged cities to rebuild, the newly supercharged industrial infrastructure could be retooled to fuel a remarkable economic boom. As it seemed to one Catholic Iowan, born in 1951, this was a veritable 'Age of Excitement', in which 'Every week brought exciting news of things becoming better, swifter, more convenient' (Bryson 2006: 78).

Nevertheless, as we saw in Chapter 2, the Baby Boom generation represents a significant transition in patterns of Catholic retention and disaffiliation. This is by no means as sharp as in Britain; there are no 1945/6 'cliff edges' in the US data. But we can indeed trace (see Figure 2.4 and commentary) a phased period of weakening retention in the 1940s and, more sharply, the 1950s. Despite appearances, it is my contention that this was largely due to the same *sorts* of underlying factors to the ones we have already identified at play in the British case. In America, these basic factors were, one might say, substantially remixed: they happened differently, for different reasons, and at different times, than in Britain. But this does not alter the central point: that in America too 'the passing away of a religious culture, sometimes disparagingly referred to as a "ghetto", which reinforced participation and identification with the Church' (Benedict XVI 2008) was already well underway in the 1940s and 1950s, due largely to suburbanization and middle-class-ization.

Worrying indications were also, here and there, starting to be noticed. In the late 1940s, Joseph Fichter's pioneering studies of New Orleans parishes were causing concerns—or rather, confirming existing ones. The Archbishop of New Orleans wrote to the Jesuit sociologist, commenting that he had 'practically confirm[ed] what I have long since deducted from other sources, namely the fact that not more than fifty to sixty percent of our so-called church member-ship can be classified as practicing Catholics' (quoted in Anderson 2006: 23). In follow-up research, Fichter focused on two characteristic 'types' of the lapsed or semi-lapsed: *marginal*, 'conforming to a bare, arbitrary minimum of the norms expected in the religious institution', and *dormant*, 'who have "given up" Catholicism, but have not joined another denomination'. He reports that, across the three parishes studied, some 20 per cent of those surveyed did not come close to fulfilling the Church's expectations of attending Mass on all Sundays and other holy days of obligations. A good proportion of these had attended church only once, or never, in the past year. By today's standards, of course, such levels of lapsation are the stuff of parish priests' wildest dreams. But for Fichter, as indeed his Archbishop, such numbers were heading in an ominous direction. The subsequent sixty-odd years, it must be said, have rather proved them right.

In America as a whole, Mass attendance, which had climbed steadily over the previous decade, finally peaked in 1958, with 74 per cent (!) of Catholics telling Gallup they had attended church in the previous seven days. It then started, albeit slowly at first, to decline (Hout and Greeley 1987: 332). Retention levels were still, admittedly, holding up. A nationwide sample of white American adults in 1965, found that 14 per cent of those with Catholic fathers (a reasonable, though far from perfect, proxy for Catholic upbring-ing) were themselves something other than Catholic, with 13 per cent identifying as some kind of Protestant. Next to the disaffiliation rates for several other denominations—Baptists' 18 per cent, Methodists' 43 per cent, Lutherans' 35 per cent—this was good going (Stark and Glock 1968: 195). Nevertheless, it suggests that Catholic disaffiliation was already by the mid-1960s very much 'a thing'. And with Ameri-can Catholicism poised 'on the brink' (Greeley 2004a: 30), it would very soon become a much bigger one.

But what was causing it all? Again, let us first consider the generation who *produced* the Baby Boomers: the young men and women who had fought and worked in the Second World War. As with their British counterparts, for those brought up in insular Catholic neighbourhoods, this experience brought with it an unprecedented amount of social mixing. The social historian Colleen McDannell, born in 1953, relates the experiences of her own mother, raised in a German Catholic neighbourhood of Erie, Pennsylvania.

> Margaret was eighteen when she married a soldier. At that point in her life she had barely even left her hometown. [...] When Ken shipped out for training to Oregon and later to Nebraska and Texas, the young bride traveled for days on crowded trains to be with her husband for a few hours on the weekends. [...] Looking at the world outside the train window, she learned the same thing that many formerly provincial young Americans were learning for the first time: The United States was an immense country full of all kinds of people. [...] As Catholic men formed platoons and women talked during breaks from their factory work, they discovered that Protestants and Jews and even atheists shared their fears and aspirations. (2011: 29–30)

Here too, this led to the increasing prevalence, and thus ultimately acceptance, of religious intermarriage. While by no means an unknown phenomenon before the War—indeed Ken McDannell was himself raised Methodist—they soon accounted for a large minority of marriages, both in or outside the Church, involving Catholics (Greeley 1970; Walch 1989: 87; McDannell 2011: 37–8).

The so-called 'GI Bill', guaranteeing a range of benefits for returning servicemen, had far-reaching implications. The commitment to fund veterans' training and education 'made college education a practical reality for millions of young people from Catholic homes in which they were the first family members ever to attend college' (Marty 1995: 168). That large numbers of Catholics were among them is amply evidenced by the resulting admissions boom at Catholic colleges nationwide (Edmondson 2002). And in fact, the existing networks of Catholic higher education meant that, at least at this time, going off to college had a less faith-disorienting effect than it had on the new crop of British working-class Catholic students twenty years later who, unless they were training to be teachers, had no Catholic options to choose from. That said, not every Catholic ex-GI attended a Catholic college, not least because of the rush for places, and the fact that many were looking to live at home while simultaneously embarking on married—and soon, family—life: in a big city like New York or Chicago one might have several Catholic options to choose from, but elsewhere one might simply be glad to get a place at a college, any college, commutable by bus (cf. Carey 2004: 93–4). Furthermore, not every veteran chose to use his education allowance on a college degree: vocational training was also covered, and trainees at these were accordingly more likely to mix and maintain friendships with non-Catholics.

The expansion of education, and with it career prospects, would itself in time have fuelled a growth in suburban, middle-class living. But the GI Bill also guaranteed preferential rates for home loans, at the same time as government subsidies and benefits were offered to developers to assuage an acute housing crisis. This combination, along with federal road building and other infrastructural initiatives, led the annual rate of new houses built to leap over tenfold from 140,000 in 1944, to an average of 1.5 million through each year of the 1950s (Nicolaides and Wiese 2017). Whole new communities, largely consisting of starter homes of modest size and price, were started from scratch. Among these, the half-dozen townships built by Levitt and Sons in the North East have become the most iconic. These 'Levittowns', whose houses came replete with a lawn and white picket fence, proved naturally attractive to young Catholic couples on the up. Their Protestant and Jewish counterparts, as well as an ever-increasing number of inter-religious couples, felt the same way. Whereas in their old New York or Pittsburgh neighbourhoods, religion was the common factor, in Levittown it was everything from age, wartime experience, class, stage of life, outlook, and aspiration. Race too, given that home-ownership in Levittowns, as in many other such communities, was originally denied to blacks (see Brodkin 1998: 44–52). This, in itself, would have profound ramifications: blacks, even affluent, college-educated, middle-class ones, were forced to remain in the inner cities, often paying more in rent than their white counterparts did on mortgages. As southern blacks migrated to northern cities in search of jobs, and new waves of Latino—not least Puerto Rican—immigrants joined them, the situation would only become even worse. Over time, those who could get out—disproportionately whites—increasingly did so, gradually eroding the distinctive character of the different ethnic neighbourhoods (see McGreevy 1996: 101–32; Opdycke 2007: 18–20).

As in our British suburbs, the building of churches was not always a first priority for the new suburbanites. Nor even, for that matter, the second. As reported by the sociologist Herbert Gans, who lived in Levittown, New Jersey, during its first few years, the local Catholics, while commendably gung-ho in building up a new parish community, were 'more interested in the parochial school than in the church'. Since both their bishop and priest required the parishioners' support to raise the necessary funds to build a parish, the laity's prioritization won the day (Gans 1967: 72–3). Admittedly, Catholics were still going to church—even if, for several years, in the sports halls of shiny new schools—in robust numbers, and bringing their children up to do likewise. But in these new mixed neighbourhoods, it was no longer the taken-for-granted *given* it had been during their own childhoods. From having been somewhere that you and a large proportion of your close neighbours *walked* to, church was now a place that you and your widely dispersed fellow parishioners *drove* to. It was, moreover, now one among many potentially more enticing options one might drive to on a Sunday. Where better to keep the kids happy *and* show off pop's new Edsel Corsair: Benediction in a 'dual-purpose' school hall, or the new drive-in movie theatre? Hence it is for various reasons that Gans, even without the benefit of hindsight, notes the growing homogenization of suburban religious sensibilities:

> They are Protestants, Catholics, and Jews who believe in an increasingly similar God, share an increasingly similar Judeo-Christian ethic, and worship in an increasingly similar way with similarly decreasing frequency. (Gans 1967: vii; cf. Wuthnow 1988: 71–99)

After the newness of the social environments in which they were raised, the next thing to note about the Baby Boomers is that there were an awful lot of them: 'America had thirty-two million children aged twelve or under in the mid-1950s [. . .] so there were kids everywhere, all the time, in densities now unimaginable' (Bryson 2006: 41). This effect was magnified through coming after a long birth rate slough during the Depression and War period. Here was suddenly a new generation, both moulding and moulded by a whole new era of equal parts 'joy and hope' and, given the ever-present threat of nuclear catastrophe, 'fear and anxiety' (cf. *Gaudium et Spes* 1). Through force of sheer numbers alone, they were destined to exert a powerful influence over American life and culture

for decades to come: 'Because the baby boom dominates the demographic landscape, its mood becomes the mood of the times'
(Russell 2013: 1).

By the early 1960s, the existence and significance of a new cultural
outlook among America's adolescents had been apparent, and anxiously fretted over, for some time. For example, a March 1957 issue of
National Review, admittedly not a periodical at the vanguard of the
burgeoning youth culture, offered this puzzled commentary on whom
it calls 'stompin' rock 'n' roll 'teen-agers':

> The office pessimist tells us that rock 'n' roll is a bored and empty
> generation's attempt to multiply the kicks which alone make life bear-
> able to it. The office activist says that kids wouldn't be rock 'n' rollers if
> they were taught, say, to figure-skate, or even allowed to stay a few more
> years with marbles. Such explanations are as good as any, but they don't
> tell us what's the matter with an adult world that fails to make it possible
> for kids to enjoy themselves within the bounds of sanity.
>
> (National Review 1957)

This was also, naturally, a topic of growing concern in Catholic
circles. The same month as the *National Review* piece, the *New
York Times* reported on the National Catholic Family Life convention
held in Milwaukee (again, the *Times*' assumption that such an event
would interest its readers enough to send along a correspondent
is worth noting). Among several talks addressing contemporary
'youths' rebellion against authority', the *Times* singled out remarks
by an Illinois priest and high school teacher:

> 'The solution to rock 'n' roll music and the comic books,' [Fr Dennis
> J. Geaney] declares, 'is simply not a war against them. There is a void in
> these people's lives that must be filled. Good music and good reading
> could do this.' [...] While high school freshmen may still heed their
> parents, they do so with diminished confidence. Older high school
> children, he declared, may even question the parental position of
> authority. (Johnston 1957)

These widespread feelings of intergenerational alienation, ranging
from mutual incomprehension to outright antagonism—from the
parents' perspective, all the more mystifying from a generation lav-
ished with luxuries and opportunities undreamt of during their own
childhoods—is summed up well in the title of Andrew Greeley's
tellingly successful 1961 book *Strangers in the House: Young Catholics*

in America (see Kotre 1978: 11–30).[15] At this early point, however, Greeley's main criticism of the youth concerned their—sex and drinking notwithstanding—perceived apathy and conservatism: 'There are no more battles to fight, no more mountains to climb, no more crusades to go on, nothing more important to be done' (1961: 9).

Within just a few years, however, Greeley had rather changed his tune. Referring back to his earlier work in an *America* article, he now wished to qualify it with a 'change of emphasis':

> There has risen up a New Breed that was all but invisible five years ago. There are not very many of them; they might not show up in any sample; the majority of their classmates [. . .] continue to be listless and indifferent. But the New Breed is making so much noise that one hardly has time to notice the majority. Almost any college president or seminary rector will admit their existence and will confess puzzlement about what they want. [. . .] There are many things about the New Breed that I like, but many things that baffle me. I think I understood the 'Strangers in the House' of whom I wrote half a decade ago; but the New Breed are different, and I fear I do not know them. (1964)

In pointed contrast to his eponymous 'Strangers', this 'New Breed' are defined by their enthusiasm, keenness, and radicality. Nevertheless, although 'they are greatly concerned about things like honesty, integrity and authenticity [. . .] they seem so eager to make almost any question a matter of principle that one is tempted to feel that they are looking for a fight—though perhaps they are only looking for a cause.' In light of what would soon transpire within American Catholicism (some, though by no means all, of which will be discussed in the following two chapters), a number of Greeley's observations are uncannily prescient. For example, he quotes the view of a Jesuit priest that the Order's 'seminarians are the most radical people in the American church—bar none'. More germanely still to our concerns, he notes:

> The New Breed is not flexible, it is not gradualist. It wants a Church that is relevant to its own needs and the needs it sees in the world, and it wants it now, not next week. Unfortunately, it is not able to say exactly what that relevance involves, and at this stage of the game neither is

---

[15] The 'strangers' metaphor was also applied to British Catholic teenagers in the early 1960s, apparently independently of Greeley (e.g., Kirwin 1965).

anyone else. [...] As much as we are annoyed by the inconsistencies and irrationality that the New Breed often seem to display, we must not overlook what they are trying to tell us; they are trying to say that you cannot have a half-souled aggiornamento, that if you open the window you are not going to be able to close it again and that the wind that blows in is likely to bring [all] sorts of strange things with it. (1964)

Note especially the mention here of 'relevance'—soon to become the *cri de cœur* of, if not the New Breed themselves, then of churchmen and liturgists trying ever more experimental means of attracting and appeasing them.

For all their dissatisfaction with the status quo, Greeley is nonetheless convinced of the New Breed's religious stickability: 'It would be a terrible mistake to think that they are going to leave the Church, either by apostasy or alienation. It is their Church and it would be difficult even to drive them out of it.' Still, given simple demographic realities, Greeley foresees a turbulent future:

It should be clear that I am ambivalent about the New Breed. I am fascinated by them and I admire their courage; yet they frighten me. In another quarter of a century they will be taking over the American Church. They will be the bishops, the mothers general, the rectors, the pastors, the provincials, the superiors, the scholars, the politicians, the organizers, the editors, the leaders of lay organizations. I don't know quite what their Church will look like and I wonder how much room there will be in it for someone like me. The New Breed has reason to be confident. Everything is on their side—their youth, time, the wave of history, and, one suspects, the Holy Spirit. (1964)

CONCLUSION

My purpose here has been to show *both* the richness and vitality of British and American Catholic life in the post-war decades, *and* the simultaneous fact that much of this richness and vitality was, already, demonstrably in a process of eroding. To be more precise: it was the underlying social structures, making such richness and vitality not only possible but natural, that were gradually crumbling.

Let us return to the first of our three master ideas, namely, the centrality of social plausibility structures in maintaining the reality and givenness of a certain worldview with all its associated beliefs, identities, and practices. Our close-knit Catholic parishes, where one's neighbours, friends, workmates, and fellow-parishioners were often coextensive, and in which one's social, ethnic, cultural, and sporting senses of community and belonging—as well as, of course, one's religious life—were often closely intertwined, are paradigmatic examples of such social 'deep architecture'. Though still seemingly going strong throughout much of the post-war period, the writing was already on the presbytery wall. The Second World War, among much else, lifted large numbers of young people out of these environments, before a slew of post-war social and economic changes—everything from expansions of education leading to social and geographic mobility, to mushrooming television and automobile ownership—were already fracturing these semi-closed subcultures. Meanwhile, centrally planned programmes of slum clearance, urban renewal, and suburbanization had the knock-on (or in some cases, as noted above, apparently deliberate) effect of breaking up the inner-city neighbourhoods once and for all. Such processes did not occur identically in Britain and America. But *mutatis mutandis*, they did occur. And as they did, they likewise impacted upon the second of our master ideas: the understanding of a wide range of time, effort, and (often) cash-consuming Catholic devotions and practices as forms of Credibility Enhancing Displays or CREDs. The *real* neutering of these, however, will have to wait until the next chapter.

Deep structural changes do not, of course, tend to show their fruits with immediate effect. This follows inevitably from our axiom that a person's upbringing exerts a powerful effect over their adult religiosity. Thus a generation of persons brought up differently from their parents'—as we have been arguing the Baby Boomers certainly were—will typically not reveal the effects, if any, of these differences until they themselves begin to enter adulthood. At the most prosaic level, for instance, children and young teenagers do not typically get to choose when, where, or if they want to go to church, just as they do not get to pick whether to get baptized in the first place; their religiosity, to a very large extent, mirrors their parents'. Accordingly, if our 'generational approach' to explaining Catholic lapsation and disaffiliation is correct, and the Baby Boomers do indeed mark a genuine watershed, then one would not expect to start seeing real hints of it before, say, the late 1950s. And one would not expect it to reach full fruition until, say, they reach home-leaving or college-going age: which is itself, of course, a critically important phase of personal, social, and religious development.

Critically, the first wave of true Baby Boomers, born between 1945 and 1950, hit 18 in the years 1963 to 1968. In secular terms, that is precisely the same period from The Beatles' *Please Please Me* and the assassination of John F. Kennedy, to campus riots, Dr King's killing, and, well, a great deal else (see Kurlansky 2004). In Catholic-specific terms, moreover, it is the span of years between *Sacrosanctum Concilium* and *Humanae Vitae*. To put it mildly, rather a lot was about to happen at once. As Hugh McLeod remarks of the end of the 1950s with—note well—his eye on *all* mainstream Christian denominations and not simply the Catholic case: 'The ground was well prepared for the crisis of Christendom in the 1960s' (2007: 29).

Before moving on, let us briefly return full circle—aptly enough, given its liturgy-in-the-round design. Like a great many less-famous Catholic churches built in this period, the radical design of Liverpool Metropolitan Cathedral was understood to constitute a bold statement that 'religion accepts the challenge of the twentieth century, while planning to exist in this edifice for at least five hundred years' (British Pathé 1966). Yet before even the next ten years were out, the roof of this confidently future-facing icon was leaking badly. In 1981, the Archdiocese issued a writ claiming millions in damages from its architect, engineers, and builders 'for negligence and breach of contract' (*Liverpool Roman Catholic Archdiocesan Trustees v. Gibberd and others* [1986] 7 Con. L.R. 113). It eventually received £1.3 million in an out-of-court settlement. Since then, millions more pounds from various charitable foundations have been used for upkeep and repairs.

5

Gaudium et spes, luctus et angor

On 7 December 1965, Vatican II's penultimate day, Pope Paul VI promulgated the 'Pastoral Constitution on the Church in the World of Today',[1] whose opening words—'the joy and hopes, sorrows and anguish'—adorn this chapter. According to this, the Council's valedictory document, one of the contemporary world's chief hallmarks is its sheer pace of change.

> Today, the human race is involved in a new stage of history. Profound and rapid changes are spreading by degrees around the whole world. Triggered by the intelligence and creative energies of man, these changes recoil upon him, upon his decisions and desires, both individual and collective, and upon his manner of thinking and acting with respect to things and to people. Hence we can already speak of a true cultural and social transformation, one which has repercussions on man's religious life as well.
>
> As happens in any crisis of growth, this transformation has brought serious difficulties in its wake.   (*Gaudium et Spes* 4)

By the mid-1960s, this assessment was hard to contradict. In just over three years since it opened in October 1962, the Council had witnessed the Cuban Missile Crisis, the first woman in space, America's (formal) entry into the Vietnam War, a future Nobel laureate's transition from 'Blowin' in the Wind' to 'Like a Rolling Stone', two

---

[1] My rendering of the Latin here is different than the one normally given: i.e., '...in the Modern World'. However, the original '*in Mundo huius Temporis*'—literally, 'in the World of This Time'—implies a far tighter frame of reference than is captured by 'the Modern World'. The Council is not making a generic statement about the Church vis-à-vis modernity, but rather a series of concrete ones it thinks relevant to the immediate, present situation. For instance, *urgens* ('urgent') and its cognates appear no less than thirteen times in the document.

US presidents, and three British prime ministers. Furthermore, though he only replaced the late John XXIII in June 1963, Paul had already become the first Bishop of Rome to meet a Patriarch of Constantinople since 1438, and the first ever to set foot in the New World with a fourteen-hour visit to New York. Viewed in this light, 'profound and rapid changes' sounds like something of an understatement.

Yet in many ways the decade, in both 'Church' and 'World', was only just getting into gear. We have already noted the large numbers of young people, born in the post-war Baby Boom and thus coming of age in the 1960s, who 'In outlooks, values and expectations [. . .] were to show themselves to be less like their parents than any previous generation in modern times' (Donnelly 2005: 1). But they can scarcely be seen as the sole agents of change. Indeed, most of the era's most iconic legal and political causes—Civil Rights, the Women's Move-ment, anti-War protests—had been picking up speed for years, long before there were Boomers old enough to join the bandwagon (or indeed, Freedom Ride). Very few of their cultural icons and leaders—whether Che Guevara, Martin Luther King, Gloria Steinem, Jane Fonda, Muhammad Ali, or John Lennon—were Boomers themselves. Donovan, born 1946, may have been one; but Dylan, born 1941, was *not* (O'Rourke 2014: 181–2). For all their enthusiasm and visibility, then, the Boomers themselves were arguably as much 'changed against' as changing. They were the objects, guinea pigs even, of social and cultural upheaval, just as much as they were its subjects. And the same was true, as we shall see, in the Catholic Church.

But *change* is not, in and of itself, sufficient explanation for the kind of long-term religious downturn that followed in the decade's wake. Periods of serious social, cultural, economic, and/or technological turmoil are by no means rare in western history (see Mortimer 2014). Naturally, it is not unknown for these to have significant religious repercussions. One thinks, for example, of the flourishing of new religious ideas and groups in the 1300s' 'shipwreck of a century which is going from bad to worse', as the Italian chronicler Filippo Villani put it (quoted in Jones 2000: 1; see McGinn 2005), or the political turmoils both fuelling, and in turn being fuelled by, the various Reformations engulfing Europe in the 1500s. As a general rule of thumb, times of turbulence—'existential insecurity', in contempor-ary sociologese—tend to reinforce and reinvigorate religious beliefs, practices, and identities (cf. Norris and Inglehart 2015). To be sure, the 1960s were not immune from this either, engendering a wealth of new religious experimentation and innovation, both in and out—*far out*—of the traditional Christian offerings, especially in America. This was true of the Catholic Church too, not least with the Charismatic Renewal and the birth and/or flourishing of a number of new ecclesial movements (Faggioli 2014; Schreck 2017). But overall, despite the enthusiasm and strength of diverse and sizeable minorities, the 1960s' primary religious bequest to later decades was one of decline. This was not, it is once more worth reiterating, purely a Catholic phenomenon. American estimates suggest that mainline Protestant denominations lost between a quarter and a third of their members between the 1960s and 1980 (FitzGerald 2017: 328–9; also Kelley [1972] 1986: 1–11). Likewise, the Anglican churches of England, Wales, and Scotland lost a quarter of their communicants from 1960 to 1980 (Field 2017: 51). In neither place have mainline numbers since rebounded. A quarter-century further down the line, Britain's pre-eminent church statistician could report as good news that while overall levels of English churchgoing were still falling, the *rate* of decline was at least easing: 'We are coming out of the nosedive, but no U-turn is yet in sight—we are still dropping' (Brierley 2006: 18).[2] Not for nothing has Callum Brown recently observed:

> For organised Christianity, the sixties constituted the most concentrated period of crisis since the Reformation; but what was at stake became perceived as the very survival of Christian society and values. In this respect certainly, the sixties may turn out to have been more important than even the Renaissance and Reformation.   (2012: 29)

Seemingly, there was something about the *specific* changes afoot in British and American society, and about their *specific* repercussions, which served to weaken the traditional indicators of mainstream Christian religiosity.

'Profound and rapid changes' were not, though, something that simply *happened to* Christians in the 1960s. Neither individually nor collectively were Christians wholly passive beneficiaries or sufferers of the social, cultural, and political upheavals of the 1960s; they actively participated. What is more, they often themselves added large doses of change, of various types, into the mix. These could be far-reaching.

---

[2] This is, I readily and unrepentantly admit, an example I have used in print more than once before.

Whatever the actual nuances in the views expressed in John Robinson's *Honest to God* (1963), or in the works of the various scholars cited in *Time*'s iconic 'Is God Dead?' issue (1966), they certainly gave the *impression* that one could now be an Anglican bishop or a professor at a respected religious college without unambiguously believing in God's existence: quite the shaking of the foundations.

Such radical posturing, for all of its media attention and accompanying book sales, was only ever the preserve of a tiny minority: it is not as though there were major Protestant denominations inserting the Nietzschean 'death of God' into their articles of faith, alongside the Good Friday one. Instead, the *real* example of comprehensive, systematic, and often very practical changes being enacted by a significant Christian body in this period is, of course, the Catholic Church. Referring to the US case, though with equal relevance to the British situation also, the historian Patrick Carey observes:

> The Catholic community, perhaps more than any other religious community in the United States, experienced the simultaneously stimulating and disintegrating winds of social and religious reforms and upheavals that blew across the country in the 1960s and early 1970s. The implementation of the Second Vatican Council's liturgical and structural reforms and the corresponding transformation of American Catholic consciousness that accompanied them took place at a time of revolutionary change in American political and cultural life. [...] When combined, the religious and cultural reformations produced a period of unprecedented religious turmoil and change. (2004: 115)

Or as Joseph Komonchak has arrestingly put it, at precisely the moment that the storms of modernity 'became more common, larger, and more violent [...] it seemed that the Catholic Church had ceased to be a rock and was now more like a raft, which went up and down with the latest waves, making many people very seasick' (2018: 283).

Our interests in this chapter are not with changes in their own right, no matter how intrinsically interesting or significant. Detailed accounts of the multifarious changes—doctrinal, liturgical, pastoral, demographic—in the Catholic Church during the 1960s and beyond already exist, many of which will be gratefully drawn upon here. Our overarching focus, however, will be on those topics that are most necessary for comprehending the timing, nature, and extent of Catholic disaffiliation in the five-or-so decades since Vatican II. Guided by the various forms of sociological data adduced in Chapters 2 and 3, and the historical evidence and theoretical arguments advanced in Chapter 4, I wish to highlight four such topics. Three of these are clear-cut instances of change (or rather, especially in the first and second cases, clusters of very many changes): (i) the liturgical reforms, inspired by Vatican II's *Sacrosanctum Concilium*; (ii) the accompanying de-emphasis of many traditional devotional practices, and their concomitant theological foci, in the wake of the Council; and (iii) the so-called 'abolition' of Friday abstinence. The fourth is conversely, on the face of it, not a change at all, but rather the conspicuous absence of a change: (iv) the publication, and resulting furore surrounding, *Humanae Vitae*. On deeper analysis, however, we will see how this 'non-change' precipitated some very great changes indeed. For a book with 'Vatican II' placed prominently in its title, it will perhaps be noted that, of these four, only two are more-or-less *directly* ascribable to the Council. For the time being, however, let us simply state that, with so much going on in the 1960s, it is often very difficult to separate cause from symptom, substance from acci-dent, intended consequence from unforeseen side-effect. And as we will see in the sections of this chapter devoted directly to Vatican II itself, not everything that occurred because of the Council was neces-sarily intended or anticipated by it.

Before exploring each of the four main 'changes' in turn, with specific reference to their concrete repercussions in Britain and America, it is necessary to provide some interpretive background on the Council, as *the* Catholic event of an eventful decade, itself. In the next two subsections, therefore, we will first consider what, precisely, the Second Vatican Council was *for*. Secondly and relatedly, we will dig a little into Vatican II's vision for liturgical and ecclesial reform, as expressed in its maiden document *Sacrosanctum Conci-lium*: 'a magna carta capable of inspiring the renewal of the Church' (Marini 2013: 21) and moreover, 'the firstfruit and the ultimate theological-pastoral expression of Vatican II' (Faggioli 2012b: 155).

A COUNCIL FOR THE NEW EVANGELIZATION

If we are to understand both the Council's liturgical vision as expressed in *Sacrosanctum Concilium*, and—critically—how this vision came to be received and implemented 'on the ground' within our particular contexts, we must first pose some simple questions. What was the purpose of the liturgical reforms? What was it hoped that they would achieve, and why?

In order to answer them, I wish to repeat an argument that I have made more fully elsewhere (Bullivant 2017). My basic contention is that the liturgical reforms mandated by the Second Vatican Council were in large measure motivated, and justified, by what later Catholics would come to call the 'new evangelization'. And further, a concern for the new evangelization guided the interpretation and implementation of the reforms (in all their superdiversity). I admit that this all may sound quite strange. While it is uncontroversial enough to aver that the neo-evangelistic project is 'grounded firmly in the Vatican II documents' (Barron 2017: 202), my rather stronger proposal seems to suffer from the brute fact that the phrase 'new evangelization' did not appear until years later, in the pontificate of John Paul II. But that is merely a minor detail: I will argue that what St John Paul II actually meant by that phrase—'a "new evangelization" or a "re-evangelization" [. . .] of those peoples who have already heard Christ proclaimed' (*Redemptoris Missio* 33, 30)—was demonstrably at the forefront of many of the Council Fathers' and *periti's* minds long before the term itself was coined. This recognition has a great deal of significance.

In his 1990 encyclical letter, *Redemptoris Missio*, John Paul distinguishes between three kinds of pastoral situation. The *first* is 'peoples, groups, and socio-cultural contexts in which Christ and his Gospel are not known, or which lack Christian communities sufficiently mature to be able to incarnate the faith in their own environment and proclaim it to other groups' (33). The Church's primary task here is hence what he calls *missio ad gentes*—proposing the good news about Jesus Christ and the Church he founded to people who haven't ever heard, or heard much, about it, and carefully nurturing it once it is established. This is, if one likes, the 'classic' mode of evangelization throughout Christian history. The *second* setting is that of cultures where such 'classic evangelization' has been successful: where Christianity has taken root, matured, and is self-sustaining (even to the extent of sending missionaries elsewhere). These are, he writes: 'Christian communities with adequate and solid ecclesial structures. They are fervent in their faith and in Christian living' (33).

The *third* situation, and the critical one for our purposes, is where this solidly established Christianity is beginning to crumble within a culture:

> countries with ancient Christian roots, and occasionally in the younger Churches as well, where entire groups of the baptized have lost a living sense of the faith, or even no longer consider themselves members of the Church, and live a life far removed from Christ and his Gospel.   (33)

This is specifically called 'an intermediate situation'. In context, it is clear the meaning here is *intermediate between the second and first situations*: that is, a situation in which a culture where the Church has been firmly established is in the process of lapsing back into a position where, for the most part, 'Christ and his Gospel are not known'. It is here that what is needed is 'a new evangelization of those peoples who have already heard Christ proclaimed' (30). The newness, then, refers primarily to a difference of socio-cultural context. And it is this *difference of context* which requires a different evangelistic approach: one indeed, to quote another of the Polish Pope's famous formulations, 'new in its ardour, in its methods, and in its expression' (1983). The *concept* of new evangelization therefore refers to the Church's missionary activity in socio-cultural contexts where a long-established Christian (or indeed specifically Catholic) culture is significantly weakening. The *phrase* itself is naturally a handy label, a shorthand description, to have. But obviously, it is perfectly possible for the concept to have existed before the coining of the phrase.

And so it had. Albeit *avant-la-lettre*, the Second Vatican Council's documents are shot through with the new evangelization. And in fact, this is true of the very rationale for calling a Council in the first place. Why, after all, would one embark upon so vast an undertaking if everything was already going swimmingly? As was quoted in this book's maiden paragraph, St John XXIII's opening address spoke of an urgent need to 'introduc[e] timely changes [. . . to] really succeed in bringing men, families and nations to the appreciation of supernatural values', and without abandoning 'that sacred patrimony of truth inherited from the Fathers', to keep up to date 'with the changing conditions of this modern world, and of modern living' (John XXIII 1962).

We have seen how, by the 1960s, these were far from idle concerns in Britain and America, what with worrying statistics emerging around 'leakage', and unease about connecting with the rising Boomer generation.

More critically for the Council's orientation and direction, they had been major concerns across much of western Europe for several decades, including in those nations with the most organized and influential groups of bishops (see Bullivant 2012a: 55–9; Üffing 2013; Horn 2015). In Germany, for example, talk of a growing need for re-evangelization began in the mid-1930s. In 1941, the Jesuit Alfred Delp—later martyred for resisting the Nazi regime—wrote: 'We have become a mission country. The environment and the factors determining all life are not Christian anymore' (quoted in Üffing 2013: 37). In the following decade, Joseph Ratzinger worried in print that Catholicism was increasingly becoming 'a Church of pagans who still call themselves Christians but in truth have become pagans' (1958: 1). Around the same time, Karl Rahner could describe, as a readily recognizable and common figure, the Christian who:

> lives in a family circle whose members although originally Catholic, not only are not zealously 'practising', but if the truth is to be told have become completely without faith, sometimes to the point of being actively hostile, of officially leaving the Church.   ([1954] 1967: 355)

In France, the bishop of Bayeux and Lisieux lamented in 1929: 'There is a whole region around Caen containing all our great factories, where Christ is unknown: this is our true mission territory' (quoted in Hebblethwaite 2010: 104). Over the course of the 1930s, leading intellectuals such as Yves Congar and Étienne Gilson extended this description to huge swathes of the country. In 1941, the French hierarchy opened a new seminary, *Mission de France*, dedicated to training a new kind of missionary priest: *prêtres-ouvriers*, 'priest-workers', who would take up blue-collar jobs in factories and dock-yards in order to minister to the country's working classes as peers. The urgent need for so bold an experiment, which was swiftly copied by the Belgian bishops, was soon underlined with a report on the religious state of the working classes by two priest-sociologists, *La France—La Pays de Mission?* (Godin and Daniel [1943] 1949). In 1944, the French bishops received a new Nuncio from Rome, who would himself soon write to his family that 'Paris is a city of five million inhabitants, and many of them lead a life that is completely cut off from the Church' (quoted in Hebblethwaite 2010: 104). Fifteen years later, that same Nuncio, Angelo Giuseppe Roncalli— now known to the world as Pope John XXIII—announced his desire to convoke 'a general Council for the universal Church' for 'fostering the good of souls and bringing the new pontificate into clear and definite correspondence with the spiritual needs of the present day' (quoted in Alberigo 2006: 1).

Finally, in Italy itself, the distance of large numbers of baptized Catholics from the Church was a recognized problem. As in other countries this was especially so in major cities, among the urban working classes. Beginning in the 1940s and 1950s, dedicated factory chaplaincies began to be established, as for example in Turin among Fiat autoworkers (Horn 2015: 71–3). Readers of Giovanni Guareschi's 'Don Camillo' stories, set in the post-war Po Valley of northern Italy, will be aware that lapsation from, and politically motivated hostility towards, the Church was a feature of rural life too: one common enough to be satirized with evident affection for all sides. Surveys also confirmed that Mass attendance was falling rapidly, from around 69 per cent of adults in 1956 to just 53 per cent in 1961, and lower still in big cities (Pollard 2008: 144–5). Arriving in 1955, the new Archbishop of Milan was so saddened at the Church's failure to reach vast numbers of the city's working people—his own friendly overtures to factory workers were often met with jeers (Pollard 2008: 146)—that he organized a 'Great Mission of Milan' two years later. This huge, three-week affair involved over a thousand preachers, including twenty-six cardinals and bishops:

> For three weeks Milan was a city under siege, and the archbishop was the field commander of the troops. In and out of department stores, into banks, the stock exchange, the inevitable factories, visiting thirty churches a day, he exhorted and pleaded [. . .] And always there was the special pleading to the fallen away: 'We are determined to place those estranged from us in the first position of our activity and our prayer [. . .] If there is a voice which can reach you, those of you who have left the Church, the first will be one which asks pardon of you. Yes, we of you.' (Clancy 1963: 117–18)

Evidently, here was a prelate filled with a missionary zeal 'new in its ardour, in its methods, and in its expressions' in re-evangelizing the 'baptized [who] have lost a living sense of the faith, or even no longer consider themselves members of the Church' (*Redemptoris Missio* 33). The archbishop was, of course, Giovanni Battista Montini: the future Pope Paul VI.

'PASTORALLY EFFICACIOUS TO
THE FULLEST DEGREE'

The 'Dogmatic Constitution on the Sacred Liturgy' was the first of the Council's sixteen documents to be formally promulgated, during the Second Session in December 1963. Following long-established precedent, it would forever be known by its opening Latin words *Sacrosanctum Concilium*, '[This] Sacred Council'. This deliberate and symbolic decision (in Latin, word order can be bent to suit one's allusive desires) suggests the text should be read as making a general statement, beyond the subject of liturgy alone, regarding Vatican II's overarching purpose and intention. Indeed, Ratzinger's observation at the time has been echoed, with different emphases, by many commentators since:

> The decision to begin with the liturgy schema was not merely a technically correct move. Its significance went far deeper. [...] The text implied an entire ecclesiology and thus anticipated (in a degree that cannot be too highly appreciated) the main theme of the entire Council—its teaching on the Church.
>
> (Ratzinger [1966] 2009: 31; see also Faggioli 2012b;
> Driscoll 2017: 25–7)

Accordingly, *Sacrosanctum Concilium* (*SC*) is perfectly upfront about its, and the Council as a whole's, (neo-) evangelistic inclinations (see O'Malley 2014: 22–34). Its very opening sentence affirms that, among the Council's four main aims, two of them are 'to impart an ever increasing vigour to the Christian life of the faithful' and 'to strengthen whatever can help to call the whole of mankind into the household of the Church' (*SC* 1). The task of 'undertaking the reform and promotion of the liturgy' (*SC* 1) is then explicitly linked to fulfilling these aims. Moreover, the text's expressed desire of imbuing the liturgical rites with 'new vigour to meet the circumstances and needs of modern times' (*SC* 4) is a clear admission that the rites, as they currently stood, were felt to be somewhat less than optimally 'vigorous' for achieving these ends. This same impulse is clear in the document's leitmotiv— that is, in its repeated insistence on 'fully conscious, and active participation' (*SC* 14) which, albeit developing an emphasis already present in the writings of St Pius X (*Tra Le Sollecitudini*, 1903) and Pius XII (*Mediator Dei*, 1947), is strikingly asserted here to be 'In the restoration and promotion of the sacred liturgy, [...] *the aim to be considered before all else*'(*SC* 14; emphasis added).

It is these pastoral and evangelistic motivations—a desire, indeed, 'that the sacrifice of the Mass, even in the ritual forms of its celebration, may become pastorally efficacious to the fullest degree' (*SC* 49)—which undergird and justify many of Vatican II's most distinctive reforms: the simplification of the Mass, removing repetitions and accretions (*SC* 50); the greater involvement of the people through responses, singing, actions and so on (*SC* 39); use of the laity's 'mother tongue' (*SC* 36); the permission of vernacular musical styles and a wider range of instruments (*SC* 119–20); even the call for new norms for 'the worthy and well planned construction of sacred buildings, the shape and construction of altars, [and] the proper ordering of sacred images, embellishments, and vestments' (*SC* 128).

Such reforms did not, naturally enough, come out of nowhere. Much attention has rightly been given to the role of the Liturgical Movement, first centring around several continental Benedictine centres of learning, but then exported much further afield by enthused students and scholars returning home (Pecklers 1998: 25–79). In 1936, Virgil Michel OSB of St John's Abbey in Minnesota was already prophesying 'considerable changes in [Catholic] Liturgy made in terms of the new conditions and needs of our day' (quoted in Reid 2005: 98)—although the changes he had in mind were markedly less 'considerable' than what would eventually became the norm.

Less well-documented, though, is the extent to which this vogue for liturgical experimentation was taken up, often far more informally, in the kinds of neo-evangelistic spheres identified above. From the 1940s, we read fulsome testimonies about the evangelistic potential of vernacular languages, evening Masses, and altars facing the people from French priest-workers, operating clandestinely as conscripted labourers in Germany, and attending Mass at Dominican churches (e.g., Perrin 1947: 51). After the War, such practices were soon introduced in the Parisian slums. Further evidence of informal innovations—the Latin *Dominus vobiscum* ('The Lord be with you') replaced with '*Salut, les copains!*' ('Hi, pals!'), for example—may be derived from complaints received by the nuncio Roncalli (Hebblethwaite 2010: 105; see also Welton 1961: 10–13).

While the reforms as a whole were at least in part motivated by neo-evangelistic considerations, this general pattern becomes all the sharper where *Sacrosanctum Concilium* speaks explicitly on the topic of 'mission territories'; something it does, by my own count, on six occasions (*SC* 38, 40, 65, 68, 119). Article 40, for instance, acknowledges that 'In some places and circumstances, however, an even more radical adaptation of the liturgy is needed'. Although what 'places and circumstances' these might be is not clearly defined, it is later implied that these are to be found 'especially in mission territories (*praesertim in Missionibus*)' (*SC* 40). Elsewhere, the Council states that 'Provisions shall also be made, when revising the liturgical books, for legitimate variations and adaptations to different groups, regions, and peoples, *especially in mission territories*' (*SC* 38; emphasis added). And while Gregorian chant is to be given 'pride of place in liturgical services' (*SC* 116) and 'the pipe organ is to be held in high esteem' (*SC* 120), other possibilities are permitted. And once again, this indult applies 'In certain parts of the world, especially in mission territories, [where] there are peoples who have their own musical traditions, and these play a great part in their religious and social life' (*SC* 119).

If the above reading of *Sacrosanctum Concilium* is correct, then these specific comments about 'mission territories' are not *exceptions* to the overall thrust of the document's liturgical vision, but are rather the logical outworkings of it. They are, in short, simply particularly clear instances, as per article 14, where the 'full and active participation by all the people', 'demanded by the very nature of the liturgy', is indeed 'the aim [being] considered before all else' (*SC* 14). True enough, the primary referents of *terrae Missionum* are surely 'classic' mission territories (i.e., areas where the *missio ad gentes* is the Church's primary task, as per *Redemptoris Missio*). But we have also seen how vast regions of continental Europe, the very heart of Christendom, were with good reason already being regarded as mission territories in their own right, not least by both Popes of the Council. What is more, our previous chapter showed in detail how analogous ideas, undergirded by similar concerns, had been steadily building in Britain and America for a good decade or more.

This realization is critical for understanding the ways in which *Sacrosanctum Concilium* was then interpreted and implemented: an issue at the very heart of the postconciliar 'liturgy wars'. As is often pointed out, the Council Fathers voted overwhelmingly, 'almost triumphantly so' (Congar 1963: 1971), in support of the liturgy Constitution: even some of the most conservative bishops, recognizing the merits of (some) reform, were happy enough to sign their names to it. And indeed, the overall tenor of the document is far from radical. Much of it is devoted to extolling the wonderfulness of the centuries-old status quo, as a resplendent jewel deserving to be polished, just a little and ever-so-carefully, in order to sparkle with its original brilliance.[3] Critically, the same document then allows that, in exceptional circumstances and with very good reasons, a more substantial deviation from the status quo may be permitted by the proper Church authorities. Vatican II grants a huge degree of latitude here to the 'competent territorial bodies of bishops legitimately established'—the forerunners of our modern Bishops' Conferences—on the question of how, precisely, to interpret and apply the mandated changes (*SC* 22). Such 'decentralization of the liturgical decision-making' (Ratzinger [1966] 2009: 34) is most clear with regard to the use of vernacular languages, the Council's signature liturgical reform (see Bouyer 1965: 93–7).

On the face of it, *Sacrosanctum Concilium* presumes that the Latin language is simply the norm for Mass in the Latin rite. It does allow that 'a suitable place may [*possit*] be allotted to [the laity's] mother tongue' (*SC* 54), for instance for the scriptural readings, although in part this paragraph repeats permissions already in place from before the Council (Reid 2005: 268–70). Elsewhere, while stating unequivocally that 'the use of the Latin language is to be preserved', the Constitution defines the parameters within which a further broadening of 'the limits of [the mother tongue's] employment' might be prudently explored (*SC* 36). Yet critically, 'it is for the competent territorial ecclesiastical authority [. . .] to decide whether, and to what extent, the vernacular language is to be used' (*SC* 36).[4]

---

[3] Cf. 'The hesitant could be carried along because the draft itself made clear that what was at issue here was not negative or destructive criticism, but rather greater fullness' (Ratzinger [1966] 2009: 29).

[4] The whole paragraph is important enough to reproduce here in full. I have added my own emphases in bold:

36. 1. Particular law remaining in force, the use of the Latin language is to be preserved in the Latin rites.

2. **But since the use of the mother tongue,** whether in the Mass, the administration of the sacraments, or other parts of the liturgy, **frequently *may be* of great advantage to the people, the limits of its employment *may be* extended.** This will apply in the first place to the readings and directives, and to some of the prayers and chants, according to the regulations on this matter to be laid down separately in subsequent chapters.

3. These norms being observed, **it is for the competent territorial ecclesiastical authority** mentioned in Art. 22, 2, **to decide *whether, and to what extent,* the vernacular language is to be used**; their decrees are to be approved, that is,

Alongside local episcopal authority, soon after the Council a central body was formally instituted in Rome for guiding the roll out of the liturgical reforms. This 'Consilium' swiftly set to work, producing many of the 'bewildering assortment of documents' (Davies [1980] 2009: 19) issuing from the Vatican over the coming years, covering all aspects of liturgical practice. As such, it is notoriously difficult here to distinguish sharply between 'the letter' of *Sacrosanctum Concilium* and its subsequent interpretations and implementations (Baldovin 2008: 2; Faggioli 2012a: 104–5). For while the Council does demand reforms, it is notably non-specific as to the precise form that these should take. The Constitution opens up a great many possibilities, albeit usually accompanied by a good deal of caution and circumspection. But it deliberately leaves to others the details of how best, within these designedly broad parameters, to foster 'full and active participation by all the people' (*SC* 14). In the concrete, therefore, it was possible for the reforms to proceed far more swiftly and radically than many of the Council's participants had either anticipated or imagined (see Gamber [1981] 1993: 9–10). Nevertheless, the *potential* for most, if not all, such unintended consequences—or 'liturgical time bombs' (Davies 2003)—was codified in the letter of *Sacrosanctum Concilium* itself.

In the following section, we will discover how the Council's notably guarded *opening up of possibilities* was almost immediately taken up and run with, and in many different directions, in parishes across Britain and America (as far beyond). Presumably, this was because these were regarded as akin to mission territories, and that there were specific neo-evangelistic reasons for doing so, in the interests of leading 'all the faithful [. . .] to that fully conscious, and active participation in liturgical celebrations which is demanded by the very nature of the liturgy' (*SC* 14). As we will also discover in this and the following chapters, 'pastorally efficacious to the fullest degree' (*SC* 49)—the Council's self-imposed justification for all that followed,

confirmed, by the Apostolic See. And, whenever it seems to be called for, this authority is to consult with bishops of neighbouring regions which have the same language.

4. Translations from the Latin text into the mother tongue intended for use in the liturgy must be approved by the competent territorial ecclesiastical authority mentioned above.

and therefore the reforms' own in-built criterion for judging success or failure—is a rather demanding benchmark.

PERMANENT REVOLUTION

This brings us, if via a decidedly scenic route, to consider the impact of the liturgical reforms in Britain and America. It is not *quite* true to imagine that, in the decades before the Council, the Mass was characterized totally by 'rigid uniformity' (Dolan 2002: 238). Even within the Latin rite, a parish weekday Low Mass would have a markedly different feel (and length) to a Sunday *Missa Solemnis* at an Abbey or Cathedral. In churches whose pastors were at the Liturgical Movement-inspired cutting edge, 'dialogue Masses' (in which the congregation gave some of the Latin responses)[5] might also be offered, though these were not widespread in either of our contexts (Pecklers 1998: 55; Hornsby-Smith 2010: 69, 207). All that said, these were all self-evidently variations on a common theme—variations, moreover, with a decidedly low standard deviation. There was only so much customization of the 'standard model' one could reasonably do. Refinements to, say, the rubrics or calendar would occasionally came out from Rome, but these were mostly minor. The most significant was Pius XII's reform of Holy Week in 1955 (see Reid 2005: 219–34), which, at the time, was seen to be a radical reshaping. Thus in the words of the American liturgist Frederick McManus, who as a conciliar *peritus* would later have significant input into *Sacrosanctum Concilium*, 'The news accounts have been concerned with the radical changes, the upset of traditional practices [. . .] No change thus far introduced is equal to the reform of Holy Week in its extent and significance and no change is of greater spiritual and pastoral worth' (1956: v, viii). Arguably, McManus' reaction here tells us far more

---

[5] Such dialogue Masses were held every morning at the Council itself, if not to the full satisfaction of the true liturgical *cognoscenti*:

> Unfortunately, practically none of the successive celebrants have grasped the fact that a congregation of 2,500 will have a different pace from a single altar server; almost all rushed the prayers so that the *Gloria*, *Sanctus* and *Pater*, instead of having the moving dignity befitting such a throng, were hurried through in a way that was somewhat trying to those used to communal celebrations worthily performed.   (Congar 1963: 45 n. 1)

about how slight and gradual changes to the Roman rite had traditionally been, than it does about the magnitude of the Holy Week renovation in the grand scheme of things (Davies 1997a: 45–6).

As it happens, it was McManus himself who, less than a decade later, would demonstrate to English-speaking Catholics just what truly 'radical changes' in the liturgy might look like. The *New York Times*' breathless reportage here is worth quoting at some length:

> St. Louis, Aug. 24 [1964]—Facing the congregation in the vast Kiel Auditorium across a plain, slate-gray altar, the Rev. Frederick R. McManus of Catholic University of America celebrated today the first full English mass in the United States.
>
> More than 11,000 Bishops, priests, nuns and laymen, supplemented by a hundred invited Protestant observers, heard the historic celebration in the horse-shoe-shaped arena. The event opened the 25th annual Liturgical Week here. [...]
>
> Besides the use of the vernacular in the mass today and the participation of the congregation in responding to the words of the priest, there were a number of other innovations.
>
> One was the celebration with the priest facing the congregation across the altar. Another was the use of Protestant hymns as the opening and closing songs. [...] Tomorrow morning, when Cardinal Ritter celebrates the second vernacular mass, the entrance song will be Martin Luther's hymn, "A Mighty Fortress Is Our God."
>
> Communion was also served in an unusual way today. When the worshippers entered the auditorium before the mass, they were asked to take thick wholewheat communion wafers from a stainless steel tray and place them in a covered receptacle.
>
> These were taken to the altar, consecrated during the mass, then distributed to communicants at the communion rail.
>
> (Montgomery 1964)

There is much that is striking here. First of all, note how early this was. Fewer than nine months had elapsed since the promulgation of *Sacrosanctum Concilium*, and it would be a further two before the Consilium—of which McManus was a consultor—would issue *Inter Oecumenici*, its own 'Instruction on Implementing the Constitution on Liturgy' (the first of a great many). Second, this was clearly intended as a 'model Mass': a showcase of what the reformed liturgy *should* be like, authoritatively demonstrated by a Council *peritus* and (now) a member of the Vatican's own body entrusted with interpreting, and overseeing the execution of, the Council's liturgical desires. The 'North American Liturgy Week', which began life in 1940 organized by Benedictines including the aforementioned Virgil Michel, attracted thousands of liturgical scholars and enthusiasts from across the USA: many of whom would soon form an all-powerful, professionalized 'mandarin class' on diocesan and parish liturgy committees up and down the country (Maines and McCallion 2007: 31–64; Greeley 2004a: 179–89). Third, the inclusion of Protestant hymns, while in keeping with other ecumenical initiatives of the period, is an advanced example of the kind of denominational boundary-blurring previously noted as both symptom and cause of the weakening of Catholic identity. And while the symbolism was surely deliberate—Luther at a vernacular Mass celebrated by a cardinal rather more trumpets than dog-whistles the demise of 'Tridentine Catholicism'—it was also true that Anglophone Catholics did not yet have a huge repertoire of their own to draw on. Though that too was starting to change (see Canedo 2009: 37–8). Fourth, for all its avant-gardism in certain practices soon to become commonplace, this Ground Zero of liturgical change in the USA nonetheless appears quaintly traditional in others. This 'first full English Mass' was, in point of fact, still half in Latin (plus a Greek *Kyrie*). It also preserved elements—the prayers at the foot of the altar, for instance—ultimately to be swept away as unwanted 'accretions' in the eventual *Novus Ordo* of 1969. And for all the active participation with the hosts before Mass, apparently using the kind of home-baked altar breads that would soon be widespread, they still received communion—under *one* species—on the tongue, while kneeling at an altar rail. This custom too would rapidly disappear, along with the altar rails themselves, though nothing in *Sacrosanctum Concilium* suggests that it should or could (see Gamber 1993: 137–79; Davies 1997b).

That said, in two other respects, the liturgical reforms in August 1964 were already outpacing the explicit mandate of the Council. While the new Catholic penchant for plain, bare, freestanding altars would become enough of a cliché to be sent up by non-Catholic humorists,[6] there is nothing in the Council's own words that demands it. However, one certainly *could* make a case either strongly

---

[6] 'St Mary's was a gorgeous church until the Benedictines came through and told people they ought to clean out the statuary and the high altar, which the people did, and do you know what they used for an altar? A *lunch* table! From the cafeteria! Set

for, or alternatively dead against, it—all depending on how one parses *Sacrosanctum Concilium*'s distinction between 'noble beauty' and 'mere sumptuous display', or indeed what count as 'sacred furnishings [that] worthily and beautifully serve the dignity of worship' and those 'offend[ing] true religious sense [. . .] by lack of artistic worth, mediocrity and pretense' (*SC* 122–4). Bearing in mind the trump card of 'full and active participation by all the people is the aim to be considered before all else' (*SC* 14), *anything* could be justified on this hoped-for basis, and indeed formally permitted under the catch-all rubric that 'the territorial bodies of bishops are empowered to adapt such things to the needs and customs of their different regions; this applies especially to the materials and form of sacred furnishings and vestment' (*SC* 128). The same goes for McManus' orientation *versus populum* (i.e., 'facing the congregation across the altar'): another practice, though well-established within the canon of pre-conciliar liturgical experimentation, on which the Council itself is resolutely silent. Despite this, it rapidly became one of the chief hallmarks of the liturgical reform (cf. Lang 2009: 21–31), justified on the basis of its presumed aid to active participation (and thus according fully with the spirit of the liturgy Constitution), and popularized no doubt by its employment in 'model Masses' such as the one in St Louis.

One Mass does not, however, a revolution make. In Britain and America both, the national rollout of the first wave of reforms was decreed to commence on the first day of Advent, 1964. Experimenting among likeminded liturgists might be one thing—the reception of those attending the Liturgy Week was, reportedly, rapturous (Canedo 2009: 38)—but the impact of such changes on the faithful in ordinary parishes was a rather more uncertain proposition. In England and Wales, it seems that 'Vernacular Sunday' was a somewhat tentative affair. Speaking on the Council floor six weeks prior, Bishop Dwyer of Leeds had struck a decidedly apprehensive note, observing that the liturgy Constitution has 'launched a movement that will uproot all kinds of age-old habits, cut psychological and emotional ties, shake to the foundations the ways of thought of three to four million Catholics—all this so that the emphasis on the individual's personal concern will give place to an emphasis on communal responsibility'

right out on the floor were everybody could see it—why? Why tear the church apart so you can see the priest say Mass?' (Keillor 1986: 148).

(Tablet 1964c: 1245). Even if Dwyer thought this to be ultimately necessary or beneficial, it hardly sounds as though he were looking forward to it. Thus while most dioceses prescribed the vernacular (i.e., English; a Welsh translation, though planned, was not yet forthcoming) for all Low Masses on Sundays, this was not so everywhere. In Westminster and Brentwood, for instance, churches with more than two Masses on a Sunday were ordered to offer at least one as an all-Latin affair (Tablet 1964a). According to the *Observer*, this was specifically to 'temper the wind' of disquiet from 'a conservative element, particularly among older people and converts like Mr Evelyn Waugh, who disapprove of the descent into English'. Despite this, the newspaper also noted, 'Many Catholic priests are on tiptoe with excitement this weekend wondering how these changes will go down' (Yates 1964). This sense of ambivalence towards even the first round of liturgical changes is also conveyed in the following weekend's issue of the *Tablet*:

Vernacular Sunday must have been an exciting one for most Catholics in England, whether they went to Mass to welcome the change, to have their worst fears confirmed, or to make a gesture of loyalty to the old Latin by going to High Mass. (1964b)

The response to this first round of changes, on both sides of the Atlantic, is difficult to gauge from 'vox pops' in the Catholic press. Overall, the mood seems generally to have been positive—in America, perhaps, more clearly so than in Britain—though by no means unanimously so (e.g., Dinges 1987; O'Toole 2008: 208–10; Massa 2010: 15–16; Harris 2018a). It is crucial to realize, however, that 'Vernacular Sunday' did not simply enact *a* change to the liturgy. Rather, it inaugurated a decade of seemingly endless—and endlessly unpredictable—*changes*. As mentioned above, a profusion of instructions and guidelines began appearing out of Rome, spawning still others at both national and diocesan level, supposedly improving this or that aspect of Catholic pastoral or liturgical life. Also bear in mind that over five years separated 'Vernacular Sunday' in 1964 and the promulgation of the new Roman missal in 1970, precipitating yet another period of adaptation and adjustment.

Constant changes at the official level were, moreover, outstripped in rapidity and (often) radicality at the level of the local parish or Catholic campus. It was here that the new liturgical directives principles were interpreted, implemented, and/or ignored—for who better to judge what would be 'pastorally efficacious to the fullest degree' at the local level than the People of God (or often, the People of God's self-appointed liturgical experts) *actually there*, reading the signs of the times? This was most obviously the case in America, where James White speaks, plausibly enough, of a 'period of liturgical euphoria [. . .] when pent-up energy for reform burst the bounds of legitimate change and erupted in unofficial experimentation' (2003: 130; see Day 1990: 32; McDannell 2011: 132–5). Viewed sympathetically, one might ascribe much of this to the desire to connect with those young people over whom, as we saw in the previous chapter, Catholic commentators were *already* fretting during the relative calm of the early 1960s. Declarations like this one in *America*—'If the Church wants to sweep the world like the Beatles, it must use language as contemporary as theirs' (Edwards 1966: 484; cf. Rowland 2010: 41)—seem, in retrospect, rather more like desperation than prophetic boldness. Likewise the introduction of Simon and Garfunkel's 'Bridge Over Troubled Water', Peter, Paul, and Mary's 'Michael, Row the Boat Ashore', or Pete Seeger's 'If I Had a Hammer' into the liturgical oeuvre. True enough, the Council recognizes that:

> In certain parts of the world, especially mission lands, there are peoples who have their own musical traditions, and these play a great part in their religious and social life. For this reason due importance is to be attached to their music, and a suitable place is to be given to it, not only in forming their attitude toward religion, but also in adapting worship to their native genius.   (*SC* 119)

From this foundation, all it takes is the open-minded chaplain of a Catholic high school in Wichita to recognize his domain as a *de facto* mission territory, and one may appreciate the seductive appeal of finding 'a suitable place' for 'their music'.[7] Nor, incidentally, were such temptations exclusive to Catholics trying to engage the youth: an identical folk-lite repertoire was trendy in Reform Jewish circles too, for example (Lipstadt 2014). Without denying that this may well, with the right group of people, have genuinely helped to ensure that the 'faith of

---

[7] Or rather, what one *supposes* to be 'their music'. Personally, I don't imagine any self-respecting American teenagers were still listening to Peter, Paul, and Mary after about 1963—and even before then, only because their parents were too square to let them listen to Dylan, Van Ronk, or Ramblin' Jack Elliott.

those taking part is nourished and their minds are raised to God'
(*SC* 33)—indeed, it certainly sometimes did (Middendorf Woodall
2016)—it is equally clear that the novelty normally soon wore off.

The important point here is neither liturgical nor aesthetic, but
rather sociological. As explained at length in Chapter 4, religious
worldviews—and, *ipso facto*, the religious identities of those inhabit-
ing them—are at their strongest when they are simply taken for
granted (Berger [1967] 1990: 150). This is just the way things are,
and moreover, the way things always have been and will be: *Sicut erat
in principio, et nunc, et semper, et in saecula saeculorum*. For generations of Catholics, the Mass itself was the most obvious symbol of
such apparent timelessness, all the more so, for its obvious 'set-apart-
ness' from contemporary language and custom (Dinges 1987: 145–6).
Its centrality to the Catholic imagination in the wake of—and in
opposition to—the Protestant Reformation, moreover, further
reinforced this: this was perhaps especially so among English and
Irish-diaspora Catholics, in the light of penal history and the accompanying folk-memory of priest holes and hedgerow Masses. In this
light, the occasional tinkerings with the rubrics in the decades preceding the Council—enacted uniformly everywhere, on the same
date, and in the same way—were barely if at all noticed by ordinary
Mass-goers: mere ripples on the surface of deep, unchanging (indeed
seemingly unchangeable) stability. It was, therefore, not only the
language and outward forms of the Mass that changed on Vernacular
Sunday, but ultimately rather—as Mark Massa has argued in persuasive detail—the 'givenness' of the whole Catholic package.

> Catholics were now asked to adjust to a new awareness, a historical
> awareness, that even the most sacred of religious symbols, the eucharist
> no less than the texts of scripture, evolve over time and bear the marks
> of that historical evolution. [. . .] After the actual experience of change
> on the ground, the unsettling new historical consciousness unleashed by
> the council's reforms could not be stopped by anything so simple as an
> appeal to the intentions of the council's participants, or to some pur-
> ported 'law of continuity' within the tradition that existed above the
> realm of historical experience. [. . .] Change the experience, which the
> Second Vatican Council did with breathtaking historical innocence, and
> what the belief means changes with it.   (Massa 2010: 9, 13–14)

In fact, I would go further than Massa. For it was not simply a case of
a single change, however substantial. Rather, it was the constant
changes, all happening differently, and at different rates, in each

parish—an experience as exhausting for some as it was exhilarating for others—that really eroded any erstwhile sense of permanence.

> Only rarely did the ordinary Catholic have any control over the liturgical innovations that occurred in his parish; more typically he would learn about the latest changes only when he arrived in church on Sunday morning. From week to week, year after year, bewildered parishioners did not know what to expect at Sunday Mass, and the experiments would continue whether or not they approved.
>
> (Lawler 2008: 72)

The sheer adaptability of the postconciliar liturgy is, viewed from one perspective, its greatest strength. The same basic template may, within certain parameters, be 'customized' to suit the needs of different congregations. Those who find their faith best nourished, or their soul most uplifted, by a Mass in Latin with plainchant accompaniment can seek one out. Likewise, if a polka Mass performed by 'Fr Frank Perkovich and the Perkatones', or 'Joe Cvek and the Polka Mass-ters', would indeed be 'pastorally efficacious to the fullest degree', then such things are indeed possible (see Walser 1992).

Yet taken as a whole, this multiplicity of options might feasibly undermine one's weddedness to any one of them. Prior to the reforms, most Catholics likely did not have liturgical 'preferences'. Now, as amply proven by the qualitative studies presented in Chapter 2, the liturgy presents limitless possibilities for dissatisfaction, whether great or small.[8] Worshippers are now free to gravitate to Mass at a particular parish, or at a particular time, which best suits their taste (and/or schedule). But they are unlikely to find one that is, in all its details, perfectly satisfactory. Music, in particular, seems to be a special source of complaints—and no wonder. The quest for a musical vernacular common to the multigenerational, multicultural, multitaste denizens of a typical British or American congregation,

---

[8] Compare Peter Berger's observation:

As a sociologist of religion I was already struck at the time of the Second Vatican Council by the fact that there was little if any empirical evidence to indicate that ordinary Catholics found the Latin mass remote or difficult to understand (especially with English missals in hand). The remoteness and the incomprehensibility were posited a priori by theologians and prelates. The same lack of evidence pertains to all the other programs of vernacularization. I'm not aware of any studies showing that ordinary people in England or in the United States had problems with the language of the old Book of Common Prayer. (1995)

and hence the better able to foster their collective *participatio actuosa*, is a doomed one (see Bullivant and Bullivant 2011). Matters of personal taste aside, the introduction of choice to Catholic liturgy arguably has had a more fundamentally eroding effect on practice and, thereby ultimately, identity. After all, it is not necessarily so big a step from choosing *which*, to choosing *if*.[9]

The 'effervescence' (cf. Greeley 2005: 191–2) of the immediate postconciliar years could not, of course, last forever. Eventually, the liturgy in most parishes settled down into a set menu of more-or-less predictable offerings, if with a *much* higher 'standard deviation' than prior to the Council—and not before overall Mass attendance had fallen sharply. We will consider these statistics in the following chapter, since how they are to be interpreted is a matter of some dispute. Until then, I shall confine myself to the comment that, whatsoever other factors may also have played a role, it seems obvious that this decade or so of liturgical turbulence did not exactly help matters. As a more general point, it is worth noting that the people best suited to weathering the storm were those *already* settled down into a parish, and with an established routine of attending it every Sunday. (As we saw in Chapter 2, such ingrained habits have a powerfully conservative influence over Mass-going, even when one is no longer getting much out of the experience.) Even the eldest of the Baby Boomers were still (just) in their late teens on the original

---

[9] This is, be it noted, simply a narrower application of the standard Bergerian 'pluralization leads to secularization' hypothesis, exposited in Chapter 4. An obvious objection to this Catholic-specific elaboration of the argument would be to point out that, even before the Council, a plurality of liturgical options *already* existed at the local parish level. As noted above, especially among the national/ethnic parishes or (in Britain) 'missions', different traditions of liturgical music were in existence (e.g., German-American churches were known for congregational singing, in a way that the largely Irish-American territorial parishes were not). And while these differences tended to be minor, if one adds in non-Latin-rite parishes, there was a genuine breadth of liturgical possibility and, therefore, of preference. Indeed, 'Uniformity in liturgy throughout the Church has never been a Catholic ideal' (Fortescue 1922: 208).

This objection fails, however. Even if I was aware of significant liturgical differences between my own church and nearby German or Maronite ones, it is unlikely that I would regard these as being 'live options' *for me* or *my* parish's liturgical offering. In a similar way, the fact that medieval Christians were *aware* of the mere existence of Jews and Muslims (or even, in the former case, had perhaps even seen them in big cities) is not, on Berger's schema at least, sufficient to undermine the taken-for-granted-ness, and hence security, of their own Christianity. Followers of different religions are not, one might say, present to them 'existentially'—that is, as genuinely imaginable options *for them*.

Vernacular Sunday, however, and thus typically had several years of college and/or 'finding themselves' ahead before putting down any roots. For reasons previously noted, this stage in life is *already* disruptive in terms of the regularity of religious practice. For the Boomers, however, this period saw the sweeping away of the religiosity they had grown up with—their impressions of which would forever remain those of a bored child or teenager—with nothing specific replacing it for a long time. So having lost the habit of regular Mass attendance, by the time they might have been ready to return (i.e., as they started to get married, get jobs, and put down roots of their own), they could no longer 'go back home to the old forms and systems of things which once seemed everlasting but which are changing all the time' (Wolfe [1940] 2011: 602; cf. Gamber 1993 105–11). Critically, they had *also* missed out on the long, slow, uneven period of acclimatization to the new liturgical normal.

CHOOSING ONE OR THE OTHER

The previous chapter dwelt in detail on the rich devotional life of post-war-but-preconciliar Catholic life: *popular* religiosity in both senses of the term. It was argued, moreover, that these were clear examples of what cognitive anthropologists refer to as Credibility Enhancing Displays (CREDs). *Ex hypothesi*, the profusion of Catholic devotional CREDs had a mutually galvanizing effect within the communities in which they were practised. (In Chapter 7, we will explore how Credibility *Undermining* Displays, or 'CRUDs'—that is to say, revelations of religious figures failing, horrifically, to live up to their professed ideals—can contrarily corrode Catholic identity.)

There is some evidence that the 'close-knit unity of texture and imaginative hold [. . .] of the pre-Conciliar devotional world' (Duffy 2004: 24) was already, by the late 1950s, showing the beginnings of decline. This was largely due to the same basic factors detailed in Chapter 4: suburbanization, middle-class-ization, other things to do of an evening, and so on (e.g., Kane 2004). That cracks were developing beneath the shamrock—or in Polish parishes, white eagle— wallpaper does not, however, account for the startlingly swift collapse of the entire edifice, beginning in the mid-1960s. That required an 'inside job'.

Sacrosanctum Concilium, once again, does not itself mandate any policy of suppression. On the contrary, 'Popular devotions of the Christian people are to be highly commended' (*SC* 13), and 'The practice of placing sacred images in churches so that they may be venerated by the faithful is to be maintained' (*SC* 125). Nevertheless, these affirmations are accompanied by cautionary comments, which imply that Catholic devotionalism, as currently practised, could use some reining in. Hence one gets the impression that sacred images, though fine enough in themselves, are prone to being problematic: 'Nevertheless, their number should be moderate and their relative positions should reflect right order. For otherwise they may create confusion among the Christian people and foster devotion of doubtful orthodoxy' (*SC* 125). Furthermore, the Council's statement that devotions 'should be so drawn up that they [...] accord with the sacred liturgy, [...] and lead the people to it, since, in fact, the liturgy by its very nature far surpasses any of them' (*SC* 13) rather suggests that, as things stand, this is far from always the case.

These warnings are consonant with the document's overriding emphasis on the Mass—especially that of Sunday, the Church's pre-eminent communal celebration 'as the foundation and kernel of the whole liturgical year' (*SC* 106)—as 'a sacred action surpassing all others; no other action of the Church can equal its efficacy by the same title and to the same degree' (*SC* 7). Nothing, therefore, may be permitted either to *detract* from this 'summit toward which the activity of the Church is directed' and 'the font from which all her power flows' (*SC* 10; cf. *Lumen Gentium* 11), or to *distract* 'the faithful [from taking] part fully aware of what they are doing, actively engaged in the rite, and enriched by its effects' (*SC* 11).

For many influenced by the Liturgical Movement, that is *precisely* what devotional practices did. In fact, the sheer popularity of such practices was taken as conclusive and damning proof that the laity were being insufficiently nourished by the liturgy itself. In Pecklers' paraphrase:

> These popular devotions were religious exercises often enacted in common, but separate from the Church's official liturgy. Over the centuries, as the liturgy was increasingly removed from the laity, these devotions grew in number and variety. Since they were often celebrated in the vernacular, they had an appeal which was lacking in a Mass celebrated in a language no one could understand. Further, in a Church whose

public rituals had become increasingly clericalized, popular devotions offered the possibility of an experience of prayer that was authentically of the people. (1998: 41)

This type of attitude explicitly pits Catholic devotionalism against authentic liturgical participation in a kind of zero-sum game; in biblical terms, the one must decrease for the other to increase. For Yves Congar: 'Surely we must choose one *or* the other' (1963: 49). Later clarifying his position, in the face of 'several letters of protest, including one or two that were insulting' (1963: 110), Congar adds 'We urge nothing against devotions, so long as they keep their place'. Nevertheless, he continues:

> In religion, as in other matters, space is in practice limited and our powers of attention have their saturation point. If exuberant development and over-emphatic emphasis are allowed to those devotions which satisfy man's religious instinct only too well [. . .] then all these things, which do have their place in the most authentic traditional Christianity, will be found, *in practice*, to have taken up the available room. [. . .] The centre may well continue *in theory* to be the paschal mystery of Christ, but *in practice* that space will have been occupied by devotions, in the life of the people, in the activities of their pastors, and even in the practical questions such as the lay-out of churches and the organization of worship. (1963: 113)

Howsoever proponents of this new spirit of liturgical prioritization imagined it might play out *in theory*, as it was filtered down to the bishops, parish priests, architects, liturgical experts, and others responsible for fostering it among the People of God, the result *in practice* was a remarkable sweeping-away. In Britain, 'Many props to piety, sacramentals hallowed in use through custom and tradition, were ruthlessly set aside' (Flanagan 1987: 66), and a large number of 'hitherto essential features of Catholicism simply disappeared overnight in a wholly inexplicable fashion' (Archer 1986: 132). Meanwhile:

> A number of traditional practices disappeared from American Catholic practice. Vespers and Benediction, for examples, staples in churches on Sunday afternoons since the early nineteenth century, were abandoned nearly everywhere. Some liturgists thought these services distracted from the Mass itself [. . .] The rosary, visits to the Blessed Sacrament, devotional confessions, and other practices were deemphasized. Statuary and banks of votive lights were relegated to the church storerooms, on the theory that these, too, diverted the attention of worshipers. These

changes led some Catholics, who had enjoyed the older forms and found meaning in them, to discern a 'piety void.'

(O'Toole 2008: 222–3)

In both countries, the concern to ward off liturgical 'distractions' was reflected in the art and architecture of the churches themselves. Bare walls and abstract art replaced plasterwork statues of Mary and dreamily soft-focus depictions of the Sacred Heart (Proctor 2014: 219–49). Most controversial, though, was the habit of removing the tabernacle away from the altar, and off to a side chapel (themselves a dying breed) or corner somewhere. From the liturgists' point of view, this served two functions: to 'help' the laity focus their full attention on what was happening on the altar, and as a symbolic downplaying of alleged 'superstitions' surrounding the Eucharist.

> Transubstantiation (the substantial change of the bread and wine), the adoration of the Lord in the Blessed Sacrament, eucharistic devotions with monstrance and processions—all these things, it is alleged, are medieval errors, errors from which we must once and for all take our leave. 'The Eucharistic Gifts are for eating, not for looking at'—these and similar slogans are all too familiar. The glib way such statements are made is quite astonishing.   (Ratzinger 2000: 85–6)

For their part, the laity tended rather to like their tabernacles, and moreover, didn't like the idea of Jesus, really present inside of them, being relegated to a backroom. On this subject, as so many others, the laity—'dedicated to Christ', 'anointed by the Holy Spirit', 'marvellously called and wonderfully prepared' (*Lumen Gentium* 34) as they might be—were a grave source of disappointment to their liturgical overlords (see, in entertaining detail, Maines and McCallion 2007: 103–19).

The postconciliar downplaying of Catholic devotional life was not completely due to the reform of the Mass. Marian devotion, central to so many pious practices as indeed to Catholic identity as a whole, also shrank sharply around the time of Vatican II (Spretnak 2004: 1–25; Kane 2004). This was due to the confluence of several impulses, none of which was necessarily intending to produce this dramatic effect, or (probably) even imagining it possible.[10] Some of these were biblical,

---

[10] Cf. 'This most Holy Synod deliberately teaches this Catholic doctrine [concerning Mary's significance] and at the same time admonishes all the sons of the Church that the cult, especially the liturgical cult, of the Blessed Virgin, be generously fostered,

some intellectual, some ecumenical, in inspiration. In whatever combination they interacted, the outcome was such that: 'after the Second Vatican Council, the level of devotion to Mary, at least in the Catholicism of much of Europe and North America, plummeted and remains very low' (Cavadini 2017: 1). In England and Wales, the popularity of 'Mary' as a name for baby girls also took a dramatic downturn around this time. Having been a perennial Top Four favourite throughout the first half of the century, it was down to ninth place by 1954. In 1964, this was 37th, followed by 77th in 1974, and 98th in 1984. It has never troubled the Top Hundred since.[11]

Nor was Mary alone among the saints to lose a significant part of her devotional following. Following the Council's prompts (e.g., *SC* 111; *Lumen Gentium* 51), the liturgical calendar was reconfigured by Paul VI in 1969. Among the rationales given, Pope Paul notes that 'over the course of centuries the feasts of the saints have become more and more numerous' (*Mysterium Paschalis* II), and moreover, 'the multiplication of feasts, vigils and octaves, as well as the progressive complication of different parts of the liturgical year, have often driven the faithful to particular devotions, in such a way that their minds have been somewhat diverted from the fundamental mysteries of our Redemption' (*Mysterium Paschalis* I). Accordingly, 'the names of some saints have been removed from the universal Calendar' (*Mysterium Paschalis* II), while the rank of others' Feast days was lowered. Although some new saints were simultaneously drafted in, partly to reflect the global nature of the Church (e.g., the Ugandan Martyrs), the saints still suffered a significant net loss.

The stated *intention* of these changes was to focus the calendar more clearly on the 'fundamental mysteries of our Redemption', hence the celebration of Sunday, and thus of Christ's resurrection, would now trump all but the most prominent of Feast days (cf. *SC* 106). However, in a pattern frequently repeated, this was not

and the practices and exercises of piety, recommended by the magisterium of the Church toward her in the course of centuries be made of great moment, and those decrees, which have been given in the early days regarding the cult of images of Christ, the Blessed Virgin and the saints, be religiously observed' (*Lumen Gentium* 67).

[11] These data are taken from the Office for National Statistics' website: https://visual.ons.gov.uk/baby-names-since-1904-how-has-yours-performed/ (last accessed 21 February 2018). The picture is, admittedly, somewhat complicated by the existence of several Marian variants, such as Marie and Maria. These and others have waxed and waned. None, however, has featured in the Top Fifty since the mid-1970s.

quite how the message was communicated by the world's press. On the evening of Friday, 9 May, sub-editors the world over gleefully set to work, with varying degrees of subtlety: 'The Saints Come Marching Out' (*Guardian*; Armstrong 1969), 'The Pope Sacks 30 Saints' (*Mirror*; Checkley 1969), 'Church Demotes 200 Saints: St. Christopher Included' (*Washington Post*; News Dispatches 1969). As highlighted in the latter example, particular attention was given to the fact that, among those 'suppressed', were a significant number of beloved favourites. In addition to Christopher, these included George, Nicholas, Valentine, Ursula, and Barbara. This did not, to put it mildly, go down very well. In Britain, colourful reports of protests against 'Paul's purge' (*Spectator*; Brogan 1969) reliably filled column inches for weeks thereafter. These ranged from a patriotic Essex MP and the head of the Coptic Orthodox Church united in their 'astonishment and dismay' at the slight to St George, to the head of Italy's automobile association plaintive 'We have been abandoned' reaction to Christopher's diminution (Hirst 1969; Observer 1969; Mirror 1969). Most memorably, the *Daily Mirror* even managed to report dissent coming from heaven itself. Under the eye-catching headline, 'A "Miracle" from the Demoted Saint', it began: 'The preserved blood of St. Januarius, one of the Roman Catholic saints demoted by the Pope last week, was said yesterday to have turned to liquid after a Naples crowd prayed for a miracle' (Mirror 1969). In the late 1960s, the *Daily Mirror* was Britain's best-selling newspaper with a circulation of around 5 million. Significantly, not the smallest proportion of these hailed from the northern, working-class Catholic heartlands.

Alongside this perceived affront to several cherished staples of Catholic piety, the long-established cults of certain other, important saints were undermined from other directions. In Britain, though St Thomas More was among those *added* to the calendar in 1969, as a genre the Reformation-era martyrs of England, Wales, and Scotland were undeniably problematic within the new context of ecumenical openness precipitated by the Council. These martyrs had formed a cornerstone of identity and, especially regarding their relics, devotional practice for generations of British Catholics. While several of the 'big names', most notably More and Fisher (canonized together in 1935), inspired national devotion, their sheer numbers—two hundred had officially been declared 'Blessed' by this point, with causes in process for over a hundred others—meant that many were the focus of intense localized cults. This was especially so in the North West, which could lay claim to dozens. (By way of illustration, from my childhood home in Preston, Lancashire, I could easily walk to the birthplaces of six of these, and comfortably hike there and back to those of a further six.[12]) Formal moves, spearheaded by the Jesuits, to canonize forty of the existing Blesseds had been made in 1960. Such things move slowly in Rome, however. And a decade later, when Pope Paul was due to raise them to the altars, the cause was now clearly a cause of embarrassment in official circles. As the Anglican historian Andrew Atherstone notes, in his absorbing account of the ensuing 'great English Martyrs hulla-baloo' (as it was dubbed by the Jesuit journal the *Month*):

> Many commentators believed that the cause of the English martyrs and the cause of ecumenism were incompatible. Some Catholics threw their weight behind the canonisation for that very reason, as a protest against the innovations of Vatican II. After all, had not the martyrs been put to death for their resolute defence of the 'old faith' which was now under threat from conciliar reforms? [. . .] Meanwhile other Catholics decried the canonisation, believing it to be nothing more than a celebration of counter-reformation resistance. As [one of the cause's vice-postulators, James] Walsh observed: 'In many quarters, it had become the fashion to see devotion to saints as *démodé*; the cult of the Martyrs as a sign of the state of siege; and the Cause as inopportune for the ecumenical movement.' (2011: 574)

Faced with this, as early as 1965 there were official attempts to spin the martyrs, somewhat hopefully, as 'ideal Patrons of the Ecumenical Movement' and 'standard-bearers of the Christian unity movement' (Atherstone 2011: 575).

The emerging 'signs of the times' were not, meanwhile, looking too kindly on North America's own martyrs: the eight seventeenth-century Jesuits killed by Iroquois warriors in various locales of New France, on both sides of what would later become the US–Canadian border. Though generally more popular in Canada, devotion to the 'North American Martyrs' received a south-of-the-border fillip from

---

[12] For the curious, in the walkable category I count: Bl. William Marsden (Goosnargh), Bl. Richard Hayhurst (Broughton), Bl. George Haydock (Cottam), Bl. George Beesley (Goosnargh), St John Southworth (Samlesbury), and St John Wall (Goosnargh). In the hikable—that is, within a twenty-or-so mile round trip—I include: St John Plessington (Garstang), Bl. John Finch (Eccleston), Bl. William Harcourt (Weeton), Bl. John Woodcock (Clayton-le-Woods), Bl. Roger Wenno (Chorley), and Bl. Thomas Cottam (Dilworth). Note that these lists *only* include those formally beatified or canonized. For example, Fr Germanus Helme, yet another Goosnarghian and reputedly the most recent of England's martyrs (in 1746), does not make the cut.

their collective canonization in 1930. That same year, a shrine was opened in Auriesville, New York, close to the presumed site of three of their deaths: Isaac Jogues, René Goupil, and Jean de Lalande. By the late 1960s, however, the 'Saint among Savages'—as the subtitle of a popular 1935 biography of Jogues put it—trope of the previous generation's devotional literature was embarrassingly dated, not least in light of the emergent 'red power' movement (Deloria [1969] 1988: 182), and wider reappraisals of the period of American colonialism and expansion (Monson 2014). The new Catholic spirit of dialogue and intercultural respect, closely associated with the Jesuits themselves, did not sit well with the 'converting and civilizing' mode of evangelization associated with the North American Martyrs (Anderson 2013: 214–54). For all of these reasons, and perhaps several others,[13] ornate reliquaries holding the (im)mortal remains of these and other saints were quietly stashed away in sacristy cupboards over the next decade or so; relics, literally, of a bygone era.

Catholic devotional culture was not, it is true, wiped out suddenly and altogether (see Orsi 1996: 32–8; Harris 2013a: 202–57). Naturally, assiduous daily rosary-prayers did not collectively 'down-bead' one day in the early 1970s, never to pick them up again. And while attempts from some quarters to mint new rituals embodying what was 'understood to be "the spirit of Vatican II" [. . .] Reform, relevancy, experimentation, collaboration, youthfulness, intentionality, openness, humour, protest, and the vernacular were the values taken from the Council debates and documents' (McDannell 2011: 135) generally did not catch on, some older ones undoubtedly grew in popularity. The ancient monastic practice of *Lectio Divina*, involving prayerful meditation on a short passage of Scripture, was, for example, perfectly suited to the Council's scriptural emphasis (cf. *Dei Verbum* 25). For similar reasons, the Spiritual Exercises of St Ignatius proved eminently adaptable to the needs of those encouraged by the Council to explore the lay state's 'own form of the spiritual life' (*Apostolicam Actuositatem* 29). Nevertheless, these were all undoubtedly minority pursuits.

It is irrefutably true that the rich devotional life of mainstream Catholicism did not survive much beyond the 1960s. The novenas, pilgrimages, processions, and rosary recitations, which had been so large and 'given' a staple of *ordinary* parish life for much of the

---

[13] Around this time, concerns about 'cultural imperialism' were also dampening, or rather dousing, the missionary zeal of many Protestant denominations (Stark 2015: chap. 5).

previous century, largely disappeared. And while the Boomers' parents or (much more likely) grandparents may still have persevered, at least for a while, the Boomers themselves by and large did not. When they themselves, soon enough, began having children of their own, the sheer colourfulness—the new penchant for felt banners and bold vestment designs notwithstanding—of preconciliar Catholic parish life was gone. But this is a subject for the following chapter.

The theoretical point here, though, is worth emphasizing. If it is true that exposure to CREDs, especially though not exclusively in childhood, is a critical contributor to the 'stickiness' of a given belief or commitment, then this sea change in Catholic parish culture can scarcely have failed to have a significant effect. As we have detailed above, it was an axiom of the liturgical reformers that the 'extras' with which the laity filled up the week served primarily to distract them from the singular importance of the Mass. According to this view, attending Mass had become simply *one more* devotional exercise, and given its mysteriously Latinate opaqueness, far from the most engaging and involving of them. By both downplaying or discouraging the 'competitors', and judiciously borrowing some of their more accessible elements (the vernacular, group participation, 'relevance'), then Sunday Mass would stand out all the taller and more attractively.[14]

---

[14] Perhaps the clearest expression of this view occurs in a short, popular work by Hans Küng, originally published in German in 1962, with British and American editions swiftly following in 1963. He begins by describing the upshot of the liturgical reforms of Trent:

Everything, down to the smallest detail was made the subject of an official ruling [...] No opportunity was opened up for the people to take any active part. More and more, 'devotions' came into existence, which the people liked better. More candles were lit at them than at Mass. You could understand the prayers and readings at the devotions; you could join in the praying and singing yourself. None of this was possible at Mass. Only too often, in consequence, Mass was regarded as just one more devotion amongst others (if perhaps the most important), whereas the Mass was instituted by Christ himself, and devotions only by men.

In these circumstances it will certainly not surprise you that quietly, all over Europe, there took place a withdrawal from the Mass. In one country after another it was realized, with dismay, that often only a fraction of the faithful was still going to Sunday Mass. This naturally, as you can imagine, had a bad effect on the people's religious life. Certainly it was not *only* the strange and unintelligible form that Mass had taken which was to blame for the fact that people were no longer coming in such numbers to the liturgy. But it certainly was *partly* to blame. (1963: 68–9)

However well-intentioned, such a view was, at best, woefully naïve. Without denying the possibility of such excesses as the Council warns against, there is simply no reason for thinking that, as confidently stated above by Congar, the laity possess a set amount of religious 'space' which, if filled up with devotions, leaves no room left for the Mass. Are we meant to suppose that increasing levels of lapsation after the War were due to swathes of teenagers and the working classes so sating their religious urges on pious practices that they no longer went to Mass? To put it mildly, it is rather more plausible to posit a strong, positive correlation between time expended on traditional devotions and not merely *attending* Mass, but doing so 'fully aware of what they are doing, actively engaged in the rite, and enriched by its effects' (*SC* 11). The kind of person who, say, gathers on a Thursday night with other overworked mothers to sew tiny sequins on a new nightie for an Infant of Prague figurine (cf. Orsi 1996: 33), or who gets up at 2 a.m. to fill his allotted *Quarant'Ore* slot before a full day at the factory, is probably not the kind of person who frequently skips Mass in favour of a—frankly, well-deserved—lie-in. In this regard, it is worth recalling the statistics presented in Chapter 2, showing markedly higher levels of both Catholic retention and Mass attendance among first- and second-generation American immigrants, compared to either third-generation or 'native' (i.e., those with four US-born grandparents) Catholics. While there are undoubtedly many factors for this, the typically higher incidences of devotionalism and popular religiosity within, say, Latino or Filipino communities (see Matovina 2011: 140–61; Cherry 2014: 1–22) are at least suggestive here.

'LIKE EVERYONE ELSE'

A good deal of the above argument applies, *mutatis mutandis*, to the third of our four 'changes'—i.e., the 'abolition' of fish on Fridays— and as such, may be dealt with somewhat more cursorily. The facts of the matter are, indeed, easily stated. Within months of the close of the Council, Paul promulgated the apostolic constitution *Paenitemini*. This was, on the face of it, a stirring reiteration of traditional fasting and penitential practice. He notes, for example, that 'almost everywhere and at all times penitence has held a place of great importance', and dwells in some detail on its deep roots in both the Old and New Testaments. True penance, as Christ himself stresses, demands more than simply external observance. Accordingly, as the Pope affirms, the 'intimate relationship which exists in penitence between the external act, inner conversion, prayer and works of charity is affirmed and widely developed in the liturgical texts and authors of every era' (1966). Prior to the release of the document, there had been some speculation that Paul might abolish the requirement for Catholics to abstain from meat on Fridays. But while *Paenitemini* relaxes other long-standing rules, most notably those during Lent, it leaves those hopeful of eating steak on Fridays sorely disappointed.

That, at least, is the natural reading of the document. In the words of the *New York Times*' write-up, 'meatless Fridays will stay' (Fiske 1966). True, Paul does allow the possibility 'in countries where the standard of living is lower' that 'members of the Body of Christ' might instead 'offer their suffering'—i.e., their involuntary abstinence, the whole week long—'in prayer to the Lord in close union with the Cross of Christ'. However, this makes the onus on those 'where economic well-being is greater' all the greater: 'so much more will the witness of asceticism have to be given in order that the sons of the Church may not be involved in the spirit of the "world," and at the same time the witness of charity will have to be given to the brethren who suffer poverty and hunger beyond any barrier of nation or continent.' Thus the plain reading of *Paenitemini* is that, in affluent western countries, *more* fasting and abstinence is the order of the day, in order both to fend off worldliness, and to inculcate a sense of solidarity with their less fortunate brethren. However, true to the decentralizing trend pioneered in *Sacrosanctum Concilium*, Paul devolves a great deal of latitude to national episcopal conferences. Should they see fit, then they might 'Substitute abstinence and fast wholly or in part with other forms of penitence and especially works of charity and the exercises of piety', and are obliged simply to inform the Apostolic See 'for information' if they do so.

Given the overall thrust of *Paenitemini*, it is striking just how very swiftly various bishops' conferences, and especially those comfortably within Paul's 'where economic well-being is greater' bracket, chose to exercise this right. The French and Canadian bishops abolished obligatory meatlessness more or less immediately, in early 1966. The US bishops were not far behind them, introducing new norms—discussed below—that November, to come into force at the start of Advent. The bishops of England, Wales, and Scotland, for their part, thought it necessary to consult widely before making any decisions. The *Tablet*'s commentary on this turn of events is, in light of some of the earlier points made in this chapter, worth quoting:

> Fish on Fridays has long been a mark of the tribe [...]. Now, like everything else, it has been brought into question, with the opinion of the pews being sought by the bishops. The Catholic laity are a good-tempered and docile lot, and on general issues only a few, though rather a loud-voiced few, show disgruntlement. But on this issue, I have found a good deal of mild irritation. It rests on the fact that, after the laity have been presented with so many real and far-reaching and, to many of them, devastating changes, without having their opinions publicly asked, they are now being asked about this with great elaborateness.
>
> (Tablet 1967)

Seemingly inevitably—the article also complains about 'loaded' questions—obligatorily meatless Fridays ended in December 1967. For the *Guardian*, 'The lifting of the rule will be no comfort to the British Trawlers' Federation, which says it is having one of its worst years since before the last war' (Guardian 1967).

The American bishops' 'Pastoral Statement on Penance and Abstinence' will repay some scrutiny. In this, they note that 'Changing circumstances, including economic, dietary, and social elements, have made some of our people feel that the renunciation of the eating of meat is not always and for everyone the most effective means of practicing penance' (National Conference of Catholic Bishops 1966: 19). (Evidently, Lou Groen's Filet-O-Fish sandwiches were just too darn festive.) Oddly enough, such considerations do *not* prevent them from: 'In keeping with the letter and spirit of Pope Paul's Constitution [... *preserving*] for our dioceses the tradition of abstinence from meat on each of the Fridays of Lent, confident that no Catholic Christian will lightly hold himself excused from this penitential practice' (National Conference of Catholic Bishops 1966: 13). Fridays all the rest of the year, however, are a rather more complicated story. Framing their new regulations as 'far from downgrading the traditional penitential observance of Friday, and motivated precisely by the desire to give the spirit of penance greater vitality', the bishops proceed to affirm that 'Friday itself remains a special day of penitential observance throughout the year' (21–2). Then, in a single sentence, they simultaneously 'especially commend' abstaining from meat on Fridays, while abolishing the requirement to do just that:

> Among the works of voluntary self-denial and personal penance which we especially commend to our people for the future observance of Friday, even though we hereby terminate the traditional law of abstinence binding under pain of sin, as the sole prescribed means of observing Friday, we give first place to abstinence from flesh meat.

The bishops add, 'We do so in the hope that the Catholic community will ordinarily continue to abstain from meat by free choice as formerly we did in obedience to Church law' (24).

To call this a 'mixed message' would be something of an understatement. All the more so, in fact, since it is followed by an implied slight on those who do indeed opt to follow their bishops' 'especially commend[ed]' suggestion: 'Perhaps we should warn those who decide to keep the Friday abstinence for reasons of personal piety and special love that they must not pass judgment on those who elect to substitute other penitential observances' (26). On the subject of these 'other penitential observances', the bishops express hope that 'Friday, please God, will acquire among us other forms of penitential witness which may become as much a part of the devout way of life in the future as Friday abstinence from meat.' In this regard, they have 'foremost in mind the modern need for self-discipline in the use of stimulants'—given the context, presumably abstaining from coffee (rather than, say, amphetamines) is imagined—'and for a renewed emphasis on the virtue of temperance, especially in the use of alcoholic beverages'. Furthermore, they add:

> It would bring great glory to God and good to souls if Fridays found our people doing volunteer work in hospitals, visiting the sick, serving the needs of the aged and the lonely, instructing the young in the Faith, participating as Christians in community affairs, and meeting our obligations to our families, our friends, our neighbors, and our community, including our parishes, with a special zeal born of the desire to add the merit of penance to the other virtues exercised in good works born of living faith. (27)

A very similar set of 'substitutes' was, incidentally, mooted by the English, Welsh, and Scottish bishops the following year (Guardian 1967).

It is easy enough to see, and sympathize with, what the bishops of America and elsewhere were *trying* to achieve. The loss of the true meaning of Friday had been a common complaint for decades (see Feeney 1934). *Voluntarily* abstaining from meat, or imposing upon oneself some other ascesis, in a spirit of true penance and prayer would indeed be more meritorious than doing so unthinkingly and automatically. The *hope* that these new freedoms would engender a penitential equivalent to the liturgical dream of the People of God being 'fully aware of what they are doing, actively engaged in the rite, and enriched by its effects' (*SC* 11) was, one can only presume, a wholly sincere one.

Yet however sincere the intention, it was at least as much—and arguably, very much more—sociologically, psychologically, and religiously naïve. In the first place, irrespective of anything else that was said, the singular take-home point of the various episcopal statements was that 'meatless Fridays' were henceforth abolished. This was, naturally enough, precisely how the newspapers reported it. Thus the *Washington Post* devoted its front-page banner headline to 'Catholic Bishops End Friday Meat Ban', while reproducing inside the full 'Text of Statement Abolishing Meatless Fridays' (MacKaye 1966; Washington Post 1966). In its end-of-the-year religion review, the *Chicago Daily Defender* whimsically expressed the central points like so:

Men in robes . . . devout . . . deceitless,

Did away with Fridays meatless.

Breaking up an old tradition . . .

Lousing up commercial fishing.   (Davis 1966)

Although the media dutifully reported that Catholics were now being urged instead either to abstain voluntarily, or else commit themselves to charitable acts, this was clearly not the story. Furthermore, the suggested substitutes were too wide-ranging for any one of them really to impress itself upon the mind. Had the bishops put their (still, by this point, substantial) collective authority behind a single prescription, or perhaps a choice between two—keep fasting from meat *or* devote at least one hour to a specific charitable endeavour, say—then things might potentially have turned out differently. Instead, Catholics were, with less than a fortnight's notice, simply condemned to be free. And so Friday became just another day. And with it, of course, an entire daylong CRED—from skipping bacon with one's morning waffles, to eating fried fish in the evening—simply disappeared.

On Andrew Greeley's estimation, this 'may have been the most unnecessary and the most devastating' of several 'crucial changes that transformed the structures of the preconciliar church' in these years (2004a: 54):

> You couldn't eat meat on Friday and that was that. Then the rules began to change and Catholics heard, well, you can eat meat on Friday, but you should voluntarily do other forms of penance. The laity didn't know from voluntary; they engaged in prescribed rituals of self-denial because they had to. They had no experience in making up their own rituals. Their identity was tied to obligatory fish on Friday. How did you establish a new, freely chosen identity? (2004a: 30)

Greeley's emphasis on identity chimes with the trenchant comments of British anthropologist Mary Douglas. She starts from the premise that while 'The official symbolism of Friday abstinence [...] could hardly have a more central load of meaning for Christian worship', with time and familiarity the practice has become, concretely, disassociated from its source: 'its symbols are no longer seen to point in that direction or anywhere in particular' ([1970] 1996: 37). Critically, however, this does not mean that the symbolism is now either empty or meaningless: 'symbols which are tenaciously adhered to can hardly be dismissed as altogether meaningless. They must mean something.' She points, for example, to the hardships and humiliations of Irish immigrant workers, who cling doggedly to the Friday rule: 'No empty symbol, it means allegiance to a humble home in Ireland and to a glorious tradition in Rome. These allegiances are something to be proud of in the humiliations of the unskilled labourer's lot' ([1970] 1996: 37).

Douglas' wider point is that the 'meatless Friday' rule has traditionally functioned, in a smaller way, as something akin to the Jewish avoidance of pork: regardless of its original social and religious aetiology, it principally acts as a cultural marker. It serves to root the individual Catholic firmly within a wider historical, cultural, and religious identity, while simultaneously setting this specific identity apart from other identities. Such shibboleths, and the identities with which they are bound up, cannot simply be conjured up out of nowhere. And nor can one hope substantially to alter or replace them, while retaining their original power—a point to which, as Douglas alludes, may be applied to other contemporary topics also:

> To take away one symbol that meant something is no guarantee that the spirit of charity will flow in its place. [...] But we have seen that those

who are responsible for ecclesiastical decisions are only too likely to
have been made, by the manner of their education, insensitive to non-
verbal signals and dull to their meaning. This is central to the difficulties
of Christianity today. It is as if the liturgical signal boxes were manned
by colour-blind signalmen.   (Douglas [1970] 1996: 42)

As she puts it, with a final phrase that has been quoted by several
commentators on postconciliar British Catholicism (and with a sen-
timent echoed by plenty of commentators on post-war American
Catholicism too):

Now there is no cause for others to 'regard us as odd'. Friday no longer
rings the great cosmic symbols of expiation and atonement: it is not
symbolic at all, but a practical day for the organization of charity. *Now
the English Catholics are like everyone else.*

([1970] 1996: 44; emphasis added)

THE CHANGE THAT DIDN'T

In the historiography of the 'Catholic sixties' (Massa 2010), and
indeed of everything that followed in its wake, Pope Paul's release
in July 1968 of a shortish (a mere five thousand words in the original
Latin, footnotes excluded) encyclical 'on the right ordering of the
propagation of human offspring' (cf. Smith 1991: 381 n.1) looms
large. So large, in fact, that it risks overshadowing the Council itself
as *the* key event. A kind of arms race exists among Catholic writers,
striving to distil the significance of *Humanae Vitae* into a suitably
apocalyptic idiom. Its impact, we are told, 'was the equivalent of a
tsunami' (Corrin 2013: 161) that 'shook the Catholic world to its
foundations' (Murphy-O'Connor 2015: 77), and precipitated 'the
gravest crisis of authority the church had faced in centuries' (Fisher
2007: 142). This 'unfashionable, unwanted, and ubiquitously deplored
moral teaching' (Eberstadt 2012: 134) initiated 'the Vietnam War of
the Catholic Church' (Steinfels 2003: 257). The year 1968 was hence
'The Year the Church Fell Apart' (McInerny 1998: 39).

As briefly adverted in Chapter 1, *Humanae Vitae* and its
varied repercussions have often been identified as critical catalysts
of Catholic lapsation and (increasingly) disaffiliation. With so seemingly cataclysmic an ecclesial occurrence, is it not plausible that the
large numbers of cradle Catholics who have left the Church in the

fifty years following it, have done so precisely *because* of it? This genus of argument comes, as noted much earlier, in two species, which, in the care of certain keepers (rather to run with this metaphor) can sometimes be persuaded to interbreed. The first form, promoted most clearly by Andrew Greeley in a number of publications, ascribes almost the entirety of post-1960s Catholic lapsation to Catholics either directly boycotting Mass in protest at *Humanae Vitae*, or else becoming so frustrated and disillusioned with an institution (officially) committed to upholding its teaching that they ultimately gave up and left. His strong statement of this view in 1985 was quoted in Chapter 1. Here's an even stronger follow-up from a few years later:

> Might the encyclical account for the decline in religious devotion? [. . .] Maybe the Council was a huge success. Maybe the encyclical had canceled it out. Maybe if it had not been for the surge in devotion after the Council, the decline after the Council would have been worse. If one put the decline in acceptance of papal authority and the decline in support for the birth-control teaching into an equation, how much of the change in the various devotional measures might be accounted for by the sex and authority change?
>
> The answer was that all of the change could be traced to the sex and authority issue. The Council had been a success and the encyclical a disaster.   (Greeley 1990: 23)

According to the second form, the problem was not so much the encyclical itself; indeed, wranglers of this approach tend to be all in favour of it. Nor was the primary issue the laity's distaste for it. Rather, commentators including Ralph McInerny and Philip Lawler cite the unwelcoming reception the encyclical received from some bishops, priests, theologians, and journalists—creating, in Russell Shaw's phrase, 'an organized culture of dissent' (2013: 125)—as having far-reaching implications, ultimately weakening Catholic identity, and with it belief, practice, and affiliation (McInerny 1998; Lawler 2008: 78–9). Before adding our own thoughts into the gene pool, it is necessary first to give some background. This history, recounted in fascinating detail elsewhere (e.g., Smith 1991: 1–35; Tentler 2004), must be recounted here quite briefly.

In 1930, 'Resolution 15' of the Anglican Churches' Lambeth Conference permitted, albeit it with heavy qualifications, 'in those cases where there is such a clearly felt moral obligation to limit or avoid parenthood, and where there is a morally sound reason for avoiding complete abstinence, [. . .] that other methods may be used' (Anglican Consultative Council [1930] 2005: 7). Around this time also, growing numbers of American Protestant denominations, often explicitly motivated by then-respectable eugenic concerns, began making their peace with contraception, if not for their own members, then at least for other, 'undesirable' groups.[15] Responding to these developments, with the bombast typical of papal demurrals in this period, Pope Pius XI released the encyclical *Casti Connubii*. Against 'the false principles of a new and utterly perverse morality' (1), this bracingly reaffirmed that:

> the Catholic Church, to whom God has entrusted the defense of the integrity and purity of morals, standing erect in the midst of the moral ruin which surrounds her, in order that she may preserve the chastity of the nuptial union from being defiled by this foul stain, raises her voice in token of her divine ambassadorship and through Our mouth proclaims anew: *any use whatsoever of matrimony exercised in such a way that the act is deliberately frustrated in its natural power to generate life is an offense against the law of God and of nature, and those who indulge in such are branded with the guilt of a grave sin.* (56; emphasis added)

Three decades on, however, the issue had failed to go away. These years witnessed the growing women's movement and the suggestive first stirrings of a sexual revolution (Collins 2009: 178–209); the invention of the Pill, and by a Catholic doctor no less (Rock 1963); growing worries about Third World overpopulation, which would reach fever pitch in 1968 with Paul Ehrlich's *The Population Bomb* (Gardner 2011: 161–75); increasing publicity for the often tragic plight of Catholic parents faced with severe medical, domestic, and/or economic pressures (Tentler 2004: 173–203; Harris 2015b); and, of course, for our new Catholic suburbanites and co-eds, conversations with one's non-Catholic neighbours and friends. All of these factors contributed in different ways to a climate in which the

---

[15] In support of this remarkable assertion, I refer the reader here to Wilde and Danielsen's exhaustively evidenced *American Journal of Sociology* paper, amply justifying their contention that 'the stances religious groups took at this time [i.e., 1929–31] can be explained by their position within the United States' system of racial and class stratification. We argue that religious organizations' advocacy for birth control was a critical component of a "racial project" to curtail the fertility of (mainly Catholic, but also Jewish) immigrants' (2014: 1711).

pros and cons of birth control were much talked-about by Catholics, including—at least for now—in the confessional (Tentler 2004: 130–72; Morrow 2018: 142–5).

The one place where they *weren't* talked about, however, was in the formal proceedings of the Second Vatican Council. While the Preparatory Commission's interest in sexual matters was wide-ranging—'discussing sexual morality and the dangers of "stardom, nudism, so-called sexual education, pan-sexualism, and the worst aspects of psycho-analysis"' (Tablet 1962: 459)—very little of this ended up reflected in the Council's documents. This was because by far the biggest issue, i.e., birth control, was lifted out of the Council's direct purview by John XXIII in 1963, and entrusted to a special committee. The final report of this Pontifical Commission on Birth Control, which Paul VI had continued and expanded, was finally completed in 1966. It argued that modern hormonal contraceptive methods were not, in themselves, intrinsically opposed to Catholic sexual ethics. Thus they might, by the right people (i.e., a validly married couple), and with the right intentions, be used morally. While this report was meant to be 'for the Pope's eyes only', it leaked the following year, along with a dissenting opinion (the so-called 'Minority Report') composed by only a handful of the Commission's members, thus raising rampant expectations of change. Even before this apparent confirmation, those expectations had been growing. As early as June 1964, for instance, the *San Francisco Chronicle* ran the front-page headline 'Pope Hints at New View of Birth Control', due to a passing comment that the subject was 'being considered as deeply and amply as possible . . . and we hope soon to conclude these studies' (1964). What, after all, was there to consider and study, if the subject really had already been closed?

Famously, no change was forthcoming. When Paul VI finally released *Humanae Vitae* to the world on 29 July 1968, he fundamentally reaffirmed the basic position, though not the bombast, of Pius XI's *Casti Connubii*. Paul was not, however, naïve enough to think the repeated teaching, howsoever much 'a promulgation of the law of God Himself', would be accepted joyfully in all quarters. Indeed, he freely admits 'there is no doubt that to many it will appear not merely difficult but even impossible to observe' (*Humanae Vitae* 20).

As the descriptions quoted above attest, the fallout in Britain and America, as elsewhere, was considerable. Reports of the encyclical's contents being mockingly announced, or else damningly denounced, from the pulpit are easy to find (McDannell 2011: 189; Shaw

2013: 125). Formal letters and expression of dissent, signed by groups of clergy and theologians, began appearing immediately. Page one of the *New York Times*, just a day after its initial announcement of 'Pope Bars Birth Control By Any Artificial Means; Tone Forthright' (Doty 1968), breathlessly reported: 'Catholic Experts in Strong Dissent on Edict by Pope; 87 Theologians, Mostly of Clergy, Say Birth-Control Ban is Not Binding; Decree Held Fallible' (Carmody 1968).[16] In Britain, the rather more demotic *Daily Mail* followed up a front-page splash on 'The Pope's Bitter Pill' by devoting much of page six to 'Why We Will Defy the Pope: By the Catholic Mothers Taking the Pill' (Churchill 1968a, 1968b). Given the tumult, not least among their own clergy, diocesan bishops were soon obliged to put out, and *be seen* to put out, their own statements in support of the encyclical. Sometimes, however, these included language that seemed calculated to signal, to those with ears to hear, the opposite—the comment by Boston's Cardinal Cushing that 'The matter is settled for now' being a case in point (quoted in Lawler 2008: 78). On the other side of the Atlantic, those desiring a contrary take from a *bona fide* Successor of the Apostles had no need to read between the lines. The London-based Jesuit, Archbishop Thomas Roberts, having retired early from the See of Bombay in favour of a homegrown successor, had been generating headlines like 'Jesuit Prelate Attacks Vatican on Pill' (Singleton 1965) for several years. Naturally, this made him the British media's go-to bishop for expert punditry on the encyclical: the BBC interviewed him on the evening of its release. Speaking to a journalist the follow day, he prophesied *Humanae Vitae* 'may result in many thoughtful people leaving the Church', swiftly followed by 'those priests who are unhappy about the present place of authority in the Church [who] may now feel driven to leave it ranks'. Always good for a quotable quote, Archbishop Roberts ended the interview:

> The birth control encyclical will not be repudiated [i.e., by future popes] but forgotten. The important lesson [. . .] is that the obedience of an

---

[16] The reference here is to the famous ten-paragraph 'Statement of Dissent', coordinated by Fr Charles Curran, then a professor of moral theology at Catholic University of America. *Humanae Vitae* was publicly released on 29 July, and thus made the next morning's papers. Having got hold of a copy on the day of release, Curran and colleagues were able to draft the Statement, and find almost ninety clerical and/or academic signatories, in time to unveil it to the press on the afternoon of the 30th (Curran 2006: 50–2). On this remarkable feat of organization and media-savviness, among much else besides, see Massa 2010: 49–74.

individual is worth little unless his intelligence enters into it; otherwise a
man's obedience is no different from a dog's.   (Beeson 1968)

This brief summary of the early unfolding of the *Humanae Vitae*
controversy, in the midst of (lest we forget) quite an eventful year in
its own right, ought to provide sufficient background for our purposes
here. It does, for one, contain the rudiments of an answer to something of a fundamental, if rarely asked, question. Of all the possible
explanations for the dramatic changes in Catholic practice and
(ultimately) identity which began and/or intensified from the 1960s
onwards, why would *something*—i.e., the Church's opposition to
artificial means of contraception—*staying essentially the same as it
always had been* be the most likely culprit? *Prima facie*, it is extraor-
dinarily odd that *Humanae Vitae* should be identified as a major
contributor to change in Catholic pastoral life, up or down, positive
or negative, in the first place. Catholic couples wishing to space or
avoid pregnancies, after all, had always had two options. *Either* they
could practise various methods of abstinence, ranging from total, to
the periodic kinds of the rhythm method and early forms of natural
fertility awareness, explicitly permitted by *Casti Connubii* (59), and
further encouraged in both *Gaudium et Spes* (52) and *Humanae Vitae*
(16, 24). *Or* they might choose to practise artificial contraception, by
various means, and with varying degrees of uneasy conscience.
Informed estimates differ, but a 'distinct minority' of perhaps
30 per cent of American Catholic women were using birth control
methods by the mid-1950s (Tentler 1990: 482–3), and perhaps 40 per
cent of British ones a decade later (Corrin 2013: 161; see Marshall
1999: 69–71). As such, it is not immediately obvious why *Humanae
Vitae* should have prompted anyone to leave the Church who had not
done so already. Is it really plausible to ascribe our 'Mass Exodus' to
Paul's simple repetition, in a far kindlier tone than that used by his
predecessors, of 'what just about everyone authoritative in the history
of Christianity had ever said on the subject until practically the day
before yesterday' (Eberstadt 2012: 155), and using reasoning that had
been 'accepted by all [Catholic] theologians until the 1960s' (Curran
2008: 47)? Why would—or rather, *how could*—this issue suddenly
become a deal-breaker for apparently so many hitherto-practising
Catholics?

   There are two answers to these questions. The first is simply that, in
contrast to the run-up to *Casti Connubii*, those desiring a change in

the teaching had strong reasons not just to hope, but actively to expect, that one would be forthcoming. The sheer fact that the topic was up for debate seemed to augur in this direction, as did the long time taken first by the Commission, and then—especially once the Commission's conclusions were widely known—by the Pope. A simple no, it was thought, could be quickly and flatly stated. But a momentous change? *That* would certainly require a bit of steeling oneself before making; biding one's time for the right moment; finessing one's arguments as to why it wasn't really a change, but instead a more faithful realization of what the Tradition had been aiming for all along. The argument that the Pill, in contrast to barrier methods of contraception, did not fall foul of the Church's expressed strictures, is one that had been made since it first appeared (McDannell 2011: 191–2).[17] Anticipating that Paul would ultimately endorse this view, therefore, confessors increasingly began either explicitly to condone the practice, or else no longer, if ever they had, to forbid it. Moreover, 'Couples preparing for marriage could hardly be expected to be guided by a prohibition whose days were numbered' (McInerny 1998: 43). All this meant that, come the end of July 1968, there was a significant proportion of the Catholic laity who could legitimately feel that they had done everything right—they had consulted their appointed moral authority figures, had been given to believe (perhaps tacitly) that there was nothing intrinsically wrong in their taking birth control, and had in good faith acted on this advice—and *now* were being told that they had, at least objectively, been sinning after all. As one English wife and mother wrote to Cardinal Heenan, the Archbishop of Westminster, in August 1968:

> During the past couple of years, when this teaching of the Church has been under revision pending a papal decision, we have been told to use our own consciences with regard to the manner in which we limit our family, by three priests in this parish. This I know to be the case with many of my Catholic friends and relations, none of whom could be classed in any way as lapsed or indifferent.
>
> (Quoted in Harris 2018b: 87)

---

[17] The idea here being, *in nuce*, that the Pill does not interfere with the actual procreative act itself, but rather simply regulates and extends the infertile ('safe') periods of a cycle.

Even more significantly, as this letter also attests, there were large numbers of priests and theologians who had staked their reputation on knowledgeably second-guessing the Pope. So when the expected change never materialized, it is surely not surprising that they would now 'double down'. This could be done either by affirming that the Pope was flat-out wrong, or, much more subtly, by honouring the teaching as upholding a true and beautiful *ideal*, but one whose pastoral application required a good deal of nuance and sensitivity, with due respect for the conscience and free will of the couple involved.[18]

The second answer is that, beyond the specifics of the birth control debate, Catholics were by now well-used to things changing that had, only a few years before, appeared immutable (Carlin 2003: 59). After all, if such totemic aspects of Catholic identity as Mass in Latin or fish on Fridays could change from one week to the next, if Tabernacles and plaster statues of the Blessed Virgin could disappear from sight, if High Altars could be abandoned in favour of cafeteria-style tables, and if altar rails could be ripped out altogether, what *wasn't* susceptible to a radical overhaul? Recall too that everything mentioned in the previous sentence had begun occurring in just four years prior to *Humanae Vitae*. Less than a year after it, the perception of change-ability would be further reinforced by the (as it was widely reported) 'demotion' of Sts Christopher and George. Such was the backdrop to Paul's bombshell: a Church in which so much had already been changed, and seemingly everything else *might* be. In contrast, the blanket prohibition of artificial birth control was not simply the 'one thing' that did not change; arguably at least, it was also the one thing that a significant portion of the laity actually *wanted* to see changed. Disappointment, frustration, resentment, disillusionment, even defiance—in the circumstances such reactions were hardly surprising.

In itself, however, there is nothing here to prove that well-documented drops in church attendance, and ultimately church

---

[18] See, for example, the official guidance issued by Archbishop Beck to his Liverpool priests eight months before the publication of *Humanae Vitae*:

No priest should ever say: 'The Church is wrong in forbidding contraception', just as he should never say that the Church is wrong in commanding Sunday Mass. But he can say to an individual 'I do not think you are committing sin by missing Mass in your circumstances'; and likewise it is suggested that he can equally say to an individual 'I do not think you are committing sin by practising contraception in your circumstances.' (Quoted in Longley 2000: 359)

affiliation, occurred out of sorrow and/or anger at the encyclical. Or that if they did, that they were either primarily or exclusively so caused. Certainly, there is no shortage of evidence that *Humanae Vitae* indeed stirred such strong emotions. As Britain's leading sociologist of Catholicism, Michael Hornsby-Smith, here writing autobiographically, recalls: 'we were, like many Catholics, shattered' (2010: 83). But what proportion of the 'shattered' upped and left in protest is not clear (and certainly didn't include the Hornsby-Smiths). True enough, when Washington, DC's Cardinal O'Boyle read out his own statement supporting the encyclical at three Sunday morning Masses in his own cathedral, some 200 protesters, by prior arrangement, did precisely that. But there is no suggestion that they planned never to return. Also worth noting here, running counter to the dominant narrative around the reception of *Humanae Vitae*, are the estimated 800–1000 worshippers who not only stayed, but greeted O'Boyle's statement with a standing ovation (Weil 1968a). No doubt there were some for whom *Humanae Vitae* was a contributor to their lapsing or perhaps joining another denomination, perhaps as the kind of last-straw 'trigger' discussed in Chapter 3. But it seems doubtful that these amounted to the huge numbers needed to fulfil Greeley's thesis that pretty much all of the 'decline in Catholic religious practice is the result of a violent reaction to the birth control encyclical' (1985: 57). After all, those most deeply disappointed by *Humanae Vitae* were those practising Catholics, either already using birth control or anxiously awaiting permission to start, for whom a 'yea' or (as it turned out) 'nay' from the Vicar of Christ was a very big deal. Precisely the kinds of people, that is to say, most likely to be highly committed Catholics with a heavy investment in Church teaching and practice. In the wake of the encyclical, such people were surely more likely to stay and work for change, possibly even joining one of several lay-led groups that soon sprang up for this purpose (Corrin 2013: 164). And at the personal level, sympathetically 'pastoral' priests—if not in one's own parish, then likely in a neighbouring one—were by no means hard to find (Lawler 2008: 125–6). There is little reason for thinking that many Catholic couples, already accustomed to using contraception, suddenly stopped after the release of *Humanae Vitae*. To the contrary, there is a good deal of at least anecdotal evidence to suggest they did *not* (Lodge 2015: 409, 429–31). There are even accounts of committed Catholic couples who had pointedly held off using birth control, while waiting on the formal green light from Pope Paul, for whom his definitive *red* light became the paradoxical prompt to start (Hornsby-Smith 2010: 83).

But if the Greeley thesis doesn't quite convince—tellingly enough, Greeley himself went notably quiet on it in his later writings on 'the Catholic revolution' and its after-effects (2005: 34–5)—that does not mean that *Humanae Vitae* is not, in fact, a critical 'moment' in the history of Catholic disaffiliation. As noted above, there exists a considerable body of commentary arguing that *Humanae Vitae*'s real contribution to the ensuing 'Catholic crisis' was the substantial weakening effect it had on the Church's authority. This was not, for many proponents of this theory, an intrinsic fault of the encyclical itself (timing aside, perhaps) or of the teaching it expressed. Rather, the blame lies with the negative reception that the encyclical received from dissenting clergy and theologians. This negative reception, though significant in itself, was greatly amplified by a media for whom priest-professors from 'Catholic U.' criticizing the Pope, or working-class mothers vowing to defy him, were understandably attractive stories. Thereafter, so the argument goes, dissent from official teaching became a normal, indeed wholly respectable, feature of the Church. Hence for McInerny:

> It is clear that 1968 marked the beginning of dissent in the Church. It would be impossible to find at any earlier time a claim that theologians had the professional task of appraising and assessing magisterial teachings, of accepting or rejecting them. Now it was as if, when the Pope spoke, the theologians first scrutinized what he had said to see whether it was acceptable to them or not. This was utterly new, and it did not begin with Vatican II, but with *Humanae Vitae*.   (1998: 102–3)

Nor, of course, was such latitude the preserve of professional theologians. If good Catholics could decide that 'Since it was agreed, even by the Pope's supporters, that he was not speaking *ex cathedra* (i.e. infallibly), there was still some room for conscientious dissent' (Lodge 2015: 430), while *remaining* good Catholics—and they could cite a large number of recognized experts, from their own parish priest right up to a former Archbishop of Bombay, that they could—then there was not a great deal left from which one might not 'conscientiously dissent', if so inclined. *Humanae Vitae* precipitated a kind of domino effect (to borrow a phrase very much in vogue in 1968). According to the British social historian David Geiringer, 'For many Catholics, [using birth control] was the first time they had knowingly contravened the Church's official teaching.' And as he revealingly quotes from one of his oral history interviewees, 'It was the starting point really. I remember thinking, if the Church is wrong about this, it could be wrong about other things' (2016: 80).

This shift, which I agree was both real and significant, is probably not best imagined as lay Catholics suddenly rejecting all claims of 'authority', in favour of simply picking and choosing—the so-called 'cafeteria Catholicism' of conservative polemic—according to their own personal whims. Arguably, the immediate controversy surrounding *Humanae Vitae* precipitated not so much a collapse of authority in the Church, as it did its fragmentation—though this would, in turn, ultimately lead to a weakening of 'authority-in-general'. Think back to our discussion of plausibility structures in the previous chapter. Regardless of how a religious group's collective authority is understood in theoretical terms, in practice, it is mediated to ordinary adherents via a complex of individual *authorities*. Concretely, in our case, these include one's parish priest(s), the half-remembered maxims of one's teachers and catechists, the editorials and op-eds in one's weekly *Universe* or *Our Sunday Visitor*, and the views of various Catholic 'experts', including learned theologians, bishops, and (sometimes) the Pope, as reported in whichever daily newspaper one happens to take. If the 'Catholic system' is working more-or-less as it ought to, there should be no meaningful disagreement between these various authorities: on most questions of faith and morals, then whatever one's parish priest says should be at least consonant with whatever the Pope himself would tell you.

This is, admittedly, a rather idealized scenario: in practice, many topics allow for some degree of discordance, either on certain points of interpretation and application, or in the relative weights assigned to particular considerations. Nevertheless, even if not always with the highest fidelity of reproduction, there is an essential, base-level agreement of 'orthodoxy' among the various types and levels of authority: enough, indeed, for a clear consensus to form that a wayward, minority position constitutes 'heresy' (see Berger 1980: 27–8). In the wake of *Humanae Vitae*, however, these mechanisms of 'authoritative self-regulation' broke down. On the prior model, Pope Paul's 'no' ought to have definitively settled the question, in accordance with the ancient dictum of *Roma locuta est, causa finita est* ('Rome has spoken, the matter is ended'). 'Settling the question' here is not, incidentally, tantamount to convincing all those who disagree, or persuading everyone who was doing what the Pope has forbidden to stop doing it. But it would, at least, be widely established that they were doing these things in opposition to Catholic teaching. That is to say, priests and theologians who thought the Pope was wrong would stop saying so in public, either out of enlightened self-interest, or under episcopal duress. And lay Catholics who chose to continue doing the forbidden would do so quietly, and likely with an uneasy conscience.

Admittedly, the above picture rather simplifies things, but I think the basic gist is an accurate one. Or rather, it *was*. For that it is not what actually happened with *Humanae Vitae*. For some of the reasons mentioned earlier, rather than silence or quieten calls for repealing the birth control ban, the encyclical served to intensify them. In the face of such widespread expression of disagreement, diocesan bishops, whatever public backing they felt compelled to give the encyclical, had little desire to reprimand all their dissenting priests. That many of the bishops, perhaps most of whom had been expecting the change along with everyone else, clearly had little appetite either for defending the encyclical or punishing those who did also, of course, added legitimacy to 'the opposition'. For ordinary Catholics, therefore, this was manifestly not a choice between 'following Church authority' or 'deciding for oneself'. Rather, it was a choice between competing sets of authorities. Discerning the precise meaning of, and magisterial weight to be accorded to, a particular pronouncement of the Successor of Peter is not a job for the vast majority of Catholics. And the people whose job it *was* evidently could not agree. For every bishop or cardinal saying one thing, one was aware of at least some saying (or dog-whistling) the opposite. For every set of theologians with highfalutin titles signing one petition, one had read of another set signing an opposing one. For every parish homily in praise of the encyclical, there was another lamenting it. This reached its most perfect expression in one DC parish, with juxtaposed *pro* and *contra* homilies delivered at the same Mass, by the pastor and assistant pastor (Weil 1968b). True enough, there was only one pope. Even he, however, could be deployed against his own encyclical: on one interpretation, appealing to what one might call the 'spirit' of Pope Paul, his delay before promulgating *Humanae Vitae* was proof of both his personally being persuaded by the case for change, and his cowardly unwillingness to contradict previous papal teaching (e.g., McBrien 2010).

Both sides, therefore, felt that theirs was a legitimately Catholic position to hold. But the very fact that one could meaningfully talk in terms of 'sides' is itself revealing. However one aligned oneself on this question, the answer was no longer something that could be automatically taken for granted. Critically, this was as true for those who were 'for' *Humanae Vitae* as it was for those 'against' it. After *Casti Connubii*, there was no serious question of what the 'Catholic position' was on the birth-control question. A Catholic who contradicted Pius XI, whether in thought, word, or deed, was fully aware of the taboo nature of their position: there was, to put it in Bergerian terms, a background of established religious authority against which this was a clear transgression (Berger 1980: 27–8). Incidentally, this is probably why no one ever speaks of an 'aftermath' to *Casti Connubii*. In stark contrast, after *Humanae Vitae* there was no longer a clear default position to which a Catholic, *qua* Catholic, could passively acquiesce. Thus as Berger writes, in a supremely important passage:

> Now, suddenly, heresy no longer stands out against a clear background of authoritative tradition. The background has become dim or even disappeared. As long as that background was still there, individuals had the possibility of *not* picking and choosing—they could simply surrender to the taken-for-granted consensus that surrounded them on all sides, and that is what most individuals did. But now this possibility itself becomes dim or disappears: How can one surrender to a consensus that is socially unavailable? Any affirmation must first create the consensus, even if this can only be done in some small quasi-sectarian community. In other words, individuals now *must* pick and choose. Having done so, it is very difficult to forget the fact.   (1980: 28)[19]

This is, therefore, the watershed moment at which tribal divisions between 'liberal' and 'conservative', or 'progressive' and 'traditional' Catholics began to carry serious meaning (cf. Cuneo 1997: 21–9; Dillon 1999: 242–56). In the past, Catholics were typically divided

---

[19] It is worth stressing that this is a strictly sociological observation, and emphatically *not* a doctrinal one. In Berger's terms, 'heresy' here means whatever is clearly opposed to the established social and religious consensus (i.e., 'orthodoxy').

My own point here is not that, after July 1968, there was no longer an *actually* correct Catholic position on artificial contraception, in terms of either dogmatic theology or absolute truth. I personally have no doubt that Pope Paul was right (Bullivant 2016c). But the simple fact that this needs *stating* by a practising Catholic theologian working at a Catholic university, and cannot—to put it mildly—remotely be taken as read, rather proves the Bergerian point I'm making.

into 'good' and 'bad', or 'practising' and 'lapsed'. But these were, in a sense, degrees on a *single* scale of being Catholic. They were not two different modes, different camps, of being Catholic. In August 1968, to be fair, they weren't either. But over the coming years, that is precisely what they would become (Smith et al. 2014: 15). Nor was this simply a matter of one's position on *Humanae Vitae*—although, in fact, fifty-plus years later it still serves as a pretty reliable litmus test. On the face of it, a person's views on *Humanae Vitae* need not correlate in any predetermined way with their positions on various doctrinal points (women priests, say, or the necessity of the Church for salvation), or on their liturgical preferences. In practice, however, they very often do.

The *Washington Post*'s report of the closing Mass of a thousands-strong liturgists' conference in August 1968 offers not just a good example, but perhaps even the best of all possible examples, of this sort of accumulation. It also illuminates just how swiftly the liturgical reforms had 'progressed' in the four years since Fr McManus' 'first full English mass in the United States':

> Modern dancers, lavender lights and an eight-piece Harlem jazz band were the backdrop yesterday for an impassioned sermon that indirectly attacked Pope Paul's encyclical on birth control as 'spiritual imperialism.' [. . .] 'All of our baggage,' said Father Hovda, 'our dogmatic and moral doctrine and our liturgy, to say nothing of the tragic misconception that nature is man's master rather than the clay he works on, must be scrutinized for its utility.' [. . .] 'Simon and Garfunkel put it this way,' he said. '"Look around, Leaves are brown, and the sky is a hazy shade of winter."' [. . .] The sermon was preceded by a modern dance performed by 12 young people. [. . .] After Father Hovda's sermon, the participants in the conference took Communion and prepared to leave for their homes. They were readily identifiable in the hotel check-out lines by their bright red, yellow and blue buttons which said, 'Damn everything but the circus,' a quote from a play by E. E. Cummings.
>
> (Satter 1968)

Less colourful examples of this trend emerge from the kinds of evidence adduced in Chapter 3. For example, many of those with a visceral reaction to Latin or *ad orientem* worship saw them as symbols of a 'turning back the clock' on moral and social progress too. Likewise, those saying that they left the Church because of 'happy clappy' worship are disproportionately likely also to cite the evils of ecumenism or (in the words of a 70-year-old woman from the Portsmouth survey) 'altering [. . .] doctrine(s) to suit the "spirit of the age" (as if that itself didn't change regularly!) and which is weasel-speak for "telling people that whatever they want to do is OK"'.

Though we are rather getting ahead of ourselves, it is important to stress the full significance of these nascent developments. The immediate reaction to *Humanae Vitae* can, in retrospect, indeed be seen as the opening skirmishes of what would, in America far more so than in Britain, become the Catholic 'culture wars'. As so often, this was not purely a product of intra-Catholic dynamics. Even more important was the fact that in the wider cultures, social and moral attitudes were shifting dramatically (see McLeod 2007: 161–87; Brown [2006] 2014: 240–53). The debate over the Pill was not, in short, a one-off. Changing expectations around the role and status of women in general—'A generation that was born into a world where women were decreed to have too many household chores to permit them to serve on juries [. . .] would come of age in a society where female astronauts and judges were routine' (Collins 2009: 8)—meant the Church's exclusion of women from the clergy was, even if correct, no longer something obviously or self-evidently so. The growing availability of divorce (and the growing numbers of Catholics duly availing themselves) gradually eroded the social stigma around both it and subsequent remarriage, with consequent pressure on the Church's prohibition on communion for those 'irregularly' yoked (Buckley 1999; Hout 2000).

The gay rights movement, which gained new visibility and impetus in the 1960s, would ultimately bring not just significant numbers of gay and lesbian Catholics, but a much larger segment of Catholics in sympathy with their family members and friends, to question—again, until recent decades, wholly non-controversial—core moral and sacramental doctrines (see Brown 2012: 139–41). In the Archdiocese of San Francisco, these issues were already coming up in the late 1960s and 1970s (Burns 2018); in a decade or two, they would be mainstream everywhere. Lastly, the legalization and/or liberalization of abortion—in Britain with the Abortion Act 1967; in America with the Supreme Court's 1973 *Roe v. Wade* decision—demonstrates most strongly the extent to which the wider moral and social climate was, even at this early stage, moving away from a point of overlap with traditional Catholic positions (see Hattersley 2017: 530). That is not to say that a significant proportion of either British or American

Catholics instantly became 'pro-choice'. But five decades later, 'pro-life Catholic' is far from being the near-redundancy it once was (Clements 2014). 'Women's reproductive rights' have, moreover, become a deeply entrenched part of both mainstream feminism, and the platforms of both the US Democratic and UK Labour Parties, both traditionally Catholic strongholds. The full outworkings of these societal shifts will be further explored in the two chapters to follow. Note, though, that these are all issues where the growing divergence between 'Church' and 'World' is played out concretely in individuals' personal and social lives. A person's position on contraception, divorce, same-sex relationships, or abortion both influences and is influenced by their relationships with partners, relatives, and friends.

To return to *Humanae Vitae*'s more proximate impacts, though, one place where the controversy really hit home was in the confessional. As noted above, word soon got around which parishes, or even which priests in the same parish, might be more sympathetic to one's particular situation. But this, too, simply reinforced the sense that the topic was not—indeed could not—*really* be a matter of profound, salvation-or-damnation moral gravity. The laity are not, after all, stupid: how could something be an absolutely forbidden mortal sin in the confessional at 9.58 a.m. under Fr O'Malley, but at 10.02a.m. on Fr McMahon's shift in the same confessional, be a topic left up to the couple's own conscientious discernment? And nor, obviously, was it simply a case of individual 'mavericks'. England's Cardinal Heenan, appearing on David Frost's popular Friday-night chat show, affirmed the encyclical's teaching while confirming that couples who couldn't 'in conscience' follow it should still receive communion. This, as one of Heenan's successors at Westminster later put it, 'established the tone for the approach the Church in England and Wales would take to the issue of contraception. It was, perhaps, a very English solution' (Murphy-O'Connor 2015: 79).

Over time, all of this appears to have had a dual effect. Firstly, a culture of 'don't ask, don't tell' gradually emerged around contraception in the confessional. This has now reached such an extent that, at least according to my own priest-informants—running the full gamut of views on *Humanae Vitae*—in both countries, today the subject is rarely brought up by either confessor or penitent. (Almost inevitably, this has extended to other areas of sexual ethics: if the conscientiously contracepting may keep receiving communion, why should this 'pastoral approach' not apply to others too?) Secondly and still more significantly, the practice of confession itself very soon began a sharp free-fall from which it has never recovered. As O'Toole observes: 'confession seemed to disappear almost completely from the fiber of Catholic identity and custom. [...] Practically overnight, the lines on Saturday afternoons vanished and the hours appointed for confession dwindled as even the most ardent Catholics stayed away' (2000).

Humanae Vitae was not, it is true, the only possible contributor to this. As we have similarly seen with the liturgy, the 'sacrament of reconciliation', as it was rebranded after the Council, suffered a great many experiments in pursuit of the ever-elusive 'relevance' (Morrow 2018). It is perfectly possible that the new brightly lit 'sitting room' confessionals, which replaced the anonymous black boxes in many parishes, had a deterrent effect all of their very own. A brief vogue in the 1970s for 'general absolutions', hitherto reserved for *in extremis* times of immediate and mortal peril (such as, most famously, on the sinking *Titanic*, or among the Union Army's Irish Brigade on the eve of the Battle of Gettysburg), perhaps also diminished the sacrament's gravity in popular eyes. Bishop Carroll Dozier's 1976 absolution of twelve thousand people in a Memphis baseball stadium has, whatever its noble intentions, become a symbol of the cheapening of penance during this period. Without denying these other factors, most informed commentators plausibly regard *Humanae Vitae* as being, against all intentions, a major factor in Catholics' much-attenuated senses of sin, its life-or-death consequences, and its sacramental remedies, in the period 'since Vatican II' (Morrow 2016; Geiringer 2018). Given the arguments put forward in Chapter 4, hypothesizing confession's critical role in both internalizing Catholic belief and identity and in serving as a very conspicuous example of a CRED to oneself and others, then the subtle impact of its precipitous decline on rates of Catholic practice and retention ought not to be underestimated.

CONCLUSION

Far and away, this chapter is the longest in this book. This is simply due to letting substance dictate structure, and not vice versa. The pivotal nature of the 1960s for understanding religious change across the whole North Atlantic world, though not wholly uncontested, is widely accepted among scholars—and with good reason. As argued in Chapter 4, it was in this decade that the first wave of Baby Boomers, in several ways brought up very differently to their own parents, came of age. As they did so, they interacted in significant, and oftentimes disruptive, ways with (i) each other, (ii) a number of social and cultural movements also coming to full fruition in the decade, and (iii) the generations of 'squares' who had preceded them. In an era whose supreme cultural value has been described as the 'New, and Modern, and Young, and New, and Shiny, and New, especially New' (Beckett 2010: 79), institutions whose strongest claims to authority depend on being in accord with what 'was in the beginning, is now, and ever shall be' were always starting from a position of disadvantage. There is no reason to suppose the Catholic Church in Britain or America was in any way immune from these trends.

Meanwhile, for those interested in the Catholic story specifically, there really is no controversy. Despite there being many suggested causes of various types of Catholic decline, all theories tend to centre around something that either happened, or didn't happen, or didn't happen swiftly and/or thoroughly enough, or started happening and then stopped doing, in the 1960s. In fact, Catholic 'Ground Zero' may be pinpointed with even greater precision. Indeed, each of the *main* events (various after-effects notwithstanding) discussed in this chapter occurred in a period of just five and a half years: from the promulgation of *Sacrosanctum Concilium* in December 1963 to Pope Paul VI's reform of the liturgical calendar, announced in May 1969.

In the following two chapters, we turn directly to the fifty years 'since Vatican II' of the book's title. As we have seen, lapsation and (less so) disaffiliation were legitimate worries in the period before the Council. Indeed, a felt need to address these phenomena demonstrably contributed to the Council's convocation. It also lay behind many of its specific proposals, especially in the realm of liturgy, and—critically—informed the atmosphere in which those proposals were interpreted and reinterpreted, implemented and endlessly reimplemented, in Britain and America. The sheer fact of people being brought up Catholics and coming, later in life, no longer to practise and/or identify as Catholics, was not something that *began* in the 1960s. But, as we are about to explore, it very rapidly picked up speed and severity in the period immediately following.

6

The Morning After

The April 1975 issue of the *Month* carried an article by British sociologist Anthony Spencer, whose 1950s studies on young people and Irish immigration were discussed in Chapter 4. Once again, Spencer averred, the English and Welsh Church was suffering a 'demographic crisis'. Only this time, not only was it 'more severe', it was of a troublingly different kind.

> The difference is that the crisis of the 1950s was one of rapid population growth, creating massive problems of investment in new schools, colleges, churches, and other institutions, whereas the crisis of the 1970s is one of rapid contraction.   (1975: 100)

Using, with due caution and caveats, two decades' worth of statistics—birth rate; sacramental indices; convert numbers; net Irish immigration—Spencer sounds several alarm bells. His longest section, however, begins with the observation that: 'During the 1950s there was much concern within the Catholic community about drop-out, "lapsing", and leakage' (1975: 102). Based on several independent measures, Spencer proposes tentative estimates of baptized Catholics who are not just absent on Sunday morning, but who are 'alienated to the extent that' they either had not been Confirmed, or 'would not use the offices of the Church at the three great turning points of life: birth, marriage, death'. In 1958, he suggests, there were 249,000 such 'drop-outs' in England and Wales, out of a total baptized population of roughly 5.5 million. In 1971, there were 2.6 million drop-outs, from a total of 7 million. He further estimates that whereas *c.*30,000 Catholics 'dropped out' in each of 1959 and 1960; by the five-year period of 1967–71 the attrition rate was over 253,000 *per annum*. On Spencer's bleak assessment:

> What emerges [. . .] is that drop-out (as distinct from religious practice levels below canonical norms) was marginal in the late 1950s, but had

assumed massive proportions by the early 1970s. *The Catholic folklore that 'once a Catholic, always a Catholic', that Catholics seldom totally abandon their religious identity even if they ceased going to Mass* and did not carry out their Easter Duties, was substantially true of England and Wales in the late 1950s; it *had altogether ceased to be true by the early 1970s.* (1975: 104; emphasis added)

Around this time, American sociologists also began noting a trend towards disaffiliation (Greeley et al. 1976: 144–9). Repeated surveys in 1955 and 1967 had found that 8 per cent of those saying they were raised Catholics, roughly one person in thirteen, now identified as something other than Catholic. By 1973/4, this had jumped to 14 per cent, or one in seven. While all age bands were affected, the increase was greatest among 18- to 29-year-olds, which in 1973/4 meant those born between 1944 and 1956—i.e., more-or-less our Early Boomers. For this age group, in whose name a good deal of the previous decades' boldest experiments had been justified, the disaffiliation rate was 22 per cent, one in five. This further rose to 30 per cent among college-educated under-30s.

Spencer's operational definition of a drop-out is not, of course, the same one used in the US study (and this book). No doubt, if asked on a survey in the 1970s, a fair proportion of Spencer's 2.6 million alienated Catholics would still have identified as 'Catholic'. But both measures are, with different tools and from different angles, attempting to 'get at' the same or very similar reality: people raised as Catholics who, at some point in their later lives, no longer feel a sense of real, tangible belonging to the Catholic Church. Herein, we have been using subjective affiliation on surveys as the deciding line. For Spencer, it is availing oneself of Catholic marriage, Catholic baptism for one's children, or a Catholic funeral upon one's death. In truth, it is not necessarily clear which is the more stringent measure. Due to the vagaries and complexity of religious identity, it is perfectly possible that some of Spencer's drop-outs would still regard themselves as Catholics, just as it is that some of our 'subjective disaffiliates' would have their children baptized into the Church or receive a Catholic burial. Both measures testify, however, to a genuine level of distance or alienation—that is, in Ebaugh's parlance, 'the phenomenon of being an ex' (1988: xiii)—far beyond that of simply being lapsed, non-practising, or indeed 'resting'.

Spencer was not alone in speaking of the 1970s (and soon enough, 1980s) as a period of crisis for the Catholic Church. The full scale of it all—sharp falls in the numbers of converts and vocations; existential crises, individual and collective, within religious orders; large numbers of priests and nuns leaving their vows, often in pairs—is, on the one hand, well beyond the scope of this book. Yet on the other hand, it is precisely this context in which both postconciliar Catholic disaffiliation, and the millions of disaffiliates themselves, 'live and move and have [their] being' (Acts 17:28). Even for many people firmly rooted in their Catholic identity and practice, this could all be very disorienting. Numerous books from this era, by Catholic authors with both diverging perspectives on, and appreciation for, the previous decade's 'changes', testify to a pervading sense of vertigo. These include Dietrich von Hildebrand's *Trojan Horse in the City of God: The Catholic Crisis Explained* ([1967] 1993), Thomas O'Dea's *The Catholic Crisis* (1968), Frank Sheed's *Is It the Same Church?* (1968), John Eppstein's *Has the Catholic Church Gone Mad?* (1971), Garry Wills' *Bare Ruined Choirs* (1972), and Peter Hebblethwaite's *The Runaway Church* (1975). The latter's opening remarks, in fact, express a feeling broadly common to all:

> The Council set in motion a process which, once started, the official Church was powerless to halt. [...] Ten years on, it is still not easy to say exactly what happened. The only point of general agreement is that nothing could ever be the same afterwards. Indeed, the very terms 'pre-conciliar' and 'post-conciliar' came to express not simply a difference in chronology, but a difference of attitude, outlook and basic convictions so deep that it seemed the two could never meet or be reconciled.
>
> (1975: 7, 9)

The 1970s and 1980s, to which our tale here turns, are largely defined by the outworkings and aftershocks of events and trends already described in connection with earlier decades. These were the years in which the Baby Boomers started to settle down, get married, and start families—if typically later, further away from extended family, with fewer children, and less strongly rooted in a specific career or community, than their own parents did. These are all factors with feasibly negative impacts on religiosity.[1] The decline of traditional Catholic neighbourhoods, whether by erosion—via

---

[1] 'Religious involvement is influenced more by whether people are married, when they get married, whether they have children, and how many children they have than almost anything else. Religious involvement is also shaped by how committed people are to their careers and to their communities' (Wuthnow 2007: 17).

suburbanization, social mobility, and economic migration of various kinds—or being actively broken up through urban regeneration, continued well into this period (cf. Marty 2006). This process has already been narrated in Chapter 4. But it was further accelerated with the waning fortunes of industries such as coalmining, textiles, shipbuilding, car-manufacturing, and steel working. These were the very reasons why earlier generations of Catholics had flocked to cities like Pittsburgh, Glasgow, Cleveland, Manchester, Chicago, and Sheffield in the first place. The new suburban parishes could, it is true, be dynamic Christian communities in their own right: no doubt many American readers, especially, will have encountered such examples. Nevertheless, when compared to the old neighbour-hood churches they were supplanting, the fighting was all uphill. As noted in a big Notre Dame study of 'the U.S. parish twenty years after Vatican II', for example:

> Catholics in suburban parishes report feeling far less attached to their parishes than do Catholics in rural areas, inner cities, and small towns respectively. The suburbanites have fewer 'closest friends' from their own parishes and report fewer conversations with fellow parishioners. Suburban Catholics feel their parishes are slightly less likely to meet their spiritual needs and substantially less likely to meet their social needs than do Catholics in other types of parishes.
>
> (Leege and Gremillion 1984: 12)

Incidentally, the same processes have been observed among America's Jews in this period, with analogous effects on Jewish practice and identity (Waxman 2001: 116–17; Marty 2006).

In America, the downsizing of traditional parishes trend dovetailed nicely with a new impetus towards ethnic integration. The web of 'national parishes' and 'missions' that were, earlier in the twentieth century, so large a feature of many cities were gradually merged into existing territorial parishes (Bruce 2017: 36–7). There is no doubt that this spirit of ecclesial *e pluribus unum* was genuinely felt. But however well-meant, the logistical expedience of combining parishes in light of declining numbers of both clergy and practising Catholics, especially in the North East and Midwest, should not be overlooked. One decent-sized township along the Ohio/Pennsylvania border, for instance, had five Latin-rite parishes (territorial, German, Italian, and two Polish) in 1972 with a combined Sunday Mass attendance of around 6000. By the time all five became a single 'super parish' in the early 1990s, it was down to 3200. Today, it is a little under 1000.[2] Meanwhile, the Archdiocese of Boston closed forty-five parishes between 1985 and 2003, half of which were ethnic ones. The suppression of a further eighty-two was announced in 2004, almost a quarter of the Archdiocese's total parishes, although—as we shall see in the next chapter—Boston's problems were by then far from being purely demographic (Seitz 2011: 3). Other factors came into play elsewhere in the country: further proof of American Catholic regionality. By the turn of the 1970s, the separate black parishes in cities like Atlanta or New Orleans were manifestly not in keeping with the spirit of the times. Things were, though, rather complicated by their often being cherished by African-American Catholics themselves. The fact that it was always the black churches, schools, and colleges, however thriving, being merged into the *de facto* white infrastructure, did not go unnoticed (Alberts 1998: 378–9; Moore 2018: 140–7).[3]

Class was also an issue. Several commentators have pointed out that many of the postconciliar developments tended to appeal more to those in the new, rising middle classes (Archer 1986: 126–46). More physical and material ways of practising one's faith, such as lighting candles or (the *bête noir* of liturgical progressives) praying the rosary during Mass, were increasingly replaced by the verbal and cerebral. Composing the bidding prayers, participating in Bible studies, attending liturgical workshops, setting up a Slant Circle, even extemporizing prayers at a charismatic worship service: all require a certain amount of literate self-confidence. But this shift was not purely a liturgical and devotional one. Empowering the People of God through 'the full participation of lay people at all levels in the life of the Church' (Hornsby-Smith 1991: 8) often meant, in practice, finding people

---

[2] I am grateful to my good friend, the pastor of the aforementioned 'super parish', for this data. He is thanked by name elsewhere in these pages.

[3] Traffic was not, however, all one way. Even as a great many of the nation's traditional national parishes were disappearing, new extra-territorial parishes and missions began springing up for the pastoral care of diverse groups (see Bruce 2017). As on the old model, these were typically ethnic in nature: from the Archdiocese of Phoenix's multiple Native American missions, to the Vietnamese and Korean parishes common throughout California, Oregon, Washington, and Texas. Others cater to different kinds of 'niche' groups. In 1984 the Archdiocese of Houston erected a personal parish for former Episcopalians and others, with Vatican permission to use an Anglican-inspired version of the liturgy. Thirty years later the (as I can personally attest) thriving Church of Our Lady of Walsingham, now under the auspices of the Ordinariate of the Chair of St Peter, was consecrated as a Cathedral.

who liked committees: parish councils, liturgy committees, Justice and Peace Commissions. This too, it seems, appealed primarily to the educated middle classes. This was all the truer at the national level, as with England and Wales' National Pastoral Congress held in Liverpool in 1980. This 'initiative in shared responsibility', while undoubtedly 'an extraordinary experience of what the Church is and a foretaste of what it can grow to be' for some its participants (Bishops' Conference of England and Wales 1980: 34, 1; cf. Hornsby-Smith 2010: 155), also served to entrench the influence of middle-class elites (Eade 2002). Appealing to the middle classes is not, of course, a bad thing in itself, especially at a time when this demographic was growing among British and American Catholics. As a 1970s Newman might well have pointed out, 'Surbiton people have souls'. However, this often came at the expense of the poorer and less educated segments of the community. The demise of religious practice among at least the 'native' white working classes—intersectional effects admittedly complicate this generalization among blacks, Latinos, and some groups of white recent immigrants—has been a fact of life for many Christian denominations (Wilcox et al. 2012; Jones 2016; Charlesworth and Williams 2017). But for a denomination whose traditional heartland parishes were built up, often literally so, out of the piety and sacrifice of the white working classes, this could be near catastrophic.

In common with its own forebears, this chapter will concentrate on a select number of topics. Given the relationship between lapsation and disaffiliation, we will first dig into what is arguably this era's signature style: ever-declining Mass attendance. Excitingly for all concerned, this will necessitate a return to the kind of statistical analyses used in Chapter 2. We will also discuss a number of theories put forward, then and since, to explain (or excuse) the clear patterns that emerge. Our attention will then turn to the children brought up in this environment—and *how* they were brought up—using several of the same theoretical ideas applied in previous chapters. In many ways, these have a claim to being the real 'Vatican II' generation, that is, those for whom the postconciliar Church was simply the way things were. Family Masses, communion under both kinds, liturgy in English (or Spanish, Polish, Tagalog, or Lakota), charismatic prayer groups, Bible studies with Evangelical or Anglican neighbours: these things were not experienced as changes for the 'better' or 'worse', improvements or deteriorations, gains or losses. They were just how things were.

What was going on within the Catholic Church is, however, only one half of the story. The whole point about disaffiliation is that people *don't* simply cease thinking of themselves as 'Catholics'. Rather, they start thinking of themselves as something else: either a different kind of Christian or other religious label, or as being a person of no religion at all. The steadily rising tide of Catholic disaffiliation over these decades has, then, a good deal to do with the relative attractiveness of other identities. It is necessary, therefore, to give some consideration in this chapter to two trends: a large proportion of cradle Catholics 'switching' to other denominations, and a large proportion of them 'leaving' religious affiliation altogether. The former is, far and away, much more of an American trend than it ever has been a British one. The latter has, for many decades, been the default setting for British Catholic disaffiliates: it is only comparatively recently (recently enough to be a topic of the next chapter, and not this one) that American cradle Catholics have similarly 'nonverted' in appreciable numbers.

Finally, one topic that is hugely significant to Catholic disaffiliation, closely associated with these decades though by no means confined to them, is not covered in this chapter. Many instances of horrific abuse, perpetrated by Catholic clergy, religious, and lay staff, and subsequently ignored, denied, and/or criminally covered up by others in the Church, have since come to light. Were this a chapter a general history of British and American Catholic life in the 1970s and 1980s, then attention would need to be given to these crimes here. But insofar as these scandals have impacted upon large-scale Catholic disaffiliation—and I will be arguing in due course that they have indeed had a powerful, though subtle, role—this influence primarily occurred beginning in the early 1990s, before exploding in the early 2000s. They are, then, topics for the following chapter.

'THE RESULTS HAVE BEEN QUITE DIFFERENT FROM THOSE ANTICIPATED'

The above quotation comes from a 1976 issue of the official newspaper of the Archdiocese of Hartford, Connecticut. It paraphrases Archbishop Whealon's assessment of the introduction of Vigil

Masses on Saturday evenings, to aid those working on Sundays to fulfil their Mass obligation. Whealon comments: 'I have not seen any increase in Sunday Mass participation as a result of this permission' (Catholic Transcript 1976a). The phrase could easily be the slogan of the entire liturgical reform, at least when considered at the level of overall national trends.

There are two main ways of gauging levels of Mass attendance. The first and most obvious way is simply to turn up in churches on a given Sunday (including the preceding Saturday vigil), and do head-counts at each Mass. If the same is done at every church in a diocese or country, then one can simply add them together to get the total Mass count. By tradition, October is the month regarded as most 'normal' for these purposes. To reduce the possibility of a 'funny week' skewing the figures—torrential rain, say, or a job-lot baptism—parishes often do their counts on all Sundays in the month, and give the average. The second main way is to use a nationally representative survey, which asks people how often they attend religious services connected with their religion, apart from various types of special occasions, and isolate the Catholic subsample.[4] Neither method is, in the postlapsarian *lacrimarum valle* inhabited by social scientists, remotely perfect. But if interpreted impressionistically—that is, as reliably indicating general *trends* over a period of time—they nonetheless reveal a good deal.

In practice, 'head-count' statistics are not always easy to come by. Not all dioceses collect the data, and of those that do, few have records going beyond a decade or two. For instance, even so large and well-resourced an archdiocese as Chicago only began systematic counts in 1987. Not every diocese, moreover, is willing to publicize even those numbers it does have. The Appendix includes annual Mass attendance figures from England and Wales, Scotland, and thirty American (arch) dioceses for which I have been able to acquire—via various means—at least two separate years' data. While there are many gaps in this dataset, the overwhelming pattern is not hard to discern: only two columns out of the thirty-two show an increase from the earliest to the latest year recorded. Unfortunately, there are only two near-complete data series

---

[4] There are several other ways of gauging religious attendance using surveys—asking people if they attended a religious service in the previous seven days or asking people to list what they did the previous weekend—but this is the simplest and by far the most commonly used.

going back before the Council: England and Wales, and the Diocese of Columbus, Ohio. Both show gradually increasing Mass attendance from the late 1950s, before peaking in 1965. Thereafter, the story is one of almost year-on-year decrease: in England and Wales, only three years represent a gain on the previously recorded year (1975, 2002, 2008); in Columbus, there are thirteen such 'growth years' out of the fifty-two between 1966 and 2017.

Figure 6.1 represents the two data series in terms of each year's percentage difference from 1960. This shows similar rates of decline from 1965 until the early 1980s. In England and Wales, this rate of decline has continued fairly steadily down to the present day, albeit with a slight shallowing out since the turn of the millennium. Absolute decline also continued in Columbus, but at a slower rate until the early 2000s (see next chapter) when the rate of decline sharpens again.

Let us turn now to our national surveys. As noted in Chapter 2, the American GSS began in 1972, but started asking about religious upbringing from 1973. The BSA added an attendance question in 1990, and an upbringing one in 1991. This means that we only have attendance data for current Catholics from 1972 and 1990, and for cradle Catholics from 1973 and 1991, respectively.

Figure 6.2 shows the proportions of *current* Catholics (solid lines) who said that they attended Mass at least weekly in Britain (grey) and

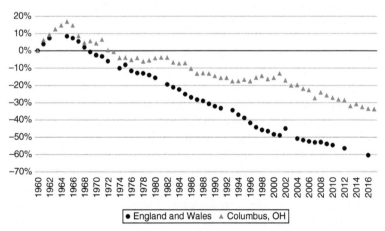

Figure 6.1. Annual 'typical Sunday' Mass attendance, depicted as % difference from 1960 level, in England and Wales, and the Diocese of Columbus, Ohio

Source: Official diocesan statistics (see Appendix)

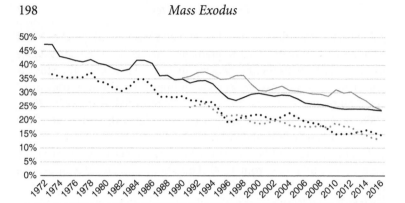

Figure 6.2. Proportions of weekly-or-more Mass attenders among all those brought up Catholic, and all those currently identifying as Catholic, in Britain and America, by year

Source: GSS (1972–2016; weighted and smoothed data) and BSA (1991–2016; weighted and smoothed data)

America (black), in each year for which we have data. (For ease of interpretation, each 'year' is in fact a rolling average of it and the years immediately adjacent to it. This allows the 'noise' of individual years to be smoothed out, to show overall trends more clearly.) It likewise shows the proportions of all *cradle* Catholics (dotted lines) who say they attended Mass at least weekly in Britain (grey) and America (black), in those years for which we have data.

As one might expect from the previous graph, the proportion of weekly-or-more Mass attenders has decreased in both Britain and America. And this holds true among both current Catholics and cradle Catholics. What we also see here is the impact that high levels of disaffiliation might have in 'inflating' the figures for weekly Mass-goers. That is to say, cradle Catholics who don't practise regularly but who still identify as Catholic 'dilute' the proportion of regular practisers in the current Catholic pool. But when they cease ticking the Catholic box on surveys, then they remove themselves from the Catholic pool—in effect, 'concentrating' the proportion of regular practisers who remain. Paradoxically, therefore, growing levels of disaffiliation could theoretically make the *percentage* of practising Catholics go up, even if the actual numbers either remain the same or possibly decline (as long as the rate of decline is slower than the rate of disaffiliation). This is an instance of what is sometimes called 'survivorship bias'. This typically applies to situations where the apparent success of a group is inflated by the removal of the least successful instances from consideration.[5]

This effect can have a significant influence. In America in the early 1970s, around 47 per cent of self-identified Catholics said they attended church at least weekly, whereas by 2016 the figure was 24 per cent. Focusing only on cradle Catholics, however, the proportion of weekly Mass-goers goes from 37 per cent in the early 1970s, down to 15 per cent by 2016: a big difference. In Britain, we only have comparable data from 1990/1 to work with. For current Catholics, this goes from 35 per cent attending Mass weekly then, down to 24 per cent in 2016. Meanwhile among cradle Catholics, it goes from 25 per cent in the early 1990s down to 13 per cent in 2016. As an aside here, it is striking just how closely the levels of weekly Mass attendance in Britain and America mirror each other.

Figures 6.3 and 6.4 show each year's relative proportions among cradle Catholics of three key categories: (i) those retaining a Catholic identity and attending Mass weekly or more; (ii) those retaining a Catholic identity but 'never' attending Mass; and (iii) all those no longer retaining a Catholic identity. This therefore allows us to put the declining 'weekly Mass attenders among cradle Catholics' lines on our previous graph into their proper context.[6] Strictly speaking, fewer weekly attenders *need not* correlate with higher numbers of lapsed Catholics or outright disaffiliates. Hitherto weekly Mass-goers might simply now go three times a month, on average (cf. Morris 1997: 308). It is even possible that while strict habits of weekly Mass attendance have fallen, the overall number of Mass-goers has risen. Perhaps—as per the National Association for Laymen's lobbying that 'It would be in the best interests of Catholics and the Church [if Sunday Mass attendance] were made optional and not compulsory under pain of any kind of ecclesiastical censure or sin' (Pittsburgh Catholic 1970)— Catholics no longer fear missing a single Mass on pain of damnation,

---

[5] For example, one might measure the 'average' success rate of investing schemes by looking at only those which are still in business. The schemes which failed to 'beat the market', presumably, went bust, removing themselves from consideration. Alternatively, one might consider how the *mean* height of the people in a pub goes up each time a short person leaves, though of course nobody actually grows any.

[6] Note that the data presented in Figures 6.3 and 6.4, unlike in 6.2, have not been smoothed—hence the 'bumpiness' of the lines. This is because, in the following chapter, the ability to pinpoint individual years will become important.

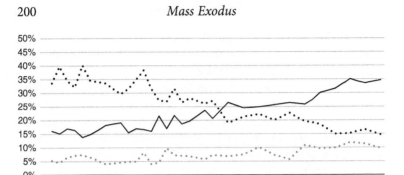

Figure 6.3. Proportions of cradle Catholics in America who are (i) weekly Mass-attending Catholics, (ii) never-attending Catholics, and (iii) disaffiliates, by year

Source: GSS (1973–2016; weighted data)

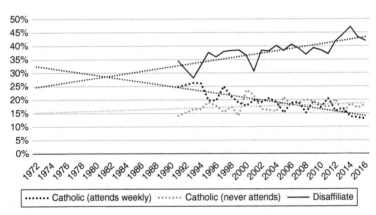

Figure 6.4. Proportions of cradle Catholics in Britain who are (i) weekly Mass-attending Catholics, (ii) never-attending Catholics, and (iii) disaffiliates, by year

Source: BSA (1991–2016; weighted data)

but much greater numbers now freely and joyfully come to Mass *almost* every week.

Alas, neither hopeful alternative is actually the case. As is clear from Figure 6.3, as weekly Mass-going among American cradle Catholics steadily declined from the early 1970s, the proportions of both disaffiliates and what one might call the 'totally lapsed' (i.e., still identifying, but never attending Mass) kept rising. In 1973, weekly Mass-goers (37 per cent) outnumbered disaffiliates (16 per cent) among US cradle Catholics by a rough ratio of five to two. By 1995, the proportions were about equal, at 23 per cent and 24 per cent respectively. By 2016, it was disaffiliates (35 per cent) who now outnumbered weekly Mass-goers (14 per cent) by a ratio of five to two. Importantly, the rise in disaffiliation cannot, as it sometimes is, simply be ascribed to previous years' lapsed Catholics now being more likely to identify as non-Catholics. Of course, that is true so far as it goes: todays disaffiliates *are*, in many cases, the non-practisers of previous years. But note that the proportion of non-practisers hasn't decreased over our period. Rather, it too has grown, albeit at a slower rate than the disaffiliates. Even as many lapsed Catholics come—no doubt gradually—to be disaffiliates, the lapsed pool is being continually refilled. This could plausibly come about *either* (i) by more regularly practising Catholics becoming less so, *or* (ii) by younger generations of cradle Catholics reaching adulthood, and hence inclusion in the data, already non-practising. Over the whole 40+ year span of our GSS data, both mechanisms have surely been important contributors, with—I suspect—(i) the stronger in the earlier years, and (ii) becoming more and more significant as time has gone on.

Figure 6.4's British data, only going back as far as the early 1990s (though the x-axis starts at 1972, to allow easier comparison with Figure 6.3), are less immediately arresting. There is, for example, no dramatic 'cross-over point' between weekly-attenders and disaffiliates in the mid-1990s, as we saw on the last graph. But this is simply because, as suggested by the backwards-extrapolating trendlines, that the cross-over happened much earlier in Britain.[7] Over the entire quarter-century covered here, there have been at least twice as many disaffiliates as weekly Mass-attenders among Britain's cradle Catholics. Since 2012 moreover, British cradle Catholics are three times more likely no longer to identify as a Catholic as they are to be a weekly Mass-goer. And once again, this is not due to a simple replacement of non-practisers with disaffiliates, for the proportion of 'never' attenders has also increased, if only very slightly.

---

[7] For example, if the overall (i.e., straight-line) trends of the data we do have are simply continued backwards, the cross-over year is 1982.

The statistical picture painted above is decidedly bleak. But by quantifying the sheer extent, in terms of both numbers and time, of the phenomenon of Catholic disaffiliation, these figures—and the patterns connecting them—are critical clues in our attempt to explain it. What then are we to make of them?

To put it mildly, they are scarcely a ringing endorsement of the liturgical reforms, at least as these were concretely applied in Britain and America. 'Vernacular Sunday' at the start of Advent 1964 precipitated a period of near-constant change. This touched almost every aspect of Sunday Mass, from the wording of the liturgical texts themselves, to the architectural environment in which they were said, to—as noted above—what day of the week Sunday actually began on. That this coincided, more-or-less exactly, with falling Sunday Mass attendance, as measured by both actual Mass counts, and the self-reported practice of Catholics themselves; that these declines have increased consistently, almost year on year, as also have the proportions of born-and-raised Catholics who never attend Mass, and/or no longer identify as Catholics; and that these downward trends have continued for fifty years, with no signs yet of abating... such brute facts cannot be denied, even if they are frequently ignored.

They also cannot simply be dismissed as a case of the '*post hoc, ergo propter hoc*' fallacy. To suppose that the liturgical reforms have had no discernible effect on the participation of Catholics in those liturgies—or to argue, even if implicitly, that changes to the manner in which the faithful worship have negligible impact on their real-life religious beliefs, practices, and identities—is to reject the foundational premise of the liturgical reforms. *Sacrosanctum Concilium* explicitly justifies 'reform and promotion of the liturgy' on the basis of the Council's own aims to 'impart an ever increasing vigor to the Christian life of the faithful', 'to adapt more suitably to the needs of our own times', and 'to strengthen whatever can help to call the whole of mankind into the household of the Church' (*SC* 1).

This is by no means to deny the role of a whole host of wider factors, in all manner of possible combinations, in contributing to the kinds of statistical trends we have been considering. That is, of course, why so much of this book has been given over to wider social, cultural, and economic trends in both our countries—a great many of which *also* impacted upon the vitality of other religious groups in this period. One cannot understand Catholic, Anglican, Presbyterian, or Methodist lapsation and disaffiliation, from the 1960s onwards, without grasping the concatenation of such disparate things as social mixing during the War, the rise of the suburbs and the higher education boom, changing patterns of both car and television ownership, the sexual revolution and its continuing repercussions. But—and this is a very big but—the Second Vatican Council's very *raison d'être* was to equip the Church to meet these things, to enable it to 'keep up to date with the changing conditions of this modern world, and of modern living' (John XXIII 1962). The liturgical reform was, moreover, the Council's flagship programme. Its whole point, that is, was to imbue the Church's liturgical rites with 'new vigor to meet the circumstances and needs of modern times' (*SC* 4), to ensure that they may be 'pastorally efficacious to the fullest degree' (SC 49). But if 'the full and active participation by all the people [*totius populi*] is the aim to be considered before all else' (SC 14), what are we to make of the ever-growing percentage of baptized Catholics who rarely, if ever, participate at all?

Might it be the case, though, that the liturgical reforms would indeed have succeeded—indeed that they were already demonstrably *succeeding*—but that this was catastrophically derailed by the release of *Humanae Vitae*? This contention, common though it is, is hard to sustain. As is evident from Figure 6.1, overall Mass attendance had already been falling (at least across England and Wales, and in Columbus, Ohio) for two years—1966 and 1967—before the encyclical. There is no evidence of a 'short, sharp fall' in Mass attendance in 1968 (that year's October count being taken within three months of the encyclical's appearance) or the years immediately following, beyond the declining trend already begun, and due to continue steadily for many years after (see also Clements 2017). As detailed in the last chapter, there are indeed strong reasons for thinking that *Humanae Vitae* and its fallout were notable contributors to the overall trend towards falling attendance and weakening identity. But if it did add fuel to the flames, then it did so gradually, and to a fire already burning. Judging by the evidence here at least, there appears to have been no sudden flare-up.

True, opinion polls from this era suggest that the laity were broadly content with the changes. This wasn't, however, wholly unanimous. By 1979, for instance, around 60 per cent of English and Welsh Catholics, and 70 per cent of Scottish ones, said they approved of

'Mass in English instead of Latin' and 'the "handshake of peace" at Mass'. Only 46 per cent in England and Wales, and 62 per cent in Scotland, felt that 'Recent changes in the Church' were 'about right', though some undoubtedly thought they had not gone far enough (Hornsby-Smith 1980: 62). In America, two-thirds felt that 'the changes' had been for the better, compared to one-fifth who thought they were for the worse (Greeley et al. 1976: 29). In both countries, though, such polls were directed only to those currently identifying as Catholics. Anyone sufficiently unhappy with changes to be among the growing ranks of former Catholics, therefore, were *ipso facto* excluded: a clear case of survivorship bias. The same polls, moreover, found that despite general approval of the reforms, actual Mass-going was down. The reforms had, it would seem, served to make the Mass more enjoyable but less *compelling*. Constant attempts were made to cure the problem of ever-declining Mass attendance. The introduction of 'Sunday' Masses on Saturday evenings was just one. In 1975, the bishops of Ohio distributed a million leaflets emphasizing the importance of going to Mass on Sundays (Catholic Transcript 1975). The following year, Bishop Curtis of Bridgeport, Connecticut, issued a letter to be read out at all Sunday Masses urging Sunday observance—a case of preaching to the converted, one presumes, in the hopes of keeping them so (Catholic Transcript 1976b). Nothing, however, seemed to work.

THE NEXT GENERATION

A major theme of recent scholarship on religious change has been the importance of generational effects (see Putnam and Campbell 2010: 27–80). Cohorts born in different decades tend, for all sorts of reasons, to have distinctive religious profiles. Within these cohorts there is naturally a huge amount of variation, and each has its shares of the hyper-religious, the militantly anti-religious, the wholly indifferent, and all possible points in between. But the relative shares of each tend to average out differently. This is something we have seen several times already. In Chapter 2, for instance, differing profiles in terms of affiliation/attendance were shown for cradle Catholics born in different decadal cohorts (see Figure 2.3). And of course, the previous chapters' focus on the differences between the Baby Boomers and their parents' generations, and how the latter's generational distinctiveness arguably laid much of the groundwork for the former's, is another instance of this.

Evidently, the children brought up in the late 1960s, 1970s, and 1980s were formed in very different milieux to those of their parents—and at a further generational remove from the old-time religion of their grandparents' generation. Few cradle-Catholic Generation X-ers (as those born between 1965 and 1985 are sometimes termed) or early Millennials would reach adulthood with fond reminiscences of accompanying their working-class fathers to *Quarant'Ore* devotions in the dead of night. Judging by the above statistics, a significant proportion likely grew up with no reminiscences, fond or otherwise, of accompanying their fathers to church for any reason. For this new generation, moreover, the excitements and/or disappointments of the 'Catholic Sixties' were as much a thing of the past as their parents' Melanie LPs.

Given the significance of religious practice during one's upbringing as a predictor of adult religiosity, it is worth noting here again the 'CRED depleted' (cf. Turpin 2018: 312–18) world in which these children of the Council were raised. The swift collapse of traditional devotional practices (later claimed in influential quarters as proof of the reforms' *success*—e.g., McBrien 2003) meant that, whether in school or at home, the frequency with which children were exposed to regular rosary, pilgrimages, novenas, and the like, was significantly reduced. The same, of course, was true of abstaining from meat on Fridays and going to Confession (or accompanying one's parents and waiting quietly outside). Inspired by his own upbringing in late 1960s and 1970s Chicago, Bishop Robert Barron famously coined the term 'beige Catholicism'. He elaborates:

> It seemed to be an overriding concern of the teachers, nuns, and priests who formed my generation to make our Catholicism as non-threatening, accessible, culturally appealing, as possible. [. . .] It seemed as though the project was to 'translate' uniquely Catholic doctrine, practice, and style into forms acceptable to the environing culture, always downplaying whatever might be construed as "odd" or "supernatural". [. . .] When I attended the twenty-fifth reunion of my eighth-grade graduating class, we reminisced about the 'banners and collages,' which were the decidedly non-doctrinal staple of our religion classes and which for most of us effectively symbolized our Catholic youth.
>
> (2004: 17)

Barron's experiences were by no means uncommon. Another American late-Boomer, born in 1960 and hence 'part of the first generation of Catholics who would have no memory of the Church prior to Vatican II', Francis Beckwith recalls his formative years in late 1960s and 1970s Las Vegas. In a section aptly titled 'Leaving the Catholic Church', he remembers 'a time in which well-meaning Catholic leaders were testing all sorts of innovations in the church, many of which were deleterious to the proper formation of young people':

> The way Mass was conducted in many parishes seemed to trivialize the liturgy of the Eucharist in such a way that its significance was diminished. Some parishes removed their kneelers, crucifixes, and statues. Newly built church buildings were constructed with modernist architectural designs. Thus, when you walked into some churches, you had an immediate sense of minimalism and spiritual barrenness, and not the majesty of God. The Blessed Sacrament was nowhere to be found. And if you were lucky, there would be a confessional, but it was rarely used. (2009: 34–5)

Due to reasons already considered, the close-knit Catholic subcultures of the 1940s and 1950s were, even then, already in the process of breaking down—along with the plausibility structures they had for so long undergirded. This process would have continued into the 1970s and 1980s regardless. Even had there been no Council, no Pittsburghian child could now grow up 'thinking the whole world was Polish', as they might still have done thirty or forty years earlier (Herguth 2016: chap. 24). But the various external pushes and pulls were substantially helped along by Catholics themselves, often intentionally. So much of what had made Catholics *different*, to both outsiders and themselves, was determinedly stripped away. The strange Catholic world 'somewhere between science and superstition'—one of spiritual warfare, holy water with supernatural properties, incantations referencing 'the blood of the martyrs', and priests and demons bantering in Latin—was already essentially an exercise in nostalgia by 1974, when it helped make *The Exorcist* a US box office hit. Remarking on Catholics' erstwhile status as 'Britain's Largest Minority', Dennis Sewell observes that 'Their recent past was repudiated as too defensive or triumphalist and they were encouraged to submerge their Catholic identity in an ecumenical anonymity, to become more a flavour than a brand' (2001: 253). This was, in effect, assimilation in the name of inculturation. Not only were Catholics now 'like everyone else', they had somehow convinced themselves that this was necessary to being more authentically Catholic. Furthermore, they became like everyone else at *precisely* the moment that 'everyone else' was starting to shift, more swiftly in Britain than in America, decisively away from traditional Christian moral and doctrinal norms. Thus, in the words of Peter Berger:

> The Second Vatican Council was supposed to open the windows, specifically the windows of the Catholic subculture that had been constructed [...] The trouble with opening windows is that you can't control what comes in, a lot has come in—indeed, the whole turbulent world of modern culture.   (1999: 5)

Education was one area where the erosion of Catholicity became increasingly evident. Catholic schools had for decades played a critical role, in partnership with the home and parish church, in expressing and transmitting Catholic identity. Differences in administrative models on each side of the Atlantic make direct comparisons awkward.[8] Nevertheless, the importance given to Catholic schooling in both is not in dispute. We saw earlier how church and school construction often went hand-in-hand, with the latter often built first, serving as an interim Mass venue until the former was completed. The large numbers of priests, nuns, and lay brothers who left their vocations in the decades following the Council hit this sector hard. Low rates of vocations, especially to women's religious orders, throughout the ensuing decades have compounded this issue. Arguably, this has produced a vicious circle. With fewer and fewer priests and nuns available to be deployed, and those remaining being on-average older than they used to be, the chances of students being inspired by a particular teacher or chaplain to discern a vocation for themselves decreases. This is especially so in America, where a much greater share of teaching in parish schools has traditionally been done by priests and especially nuns (Morris 1997: 315–19; Steinfels 2003: 211–19). A number of British schools run by religious orders, thus hitherto heavily staffed 'in house', have also either closed or are now staffed almost exclusively by laypeople.

---

[8] In very simple terms, whereas American Catholic schools are all private, in Britain there exists both an extensive network of Catholic schools within the state education system (i.e., 'public schools' in US parlance) which do not charge fees, as well as a significant number of (in some cases, highly prestigious) private, Catholic schools.

Other developments were also afoot. In 1980, Vincent McLelland, Professor of Education at the University of Hull, observed regarding British Catholic schools:

> Time-honoured religious observances within the daily routine of school organizations have been designated 'mawkish' and abandoned as conflicting with notions of 'religious freedom' and 'personal maturity'. [. . .] In recent years, together with widespread abandonment of traditional prayerful practices punctuating the various secular activities of the school day, there has emerged a distinct tension in the mode of presentation of dogmatic truth.   (1980: 110–11)

Staples of earlier Catholic schooling—the rosary, the noon Angelus, grace before meals—were, as elsewhere, abandoned as outmoded. Writing in the mid-1980s, Dominican sociologist Anthony Archer repeats the following, from one of his interviewees in north-east England:

> When we went to Ireland for a holiday, there were statues of Our Lady all over the place. 'Who's that woman standing there?' (asked the children). I thought, my goodness, ee, I was absolutely ashamed of them. And they went to the Catholic school.   (1986: 157)

Meanwhile, a combination of confusion as to what, post-Vatican II, the Catholic Church actually now taught, and new pedagogical trends downplaying the importance of learning 'facts' presented by an 'authority', were seriously disruptive to both Catholic religious education and sacramental catechesis (Welsh 2012: 211–60; Franchi 2016: 73–87). Rote learning from the *Penny* or *Baltimore Catechism* was, naturally, out. But it was not until 1992 that the Vatican issued an updated *Catechism*, incorporating the teachings of Vatican II with all that had gone before. In the meantime, a generation or more of Catholic pupils and catechumens were at the mercy of both experimental teaching methods, and—at least sometimes—still more experimental theological speculation (see Ratzinger [1983] 2006: 13–17; Steinfels 2003: 206–8). Summing up these trends, Christian Smith and his colleagues remark understatedly: 'it is not clear that ongoing effective catechesis of the young was among the results of the reforms' (2014: 15).

The Catholic side of things is, however, only one half of the story—and perhaps, as time went on, only a third, quarter, or tenth of it. Those brought up in this period were not merely socialized, however partially or temporarily in many cases, into Catholicism, but into a wider society increasingly at odds with it in significant areas (see Wuthnow 2007: 136–56; Regnerus 2007). Surveys consistently show, for example, that large numbers of even practising Catholics disagree with key areas of Church teaching, not least on a cluster of marriage, sex, and family issues. This is, not implausibly given the above, sometimes attributed to inadequate catechesis. But that cannot be the sole explanation. For irrespective of what and how one was taught in one's RE or CCD classes, it is nonetheless true that the wider culture exerts its own influences, in thousands of subtle ways. A plausibility structure that consists primarily of a few perfunctory lessons during high school plus perhaps—though by no means guaranteed—the odd remark heard during a homily and parental reinforcement at home will understandably struggle in competition with a plausibility structure consisting of the prevailing consensus, explicit or implicit, of one's friends, extended family, plus favourite magazines, books, song lyrics, films, adverts, and sitcom characters.

In this connection, it is striking how often even those brought up in committed Catholic homes, and who still practise themselves, describe their identities in terms of opposition and conflictedness. This is evident, for example, in an absorbing anthology of 'twenty-nine memoirs about being Catholic and young and a woman written by authors born in the 1970s and 1980s' published a decade ago. The editors, themselves firmly in this demographic, note 'a theme we noticed in many memoirs—a tension between being Catholic and being a woman in the twenty-first century United States' (Dugan and Owens 2009: xxi). The contributors themselves variously speak in terms of 'a choice between staying true to myself and surrendering to the mandates of a communal identity [. . .] that larger struggle to be both Catholic and a modern American [. . .] the push and pull of living in two worlds, two times, and two histories' (Campbell 2009: 14); of 'simultaneously lov[ing] and loath[ing] my church' (Scanlon 2009: 95); of groups 'struggl[ing] to reconcile their identities with the church's imperatives' (Coblentz 2009: 120); and of 'Figuring out how to hold the tension between the institution's gender norms and our twenty-first century expectations of being a woman' (Dugan and Owens 2009: 91). Different authors trace such 'excruciating frustration with my faith tradition' (Bischoff 2009: 156) to different sources. But broadly speaking, all concern normative Catholicism's dissonance vis-à-vis one or more taken-for-granted aspects of being a 'modern American woman': gender equality (i.e., vs. the non-ordination of women), contraception, abortion, and/or LGBT rights. These are, note well, young women whose commitment to Catholic identity is sufficiently ingrained or cherished for them to find some way of negotiating its accommodation alongside, and despite its dissonance with, other core aspects of their sense of self. This is by no means easy:

> At times, I've been so angry I've wanted to leave the church altogether, and sometimes I even have. But I can never stay away for long—I always feel pulled back to the church that helped raise and form me, the way we feel drawn back to our families, even after a bitter fight.
>
> (Averett 2009: 144)

It is not every young Catholic woman who has the energy, patience, or investment to keep up the fight.

This fundamental point is not exclusive to Catholic women, American or otherwise. To give another example, the English journalist Mark Dowd writes movingly of his own experiences of 'trying to hold together the potentially uncomfortable bedfellows of Catholicism and same-sex attraction [. . .] The tectonic plates of queerdom and the Holy Roman Church nestled uneasily alongside each other' (2017: chap. 4). He notes that:

> Alas for many LGBT Catholics in the past, life has framed itself as a stark binary choice: queer *or* Catholic. Hundreds of thousands have abandoned the faith of their upbringing on account of Church teaching on LGBT issues, and its description of homosexuality as an 'objective disorder'. I have been near to throwing in the towel myself at times, but something—or Someone—has always called me back from the brink.
>
> (2017: chap. 10)

As is clear from Chapter 3, Dowd's 'tectonic plates' metaphor could be adapted to include any number of ways of thinking or being, which have become socially acceptable or even celebrated over the past several decades, but which—to say the very least—'nestle uneasily alongside' Catholicism (see Dillon 1999). This is again abundantly clear from the testimonies drawn upon in Chapter 3. Even where, say, Church teaching on divorce, or sex outside marriage, or same-sex relationships, or contraception, or abortion, or IVF, or stem-cell research were not, in themselves, the trigger for lapsation or disaffiliation, they are still areas where the Church is widely held to be in error. Increasingly, the normative Catholic view on these questions is towards the periphery, if not indeed well outside, of the 'Overton window' of British and American society as a whole. For those more-or-less thoroughly socialized into those societies, it is therefore very difficult to embrace 'the Catholic package' with an unqualifiedly whole heart.

Naturally, this is not necessarily the experience of all Catholics brought up in these decades. There are undoubtedly those, where they do perceive a disjunction between contemporary mores and Catholic teaching, have gratefully opted for the latter. But such an option is, and increasingly has to be, a consciously countercultural one: precisely the opposite of being naturally taken-for-granted as the way things are (Dreher 2017: 7–20). More to the point, probably a far larger proportion do not have any existentially troubling sense of 'living in two worlds'. This is because, for all intents and purposes, they don't and quite likely never did. Indeed, it is striking just how *Catholic* the upbringings of those quoted above were (in Dowd's case, sufficiently strong for him to try out a vocation to the Dominicans). Even in the 1970s, and certainly by the 1980s, this CREDs-rich world of rosaries, grace before dinner, bedtime prayers, pictures of popes (and Kennedys) on Irish grandmothers' walls, was already fading. With each passing year, the proportion of baptized Catholics whose upbringing has impressed upon them a 'distinct Catholic birthmark [as] an inescapable part of the identities' (Dugan and Owens 2009: 1), indelibly instilling Catholicism into 'my blood and bones and sinews and inner world, despite what seemed like my best efforts to keep it out' (Campbell 2009), has undoubtedly shrunk. For the very most part, Catholics, certain groups of first- and second-generation immigrants notwithstanding, no longer 'grew up different' (Wills 1972: 15).

'TO WHOM WOULD WE GO?'

The growing proportions of Catholic disaffiliates, clearly evidenced in Figsures 6.2–6.3, prompt an obvious question. If they no longer identified as Catholics, then what were they now identifying as instead—and why?

So far in this book, the broad contours of Catholic disaffiliation have been traced in a loosely parallel way between Britain and America. That is, without downplaying the clear differences of context and detail, one can tell a reasonably coherent narrative of how the same or similar factors (of many different kinds) have had the same or similar effects upon the strength of Catholic identity and practice over our chosen period. At this point, however, we must note a serious point of divergence. As noted in Chapter 2, among the most striking differences between today's British and American disaffiliates are the relative proportions of switchers (i.e., those who have adopted a different religious identity) and leavers (i.e., those who now identify with no religious identity). Whereas in Britain, five out of every six is a leaver, in America it is one in two (see Figure 2.1). Furthermore, this American preference for switching over leaving was even more pronounced in earlier decades. In GSS 1973, three out of every five Catholic disaffiliates divulged a new religious—and in the vast majority of cases, Christian—identity. Almost two decades later in 1991, the proportion was two in three. In Britain that same year, the first for which we have comparable BSA data, leavers outnumbered switchers among Catholic disaffiliates by a ratio of five to one: more or less the same proportion as it is today.

These differences have several explanations. The first is simply what one might call the ambient religiosity of America when compared to Britain. The relative vitality and competitiveness of the American 'religious marketplace' has long been remarked upon, though whether it is a true free market or lots of locally dominant quasi-monopolies is a point of some debate.[9] Regardless, the situation has two main knock-on effects here. The first is simply a social presumption that a normal person has, and should have, a religious affiliation. And ideally, unless one has a good reason—e.g., was raised Jewish or Muslim or, if perhaps only in certain areas of California or Oregon, found oneself while trekking in the Himalayas—that it be chosen from an admittedly long menu of recognized Christian ones. Cold War contrasts between 'Christian America', and thus American-*ness*, and 'godless Communism' undoubtedly also played a role, at least for those raised before the early 1990s (see Bullivant 2010). In some areas, particularly but not only southern ones, this assumption might be constantly reinforced at the level of normal conversation. 'What church do you go to?', a small-talk icebreaker since time out of

---

[9] We need not adjudicate on this dispute here, since even on the 'multiple monopolies' model, high geographical mobility would mean that plenty of people born in Catholic-dominant areas would end up moving to, say, Southern Baptist ones anyway (and vice versa).

mind—Weber, writing over a century ago, called it 'the inevitable question' ([1906] 2002: 204)—underlines the normativity of *having* a church, irrespective of how frequently one actually goes. The second is an increased likelihood of finding a different church sufficiently attractive to want to join (Stark 2015: chap. 10). Indeed, for many switchers the 'pull' of a new church (and the denominational identity that goes along with that) is probably a much stronger influence on disaffiliating than the 'push' of the old. Even in the Portsmouth study of non-practising Catholics, discussed in Chapter 2, a fifth of respondents agreed or strongly agreed with the statement 'I found a religion/denomination that I like more' (Bullivant et al. 2019: 25). Given the much higher rates of switching among American Catholics, the proportion there is likely to be very much higher.

It is no coincidence that, as Catholic and mainline Protestant congregations were steadily declining, a new breed of church was on the rise: the Evangelical megachurch. From the mid-1970s, huge new church plants started springing up in the suburbs of major conurbations. Typically built around a large auditorium-style 'worship space' with row upon row of (comfortable!) seats, these sprawling campuses often featured vast parking lots, coffee-shops, bookstores, crèches, sports facilities, and all manner of other amenities. Though often disparagingly compared to shopping malls or corporate headquarters, this was in fact precisely the point. Early megachurch strategists were specifically aiming to emulate the convenience, comfort, and sheen of such upscale places, the better to tempt unchurched Baby Boomers and their own growing families (Loveland and Wheeler 2003: 114–53; Putnam and Campbell 2010: 54–69). Like malls, in fact, the new megachurches were deliberately sited outside of cities, where large plots of building land are cheap, and near major highway intersections, the easier to lure congregants from a large, dispersed catchment area. They were, in short, calculated to capitalize on the very same social shifts—suburbanization, middle-class-ization, new infrastructure, and a populace used to driving everywhere—that contributed significantly to the erosion of traditional church communities. The location of one of the first of the 'classic' megachurches, Willow Creek Community Church— 'Founded in 1975 on the basis of a door-to-door market research survey to learn why suburbanites stayed away from church' (Balmer 2014: 327)—in the north-west suburbs of Chicago, one of America's great Catholic centres, cannot go unnoticed here. Its success in attracting, or rather creating, ex-Catholics, is widely acknowledged: 'Willow Creek proudly counts among its members many disheartened, bored, and hurt Catholics' (Florian 2004: 25). It is also confirmed by the Archdiocese of Chicago's opening—'like Sears belatedly mimicking Walmart' (Putnam and Campbell 2010: 113)—of Holy Family Catholic Community, a self-described 'evangelical church in the Catholic tradition', just three miles away from Willow Creek, in the mid-1980s.

On the traditional criterion of a 2000-plus weekend attendance (*not* necessarily at the same service) there are currently over 1500 megachurches in the USA. These are mostly concentrated in the southern States, though like Willow Creek, with its typical weekend attendance of over 20,000, there are plenty of northern exceptions. Four-fifths of America's megachurches reported having grown between 2009 and 2014 (Thumma and Bird 2015: 2), during a period of declining church attendance across the country as a whole. The growth of megachurches, and more generally of the wider Evangelical milieu in which they are rooted, has come, to a large extent, at the expense of other churches. According to 2014 Pew data, one-tenth of all cradle Catholics now identify as Evangelical Protestants (Pew Research Center 2015a: 39). What is more, it is not only White suburbanites who are drawn to worship at Evangelical Protestant churches. The large, and by all accounts growing, Latino/a presence within the Evangelical subculture has long been recognized (e.g., Balmer 2014: 339–50). Less well-known are the existence of Protestant congregations catering specifically to Filipinos, most of whose worshippers still also attend Mass and identify as Catholics—though whether the next generation will, rather remains to be seen (Manalang 2018). Evangelical growth cannot, however, simply be ascribed to a canny exploitation of demographic trends. Rather, the original appeal of megachurches within the American 'religious marketplace' of the 1970s and 1980s arguably came down, paradoxically enough, to doing well that many Catholic churches were trying and, by-and-large, conspicuously failing at: *inculturation*.

As previously discussed, *Sacrosanctum Concilium* actively encouraged, at least *in partibus missionum* (which America was, with growing plausibility, treated as being) judicious customization of the liturgy in order to suit the specific cultures of the people gathered together. Hence the recognition that 'there are peoples who have their own musical traditions, and these play a great part in their religious and social life. For this reason, due importance is to be attached to their music [. . .] in adapting worship to their native genius', or indeed that 'In some places and circumstances, however, an even more radical adaptation of the liturgy is needed' (*SC* 119, 40). However, *in practice*—and referring here solely to the American (and indirectly British) situation—the dream of perfectly adapting the liturgy to the 'native genius' was impeded by two critical factors. The first, also previously discussed, is that there was no single 'vernacular culture' common to all members of a normal Catholic parish—*least of all* in terms of music. As such, the dominant 'vernacular' repertoire settled down into a strange kind of folk-lite idiom, mostly inspired by the naffer end of the 1960s Folk Revival. Without denying that some fine tunes exist within this repertoire, it expresses the 'native genius' of precisely zero 'peoples'.

Meanwhile one's local megachurch, unconstrained by a defined catchment area and thus an obligation to appeal to all within it, could tailor itself to a single demographic. Rapidly, American Evangelicalism embraced American young adults' 'own musical traditions', offering Christianized versions of the music their intended congregations were *actually* listening to (Thompson 2000: 41–86). This was, moreover, typically played by professional musicians, and in a space with the proper acoustics and equipment. Easy as it is to deride 'Christian rock' as a genre, it remains true that a decent subsection of the American population listen to it even when *not* in church: enough to support commercial Christian radio stations in every major city, and annual sales revenues in the hundreds of millions of dollars (Cusic 2009: 385–90). A Catholic young adult impressed by, say, Bob Dylan's fervently Evangelical, rock-driven gospel albums of the late 1970s and early 1980s, might understandably find the local Evangelical church, full of keen young people just like themselves, rather tempting (cf. Beckwith 2009: 28–9). For someone raised to view non-Catholic churches and Christians in a non-prejudicial light and schooled to recognize Christ's presence in the scriptures and 'gathered community' as much as, if not more so than, in the Blessed Sacrament, accepting a friend or colleague's invitation to come along one Sunday would not have felt like any big deal. Certainly, it would not have felt like being a seriously transgressive step, as it might have for their parents, and would have for their grandparents.

But if people come to Evangelical congregations for the contemporary music, ample parking, dynamic 'message', and free coffee and donuts, that is by no means the full story of why they stay. A thousands-strong congregation thronged together in a state-of-the-art auditorium for Sunday 'praise and worship', may be many people's enduring image of a thriving megachurch. However, arguably the real engine of their success lies in their 'very high level of intentional use of small groups' and 'multitude of social, recreational, and aid ministries' (Thumma and Bird 2015: 4): *dense clustering*, in the jargon of social networks. Champion Forest Baptist Church in Houston, which I visited in 2017, explicitly foregrounds its 'Adult Life Groups—small groups where we make friends, share in discussion about the Bible, and lift up one another's needs in prayer' (Champion Forest 2017). At its main campus, you can sign up for one of *seventy* such groups, on different days, and targeting different age groups, states of life (e.g., couples, singles, widowed), and language prefer-ences (English, Spanish, Portuguese, Farsi, and Vietnamese). These are in addition to various other ministries, plus a full suite of sports, music, and social groups, meeting throughout the week. Journalist Rich Benjamin recounts of his first visit to another Baptist mega-church, on the outskirts of Atlanta:

> Before I know it, I find myself welcomed into a cheerful quasi-community embarking on safe adventures: ice skating, pickup basket-ball, boardgames, lollygagging. Friday movie nights, and lunch after Bible study and church service every Sunday I'm in town.   (2009: 238)

Taken altogether, this forms a rich web of activities and meaningful interactions from Sunday to Sunday. These build up, as a growing research literature amply attests, densely-clustered social networks and consequent plausibility structures: 'Persons involved in small groups devoted to prayer, discussion, or Bible study report a greater sense of belonging, more frequent attendance, and higher rates of giving. [. . .] We find that the extent of small group involvement positively relates to commitment and participation' (Dougherty and Whitehead 2011: 91; see also Everton 2018: section 4.1).

Being a committed Evangelical, moreover, often involves dedica-tion to a wide range of other faith-related practices—tithing, mission trips, volunteering, witnessing to co-workers—with attached costs of time and expense: CREDs, in other words. On the surface, such 'new ways of being church' look very different to the kinds of traditional Catholic parishes described in Chapter 4. But the deep architecture here—i.e., precisely as a mutually-reinforcing community of religiously like-minded 'significant others', combined with high-cost 'culturally prescribed religious practices' (Smith 2018: 55–8)—is not perhaps so very different:

> Today we call them megachurches—huge institutional complexes capable of sponsoring groups and activities that embrace virtually all aspects of their congregants' lives. American Catholics had already invented megachurches a century ago and created thousands more in the decades that followed. (Steinfels 2003: 103)

Britain is not devoid of Evangelical success stories, at least some of which have parallels to the classic American cases—e.g., contemporary Christian music *done well*, catering to the needs of young people and families, a 'seven-day approach' to church life—though typically on a much smaller scale (e.g., Goodhew 2012). In the overall ambit of British religion, however, the thriving and youthful congregations of a Holy Trinity Brompton (plus satellites), Hillsong, or Audacious—to name fully 20 per cent of the country's fifteen 'official' megachurches[10]—are chiefly striking as rare exceptions to overarching Christian decline. Steadily falling levels of Catholic church-going and retention, from the mid-to-late 1960s onwards, have already been noted. Similar-looking graphs could also have been given for other measures of Catholic vitality, including baptisms, conversions, and marriages (see Latin Mass Society 2013). But Catholics are only 'Britain's largest minority' (Sewell 2001). To understand the place of religion in the wider culture (into which Catholics have, as has been detailed extensively, been substantially absorbed) one must instead look elsewhere.

Overall it is a bleak picture, bleaker even than the Catholic-specific one. To give just one concrete example: in 1950, the Church of England baptized 67 per cent of English babies; in 1960, 55 per cent; in 1970, 47 per cent; and in 1980, 36 per cent (Archbishops' Council 2011: 27). By 2016, the proportion was just 10 per cent (Research and Statistics 2017: 8). Similar tales could be told in all mainstream denominations. And while there is indeed a judicious amount of qualification and nuancing to be added—there *are* pockets of growth; expressions of (vestigial?) religiosity occasionally spring up in surprising ways; widespread nonreligiosity does not imply that a

---

[10] I.e., as listed in leading megachurchologist Warren Bird's 'World Megachurches' database' (2018), using the same definition as that cited above.

majority of Britons are thoroughgoing philosophical naturalists (cf. Davie 2014: 71–90; Lee 2015)—Callum Brown's sketch of the big picture is difficult to gainsay:

> The last quarter of the twentieth century witnessed the increasing marginalisation of religion from British public life, intellectualism and popular culture. Religion appeared to become steadily more unremarkable and less remarked upon in daily life and rhetoric. As sixties' youth grew older, their values became slowly dominant as the drift from the traditional Christian churches continued and as the new age developed as a more embedded element in secular culture. [...] The major religious trend of the period was that the Christian faithful dwindled in Britain. Church adherence fell by about 45 per cent and churchgoing by about one-third. [...] In terms of age, the haemorrhage of the young continued, sustaining the reversal of the situation in the 1950s when teenagers were amongst the most active in terms of church connection. No parts of mainland Britain were untouched by significant de-Christianisation. (2006: 278–9)

Comparing all this to what was happening in America results in two highly salient points of contrast. The first is that the socio-cultural mood music was vastly more conducive to being, and regarding oneself as being, nonreligious. The first round of the BSA, in 1983, found that 31 per cent of the British population identified with no religion. This coheres with a series of annual Gallup polls from the previous decade, which, asking a similarly worded question, consistently put the proportion of British nones in the mid-to-high-20s (Field 2017: 27). While British nonreligiosity, in its various expressions, has deep roots in both elite and working-class cultures, Brown argues persuasively for its significant social 'mainstreaming' in the 1960s, not least on university campuses (2012: 60–70). Furthermore, 'being nonreligious' mutated from primarily a matter of philosophical or political *conviction*—as for earlier nones—to much more one of doubt, uncertainty, and live-and-let-live disinterest. In essence, this opened up a viable 'cultural space' with few and low barriers to entry. Moreover, it was one which could coexist very easily with (and was, to most practical intents and purposes, indistinguishable from) an ever-vaguer, cultural sense of Catholic or Anglican or Methodist belonging. This was precisely the situation noted in Chapter 3's discussion of the Portsmouth study: a gradual, easy, imperceptible drift from irregular practice to non-practice to non-affiliation. Linda Woodhead's characterization of 'the rise of the nones' in Britain as 'a slow, unplanned and almost unnoticed revolution' (2016: 245), and in no religion having become 'the new normal' (2017: 247), is apposite. As she rightly states, this is not purely a matter of numbers, though according to BSA 2016 over half of the population do indeed now identify with no religion. Rather, referring specifically to the normality of nonreligious funerals (and, *ipso facto*, the increasing oddness of avowedly Christian ones) but making a wider point too, she notes, 'I also mean socially, culturally, and emotionally normal. I mean the point at which people feel perfectly comfortable with something and expect it' (2017: 248).

The second point is closely related to this. It is simply that, unlike in America, there weren't any new, shiny, disciple-making churches springing up on the outskirts of major cities, specifically targeting young adults and families. A twenty- or thirty-something gradually drifting from, or at least not terribly satisfied in, the Catholicism of their upbringing was unlikely to find anything more enticing anywhere else. Still less, given the differences between British and American social norms, were they likely to be actively invited to come along to another congregation by a friend, neighbour, co-worker, or, for that matter, recent acquaintance.

Other, subtler cultural differences perhaps come into play too. A key item of megachurch strategy lies in Americans' willingness to drive long distances. This follows naturally from the sheer scale of the country, and indeed the emptiness of a great deal of it. For many Americans, having one's folks a mere full day's drive away counts as being 'near to family'. Staying in southern Kansas some years ago, I once took a 450-mile round daytrip to visit the World's Largest Ball Twine, *also* in Kansas. Even if Britain possessed comparable cultural treasures, one would not dream of nipping up to York from London for an hour's sightseeing, however much Dr Pepper and Sonic tater tots one had to fuel the adventure. Very few Britons, I suspect, would choose somewhere even 10 miles from their home as their regular church. Data from the 2017 US National Household Transport Survey suggest, however, that over a fifth of Sunday journeys to a place of worship are of such a length or longer.[11] Meanwhile, a 2005 study of two Atlanta megachurches found 14 per cent and 20 per cent of

---

[11] Based on my own analysis of (weighted) data collected and made available by the US Department of Transportation's Federal Highway Administration. Available online at: https://nhts.ornl.gov (last accessed 12 June 2018). The actual category used

members lived over 20 miles away, and both had regular worshippers living over 100 miles away (Ingram 2005: 47–8).

Naturally, some British cradle Catholics do end up identifying with a different denomination or even religion. Judging by the Portsmouth study, a good number of these appear to be motivated by family-related reasons, either through adopting a spouse's allegiance, or finding another church more children-friendly (Bullivant et al. 2019: 25–7). British switchers also exhibit relatively high levels of belief and prayerfulness (Bullivant 2016a). This is not surprising, given the main default options of being a weakly practising and believing retainee, or else disaffiliating from religion altogether. To escape either fate, either as a committed Catholic or to actively affiliate with another denomination or religious tradition, is itself a mark of conviction. It takes a living thing to go against the stream (Chesterton 1926: 321).

CONCLUSION

In January 1979, a headline on the *New York Times'* front page declared: 'U.S. Catholics Finding Bearings After Long Period of Upheaval'. The accompanying article begins by noting:

> No region within the domain of Pope John Paul II more closely reflects the tensions, disarray and opportunities of modern Catholicism than the church in the United States. [...] Fifteen years ago, the church appeared, on the surface at least, to be a rocklike center in the lives of one out of every four Americans. Since then, it has undergone profound change, tearing millions of Catholics from familiar moorings.
>
> (Briggs 1979: A1)

Now, finally, it seemed that the tide had finally turned:

> But there is evidence that the church has begun to emerge from its darkest period of perplexity [...] There is a widespread feeling that the church's lowest point was passed about four or five years ago, when statistical data reflecting the vitality of church practice hit the lowest level in modern times, with attendance at mass falling off precipitously

here is 'religious or other community activities', though it seems reasonable to assume that most of these on a Sunday would indeed be church-related.

and the recruitment of young men for the priesthood reaping a critically meager harvest.   (Briggs 1979: A1, D8)

According to Archbishop Quinn of San Francisco, then-president of the US Bishops' Conference, moreover: 'I contend that the church has never been stronger' (Briggs 1979: D8). Eight years into this bright new dawn, in September 1987, the *Times* carried another article: 'Poll Finds Catholics Defecting from Church'. In the words of its lede: 'About one person in five who was brought up Catholic no longer considers himself or herself an adherent of the faith, the latest New York Times/CBS News Poll shows. The loss through such defections is about three times as large as the church's gain through conversions' (Clymer 1987).

Without doubt these were dispiriting years. Nothing seemed to work. Each 'new low' seemed to be followed, a year later, with a newer and lower one. Every bold initiative aimed at turning things around appeared to have, at best, no impact, and at worst, a negative one. Parishes which could, with much justification, claim to have been doing everything *right* for years—to be the very model of a modern Catholic community—might nevertheless admit 'total failure' in 'retain[ing] young people within the Church' and 'hav[ing] any impact at all upon the working class section of the community', as well as a 'not at all impressive' record of making converts (Hornsby-Smith 2010: 184–5). All of this *despite* being a parish 'well-known as an exemplar of the post-Vatican II era', shepherded by priests who 'have all espoused a "People of God" model [and] facilitated the full partici-pation of the laity', and during a 'golden age when the Spirit blew her favours freely and widely' (Hornsby-Smith 2010: 185, 197, 184).

Towards the beginning of the period covered in this chapter, the Church's various pastoral troubles, coming immediately after the hopes sparked by the Council, came as something of a shock. Most famously, Pope Paul VI preached a homily in Rome observing, with evident emotion, that 'It was believed that after the Council would come a sunny day in the history of the Church. Instead, a day of clouds, storms, gloom, searching, and uncertainty has arrived' (1972).[12] As the years wore on, however, ever-falling Mass counts,

---

[12] Judging by how the text is presented on the Vatican website, this is the Vatican's official paraphrase of the Pope's comments, rather than a verbatim transcription of his actual words.

low vocations, the normality of non-practice, and the recognition that an 'ex-Catholic' was a perfectly ordinary thing to have for a brother, sister, son, or daughter—'The "road to Damascus," we have been discovering, is a busy two-way street, and the traffic in the opposite direction has become disconcertingly heavy' (McBrien 1978: 5)— were simply accepted as the way things were. Such stoicism coexisted, often enough, with a hope that things were *just* about to start changing for the better. After all, as the 1980s turned into the 1990s, and the Pilgrim Church marched towards the new millennium, surely they couldn't get very much worse?

7

Unto the Third and Fourth Generations

Since the mid-1990s, more than 130 people have come forward with horrific childhood tales about how former priest John J. Geoghan allegedly fondled or raped them during a three-decade spree through a half-dozen Greater Boston parishes. Almost always, his victims were grammar school boys. One was just 4 years old. Then came last July's disclosure that Cardinal Bernard F. Law knew about Geoghan's problems in 1984, Law's first year in Boston, yet approved his transfer to St. Julia's parish in Weston.

(Investigative Staff of the Boston Globe 2002)

So began a *Boston Globe* front-page story on 6 January 2002, authored by its 'Spotlight' investigative reporting team. It was the first of a great many: the Boston daily would publish some six hundred stories relating to Catholic sexual abuse during the next year alone (Investigative Staff of the Boston Globe [2002] 2015: 4). Even a brief selection of their headlines eloquently narrates the snowballing depth and breadth of the crisis engulfing the Archdiocese of Boston and, very soon, the Catholic Church across the USA and beyond:

- 'Church allowed abuse by priest for years' (6 January)
- 'Law apologizes for assignment of Geoghan' (10 January)
- 'Geoghan found guilty of sexual abuse' (19 January)
- 'Scores of priests involved in sex abuse cases' (31 January)
- 'Outside cardinal's headquarters, protestors multiply' (18 February)
- 'Hundreds now claim priest abuse' (24 February)
- 'Bishop resigns in [Florida] over charges' (9 March)

- 'Attorneys see scope of cases still expanding' (14 April)
- 'Through Kansas parishes, a trail of suicide' (18 July)
- '[Arizona] abuse case names bishop, 2 priests' (20 August)
- 'Charges lodged in Detroit against 4 priests' (29 August)
- 'Diocese records show more coverups' (13 September)
- 'Diocese of [Manchester, NH] reaches settlement on abuse claims' (11 October)
- 'In meeting with victims, Law begs for forgiveness' (30 October)
- 'Allegations in Ireland's church mirror Boston case' (11 November)
- 'Records detail quiet shifting of rogue priests' (4 December)
- 'Law meets with pope at Vatican to discuss his future' (13 December)
- 'Pope accepts Law's resignation in Rome' (14 December)
- 'Patterns of priest sexual abuse found nationwide' (14 December)
- 'Around the world, cleric sex abuse takes a toll' (14 December)

The *Globe*'s reporting, which won a Pulitzer Prize in 2013 and (via the subsequent movie version) two Oscars in 2015, was widely viewed, then as now, as a watershed moment in the 'Catholic abuse scandals'—and rightly so. It was sparked by the case of Fr John Geoghan, a Boston priest accused of molesting over a hundred boys over a three-decade period from the mid-1960s onwards, facilitated by his being quietly moved from parish to parish by the Archdiocese each time a new set of allegations emerged. Geoghan, who had been laicized in 1998, was imprisoned in 2002 for assaulting a ten-year-old boy at a public swimming pool ten years earlier. He was killed in prison the following year by a fellow inmate, with several charges pending.

Geoghan's was not, however, the first case of a serial-abusing cleric receiving such a conviction. And nor was this the first in which, to put it mildly, very serious errors of judgement might be placed firmly at the door of Church authorities (Dreher 2002: 28). A decade before the Spotlight revelations, the journalist Jason Berry—who had earlier reported on Fr Gilbert Gauthe's crimes and their cover-up in the Diocese of Lafayette, Louisiana (1986)—could write of 'a storm of news coverage about Catholics priests who had sexually abused young people and entrenched pattern of bishops who concealed the perpetrators, shuffling many of them on to new assignments':

Between 1983 and 1987, more than two hundred priests or religious brothers were reported to the Vatican Embassy [i.e., the Apostolic Nunciature in Washington, DC] for sexually abusing youngsters, in most cases teenage boys—an average of nearly one accusation a week in those four years alone. In the decade of 1982 to 1992, approximately four hundred priests were reported to church or civil authorities for molesting youths. The vast majority of these men had multiple victims. By 1992, the church's financial losses—in victims' settlements, legal expenses, and medical treatments of clergy—had reached an estimated $400 million.   (Berry [1992] 2000: ix, xxi)

Yet for a combination of reasons, 2002 was different. Unlike Lafayette, Boston was a major urban centre, with a large population of baptized Catholics, a deeply ingrained Catholic culture, and a long history of cooperation and cordial relations between 'Church' and 'City' (the extent of which would soon come under sharp scrutiny as the revelations unfolded). As is abundantly clear from the recent history of Ireland, this is fertile ground for sexual abuse scandals, and their cover-ups, to strike very deeply. The centrality to the story of both Cardinal Law, a high-profile and divisive figure who had been Boston's Archbishop for over fifteen years, and his predecessor Cardinal Medeiros, naturally also added traction. (The same had been true the previous year in England and Wales, when serious questions were raised as to what—and when—Westminster's Archbishop Murphy-O'Connor had known about Fr Michael Hill's decades of child-abusing as a priest in his former diocese of Arundel and Brighton; see Scorer 2014: chap. 7; Murphy-O'Connor 2015: 143–5.) It also meant that a far larger amount of attention focused on the complicity on the Church *as an institution* in the crimes committed by individual priests. This was all the truer as case after case, from dioceses across America, started piling up. A more-or-less standard pattern emerged: credible allegations against an abusive priest being kept quiet, with assurances made to the victims and their families; the priest in question being quietly reassigned, perhaps after a period of 'successful' counselling at one of a small group of Church-run treatment centres specializing in precisely this, or sent to another diocese with a glowing letter of recommendation; no thought whatsoever being given to this new set of young people being put into very serious harm's way; and this process being repeated, multiple times, for years if not decades (e.g., Margolick 2011; for multiple British examples, see Scorer 2014). Not surprisingly, 'Each new story provoked a media frenzy in the city where it broke, and editorial writers thundered their denunciation of the Catholic hierarchy. Dozens of prelates were facing demands for their resignation' (Lawler 2008: 164).

Crucially, something else was different in 2002. The mid-1980s Gauthe case had been a big story in the Louisiana papers, and attracted the occasional article in the biggest of the quasi-national dailies. The *New York Times*, for example, reported on key moments in the case five times between June 1984 and December 1987; the *Washington Post* carried three stories over the same period. The nearest the story got to the front of either newspaper, however, was page four. Another notorious, pre-Spotlight case, that of James Porter, a former priest of Boston's neighbouring Diocese of Fall River, who abused scores of children in parishes spanning several states, garnered similar attention in the *Times* and *Post* in the early 1990s. Unless one happened to be near the epicentre of a particular scandal, therefore, even the most assiduous news junkie might read about sexual abuse within the Catholic Church only intermittently: enough to be aware of it as a sporadic 'problem', but not enough for it to seem like an urgent and endemic crisis. The Catholic press might, of course, feature it more prominently, but only placed within a much wider and more positive implicit context: i.e., one would read about a great deal *else* besides. In the decade separating Porter's and Geoghan's trials, however, the internet had taken off in a big way, as had online news. In fact, the *Boston Globe* was one of the forerunners here: its first website launched in 1995. No longer could major scandals be substantially contained within regional news silos: a big enough story, as the ones from Boston undoubtedly were, could not only reach readers across the country more-or-less instantly, but so could the full reporting of their horrific details (Turpin 2018: 77). Victims too could, if not Google, then at least 'Altavista' the names of past abusers. Upon finding that others had come forward, they might well feel emboldened to do so themselves. The early, primitive stirrings of social media—email, listservs, forums, instant messenger, school reunion websites—could also serve as distribution channels for news stories about one's former priests or teachers, and as catalysts for bringing painful memories to light. On these new social networks, bad news could travel far and fast. Critically, they were also catalysts for the creation of close-knit communities of survivors, most of whom had suffered for years in harrowing silence, determined to make their collective voices heard.

'ASHAMED TO BE A CATHOLIC'

'The scandals' (to use the common if insipid shorthand) cast a dark shadow over everything narrated in this final main chapter, covering the period from the early 1990s to the present day. Even for those with no immediate connection, they naturally formed a major part of 'the Catholic context': the dominant theme of news reports, TV shows, and films about the Church; a frequent topic of conversation within it; the butt of jokes or throw-away insults. Where *'aggiornamento'*, 'collegiality', and 'active participation' had been the distinctive buzzwords for a previous generation, now it would be 'safeguarding', 'mandatory reporting', and 'transparency'. Juxtaposing all this with the kinds of statistics detailed in Chapter 2—not least that 44 per cent of British cradle Catholics, and 34 per cent of American ones, now no longer identify as Catholics—it is not difficult to draw direct lines of causation. After all, the monstrous enormity of what has come to light over the past quarter-decade; the grave crimes, of commission and omission both, perpetrated by so many in the Church; the ongoingly serious and, in some cases literally life-destroying, effects wreaked upon the victims; the sorrow, hurt, and justifiable anger wrought within the communities affected; and the fact that likely only a small proportion of all the abusers, conspirers, and gross-negligents have been brought to (temporal) justice . . . given all this, it seems obvious that a significant amount of contemporary Catholic disaffiliation should be ascribable to the abuse crisis in one way or another.

We have given much attention to the role of so-called Credibility Enhancing Displays, or CREDs, in inculcating commitment to a given religious identity: 'walking the walk', especially when doing so requires a significant investment, *ipso facto* underwrites one's 'talking the talk'. But this is, surely, a two-edged sword. If those urging fidelity to a certain set of convictions fail conspicuously to live up to them, then that should undermine the intuitive plausibility of what is being proclaimed. As with CREDs, the hypothesized deleterious effect of such 'Credibility *Undermining* Displays', or CRUDs (Turpin et al. 2018; Turpin 2018: 78–90), accords well with common sense. It also features in the teaching of Jesus, whose antipathy towards 'the hypocrites' who 'do not practise what they teach' was frequently expressed (Matthew 23:1–36). Similar ideas may be found throughout the New Testament: e.g., 'They profess to know God, but they deny him by their actions' (Titus 1:16); 'faith by itself, if it has no works, is dead' (James 2:17).

There is no denying that, for some people, the abuse crisis *has* critically undermined their Catholic beliefs, practice, and identity. Such testimonies from people who have been abused themselves, or who have been affected in other ways, were cited in Chapter 3 from each of the Trenton, Springfield, and Portsmouth studies. For many survivors, the trauma of the abuse itself, and/or of how they were then treated by Church authorities when reporting it,[1] remains intimately bound up with their religious beliefs and emotions (Bain 2011; Orsi 2017: 287–9). People who, though neither they nor their family members had been abused, were deeply affected by revelations within their home parishes are also well-represented in surveys of lapsed Catholics. Remember, for instance, the comment from a 69-year-old man in the Portsmouth study:

> I discovered several awful truths about things that had happened in our small parish. [. . .] A priest that we were all very in awe of, and who we trusted with our children, committed suicide whilst awaiting trial for his sexual abuse with other children, our son's friend and several others. [. . .] The result of all this is that our lives are spoilt as we had lots of good friends through going to Mass and now they are all rather distant. Also we had a faith which has gone, and it affects our lives, present and future.   (Bullivant et al. 2019: 32)

Overall, the Portsmouth study found that 'Around half of all respondents either agreed or strongly agreed that the scandals in the Catholic Church were a factor in their decision to stop attending Mass' (Bullivant et al. 2019: 31).

Such outcomes are not, however, inevitable. Neither the experience of abuse, nor of the myriad 'ripples [spreading] far beyond the victims themselves' (Bowman 2016: 160), affect everyone in a uniform manner. Very many of those hardest and most personally hit by the scandals remain practising Catholics. Naturally enough, this has not

---

[1] See, e.g., Marie Collins' testimony: 'I was a practising Catholic and had high expectations of how the church would deal with my report. I expected them to care about what had happened to me and to act quickly to ensure no children were left in danger. As time went on I began to realize there was little concern for me. I was considered a nuisance, a threat, and eventually the enemy! [. . .] Alienation from the church has happened to victims and family members "because of the way their complaint of abuse was responded to and managed rather than as a direct result of the abuse *per se*"' (2004: 15, 18; quoting Goode et al. 2003: 201).

always been easy. The words of Irish abuse survivor Marie Collins would undoubtedly find echoes in Britain and America:

> I have remained a Catholic but not without much difficulty and struggle [. . .] There have been periods when practicing my faith has been impossible. I have tried to separate the institution of the Church from the Faith. My belief in God has never wavered.   (Quoted in Kelly 2014)

Such resilience, often channelled by survivors into seeking reform of the Church from within, is partly explained by the fact that predators within the Catholic Church overwhelmingly targeted those who were strongly practising. After all, these were the ones to whom abusers had the most regular access, who were the easiest to 'groom', and who came from the kinds of solidly Catholic families who not only trusted priests implicitly, but who would positively encourage their children spending time with them. In a sense, therefore, those with most reason to leave the Church are often also those with strong reasons to feel deeply rooted within it. The same is true, to a lesser extent, with those within the wider church community: it is those most committed to the life of a given parish, and most densely connected to both clergy and fellow parishioners, who are most devastated when abuse comes to light. The resulting shock and shame *might* lead them into leaving, but it will struggle to outweigh all that was keeping them there in the first place.

Nevertheless, one might reasonably expect to see sharp rises in the proportion of Catholic disaffiliates and 'never attending' Catholics, and a sharp fall in the proportion of weekly attending Catholics, in the wake of highly publicized revelations of sexual abuse and/or its cover-up. Interestingly, judging by the data presented in the previous chapter's Figures 6.3–6.4, this seems not to be the case—or at least, not in any immediate way.

Turning to the dioceses' own attendance statistics, however, shows a rather different picture, at least in some places. Figure 7.1 gives the annual 'typical Sunday' Mass attendance data given in the Appendix for thirteen US dioceses from 1990–2017 (with some gaps), in terms of percentage difference from the 1990 figure (i.e., 1990 is taken as the '0%' base level).[2] Representing change in this way, rather than as

---

[2] In two cases, where no data for 1990 was available, I have used modified figures from nearby years. For Green Bay, the figure used here is from 1991, with an additional 2% added. For Milwaukee, I have used 1992 data, plus an additional 4%. These added percentages are rough estimates, based on a fairly typical rate of annual decline for dioceses in the dataset.

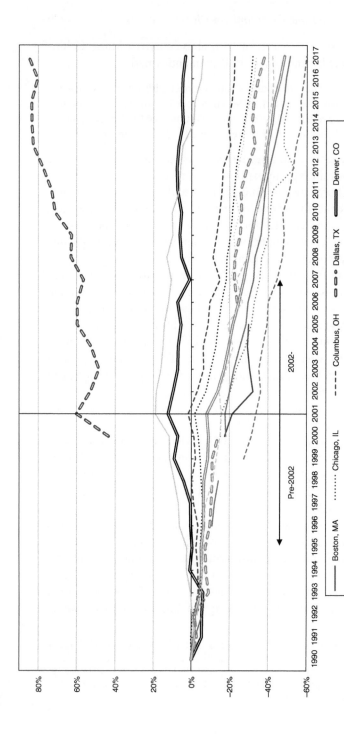

Figure 7.1. Annual 'typical Sunday' Mass attendance, depicted as % difference from 1990 level, in thirteen US (arch)dioceses (1990–2017)

Source: Official diocesan statistics (see Appendix)

the raw numbers, allows easier comparisons between dioceses of widely different Catholic populations. The Diocese of Steubenville, Ohio, has roughly one-twentieth the number of Mass-goers that the Archdiocese of Chicago has, for example.

In most (and perhaps all) of the thirteen, attendance counts for 2002 would have been taken in October: deep in the midst of the Church's self-inflicted *annus horribilis*. The figures for 2001, meanwhile, were taken a couple of months before the first *Globe* stories broke. This permits us a direct 'before' and 'during/after' comparison. While the effect is not uniform, eight of our dioceses show a clear downturn between 2001 and 2002, over and above what one might expect from pre-2002 trends simply continuing, and which might plausibly be interpreted as a reaction to the scandals. As one would predict on this interpretation, Boston is by far the clearest example. But Dallas, Rockford, Denver, Columbus, Chicago, Philadelphia, and Marquette all show similar signs. These falls from 2001 to 2002, where they occur, are not—Boston excepted—typically that large: in most dioceses, amounting to a few per cent fewer Mass-goers than one might have otherwise have expected (which perhaps explains why it does not show up clearly in the GSS). No doubt in many cases, the scandals delivered the *coup de grâce* to a gradual period of dissatisfaction for other reasons. In Boston the numbers even rallied in the following two years, suggesting that some of those absent in October 2002 later returned (I have not been able to find any data since 2005).

'Short, sharp shocks' aside, however, Figure 7.1's graph lines suggest a subtler, though perhaps ultimately more significant, longer-term trend. In a good proportion of the dioceses sampled, there are striking differences between the general trends up to and including 2001, and then from 2002 onwards. Two dioceses that were growing prior to 2002 (Denver and Rockford), and a further two that were holding fairly steady (Chicago and Columbus), begin a period decline after it. In three others—Philadelphia, Steubenville, and Marquette—existing rates of year-on-year decline becomes appreciably steeper post-2001. Even in the massively trend-bucking (in overall US terms, though likely rather less so in the border states) Diocese of Dallas, where Mass attendance has increased by 85 per cent between 1990 and 2017, the great bulk of this rise occurred prior to 2002, before stalling for the best part of a decade from 2002 onwards.

Also worth noting here is the lack of any obvious boost to Mass attendance following the 2013 papal election. Early hopes that Pope Francis' high popularity among a majority of Catholics and non-Catholics would soon spark a 'Mass Return' to the Church among the lapsed and disaffected failed to materialize. As a March 2014 headline in the Diocese of Honolulu's newspaper noted: 'The Francis Effect: Catholics Love the Pope, But for the Lapsed, Not Enough to Return to Church' (Hawaii Catholic Herald 2014). It is undoubtedly true that Francis has, at least in some circles, 'helped to detoxify the Catholic brand' (Thompson 2018). Lapsed and former Catholics, moreover, often bring him up as something positive about the Church, as indeed do many non-Catholics. This tangible 'Francis effect' is one I have observed in both the 2015 Portsmouth study (Bullivant et al. 2019: 77–8), and interviewing dozens of atheists and agnostics in a range of US states in 2017–18.[3] As an unbeliever in her fifties, who was raised Pentecostal, told me in Louisiana, 'If there was a religion I would join today, with this Pope, it would be Catholic.' This is certainly not nothing: such initial 'bridges of trust' can play a key role in drawing people (back) to the Church (e.g., Weddell 2012: 129). But such wishfully naïve headlines such as 'The "Pope Francis Effect" May Help Fill U.S. Pews' (Lesley 2015) have now dried up. As Tim O'Malley correctly summed things up: 'Pope Francis, no matter how attractive[ly] he is viewed, is not bringing people back to active Mass attendance at least within the United States. We should not be surprised that lapsed Catholics remain, well, lapsed—despite the magnetic pull of a single Pontiff' (2016).

Returning to 2002 and its immediate aftermath, our diocesan data offer modest support for the existence of an instant 'reflex reaction'— whether out of protest or disgust—on the part of the laity, mostly concentrated in specific locales. More importantly, it suggests that the full impact of the abuse crisis may well be both more subtly corrosive and much longer-lasting: a slow-burn, acting in combination with other factors (similar to what was earlier hypothesized regarding the impact of *Humanae Vitae*). Feasibly, this might work in two main ways. We shall consider the first of these here, in relation to both 'leaving' and 'switching' forms of disaffiliation. The second,

---

[3] This was part of another research project, as part of the 'Understanding Unbelief' initiative, funded by the John Templeton Foundation. Details may be found here: https://research.kent.ac.uk/understandingunbelief (last accessed 21 September 2018).

understood within the wider context of intergenerational transmission, will be explored in the next section.

The gradual nature of much disaffiliation has been discussed at several points in this book. People do not simply wake up one morning and think 'whereas yesterday I was a Catholic, today I am a "Baptist" (or a "none")'. Instead, as Ebaugh describes, the transition tends to creep up on them:

> Role exit is a social process that occurs over time. Very rarely does it happen as a result of one sudden decision. Rather, role exiting usually takes place over a time period, frequently originating before the individual is fully aware of what is happening or where events and decisions are leading him or her. In time, sometimes after years [...] the individual becomes aware of what is happening and begins to act more self-consciously and deliberately. (1988: 23)

This holds true, moreover, for both leavers and switchers. The former are, naturally, of most immediate relevance in rapidly secularizing societies. Here, where a large proportion of a population have been (however nominally) brought up as a religious 'something' but have very little tangible connection with the distinctive beliefs, practices, or expressions of identity[4] associated with that 'something-ness', a great many people are likely to be somewhere along the road Ebaugh sketches. Necessity being the mother of invention, British sociologists have minted various interpretive descriptions of this widespread form of religious ambivalence, with Grace Davie's 'believing without belonging' and David Voas' 'fuzzy fidelity' being the best-known. This need not be a transitional state—and Davie especially argues for this as being a fairly stable *modus vivendi* for much British Christianity—and at the individual level there is no inevitability

---

[4] This is, admittedly and deliberately, a rather loose and vague term. I principally mean by it such things as, say, wearing a crucifix for Catholics or marking Passover as a Jew. (Celebrating Christmas or Easter is a rather murkier area in western societies, since one can do so wholeheartedly in accordance with the secular understandings of these festivals without any real reference to the underlying Christian meanings.) All manner of other things might reasonably count here, though, depending on their wider cultural meaning. Living on a particular street in central Belfast, such as Donegall Pass, would plausibly count as 'an expression of Protestant identity' even for someone with no accompanying Protestant (religious) beliefs or practices. Being heavily involved in supporting certain football teams—cf. Sewell's observation regarding 'a Celtic supporter declaring himself a Catholic "in the football sense; but not at all religious"' (2001: 136)—would be another.

about the final destination. For a large number of people, however, it is undoubtedly precisely this. Very similarly, in Chapter 3 we noted the phenomenon of 'liminal nones' (Lim et al. 2010)—that is, of people who sometimes identify as a something, and sometimes as a nothing, despite there being no obvious change in circumstance. While such liminality might plausibly be a stable 'mode of being non/religious' for individuals, the overall phenomenon is best viewed, as will presently be explained in more detail, 'as part of the secularizing trajectory, a stage on the route to secularism' (Brown 2012: 68).

In what one might call the *balance* of liminality, the sexual abuse crisis acts as one (more) reason—and an evidently weighty one—for not thinking of oneself as a Catholic and, thereby, for thinking of oneself as either nonreligious or, perhaps, as a generic 'Christian' without any denominational marker (cf. the growth of the 'Christian – no denomination' category in surveys, discussed in Chapter 2). This effect would not, necessarily, come on suddenly and strongly, since such people typically have only a weak attachment to the Church. However, both the constant 'drip-drip' of negative stories, and the concomitant tainting of the 'Catholic brand' within the wider culture, exert an influence.

The power of 'social desirability bias' has long been noted by psychologists and sociologists: people often present themselves in what they regard (and thus believe others will regard) as their best light, both consciously and not. While it is easy to think of this as cynical calculation, a good proportion of it is undoubtedly done in good faith: the person who intends to be at church every Sunday, but— no doubt always for very good, one-off reasons—only actually makes it three weeks in four, might well still think of themselves as a 'weekly' rather than a mere '2–3 times a month' churchgoer. Viewed in this light, the power and tenacity of 'cultural', 'ethnic', or 'tribal' Catholicism, as 'a mindset hard to shift, tending to survive not only the decline of religious observance, but in some cases the deliberate and determined renunciation of faith' (Sewell 2001: 3), makes sense against cultural backgrounds where there exists a generally benign view of Catholicism. If the popular perception of Catholicism is an odd mix of weeping statues (as in an episode of *Only Fools and Horses*), habited nuns *à la* Julie Andrews or Whoopi Goldberg, and the 'absurd and irrelevant but almost lovably so' (Turpin 2018: 266) characters of *Father Ted*, then taking a certain, nostalgic pride in one's connection to Catholicism is one thing. But its attractiveness rather suffers in a world where the Catholic Church is most closely associated in the popular mind with 'paedophile priests'. Thus to quote from three different respondents to the Portsmouth study: 'Sometimes I feel ashamed to associate myself with the Church'; 'The way in which the church dealt with the priests that were paedophiles made me ashamed to be a Catholic'; and 'I am not Catholic anymore and I am ashamed that I ever felt I was.' Related to this, Hugh Turpin's ground-breaking work on the role of the sexual abuse scandals on Irish secularization, cited several times throughout this book, highlights how avowedly *ex*-Catholics often view cultural Catholicism as a form of culpably allying oneself with a 'foul, tarnished institution': 'These charged stances make Catholic affiliation into complicity, casting it as a shameful abrogation of moral responsibility' (2018: 196). While the contemporary situation in Ireland is undoubtedly *sui generis*, it nevertheless provides an instructive comparison to our contexts. This is especially so in those areas—with Boston chief among them—which might, in Catholic terms, rightly be regarded as part of the Hibernosphere. In any case, it is certainly true the scandals have severely tainted perceptions of the Catholic Church in Britain and America. As identifying as a Catholic, whether to others or oneself, becomes progressively less attractive, it would make sense if a per-centage of 'liminals' were to edge that bit nearer towards the exit.

The taintedness of Catholicism, in the wake of (ongoing) scandals, might thus have a slow-but-long burning effect in nudging weakly attached Catholics towards leaving. Among the more strongly attached, meanwhile, its effects may take time to become fully mani-fest for rather different reasons. The case of the American journalist Rod Dreher, who converted to Catholicism from cradle Methodism in 1993 during his mid-twenties, is revealing here. Covering the abuse scandals for *National Review* in 2002 and beyond, Dreher writes movingly of how, 'I had been a devoutly observant and convinced Roman Catholic for years, but had my faith shattered in large part by what I had learned as a reporter' (2011).

> [T]he scandal broke my Catholic faith, and made it impossible for me to continue [. . .] Everything that was hidden, and foul, and corrupt, and that thrived in the darkness, is being exposed. My Catholic faith was not strong enough to withstand knowing that [prominent Catholic leaders] were getting away with this injustice. My problem was that I had placed too much faith in the integrity of the institutional Church. I kept thinking that there was bound to be a bottom to this scandal, and kept finding out otherwise. (2018)

Elsewhere, Dreher describes the deleterious effect of the abuse crisis, and especially the hypocrisy with which Church leaders spoke about dealing with it—CRUDs again, note—had on his and his wife's faith over a long period.

> We [...] spent months going through the motions. It's hard for me to express how spiritually depressed we were. The only strong emotion I felt about faith in those days was [...] anger and bitterness. [...] I'd go to fulfil my Sunday duty, receiving the Eucharist and then getting the heck out of there, wanting as little as possible to do with parish life.
>
> (2006)

Finally, and only after much agonizing, they began attending a local Orthodox church and, gradually, were pulled closer and closer into Orthodox liturgical, intellectual, and community life. All this, necessarily, took time: the Drehers formally joined the Orthodox Church, and thus formally left the Catholic Church, in the middle of 2006. This was four and half years since the Spotlight revelations began and, interestingly enough, pretty close to when the national Catholic disaffiliate rate started to climb (see Figure 6.3).

While the primary cause of the Drehers' switching was clearly and unambiguously the Catholic abuse crisis, the move away from Catholicism was neither sudden nor easy: 'Leaving was like chewing my own leg off to get out of a trap' (2006). Note too, to return to a point raised in the last chapter regarding megachurches, that this story is not simply about *leaving* Catholicism. It is also about finding another Church to become one's new home. Other churches possess their own intrinsic attractions which can, and do, make Catholics want to convert (and vice versa) even apart from the scandals. But the Drehers will certainly not be the only committed Catholics for whom the horrifying revelations of 2002 served as a prompt to 'try out' a different ecclesial home, albeit with heavy and weary hearts, and ultimately, after perhaps several years, to stay.

'WORSE THAN 2002'

As a postscript to the previous section, the finishing touches to this book manuscript were made in the summer of 2018. On 20 June, Theodore McCarrick, Cardinal-Archbishop of Washington, DC, was removed from public ministry by the Holy See in the wake of credible allegations being made of his having abused minors. Following a slew of other allegations relating to sexual abuse, coercion, and harassment, McCarrick resigned from the College of Cardinals on 28 July. A month later, Archbishop Carlo Maria Viganò, formerly Apostolic Nuncio (i.e., the Vatican's Ambassador) to the USA, released an extraordinary document, alleging that not only were various accusations against McCarrick well-known to the Holy See, but Pope Benedict had placed restrictions on his public ministry in 2009 or 2010. Under Francis, however, Viganò claimed that these sanctions had been removed, and McCarrick had been promoted as a papal confidant and bishop-maker (Altieri 2018).

In the middle of all this, the official report of a Pennsylvania Grand Jury investigation into abuse and cover-up within six of the state's dioceses was published in mid-August. Its opening sentences convey something—though only something—of the horrors narrated in its 1000+ pages:

> We, the members of this grand jury, need you to hear this. We know some of you have heard some of it before. There have been other reports about child sex abuse within the Catholic Church. But never on this scale. For many of us, those earlier stories happened someplace else, someplace away. Now we know the truth: it happened everywhere.
>
> [Our investigation uncovered] credible allegations against over *three hundred* predator priests. Over *one thousand* child victims were identifiable, from the church's own records. We believe that the real number—of children whose records were lost, or who were afraid ever to come forward—is in the thousands.
>
> Most of the victims were boys; but there were girls too. Some were teens; many were prepubescent. Some were manipulated with alcohol or pornography. Some were made to masturbate their assailants, or were groped by them. Some were raped orally, some vaginally, some anally. But all of them were brushed aside, in every part of the state, by church leaders who preferred to protect the abusers and their institution above all. (Pennsylvania Grand Jury 2018: 1)

As with Boston sixteen years earlier, this new round of light-shedding had something of a domino effect, with new allegations emerging from dioceses across the country. Within just three weeks of the Pennsylvania report, the Attorneys General of New York, Illinois, Missouri, Nebraska, and New Mexico had announced similar investigations of their own (Otterman and Goodstein 2018). Meanwhile in the UK, the government-backed *Independent Inquiry into Child Sexual Abuse* released a damning report on two Benedictine-run schools. Among much else, this detailed 'appalling sexual abuse inflicted over decades on children aged as young as seven at Ampleforth School, and 11 at Downside School' (Independent Inquiry into Child Sexual Abuse 2018: iii). Further abuse scandals erupted, or continued to erupt, in Germany, Belgium, Chile, and elsewhere.

On 20 August—in retrospect, relatively early into the torrid summer—CNN published an article carrying the subtitle: 'Why this Catholic Abuse Scandal Seems Worse than 2002' (Burke 2018). This impression was one that was widely shared. If so, and if the above analysis of 2002 is broadly correct, then the after-effects of 2018 are likely to hit hard and deep.

At the end of August, *The Week* columnist Damon Linker wrote movingly of the near-constant scandals that have engulfed the American Church in the years since he converted to Catholicism in 2000. Observing that his faith in the 'beauty' of the Catholic Church had already begun 'to fade in the church scandals that broke less than two years after I entered the church'—the long tail of 2002 again, note— he continues: 'My belief has faded further over the intervening years, as I've tried to keep some spark of it alive long enough to give my children the Catholic education that from the moment of my conversion I was obligated to provide them.' The year 2018, however— with the 'toxic sludge' of the Grand Jury's findings in his home state, 'Theodore McCarrick's loathsome character and career', and the 'allegations piled up in Viganò's memo'—has proved the final straw. 'No thanks. I'm done', he concludes. 'And I bet I'll have a lot of company headed for the door' (Linker 2018).

'GOD HAS NO GRANDCHILDREN'

The scandals' effects on those who had already retained a Catholic identity into adulthood (or gained one once there) is one thing. But what of those who had yet to do so? Or indeed, of those young adults who had only recently done so?

Failing intergenerational transmission—that is, the decreasing 'stickiness' of a Catholic upbringing—already forms a major subplot in our narrativized explanation of postconciliar Catholic disaffiliation. This was discussed already in the previous chapter, referring to those cradle Catholics principally raised in the 1970s and 1980s: that is to say, the generations hitting adolescence, young adulthood, and, less reliably, marrying (or otherwise pairing) and/or raising children of their own in the 1990s, 2000s, and 2010s. And the points already raised there apply, *a fortiori*, here also—not least the decreasing likelihood of being raised in even a moderately CREDs-rich Catholic environment, and the increasing likelihood of being socialized into the mores of a wider culture increasingly in tension with normative Catholic teaching and practice. The concrete ramifications of these processes will, I suspect, be instantly familiar to both school chaplains and parish catechists: a generation of young Catholics raised mainly in non-practising homes, for whom Confirmation has become, at least in its outward effects, a Sacrament of Valediction (see Vaughan-Spruce 2018: 8, 63). Recall that, according to the BSA data cited in Chapter 2, fully 56 per cent of British cradle Catholics born between 1985 and 1994 are disaffiliates. In contrast, only 15 per cent say they are Catholics who practise at least once a month (see Figure 2.3).

For those brought up Catholic, however weakly, in this era, the sexual abuse scandals cannot but have been a major contributor to their overall understanding of the 'meaning' of Catholicism. This is obviously so for two reasons. In the first place, for a very large percentage of their lives, news reports of 'paedophile priests' have formed a dominant part of the wider Catholic story. In addition to those directly reporting on the topic itself, any major Catholic news story—not least Papal visits, funerals, resignations, and/or elections— becomes, to a significant degree, 'about' it too. Secondly, they have typically had very little other Catholic 'input' to outweigh this, with even less of it underwritten by practice. (For example, even if they *heard* a fair bit about the importance of the Eucharist during their First Holy Communion preparation classes at Catholic primary/ elementary school, this may well have been undermined by their own parents never making 'a thing' of Sunday Mass, or if they did, on their seeing very few of their peers or indeed teachers there.) Whatever else a Baby Boomer might think about his or her 1950s' Catholic upbringing, it is probably true that (i) there was a lot of it, and (ii) it made a deep and long-lasting impression.

The essential point here is simply that 'tribal' or 'cultural' Catholicism does not pass on very easily. Or rather, in order to go through life with a deeply ingrained feeling of Catholic identity even without practising it one itself, it is necessary to have been brought up in a sufficiently robust Catholic environment to ingrain it in the first place. Such clearly was the case for many British and American Catholics brought up in the early twentieth century and before. And indeed this is confirmed by the now-fading power of 'lapsed Catholic' in conveying a positive sense of identity. Consider, for example, the following from the English author Anthony Burgess, born in 1917, and writing here in 1967:

> I avoid envying the believer, but it is with no indifferent eye that I view the flood of worshippers pouring into the Catholic church at the corner of my street. I want to be one of them, but wanting is not enough. The position of standing on the periphery is one that I share with many men of good will; the state of being a lapsed Catholic is so painful that it sometimes seems to generate a positive charge, as though it had in itself a certain religious validity. Perhaps some of the prayers that go for the souls in purgatory might occasionally be used for us. Those souls at least know where they are. We don't. I don't.   ([1967] 2017)

It is hard to imagine the same sort of sensibility, a nostalgic longing for something missing, coming to afflict many cradle-Catholic millennials in later life—and not only because they have probably never heard of purgatory.

The upshot of this is that a large proportion of those brought up as Catholics today are often brought up as such in only a very weak or nominal manner. This, especially when allied to a wider cultural environment often taking a dim view of any but the most domesticated expressions of Christianity, and moreover in which Catholicism in particular is widely associated with the sexual abuse of children, means that the path of least resistance often lies in *not* thinking of oneself as a Catholic. This is all the more true if, as in the UK, one lives in a milieu in which 70 per cent of 16- to 29-year-olds identify as having no religion (Bullivant 2018b: 6). Thus again to quote Callum Brown: 'There is a new generation, those born in the late twentieth century, who agonize less over leaving religion' (2017: 12). While 'believing without belonging', 'liminality', and/or 'fuzzy fidelity' might be a reasonably stable state for people brought up by rather more religious people in rather more religious cultures, *their* children were not brought up like this at all. They are far more likely to discard even the little, vestigial religious input that they had, and to do so without even noticing it. As the influential Catholic writer Sherry Weddell rightly puts it, 'Cultural Catholicism is dead as a retention strategy is dead, because God has no grandchildren' (2012: 39). Important here is the chasm between traditional Christian teachings on marriage, family, sex, and gender and wider social norms. The beginnings of this rift were explicitly noted in connection with the 1960s, though subtler cultural roots may indeed be traced to earlier decades. We have already discussed the resulting 'push and pull of living in two worlds' (Campbell 2009: 14) as an issue for those brought up Catholic in the late 1960s, 1970s, and 1980s. This disconnect has only grown with time. In his 2017 book *The Benedict Option*—which, having sold over 60,000 copies within just eighteen months of its publication,[5] evidently touched a nerve among its target audience of 'theologically traditional Protestants, Catholics, and Eastern Orthodox Christians' (2017: 5)—Rod Dreher argues that: 'American Christians are going to have to come to terms with the brute fact that we live in a culture, one in which our beliefs increasingly little sense. We speak a language that the world more and more either cannot hear or finds offensive to its ears' (2017: 12). This general observation is perhaps nowhere so clear as in the area of LGBT rights and acceptance.

Commenting on the sea change in attitudes towards gay, lesbian, bisexual, and transgender people in the space of even a few decades, journalist and author Mark Simpson writes:

> Today, they are triumphant. Has any once persecuted, despised group in history been more rapidly and giddily promoted? [Not only have we witnessed a succession of landmark political and legal victories,] every major UK soap has at least one openly lesbian, gay, bisexual, or transgender character. At times, *Coronation Street* has so many it seems to have relocated to Canal Street. [...] Now the fluffy slipper is on the other foot, and *Christians* complain of persecution and being unable to practise their preferences in the privacy of their own home. [...] Homosexuality has become respectable. We are entering an era when the biggest problem gay people face in the UK and much of western Europe (and even, increasingly, in the US, despite its strongly religious nature) is no longer overt homophobia, but rather the rapid falling-off of it—at least, for their survival as a distinct group, with their own identity, culture, clubs. (2014)

---

[5] Personal communication with Rod Dreher, 3 September 2018.

Simpson is being deliberately provocative here; other commentators could be cited who take a decidedly less sanguine view of current LGBT acceptance. Nevertheless, the broad outlines of his position are difficult to countermand, at least at the level of dominant social values and attitudes (e.g., Jones et al. 2014).

In this kind of world, the official Catholic positions on a wide range of LGBT-related matters, however sensitively and pastorally interpreted and applied (e.g., Sarah 2017), are inherently countercultural. As such, a keen sense of 'disconnection, tension, and conflict between the realms of faith and sexuality [particularly among] wide swaths of everyday believers whose sexual values or practices transgress traditional boundaries' (Hinze and Hornbeck 2014: 3) is unavoidable. They cannot fail, therefore, to be a stumbling-block for many. Against a cultural backdrop in which same-sex sexual relationships, (legal) marriages, and parenting are positively affirmed and celebrated, and in which gender is increasingly defined in terms of subjective identity and—where desired—chemical and surgical intervention, first impressions of the Church 'as a weird mix of oppressive and exotic [. . .] vivid and visceral, but also sex hating, body hating, and life hating' (Tushnet 2014: 28) are understandable. Likewise, it should come as no surprise for some people to feel, as the head of the UK LGBT-rights charity Stonewall revealed in a *Guardian* interview, that 'It's been harder for me to come out as a Catholic than it was to come out as a lesbian—easily' (Topping 2015; cf. Martin 2017: 56). All this affects not only LGBT-identifying Catholics themselves, but also their close friends or family members. According to US survey data from 2014, around a third of 'millennials' (born circa 1980–95) who had left religion said 'that negative teachings about, or treatment of, gay and lesbian people' was either a somewhat or very important factor in their disaffiliation. Fifty-eight per cent of American adults, moreover, regarded the Catholic Church as being 'unfriendly to LGBT people', outranking Mormons and Evangelicals in perceived unfriendliness. Among LGBT-identifying individuals themselves, 71 per cent considered the Church 'unfriendly' (Jones et al. 2014: 20–2). In the 2015 Portsmouth study of lapsed Catholics, almost three-fifths of respondents cited the Church's stance on 'homosexuality' as either very much or somewhat of a factor in their distancing from the Church, and a good number elaborated on this in their answers to our open-ended questions. The disjunct between Church teaching and contemporary social mores, and thus the perceived necessity of the former 'catching up', was raised by several. For one 50-year-old woman, 'The Catholic Church needs to be representative of the time in which we live. Jesus was a changemaker and dared to challenge the old ways in his time. We should be doing the same now.' A man in his mid-30s, echoing Ruth Hunt, spoke of having 'to apologize to my "liberal" friends for being Catholic' (Bullivant et al. 2019: 40, 50–2).

For all the above reasons, the normalcy of no religion in contemporary Britain is by now well-established. Quite what this translates to, in practice, is often rather fluid and ambivalent. For the very most part, Britain's nones are not committed atheists or secularists. As Steve Bruce has adroitly observed, 'Self-conscious atheism and agnosticism are features of religious cultures [. . .] They are postures adopted in a world where people are keenly interested in religion' (1996: 58); 'you have to care too much about religion to be irreligious' (2002: 42). Then again, nor are they necessarily so indifferent to religion as they might like to think (Lee 2015; Bullivant 2012b). To give a concrete instance of this ambivalence: British politicians' non-religiosity is not generally regarded to be an issue, provided that they make anodyne affirmations of respect for 'all faiths and none'. The theologically strange stance of being a 'committed Christian' who is 'not that regular in attendance, and a bit vague on some of the more difficult parts of the faith' is equally no bar to high(est) office (Allen 2017, quoting David Cameron). However, more conventionally committed Christians from all three main parties—Ruth Kelly (Labour), Tim Farron (Liberal Democrat), and Jacob Rees-Mogg (Conservative) spring immediately to mind—have come under intense media scrutiny for taking their religion a little too seriously. 'Doing God' is fine, so long as one does it quietly, and focusing on either social justice or cultural heritage, rather than those points at which traditional Christian teachings conflict with secular sexual and ethical mores (see Crossley 2018: 30–64).

THE RISE OF THE NONES

While 'No religion' has been a large and, thus far, inexorably growing feature of the British society for the past forty or fifty years, this is not the case in the USA. Or rather, it *had not* been. While the proportion of nones was rising (and rising) in Britain and much of western

Europe in the 1970s and 1980s, US religious affiliation held remarkably steady. As can be seen in Figure 7.2, the percentage of nones in the general population hovered around 7 or 8 per cent for a solid two-decade period from the early 1970s onwards. Among under-30s, the proportion of nones was also fairly consistent: undulating between lows of 8 per cent and highs of 14 per cent. Beginning in the early-to-mid-1990s, however, the nones began to steadily rise. While the trend has been sharpest among the under-30s, among whom a third now identify with no religion, a significant slice of the population-at-large are now religiously unaffiliated: 22 per cent according to GSS 2016. These trends are confirmed by a wealth of other surveys. Pew's 2014 Religious Landscape Survey, for example, found 23 per cent of American adults to be nones of one kind or another (Pew Research Center 2015a). Data from the 2017 American Values Atlas, meanwhile, puts the figure at 25 per cent (Jones and Cox 2017). It seems that every new survey makes headlines for a 'new high'.

The full story of why, how, and when all this has happened is too large and complex a topic to attempt here. In the most general of terms, however, it is driven by two main phenomena. The first is growing numbers of people brought up in a religion, who come to regard themselves as having no religion. Such 'nonverts' currently account for 75 per cent of all US nones in GSS 2012–16. Seventy-two per cent of US nones, moreover, say they were raised as Christians;

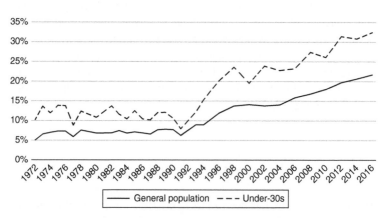

Figure 7.2. Proportions of general US adult population, and US adults under-30, identifying with no religion, by year

Source: GSS 1972–2016; weighted data

29 per cent are former Catholics. The second is the relative strength of nonreligious retention. Sixty per cent of those who say they were raised with no religion, still have no religion. Furthermore, once these two trends get sufficiently established (and strong enough to out-weigh the net religious gains from immigration and religious folk's tendency to have more children than nonreligious folk do) then a kind of feedback loop starts to kick in. As more people identify with no religion, and more media pieces report the fact, the more 'ordin-ary' it feels to do so oneself.

What triggered these trends in the first place is rather a moot point. How was it that US nonreligiosity remained so low for so long, in stark contrast to most other western societies, before suddenly start-ing to rise from the mid-1990s onwards? I have elsewhere proffered several speculations, referring specifically to the recent growth of atheism in America, though I think they apply to the nonreligious more broadly (Bullivant 2010).[6] These include the waning of Cold War oppositions between 'Christian America' and 'godless Commun-ism', and hence the equation of being a 'good American' with being a 'good Christian' (or if not, a 'good Jew'), following the collapse of the Soviet Union. This casting of the Cold War in explicitly religious terms, strongly promoted by 'hyperpatriotic' American Catholics, almost certainly lent nonreligiosity an unappealingly unpatriotic air. While an element of this no doubt persists—atheists still rank fairly high on Americans' lists of 'groups who do not share my vision of American society' (Edgell et al. 2006)—this association has surely eroded in the three decades since the fall of the Berlin Wall. Those who can remember growing up, in Freddie Mercury's phrase, 'tall and proud in the shadow of the Mushroom Cloud' are now either firmly into, or out the other side of, middle age. Replacing them, moreover, is a generation for whom the real 'bad guys' are not those with too little religion, but much too much of it: Islamist terrorists. This awareness, which began dawning in the early 1990s with Al-Qaeda's *first* attack on the World Trade Center, was then irrevocably cemented on 11 September 2001. This point was a central theme in several of the New Atheist bestsellers—themselves both confirma-tion of, and further catalysts for, the opening up of a 'space' for

---

[6] Beginning in the late 1960s, studies have consistently shown that American nones are by no means all atheists or agnostics (e.g., Vernon 1968; Gullickson 2018).

nonreligiosity within American culture (see Kettell 2013)—of the mid-2000s (Harris 2004; Dawkins 2006; Hitchens 2007).

As we have charted in relation to earlier decades, major changes in the 'architecture of everyday life' (Newman 2010)—including such things as suburbanization, the building of interstate highways, urban regeneration, the growing market for cars and televisions—can exert profound influences upon patterns of religious belonging, believing, and practice. Another such social transformation, which also gained serious traction in the early 1990s before rapidly expanding in the early 2000s, almost certainly had a hand in the growth of American nonreligiosity: the rise of the internet, and especially, of social media. The ultimate impact of this digital revolution is fundamentally unforeseeable. After all, who within living memory of Gutenberg's inventing of the printing press could correctly have prophesied its full, future significance? Nevertheless, the absorption of personal computing and social media into everyday life—and, perhaps, vice versa—has already been profound.

> Rather than virtual or second life, social media is actually becoming life itself—the central and increasingly transparent stage of human exist-ence that Silicon Valley venture capitalists are now calling 'an internet of people' [. . .] it is the architecture in which we now live.
>
> (Keen 2012: 2–3)

Recall this book's guiding Bergerian principle, that (as pithily put by Steve Bruce): 'Ideas are most convincing when they are universally shared. If everyone shares the same beliefs, they are not beliefs; they are just how the world is. The elaboration of alternatives provides a profound challenge' (2011: 37). Contrast this with the typical user's experience of major social media platforms: constant exposure to views and opinions, on a very broad range of topics, from (on Face-book) one's family, friends, and co-workers, or (on Twitter) people whose comments one is sufficiently interested in to actively 'follow' them. Naturally, unless one curates and polices one's 'feed' very strictly, a large number of these will likely express, explicitly or implicitly, positions very different to one's own. On one level, there is of course something good and healthy about all this: exposure to other viewpoints, to 'see the world differently', to walk a mile in another person's shoes, and so on, has very much to recommend it. The collateral damage comes, however, in trying to maintain any distinct worldview over and against this cacophony of contradicting 'discrepant worlds', held by (admittedly varying degrees of) one's significant others. Hence for Berger and Luckmann, presciently writing the same year as ARPANET—the forerunner to the internet— first received Pentagon funding: '[In] a society in which discrepant worlds are generally available on a market basis [. . .] There will be an increasingly general consciousness of the relativity of *all* worlds, including one's own, which is now subjectively apprehended as "*a* world*", rather than "*the* world"' ([1966] 1971: 192). Updating these basic ideas in light of the digital revolution, Paul McClure argues in a recent article:

> Whether through social media or the sheer proliferation of competing truth claims found online, the Internet is the perfect breeding ground for new "life-worlds" that systematically chip away at one's certainty. The more time one spends online, the more one is barraged with various ideas, beliefs, and truth claims about what is good, true, and of ultimate importance.   (2017: 487)

Thinking more broadly, the likely effect of the internet in fanning and spreading Boston's flames in 2002 has already been discussed. It is not hard to think of other, plausibly concrete ways in which digital technologies might have had an overall weakening effect on religiosity for those who have grown up 'at home in a digital world' (Benedict XVI 2009b; see Smith and Denton 2005: 5). For example, many ex-Mormons cite the role of the internet as a critical catalyst in their own disaffiliations. This can be for various reasons, from providing different perspectives on LDS history than they had been brought up with, to enabling them to make and maintain close friendships with people outside of their otherwise Church-centric 'offline' networks, and to finding supportive forums and Facebook groups of (many) other 'ExMos'—online plausibility structures, that is, socializing people into being *not* Mormons.[7] It is not hard to imagine the existence of multiple less-extreme versions of this: young people raised in small towns, where almost everyone expresses some version of Christianity and nobody publicly avows unbelief, finding online a space where normative Christianity is and can be questioned, and where one encounters plenty of (otherwise normal) nonreligious folks (Downey 2014: 9). There is certainly much evidence for the internet playing an

---

[7] Based on my own interviews with LDS disaffiliates in New York, Oregon, and London, as part of another book project.

important role in the formation of secular individuals and communities, from the late 1990s onwards (Cimino and Smith 2014: 85–117).

None of this is to argue that social media cannot play an important role in *affirming* individuals or groups in their religious commitments. Indeed, I have myself argued that they both can and do (e.g., Bullivant 2014). The internet's *potential* to both reinforce one's existing convictions, and generate genuine forms of community devoted to them, is a real one (see Putnam 2000: 172). Furthermore, these basic processes may be exacerbated by the advent of the 'personalized web': Google searches tailor-made to align with your existing preferences, Facebook privileging the statuses of people it knows you typically agree with, 'curated' news stories targeted to those more likely to click them. These so-called 'filter bubbles' (Pariser 2011), which serve to reinforce one's existing views while filtering out opposing ones, received particular attention in the wake of the 2016 UK Brexit and US election results. Admittedly, the resulting 'filter bubble effect' is certainly not as total as sometimes alarmingly imagined. Anyone who really imagines that social media interactions are near-always ones of mutual concord and congratulation are themselves living in a *seriously* reality-filtering bubble. But it undoubtedly exists to some extent (Bakshy et al. 2015). While the technology may be new, the underlying sociology is textbook plausibility structures.

The internet also offers new opportunities for religious individuals to gather with their own 'tribe' in a particular niche of the web's 'long tail' (Anderson 2006; Godin 2008). In fact, given the sheer pervasiveness of digital technology, the creation of such online 'Benedict Options' (see Dreher 2017) is feasibly essential for Christian communities' continuing vitality. Nevertheless, there is strong evidence for thinking that the *overall* effect of the rise of the internet on American religion—at least so far—has been a negative one. Regardless of the specific mechanisms at work, recent studies have demonstrated a clear link between internet use and religious non-affiliation (Downey 2014) and, more specifically, that use of social networking sites correlates both negatively with religious attendance, and positively with taking a relativistic and syncretic approach to religious beliefs (McClure 2016, 2017).

The above are not the only possible explanations for the rise of the nones. Perhaps the overarching factor is the gradually waning level of commitment, evident across many denominations, from the 1960s onwards. In GSS 1972, 35 per cent of American adults said they attended religious services at least weekly, and only 9 per cent said that they never did. By 1990, the respective proportions were 30 per cent and 13 per cent. By 2016, it was 25 per cent and 24 per cent. Among 2016's under-30s, meanwhile, the difference was even starker: 17 per cent and 31 per cent. In this age demographic, 'nevers' have outstripped 'weeklies' in every survey wave since 1996. No doubt a good proportion of this is due, *mutatis mutandis*, to similar forces to those driving lapsation and disaffiliation in the Catholic Church: CRED-poor, low-practising forms of Christianity do not pass on very easily from one generation to the next. As also among Catholics, the growing rift between mainstream mores and traditional Christian teaching is also a factor, hence the strong congruence between liberal social values and having no religious affiliation (Hout and Fischer 2014).

All of this raises an obvious question. Is America becoming, religiously speaking, 'western European'? Or to put it another way: is America still a glaring counterexample to secularization (Newport 2012; Schnabel and Bock 2017), or in fact a late blooming confirmation of it (Bruce 2011: 157–76)? It is undeniably true that, at the level of national trends, 'religiosity has been declining in the United States for decades, albeit slowly and from high levels', and the pattern of this decline has been chiefly a generational one (Voas and Chaves 2016: 1258). The top-level trends do, however, mask some striking regional differences. Most notably, across the South—a vast swathe of land with a population roughly twice that of the UK—only 15 per cent of the population are nones, and 31 per cent report attending services at least weekly.[8] Meanwhile, the Western states have 31 per cent nones, and weekly-or-more attendance of 20 per cent. On the one hand, even the West's figures are a long off the typically 'western European' levels of secularity to be found in, say, Britain. On quite the other, one need not delve very far into the past to realize that even Southern 'highs' were very much higher, say, twenty years ago. In 1992–6, the South had 6 per cent nones, and 40 per cent weekly-or-more attenders. To put all of this in the most general of terms: much of America remains

---

[8] All statistics in this paragraph are based on my own analysis of the GSS. Except where otherwise stated, I have used 2012–16 data. For reference, the South here includes the West South Central, East South Central, and South Atlantic regions used in earlier geographical breakdowns. The West includes the Mountain and Pacific regions.

much more religious than much of western Europe and will assuredly remain so for the foreseeable future. Nevertheless, real religious decline is demonstrably occurring, and has been for some time. There is no reason to assume it will follow any predetermined, 'typically western European' script—and not only because there is no single such script for it to follow. Religious change, even change for the worse, is not a matter of conveyer-belt determinism. As Steve Bruce, as paid-up a proponent of the secularization thesis (properly understood) as one might desire, puts it:

> The secularization paradigm [. . .] is not a universally applicable scientific law, but a description and explanation of the past of European societies and their settler offspring. Contrary to often repeated caricatures, it is not a simple evolutionary model and does not imply a single uniform future. (2006: 35)

America might still 'flagrantly stand out from other Atlantic countries' (Taylor 2007: 425) in its current religiosity. Perhaps it also will in the manner in which it goes about losing it.

CONCLUSION

These observations bring our narrative nicely up-to-date. Up to, that is, Chapter 2's contemporary profile of British and American Catholic disaffiliates, using pooled 2012–16 data. To recap briefly, these showed among much else that:

- 44 per cent of British cradle Catholics, and 35 per cent of American ones, now no longer identify as Catholic.

- In Britain, the great bulk of disaffiliates—roughly seven-eighths of them—now identify with no religion. By contrast, American disaffiliates split equally between those now with no religion, and those affirming a different (i.e., non-Catholic) religious affiliation. In both countries those who 'switch' predominantly do so to a different Christian identity.

- Patterns of retention/disaffiliation vary greatly according to region, especially in America. This is roughly in line with the overarching religious 'microclimate'. For example, the West South Central region—comprising Texas, Louisiana, Oklahoma, and Kansas—has strong retention (72 per cent), while most of those who do leave adopt another Christian identity. Meanwhile in the Mountain States from Montana and Idaho down, retention is very low (54 per cent—i.e., sub-British levels), and most disaffiliates are now religious nones.

- In both countries, Catholic retention holds up better than other mainstream denominations', though the differences are not always vast. However, ex-Catholics are typically more likely to become nones than are disaffiliates from other denominations.

- Disaffiliates are disproportionately male, young(er), and—in the USA—non-immigrants, and White or Black (as opposed to Latino/a). These statistical generalizations ought not, however, deflect from the fact that disaffiliates are present in significant numbers within all main demographic groups. In Britain, for example, cradle-Catholic women are only slightly less likely to be disaffiliates than are men. In America, a quarter of Hispanics who were raised Catholic now identify as something else.

- Those born immediately after the Second World War—i.e., the Baby Boomers—are demonstrably a 'watershed generation' with regard to both Catholic practice and retention. This is true for both countries, but the shift is sharpest in our British data.

In large measure, the foregoing four chapters have constituted 'one long argument' (*pace* Darwin [1859] 1964: 459), attempting to provide a plausibly three-dimensional backstory to these and other statistics. A great deal of evidence, of several kinds, has been brought forward to support this backstory. These have included the fruits of several qualitative studies into lapsation and disaffiliation, other items of quantitative data (including a good deal of *ressourcement* vis-à-vis earlier studies), testimonies from biographies and memoirs, contemporary news reports from both Catholic and secular media, as well as—naturally—judicious borrowing from the evidence and arguments put forward by a wealth of other sociologists, historians, theologians, and journalists (from all of whom I have learned much; from those I disagree with most of all).

While trying to do justice to the particularities and peculiarities of this history, my overall approach has been guided by insights from three theoretical areas: plausibility structures, CREDs and CRUDs, and social network theory. It is hoped these have helped to elucidate the social mechanisms and processes at work *underneath* the various historical episodes and trends narrated. They are intended to be, so to speak, the underlying 'socio-logic' explaining *why* and *how*, for example, such disparate things as wartime romances, post-war town planning, avant-garde architectural ideas, the Filet-O-Fish sandwich, the design and placing of altars, 1970s pedagogical fashions, the downsizing of heavy industries, or the advent of social media might have influenced the likelihood of a person brought up Catholic growing up to be a practising Catholic—or even (to their own mind) any kind of Catholic whatsoever. It is these theoretical perspectives, therefore, which permit one to speak of offering causal explanations. It is one thing to say that 'V, W, X, and Y happened', then 'Z happened'. It is quite another to be able to propose a serious account that Z happened *because of* V and X, which had in turn been made possible due to D, and that the hitherto-dominant explanations W and Y had little or no effect at all. Naturally, the account offered in Chapters 4–7 is not the only one that either could be, or has been, constructed to explain large-scale Catholic lapsation and disaffiliation over the past fifty-or-so years. But I think it is a plausible one, and—as I have tried to show along the way—makes better sense of *all* the available data than do various competitors.

As discussed in Chapter 1, this book uses the Second Vatican Council as a kind of framing device. This is true in both simple chronological terms (the 'since Vatican II' of my title), and in terms of my intervening in various debates, scholarly and popular, vis-à-vis the Council's reception and legacy. As has been stated many times, an awful lot happened in the period with which we have been dealing. What is more, much of it happened conterminously with the Second Vatican Council and its immediate aftermath. It is high time, therefore, that we addressed the questions raised in Chapter 1, and present implicitly throughout, head on: What responsibility must Vatican II take for the quantity and/or precise texture of Catholic disaffiliation in Britain and America over the past fifty-or-so years? Or to put it another way: Is '*since* Vatican II', properly speaking, simply a euphemism for '*because of* Vatican II'?

Epilogue

Did the Council Fail?

In the foregoing pages, much has been made of the influence of wider social, cultural, economic, and intellectual factors in explaining the quantity and nature of Catholic disaffiliation. In Chapter 4, attention was given to the various restructurings of British and American society during and in the immediate aftermath of the Second World War. These included greater social mixing, the Baby Boom, increasing educational opportunities, town planning and suburbanization, growing prosperity, sales of cars and televisions, new architectural idioms, and much else. Similar 'secular'—or rather, in some cases, 'interdenominational'—factors have featured heavily in each subsequent chapter. This should come as no surprise to students of Vatican II. For the Church is, indeed, 'a community composed of humans', and 'is truly linked with mankind and its history by the deepest of bonds' (*Gaudium et Spes* 1).

Let us be quite clear here. Even had there been no Council, no deep and rapid liturgical reforms, no raised-then-dashed hopes surrounding the Pill, no official end to Friday abstinence, no 'demotion' of St Christopher... the strong likelihood is that British and American Catholicism would have had a fairly torrid time of the past half-century. As has been shown, 'leakage' was already a recognized and worried-about problem in the 1940s and 1950s. The rising tide of *National Review*'s 'stompin' rock 'n' roll 'teen-agers' (1957), and indeed Greeley's 'New Breed' (1964), were always going to come of age in a somewhat lively manner. And possibly most significantly, the traditional urban neighbourhoods—the long-standing incubators of robustly ingrained Catholic belief, practice, and identity—were already passing away.

What is more, the occurrence of widespread lapsation and disaffiliation in other Christian denominations is an obvious riposte to any account of Catholic disaffiliation that focuses too narrowly on Catholic-specific factors. In fact, since Catholic levels of retention and practice are *relatively* strong compared to say, Methodist, Lutheran, Baptist, and Anglican/Episcopalian ones (see Chapter 2), this would seem to be a strong argument in favour of the primary Catholic-specific story being a positive one. If Catholics are doing better than (some) other Christians, then it would be reasonable to suppose that the things that the Catholic Church did but the others didn't—not least holding an ecumenical Council in the 1960s—is a clue to its success.

This line of argumentation is, again, one with which *Mass Exodus* has much sympathy. Suburbanization, road building, and the rapidly increasing number of 'better things to do' at the weekend, impacted upon other hitherto close-knit religious minorities just as certainly as they did Catholicism (Marty 2006). The rise of social media is perfectly ecumenical in fostering relativism and nonreligiosity. And other Christian groups have suffered from the rapid divergence of traditional Christian teachings and contemporary sexual norms (e.g., Brown and Woodhead 2016: 35–62, 71–90; Bottum 2008). Given the across-the-board travails of other Christian denominations during this whole period, it makes little sense to ascribe *everything* to things that Catholics did or did not, or should or should not, have done.

This point is worth stressing. Had there been no Council, scholars might now be writing books arguing that *if only* the Church had less timidly embraced the Liturgical Movement; *if only* Pope John had realized his dream for a great Council; *if only* the Church had at least discussed revisiting *Casti Connubii*; *if only* the faithful had been permitted the option of making their Friday penance more personally meaningful; *if only* the judicious use of more relevant musical styles had been allowed; *if only* Catholics had updated some of its weirder, and ecumenically unpalatable, devotional practices... then perhaps more than half of Catholics would still be at Mass on a weekly basis, and the disaffiliation rate would not be at a parlously high 25 per cent.

These considerations, while doubtlessly true and important, are not remotely sufficient for explaining the scale and nature of Catholic lapsation and disaffiliation during the past five decades. That several non-Catholic-specific factors have demonstrably influenced the trends at the heart of this book, in no way implies that no Catholic-specific ones also have. The simple fact of there being serious wider social forces at work does not, in itself, mean that the Church's own reactions and responses had either no effect, or else had a positive-but-outweighed one. Religious organizations are rarely if ever simply the passive objects of external social pressures and trends, with no agency of their own either to counteract or exacerbate them, or indeed the potential to create original problems of their own design. There need be no dichotomy between 'worldly' and 'churchy' explanations of religious growth or decline. This is another area where we need not, to borrow Congar's idiom, 'choose one *or* the other' (1963: 49).

POST ET PROPTER

With this firmly in mind, consider these four truths which I regard, more or less, to be self-evident:

(i)   Given Vatican II's scale, scope, vision, and ambition, it could scarcely have failed to impact upon *any* area of Catholic ecclesial, pastoral, or theological life in the fifty years following it. This follows naturally from it being, and/or being widely seen to be, the 'most important event in the history of the Catholic Church in the last four centuries' (Faggioli 2012c: 20). New Pentecosts do not, it is fair to say, produce null effects.

(ii) This general point applies all the more so here, given the Council's particular concern for several topics of special relevance: the 'broaden[ing] and intensif[ying]' of the apostolate of the laity, better equipping them 'to penetrate the world with a Christian spirit, [and] to be witnesses to Christ in all things in the midst of human society' (*Apostolicam Actuositatem* 1; *Gaudium et Spes* 43); the imparting of 'an ever increasing vigor to the Christian life of the faithful [. . . and strengthening of] whatever can help to call the whole of mankind into the household of the Church' (*Sacrosanctum Concilium* 1); and the 'restoration and promotion of the sacred liturgy' in order to make it 'pastorally efficacious to the fullest degree' (*SC* 14, 49).

(iii) The Second Vatican Council, in John O'Malley's much-quoted phrase, '*wanted* something to happen' (2006: 33). Its purpose was avowedly one of reform and renewal (Benedict

XVI 2005). 'By introducing timely changes', John XXIII promised, the Church would strive to accomplish 'The major interest of the Ecumenical Council': i.e., 'that the sacred heritage of Christian truth be safeguarded and expounded with greater efficacy' and 'shall be more widely known, more deeply understood, and more penetrating in its effects on men's moral lives' (1962). All of this required enacting change of one sort or another: doing different things and/or doing things differently.

(iv) And finally, the diverse ways in which human beings pray, worship, and participate in religious rituals, individually and collectively, have concrete effects on people's moral, social, and cultural lives, as they also do upon their beliefs and identities. *How* we worship matters. On the one hand, this is a fairly pedestrian anthropological insight (see Bell 1989; McDannell 1995). On the other, it is a guiding principle of much liturgical theology, including that enshrined in the conciliar texts. Most obviously, it is central to the idea of the 'full and active participation by all the people'—'the bedrock of the Constitution on the Sacred Liturgy [without which it] it falls apart' (Chupungco 2016: 266)—being 'the primary and indispensable source from which the faithful are to derive the true Christian spirit' (*SC* 14).

Given these four principles, it is difficult to imagine a scenario in which the Council's reforms are *not* causally related to the very significant decline in Mass-going among British and American Catholics—and ultimately, to the high and growing levels of Catholic disaffiliation. The beginning of this decline coincided, more-or-less exactly, with the beginning of a sustained period of far-reaching changes, first to the Mass, and then to many other aspects of Catholic life. This inconvenient fact is most easily obviously and easily explained by the hypothesis that the reforms, as actually enacted and experienced, did not achieve what the Council evidently hoped that they would.

Vatican II was, after all, specifically *intended* better to equip the Church to meet the challenges of the present and future. That 'the world of this time' might be pastorally problematic is not a topic about which the Council Fathers can plead ignorance. For one thing, it was one of the main reasons why they were there in the first place.

It is also a topic they explicitly addressed, in detail, at various points in the conciliar corpus: e.g., 'we can already speak of a true cultural and social transformation, one which has repercussions on man's religious life as well' (*Gaudium et Spes* 4). The very purpose of the liturgical reforms is explicitly stated to be 'that they be given new vigor to meet the circumstances and needs of modern times' (*SC* 4). Its various directives are, moreover, made 'in order that the sacrifice of the Mass, even in the ritual forms of its celebration, may become pastorally efficacious to the fullest degree' (*SC* 49). Since these are *Sacrosanctum Concilium*'s own justifications for undertaking the reform, they may reasonably be used as the benchmark against which to judge its success. On the basis of fifty years' evidence from Britain and America—the only ground upon which this book is qualified to pass comment[1]—one has to say that the reforms failed.

This is not to say that the reforms did not achieve their intention anywhere, or with anyone. I don't doubt that many British or American Catholics now 'take part [more] fully aware of what they are doing, [more] actively engaged in the rite, and [more] enriched by its effects' than they either did before the reforms, or would have had there been different reforms or none at all. But I am equally sure that significant numbers of those still participating now do so less fully aware, less actively engaged, and less enriched by its effects (Driscoll 2005: 40–1; McCallion and Ligas 2018). Furthermore, it is irrefutable that vast numbers of baptized Catholics are not even remotely aware of, engaged in, or enriched by the Mass—at least not in any direct sense—precisely because they are not *at* Mass in the first place.

OBJECTIONS

At this point, it will be worthwhile to pre-empt three possible objections to the above paragraphs. The first two can be dealt with fairly quickly. The third and fourth warrant a little more space.

[1] The extent to which the conciliar reforms have impacted upon retention and disaffiliation in other countries is beyond the scope of this study. Perhaps the peculiarly British-American brand of Catholicism has suffered a kind of 'pastoral collateral damage', decreasing in order that the Church in other countries may increase.

The first objection accepts the fact of declining Mass attendance, but denies that this is in any way an indication of declining devotion. For example, no less an authority than Andrew Greeley once seriously wrote that 'If many devout Catholics now tend to go to church a couple of times a month rather than every week—and there is ample evidence they do—then there will be major shifts in who is present from Sunday to Sunday' (1997; see also Untener [1999] 2007: 39). However, unless we are to suppose that, post-Vatican II, Catholics are now *so* 'aware, engaged, and enriched' that even the most pious need only go to Mass once a fortnight or so, it is hard to interpret this as anything other than a deeply dubious redefinition of 'devout'.

The second, taking a slightly similar tack, makes what is in effect an appeal to 'quality over quantity'. This is actually quite common: it is present, for example, in black-and-white contrasts between *before the Council*, when no one understood what they were watching and were only there out of fear or superstitious habit, and *after the Council*, now that the laity understand what's happening, and more-over are prayerfully participating in it all. Another variant of this 'fewer but better' canard is the appeal to the near-total collapse of Catholic devotional life as evidence in favour of the success of the liturgical reform:

> What, then, of the frequently voiced complaint from some quarters that Catholics are less interested today in private devotions than they were in the years preceding the Second Vatican Council?
>
> This should not be taken as a negative reflection on the current state of the church's spiritual well-being. On the contrary, the lessening of interest in private devotions is more likely a sign that the church is spiritually healthier now because its spiritual life is, as the council hoped it would be, rooted more directly and more deeply in the liturgy itself, and especially in the Eucharist.   (McBrien 2003; see also 2009)

This is not the first time we have seen this type of zero-sum opposition between liturgy and devotional practices (see Chapter 5). Note here, however, how decline in the practice of the latter is taken as evidence for the quality and/or intensity of the former. Of course, one can buy into the same logic, and make the (equally shaky) opposite argument: the large-scale decline in Mass attendance is proof that, since the Council, Catholic devotional practices are now so spiritually supercharged that people no longer need to attend Mass. Far more probable, however, is the argument made at length in Chapter 5: that the Church's liturgy and devotions are, for better *and* worse, intimately connected and mutually reinforcing.

Thirdly, it is traditional at this juncture to draw a sharp distinction between 'the letter of the Council' and the various ways in which it was, concretely, interpreted and implemented. It is perfectly possible to say, for example, that *Sacrosanctum Concilium* is itself a fine and inspiring document, and had it only been properly interpreted, and properly implemented, then things would have gone very differently. Writing in 1980, Nicholas Kenyon, then-music critic for the *New Yorker*—though now, as *Sir* Nicholas, Managing Director of London's Barbican—could note: 'Looking back over fifteen years, it is difficult to avoid the conclusion that the situation was bungled [. . .] liturgical reform has run faster than pastoral life can keep up with it' (1980: 83, 86).

There is, I think, a good deal of truth in this (see Bullivant 2017). There is nothing in the document that demands that the reforms were rolled out in the specific ways that they were. As detailed in Chapter 5, it was the sheer chaos of the reform's first decade or so, as much as the content of the reforms themselves, that had such a disorienting effect on the laity. Furthermore, a great deal of the liturgical 'new normal' demonstrably goes beyond the overall *tenor* of the text. One can certainly imagine a reform in which any changes made were done so much more slowly, circumspectly, and uniformly, and in which the consensus interpretations of various vague principles in *Sacrosanctum Concilium* (regarding the ordering of the Sanctuary, for example) were rather less enthusiastic in their radicalism. It didn't, in short, have to be *this* way at all.

All that said, in practice it is much harder to put *Sacrosanctum Concilium*'s 'letter' and 'implementation' asunder than is sometimes supposed. One of the most striking features of its letter lies precisely in the very great latitude it allows to concrete interpretation and implementation. Most obviously, many significant decisions are formally devolved to 'competent territorial bodies of bishops legitimately established' (*SC* 22). Far beyond this, the document is quite emphatic that 'In the restoration and promotion of the sacred liturgy, [the] full and active participation by all the people is the aim to be considered *before all else* [*summopere*]' (*SC* 14; my emphasis). Taking this sentence at its word—indeed, its letter—effectively grants *carte blanche* to any priest or liturgist in the pursuit of fostering active participation. The same is true of the document's affirmation that 'In some places and circumstances [...] an even more radical adaptation of the liturgy is needed' (*SC* 40). That an appreciable number of British and American pastors evidently felt their own parishes or chaplaincies were precisely such exceptional 'places and circumstances' has already been discussed.

For these reasons, no very sharp line can be drawn between letter and implementation. As such, it might be helpful to speak in terms of the 'permissive will' of *Sacrosanctum Concilium*. It is very difficult to lay direct blame for any single one of the liturgical reforms' 'bunglings' at the door of the Council: in signing the document, the bishops did not *intend* to consign thousands of the People of God to bad cover-versions of Peter, Paul, and Mary songs. Nevertheless, the document undoubtedly opened up the possibility—indeed, a near-infinite variety of possibilities—of such misfortunes.

Fourthly and finally, let us revisit the travails of other mainstream denominations in roughly the same period, that is to say, 'since Vatican II'. Do not these facts rather prove that the Council (and other Catholic-specific factors) *cannot* be the real issue?

In a word, no. The fact that several Churches and ecclesial communities have suffered from lapsation and disaffiliation since the 1960s does not imply that all have done so in the same way, or for *all* of the same reasons. It also does not follow that the various strategies they have employed in response have been equally ineffectual. Furthermore, the fact that, as of 2012–16, Catholic retention rates are only a little better than those of other denominations (and denominations, let us not forget, rather less likely to have been 'boosted' recently by Latino, Filipino, Vietnamese, Polish, and/or Keralan immigration) is something that might itself be thought worthy of explanation.

Prior to the Council, for example, church-going among American Catholics was significantly higher than among Protestants. According to a 1955 Gallup poll, 75 per cent of self-identified Catholics said they had attended church in past seven days, compared to only 42 per cent of Protestants. In the sixty years since then, Protestant church-going has remained fairly steady, while Catholic attendance has roughly halved. It is now slightly below the Protestant rate (Saad 2018). On these and several other types of measure, it is clear that the Catholic Church fared much worse than other denominations. While current levels may be close to, or in some cases slightly better than, those of other denominations, indicators of Catholic commitment have often fallen from a much greater height to get there.

Writing in the early 1970s with a prescience bordering on prophecy, National Council of Churches researcher Dean Kelley asked *the* awkward question of American Catholicism's 'remarkable transformation such as few would have predicted a mere ten years ago':

> What has been the result of this amazing effort to make the Roman Catholic Church more reasonable, more ecumenical, more tolerant, more relevant to today's world? Has it become stronger, more vigorous—vital—confident? Not exactly. It has suffered the defection of hundreds of priests and nuns, not to mention lay members.
>
> ([1972] 1986: 34)

He proceeds to note a number of indicators 'suggesting that the once-unshakeable church has fallen into serious disarray. It has "leaped over the wall" to join the liberal, "relevant," ecumenical churches—and is beginning to show the same symptoms. Why?' His diagnosis, while diverging from my own in several respects, merits serious consideration:

> Some would say that they are all declining because they have not modernized rapidly enough; others consider it a regrettable but temporary trauma accompanying rapid change, which will subside when things settle down.
>
> Is it possible that it is neither, but instead a direct *consequence* of modernization? [I suspect] that the declining churches are not victims of changing times but of internal failure—the inability to provide a needed product or service. They have not adequately understood or performed their essential business: the dispensing of religion.
>
> ([1972] 1986: 35)

'SLIPPERY ROAD WITH NO GUARANTEES'

In the game of chess, a *sacrifice* is when a player deliberately surrenders a piece, not for any immediate recompense (e.g., to force a checkmate, or in 'trade' for another piece), but to gain—he or she hopes—some other, less immediately tangible, strategic advantage. Since chess-players do not normally give pieces away, the true sacrifice always has an element of surprise, if not outright shock. It disrupts the natural flow of how the game is unfolding, setting it off in a radically new direction. This is all the more so when the sacrificial victim is a particularly valuable piece that, in normal circumstances, a player would jealously protect. The sacrifice of a pawn can be dramatic enough. Yet in the words of one Grandmaster, 'What captures our imagination as much as a queen sacrifice? A queen sacrifice means we have to bravely give up our most important piece in order to create some magic on the board' (Williams 2016).

When it works, a sacrifice is a thing of both beauty and genius. Chess lore is filled with tales of sacrificial derring-do: moves of apparent madness, whose method is devastatingly revealed as the game progresses. But sacrifices are exciting precisely because they are so dangerous: 'the sacrificing side is not able to calculate the consequences to a final conclusion, [. . . he] takes off on a journey, on a slippery road with no guarantees' (Sokolov 2013: 236, 7). This can certainly be a statement of strength, of seizing control of the game, of confidence in one's victory even at a material disadvantage. But it is perhaps more commonly an act of desperation, born from the need to do something—*anything*—to divert the course of the game from where it's currently heading. A player whose current strategy is making steady progress is unlikely to want to risk it all.

> In real sacrifices the player gives up material, but is unable to calculate the consequences with accuracy; he has to rely on his judgment. He obtains dynamic advantages, which he can realize gradually. Should he not succeed in this, he will most probably lose the game through deficiency in material. Therein lies the risk, and risk is the hallmark of real sacrifice [. . .] the result lies in the lap of the gods, and at most can be formulated only intuitively.   (Spielmann [1935] 1995: 5)

This metaphor should not be pushed too far. However complicated a game of chess might be, it is infinitely simpler than the interacting networks of individuals, groups, ideas, and events that make up contemporary socio-religious life. A skilled chess-player, moreover, only has to second-guess a single opponent's next few moves. Church leaders must discern the social, cultural, intellectual, political, and demographic 'signs of the times', interpret them 'in the light of the gospel', and foresee how both might play out in the years or decades to come (see *Gaudium et Spes* 4). That they do not always or immediately 'get it right' is a simple fact of church history. Ecumenical Councils are, indeed, a case in point. Given the time, effort, expense, and upheaval they require, they are usually only called once a problem is well out of hand. The Council of Nicaea did not end the Arian controversy. The Council of Florence-Ferrara did not reunite Latins and Greeks. The Council of Trent did not, among its various aims, fully accomplish 'the extirpation of heresies', 'the peace and union of the Church', or 'the depression and extinction of the enemies of the Christian name' (*Decree concerning the Opening of the Council*, 1545).

This book has traced the history and contours of large-scale 'Catholic disaffiliation in Britain and America since Vatican II'. One of its leitmotifs has been the social and cultural 'mainstreaming' of Catholicism in the post-war period. Much of this was involuntary: the products of demographics, social restructuring, and shifting cultures. A good proportion of it, though, was self-sought, done with the best of intentions. In order to bring the Church into the world, to infuse it with the light of Christ, the 'ghetto' walls needed breaking down. To do this, the Church and its practices would need to be less weird and culturally remote: for there to be 'no cause for others to "regard us as odd"' (Douglas ([1970] 1996: 44). Everything from the words of the Mass itself, to the dress habits of nuns, to the soft furnishings of confessionals, should be made more accessible and relevant. The tactic did not, as it has turned out, reap very rich rewards. Catholics 'became like everyone else' (Douglas ([1970] 1996: 44) at precisely the same moment as 'everybody else' started rapidly to become less orthodoxly believing, less regularly practising, and ultimately, less religiously identifying.

The story of British and American Catholic disaffiliation has, I fear, a while yet to run. The eventual reversal of this Mass Exodus, and what Catholic 'retainees' and converts might do to hasten it, is a subject for a different book.

Appendix: Mass Attendance Statistics for England and Wales, Scotland, and Selected US Dioceses (1958–2017)

The following table collates annual 'typical Sunday' Mass count data for England and Wales, Scotland, and 30 American territorial Latin-rite dioceses or archdioceses (out of a total of 177). All figures come from official sources, directly or indirectly. Some of these figures have been used as the basis for a number of graphs in Chapters 6 and 7. However, since these kinds of figures are very hard to come by, I thought it might be useful to present them here. They do, however, come with the caveat (one stressed, I might add, by several diocesan officials responsible for overseeing the annual 'October count') that, due to the ways in which these are collected, there is significant potential for errors to creep in. While questions might be asked about any one year, if treated 'impressionistically', they should nevertheless give valuable insights into overall trends.

Counting worshippers is a time-consuming process, especially when done at every Sunday (and Saturday evening vigil) Mass, in every parish, and—as is common practice in several dioceses—on each of four separate Sundays with an average taken. In some dioceses, the process is done more than once in the year, especially if there is significant seasonal fluctuation (e.g., due to being a holiday destination). Not every US diocese conducts a formal count, and many have only started theirs within the past decade or two. In the relatively rare dioceses that have been conducting counts for a long time, older records are often held only as paper copies in the diocesan archives: it would be a major undertaking to process and collate them all. Counts are also, of course, very dependent on individual parishes actually doing them properly, and submitting their returns. Finally, even where dioceses collect and keep these kinds of data, they are—as I have found—not always willing to share them.

In June and July 2018, I emailed (or filled out a form on the website of) each of the US dioceses, requesting as long a series of annual Mass counts as they might possess and be willing to send me. I am grateful to all of those who bothered to respond to this electronic cold-calling, and naturally even more so to those who readily collected and sent their data. In many cases, this required considerable effort in finding and collating the figures—and therefore, considerable kindness on the part of those willing to do it.

In addition to the data received 'direct', I was also able to gather some figures from diocesan websites, media reports, or academic publications (especially Chaves and Cavendish 1994 for America; Catholic Education Council 2006, Latin Mass Society 2013, and Spencer 2014 for England and Wales; and Brierley 1999 and Bruce 2014 for Scotland). Archived diocesan newspapers proved to be a particularly rich source of data for the critical period immediately after the Council. The run of eight years' worth of 1970s counts for the Archdiocese of Hartford, for example, were gleaned from back issues of *Catholic Transcript* (available and searchable online, along with several other hugely useful publications, at: https://thecatholicnewsarchive. org/).

In addition to the abovementioned sources, I am grateful to a large number of individuals for either supplying data themselves, or for suggesting people who might. These include, in Britain, Dr Peter Brierley, Prof. Callum Brown, Prof. Steve Bruce, Prof. Clive Field, and Lorraine Welch. And in America (with due apologies to anyone missed out), Sandy Riesberg, Dcn James Crowley, Linda Nichols, Mark Howard, Bernard Grizard, Thomas Bebbington, MaryAnn Bernier, Rita Gracia, Kevin Fuss, Mary Beth Celio, Mark Kemetter, Susan Skibba, Dcn Dan Joyce, John Schwob, Nancy Valtos, Annette Denton, Dr Tom Denton, Renae Bennett, Carol Brinati, Patty Young, Barry Metzentine, Julianne Stanz, Caroline Rose, Sr Jane Ann Slater, Dcn Keith Cabiles, Kimberly Carter, Ann Williams, Donald Schlegel, Robert Graffio, Antonia Velasco, and Chris Doan. Thank you!

'Typical Sunday' Mass attendance (000s)

	England&Wales	Scotland	Chicago, IL	Cincinnati, OH	Boston, MA	Columbus, OH	Dallas, TX	Denver, CO	Des Moines, IA	Dubuque, IA	Green Bay, WI	Hartford, CT	Honolulu, HI	Jefferson City, MO	Manchester, NH	Marquette, MI	Milwaukee, WI	Newark, NJ	Ogdensburg, NY	Orlando, FL	Owensboro, KY	Philadelphia, PA	Pittsburgh, PA	Rochester, NY	Rockford, IL	San Antonio, TX	San Francisco, CA	Savannah, GA	Scranton, PA	Springfield, IL	Steubenville, OH	Trenton, NJ
1958	1874					109																										
1959	1892					112																										
1960	1949	418				111																										
1961	2024					118																										
1962	2093					121																										
1963						125																										
1964						127																										
1965	2114					130																										
1966	2092					127																										
1967	2055					121																										
1968	1988					116																										
1969	1935					117						395																				
1970	1900	394				116						381																				
1971	1886					118						352																				
1972	1832			303		111						342																				
1973				297		110						334																				
1974	1753					106						328																				
1975	1791					107						323																				
1976	1722					105						314																				

(continued)

Continued

Year	England&Wales	Scotland	Chicago, IL	Cincinnati, OH	Boston, MA	Columbus, OH	Dallas, TX	Denver, CO	Des Moines, IA	Dubuque, IA	Green Bay, WI	Hartford, CT	Honolulu, HI	Jefferson City, MO	Manchester, NH	Marquette, MI	Milwaukee, WI	Newark, NJ	Ogdensburg, NY	Orlando, FL	Owensboro, KY	Philadelphia, PA	Pittsburgh, PA	Rochester, NY	Rockford, IL	San Antonio, TX	San Francisco, CA	Savannah, GA	Scranton, PA	Springfield, IL	Steubenville, OH	Trenton, NJ
1977	1699					106																										
1978	1694					104																										
1979	1675					105																										
1980	1644	369				106																										
1981						107																										
1982	1570					107																										
1983	1537					104												349														
1984	1513	346				103												331														
1985	1460					103												335														
1986	1425					100												315														
1987	1399		611			96												313														
1988	1384		581			97												311														
1989	1350		587			96												305														
1990	1323	284	582	235		95	102				149	249				40		306			33	413	296		95		115				30	
1991	1300	273	583		456	94		122			143							297				407			94							
1992		269	578			94		121									311	301				406			95						29	
1993	1278	254	555			92		121										278				394			96						29	
1994	1226	249	553			92		129			135							282				391			98						29	
1995	1190	250	554			93		128			133							283				392			98						28	
1996	1135	249	551			92		129										276				386			101					84	28	
1997	1086	239	547			94		129										274				387			102					81	28	

Year																										
1998	1056	228	552		95		134	41		130	47		34	234	272			386		106	104				81	27	
1999	1042	222	555	219	93		140								272			378		106					80	26	
2000	1006	212	561	376	94		138	42			47		34	214	263		31	376	247	107	107				80	26	
2001	994	202	572	358	96	146	144	41		124	47		33	206	232			380		101	113				79	25	
2002	1072		538	309	92	163	141	42		125	46		31	209	237			356		98	113			37	75	26	
2003			523	317	89	156	138	36	93	121	46		30	203	236			343		96	111			37	72	25	
2004	959		508	322	89	151	137	38	91	118	45	98	28	196	228			332		93	110		37	36	69	24	221
2005	941		500	320	87	155	136	38	88	113	43	101	27	194	225			323		87	109		93	37	68	25	214
2006	927		490		86	163	138	38	87	108	43	95	27	179	226		30	311		84	107	152	92	41	66	22	207
2007	916		476		81	159	130	38	83	107	42	95	25	170	217	145		300		79	105	148	89	37	64	23	207
2008	919	186	474	178	84	166	135	35	81	102	41	91	25	167	204	172		291		75	108	148	90	37	63	21	187
2009	899		463	287	82	166	136	30	78	101	41	79	24	169	209	169		283		72	105	158	86	37	60	21	192
2010	885		457		81	174	135	25	76	97	40	77	23	158	206	168	32	275		68	105	156	90	33	60	20	157
2011		161	451		80	176	138	37	74	95	39	68	23	152	199	165	30	263		66	102	152	87	34	59	19	155
2012	849		446		79	181	137	31	72	93	39	62	18	147	189	155	29	253		63	101	150	84	35	57	19	148
2013			435		75	186	134	33	72	90	38	64	21	138		157	29	249	149	60	100	156	83	36	56	19	142
2014			422		77	187	135	31	70	86	37	62	20	140		156	27	240	139	57	94	144	80	30	55	18	140
2015			411		75	187	134	29	69	82	37	60	20	134		134	27	234	124	55	94	148	78	32	53	18	137
2016	772		401		74	184	134	34	67	79	36			130		150	27	222		53	91	141	76	30	49	17	135
2017			396		74	189	133		65	74	48	60		130		143	23	213		53	90				49	17	132

Bibliography

(All weblinks last checked on 21 September 2018)

Ahlstrom, Sydney E., and David D. Hall. 2004. *A Religious History of the American People* (New Haven, CT: Yale University Press)

Alberigo, Giuseppe. 2006. *A Brief History of Vatican II*, trans. Matthew Sherry (Maryknoll, NY: Orbis Books)

Alberts, John Bernard. 1998. 'Origins of Black Catholic Parishes in the Archdiocese of New Orleans, 1718–1920', unpublished PhD thesis, Louisiana State University

Allen, Chris. 2017. '"Doing God" According to David Cameron: Evangelism and Christian Britain': http://blogs.lse.ac.uk/politicsandpolicy/doing-god-according-to-david-cameron/#Author

Altieri, Christopher. 2018. 'Viganò Letter: Awaiting Clarity', *Catholic Herald*, 13 September: http://www.catholicherald.co.uk/magazine-post/vigano-letter-awaiting-clarity/

Anderson, Chris. 2006. *The Long Tail: Why the Future of Business is Selling Less of More* (New York: Hyperion)

Anderson, Emma. 2013. *The Death and Afterlife of the North American Martyrs* (Cambridge, MA: Harvard University Press)

Anderson, R. Bentley. 2006. 'Pride and Prejudice in New Orleans: Joseph Fichter's *Southern Parish*', *U.S. Catholic Historian* 24/4, 23–46

Anderson, Robert. 2016. 'University Fees in Historical Perspective', *History and Policy* policy paper: http://www.historyandpolicy.org/policy-papers/papers/university-fees-in-historical-perspective

Anglican Consultative Council. [1930] 2005. 'The Lambeth Conference: Resolutions Archive from 1930': http://www.anglicancommunion.org/media/127734/1930.pdf

Archbishops' Council. 2011. *Church Statistics 2009/10*: https://www.churchofengland.org/sites/default/files/2017-11/2009_10churchstatistics.pdf

Archer, Anthony. 1986. *The Two Catholic Churches: A Study in Oppression* (London: SCM Press)

Armstrong, George. 1969. 'The Saints Go Marching Out', *Guardian*, 10 May, 1

Arnett, Jeffrey Jensen. 2000. 'Emerging Adulthood: A Theory of Development from the Late Teens through the Twenties', *American Psychologist* 55/5, 469–80

Atherstone, Andrew. 2011. 'The Canonisation of the Forty English Martyrs: An Ecumenical Dilemma', *Recusant History* 30/4, 573–87

Atran, Scott, and Joseph Henrich. 2010. 'The Evolution of Religion: How Cognitive By-products, Adaptive Learning Heuristics, Ritual Displays, and Group Competition Generate Deep Commitments to Prosocial Religions', *Biological Theory* 5, 18–30

Averett, Kate Henley. 2009. 'Mass in the Dining Room', in Kate Dugan and Jennifer Owens (eds), *From the Pews in the Back: Young Women and Catholicism* (Collegeville, MN: Liturgical Press), 140–4

Badawy, Adam, and Emilio Ferrara. 2018. 'The Rise of Jihadist Propaganda on Social Networks', *Journal of Computational Social Science*, 1–18 (online early publication)

Bader, Christopher D., and Scott A. Desmond. 2006. 'Do as I Say and as I Do: The Effects of Consistent Parental Beliefs and Behaviors upon Religious Transmission', *Sociology of Religion*, 67/3, 313–29

Baggett, Jerome P. 2008. *Sense of the Faithful: How American Catholics Live Their Faith* (New York: Oxford University Press)

Bain, Elaine M. 2011. 'The Abuse of Faith: The Effect of Clerical Child Sex Abuse on the Faith Life of Victims', in Brendan Geary and Joanne Marie Greer (eds), *The Dark Night of the Catholic Church: Examining the Child Sexual Abuse Scandal* (Stowmarket: Kevin Mayhew), 197–205

Baker-Sperry, Lori. 2001. 'Passing on the Faith: The Father's Role in Religious Transmission', *Sociological Focus* 34/2, 185–98

Bakshy, Eytan, Solomon Messing, and Lada A. Adamic. 2015. 'Exposure to Ideologically Diverse News and Opinion on Facebook', *Science* 348/6239, 1130–2

Baldovin, John F. 2008. *Reforming the Liturgy: A Response to the Critics* (Collegeville, MN: Liturgical Press)

Balmer, Randall. 2014. *Mine Eyes Have Seen the Glory: A Journey into the Evangelical Subculture in America*, 5th edn (New York: Oxford University Press)

Baltimore Catechism. 1941. *A Catechism of Christian Doctrine: Revised Edition of the Baltimore Catechism, no. 2* (Paterson, NJ: St Anthony Press)

Barabási, Albert-László. 2002. *Linked: The New Science of Networks* (New York: Perseus Books)

Barron, Robert. 2004. *Bridging the Great Divide: Musings of a Post-Liberal, Post-Conservative, Evangelical Catholic* (Lanham, MD: Rowman & Littlefield)

Barron, Robert. 2017. '*Optatum Totius*', in Matthew L. Lamb and Matthew Levering (eds), *The Reception of Vatican II* (New York: Oxford University Press), 191–207

Beaudoin, Tom, and J. Patrick Hornbeck. 2013. 'Deconversion and Ordinary Theology: A Catholic Study', in Jeff Astley and Leslie J. Francis (eds), *Exploring Ordinary Theology: Everyday Christian Believing and the Church* (Aldershot: Ashgate, 2013), 33–44

Beckett, Francis. 2010. *What Did the Baby Boomers Ever Do For Us? Why the Children of the Sixties Lived the Dream and Failed the Future* (London: Biteback)

Beckwith, Francis J. 2009. *Return to Rome: Confessions of an Evangelical Catholic* (Grand Rapids, MI: Brazos Press)

Beeson, Trevor. 1968. 'Archbishop Talks on the Encyclical', *Irish Times*, 10 August, 8

Bell, Catherine. 1989. 'Ritual, Change and Changing Rituals', *Worship* 63/1, 31–41

Benedict XVI. 2005. 'Address of His Holiness Benedict XVI to the Roman Curia Offering them his Christmas Greetings': http://w2.vatican.va/content/benedict-xvi/en/speeches/2005/december/documents/hf_ben_xvi_spe_20051222_roman-curia.html

Benedict XVI. 2008. 'Responses of His Holiness Pope Benedict XVI to the Questions Posed by the Bishops', 16 April: http://www.vatican.va/holy_father/benedict_xvi/speeches/2008/april/documents/hf_ben-xvi_spe_20080416_response-bishops_en.html

Benedict XVI. 2009a. 'Apostolic Letter *'motu proprio'* *Omnium in Mentem* of the Supreme Pontiff Benedict XVI on several amendments to the Code of Canon Law', 26 October: http://w2.vatican.va/content/benedict-xvi/en/apost_letters/documents/hf_ben-xvi_apl_20091026_codex-iuris-canonici.html

Benedict XVI. 2009b. 'Message of the Holy Father Pope Benedict XVI for the 43rd World Communications Day': http://www.vatican.va/holy_father/benedict_xvi/messages/communications/documents/hf_ben-xvi_mes_20090124_43rd-world-communications-day_en.html

Bengtson, Vern L., Norella M. Putney, and Susan C. Harris. 2013. *Families and Faith: How Religion is Passed Down Across Generations* (New York: Oxford University Press)

Benjamin, Rich. 2009. *Searching for Whitopia: An Improbable Journey to the Heart of White America* (New York: Hyperion)

Berger, Peter. 1980. *The Heretical Imperative: Contemporary Possibilities of Religious Affirmation* (London: Collins)

Berger, Peter. [1967] 1990. *The Sacred Canopy: Elements of a Sociological Theory of Religion* (New York: Doubleday)

Berger, Peter. 1995. 'The Vernacularist Illusion', *First Things*, April: https://www.firstthings.com/article/1995/04/005-the-vernacularist-illusion

Berger, Peter. 1999. 'The Desecularization of the World: A Global Overview', in Peter Berger (ed.), *The Desecularization of the World: Resurgent Religion and World Politics* (Grand Rapids, MI: Eerdmans), 1–18

Berger, Peter, and Thomas Luckmann. [1966] 1971. *The Social Construction of Reality* (Harmondsworth: Penguin)

Berry, Jason. 1986. 'Anatomy of a Cover-Up', *Times of Acadiana*, 30 January, 14–15

Berry, Jason. [1992] 2000. *Lead Us Not Into Temptation: Catholic Priests and the Sexual Abuse of Children* (Urbana, IL: University of Illinois Press)

Bird, Warren. 2018. 'World Megachurches' database: http://leadnet.org/world/

Bischoff, Claire. 2009. 'Saving Religion', in Kate Dugan and Jennifer Owens (eds), *From the Pews in the Back: Young Women and Catholicism* (Collegeville, MN: Liturgical Press), 152–9

Bishops' Conference of England and Wales. 1980. *The Easter People: A Message from the Roman Catholic Bishops of England and Wales in Light of the National Pastoral Congress, Liverpool* (Slough: St Paul's)

Bottum, Joseph. 2008. 'The Death of Protestant America: A Political Theory of the Protestant Mainline', *First Things*, August: https://www.firstthings.com/article/2008/08/001-the-death-of-protestant-america-a-political-theory-of-the-protestant-mainline

Bouyer, Louis. 1965. *The Liturgy Revived: A Doctrinal Commentary of the Conciliar Constitution on the Liturgy* (London: Darton, Longman & Todd)

Bowman, Marion. 2016. 'Crisis, Change and "the Continuous Art of Individual Interpretation and Negotiation": The Aftermath of Clerical Sexual Abuse in Newfoundland', *Journal of the Irish Society for the Study of Religions* 3, 140–67

Boyce, Frank. 1999. 'Catholicism in Liverpool's Docklands: 1950s–1990s', in Michael Hornsby-Smith (ed.), *Catholics in England 1950–2000: Historical and Sociological Perspectives* (London: Cassell), 46–66

Bradley, Joseph M. 2015. 'Sectarianism, Anti-Sectarianism and Scottish Football', *Sport in Society* 18/5, 588–603

Brañas-Garza, P., T. García-Muñoz, and S. Neuman. 2013. 'Determinants of Disaffiliation: An International Study', *Religions* 4, 166–85

Brenner, Philip S. 2012. 'Investigating the Effect of Bias in Survey Measures of Church Attendance', *Sociology of Religion* 73/4, 361–83

Brierley, Peter (ed.). 1999. *Religious Trends 2000/1* (London: Marshall Pickering)

Brierley, Peter. 2006. *Pulling out of the Nosedive: A Contemporary Picture of Churchgoing: What the 2005 English Church Census Reveals* (London: Christian Research)

Briggs, Kenneth A. 1979. 'U.S. Catholics Finding Bearings After Long Period of Upheaval', *New York Times*, 29 January, A1, D8

British Pathé. 1966. 'Liverpool Cathedral Progress': http://www.britishpathe.com/video/cathedral-progress/query/workmen

British Pathé. 1967. 'A Cathedral in Our Time': http://player.bfi.org.uk/film/watch-cathedral-in-our-time-1967

Brodkin, Karen 1998. *How Jews Became White Folks and What that Says about Race in America* (New Brunswick, NJ: Rutgers University Press)

Brogan, Denis. 1969. 'Paul's Purge', *Spectator*, 23 May, 13

Brown, Andrew, and Linda Woodhead. 2016. *That Was the Church That Was: How the Church of England Lost the English People* (London: Bloomsbury)

Brown, Callum G. 2001. *The Death of Christian Britain: Understanding Secularisation 1800–2000* (London: Routledge)

Brown, Callum G. 2006. *Religion and Society in Twentieth-Century Britain* (Abingdon: Routledge)

Brown, Callum G. 2011. 'Sex, Religion and the Single Woman c.1950–1975: The Importance of a "Short" Sexual Revolution to the English Religious Crisis of the Sixties', *Twentieth-Century British History* 22/2, 189–215

Brown, Callum G. 2012. *Religion and the Demographic Revolution: Women and Secularisation in Canada, Ireland, UK and USA since the 1960s* (Woodbridge: Boydell Press)

Brown, Callum G. 2017. *Becoming Atheist: Humanism and the Secular West* (London: Bloomsbury)

Bruce, Steve. 1996. *Religion in the Modern World: From Cathedrals to Cults* (Oxford: Oxford University Press)

Bruce, Steve. 2002. *God is Dead: Secularization in the West* (Oxford: Oxford University Press)

Bruce, Steve. 2006. 'Secularization and the Impotence of Individualized Religion', *Hedgehog Review* 8/1–2, 35–45

Bruce, Steve. 2011. *Secularization: In Defence of an Unfashionable Theory* (Oxford: Oxford University Press)

Bruce, Steve. 2014. *Scottish Gods: Religion in Modern Scotland 1900–2012* (Edinburgh: Edinburgh University Press)

Bruce, Steve, and Tony Glendinning. 2010. 'When was Secularization?: Dating the Decline of the British Churches and Locating its Cause', *British Journal of Sociology* 61/1, 107–26.

Bruce, Tricia Colleen. 2017. *Parish and Place: Making Room for Diversity in the American Catholic Church* (Oxford: Oxford University Press)

Bryson, Bill. 2006. *The Life and Times of the Thunderbolt Kid* (London: Doubleday)

Buckley, Timothy J. 1999. 'English Catholics and Divorce', in Michael Hornsby-Smith (ed.), *Catholics in England 1950–2000: Historical and Sociological Perspectives* (London: Cassell), 119–218

Bullivant, Joanna, and Stephen Bullivant. 2011. 'Sing an Old Song to the Lord', *Pastoral Review* 7/2, 58–65

Bullivant, Stephen. 2008. 'Introducing Irreligious Experiences', *Implicit Religion* 11/1, 7–24

Bullivant, Stephen. 2010. 'The New Atheism and Sociology: Why Here? Why Now? What Next?', in Amarnath Amarasingam (ed.), *Religion and the New Atheism: A Critical Appraisal* (Leiden and Boston, MA: Brill), 109–24

Bullivant, Stephen. 2012a. *The Salvation of Atheists and Catholic Dogmatic Theology* (Oxford: Oxford University Press)

Bullivant, Stephen. 2012b. 'Not so Indifferent After All? The New Visibility of Atheism and the Secularization Thesis', *Approaching Religion* 2/1, 100–6

Bullivant, Stephen. 2014. 'I Call You (Facebook) Friends: New Media and the New Evangelization', in Martin Lintner (ed.), *God in Question: Religious Language and Secular Languages* (Brixen: Verlag Weger, 2014), 461–73

Bullivant, Stephen. 2016a. 'Catholic Disaffiliation in Britain: A Quantitative Overview', *Journal of Contemporary Religion* 31/2, 1–17

Bullivant, Stephen. 2016b. *Contemporary Catholicism in England and Wales: A Statistical Report Based on Recent British Social Attitudes Data*, Catholic Research Forum Reports 1 (Benedict XVI Centre for Religion and Society): http://www.stmarys.ac.uk/benedict-xvi/docs/2016-may-contemporary-catholicism-report.pdf

Bullivant, Stephen. 2016c. 'This New Attack on Humanae Vitae is either Ignorant or Disingenuous', *Catholic Herald*, 15 September: http://www.catholicherald.co.uk/commentandblogs/2016/09/15/this-new-attack-on-humanae-vitae-is-either-ignorant-or-disingenuous/

Bullivant, Stephen. 2017. '"Especially in mission territories": New Evangelization and Liturgical (Reform of the) Reform', in Uwe Michael Lang (ed.), *Authentic Liturgical Renewal in Contemporary Perspective* (London: T. & T. Clark, 2017), 97–107

Bullivant, Stephen. 2018a. 'A New Finding: One in Five UK Catholics was Born Elsewhere', *Catholic Herald*, 10 May: http://www.catholicherald.co.uk/commentandblogs/2018/05/10/a-new-finding-one-in-five-uk-catholics-was-born-elsewhere/

Bullivant, Stephen. 2018b. *Findings from the European Social Survey (2014–16) to Inform the 2018 Synod of Bishops* (Benedict XVI Centre for Religion and Society/Institut Catholique de Paris): https://www.stmarys.ac.uk/research/centres/benedict-xvi/docs/2018-mar-europe-young-people-report-eng.pdf

Bullivant, S., C. Knowles, H. Vaughan-Spruce, and B. Durcan. 2019. *Why Catholics Leave, What They Miss, and How They Might Return* (Mahwah, NJ: Paulist Press)

Burgess, Anthony. [1967] 2017. 'On Being a Lapsed Catholic', *First Things*: https://www.firstthings.com/web-exclusives/2017/08/on-being-a-lapsed-catholic

Burke, Daniel. 2018. '"How Could this Happen Again?" Why this Catholic Abuse Scandal Seems Worse than 2002', *CNN*, 20 August: https://edition.cnn.com/2018/08/19/us/catholic-sex-abuse-outrage/index.html

Burns, Jeffrey M. 2018. 'Sexuality after the Council: Gay Catholics, Married Clergy, Rights, and Change in San Francisco, 1962–1987', in Kathleen

Sprows Cummings, Timothy Matovina, and Robert A. Orsi (eds), *Catholics in the Vatican II Era: Local Histories of a Global Event* (New York: Cambridge University Press), 3–27

Byron, William J., and Charles Zech. 2012. 'Why They Left', *America*, 30 April, 17–23

Cable, Vince. 2009. *Free Radical: A Memoir* (London: Atlantic Books)

Callan, Charles J., and John A. McHugh. [1960] 2016. *Blessed Be God: A Complete Catholic Prayer Book with Epistles and Gospels for Every Sunday and Holyday of the Year* (Boonville, NY: Preserving Christian)

Campbell, Eileen. 2009. 'Small Rebellions, Small Surrenders', in Kate Dugan and Jennifer Owens (eds), *From the Pews in the Back: Young Women and Catholicism* (Collegeville, MN: Liturgical Press), 12–16

Canedo, Ken. 2009. *Keep the Fire Burning: The Folk Mass Revolution* (Portland, OR: Pastoral Press)

Carey, Patrick W. 2004. *Catholics in America: A History*, rev. edn (Lanham, MD: Sheed & Ward)

Carlin, David. 2003. *The Decline and Fall of the Catholic Church in America* (Manchester, NH: Sophia Institute Press)

Carlin, David. 2005. 'The Sudden Decline of the Catholic Church in America', *Catholic Social Science Review* 10, 107–16

Carmody, Deirdre. 1968. 'Catholic Experts in Strong Dissent on Edict by Pope', *New York Times*, 31 July, 1

Casson, Ann E. 2014. *Challenges and Opportunities for the New Evangelisation: A Case Study of Catholic Primary School Parents in England and Wales*: http://www.cbcew.org.uk/content/download/52740/407267/file/research-paper-cath-parents-new-evang-051114.pdf

Catholic Education Council. 2006. *Pastoral & Demographic Statistics of the Catholic Church in England & Wales, 1963–1991*, ed. A. E. C. W. Spencer (Taunton: Russell-Spencer)

Catholic Transcript. 1975. 'Catholic Bishops Launch Education on Sunday Mass', *Catholic Transcript*, 25 April, 3

Catholic Transcript. 1976a. 'Does Vigil Permission Increase Mass Attendance?', *Catholic Transcript*, 14 May, 3

Catholic Transcript. 1976b. 'Pastoral on Sunday Observance is Issued by Bishop Curtis', *Catholic Transcript*, 3 December, 7

Cavadini, John C. 2017. 'Introduction', in John C. Cavadini and Danielle M. Peters (eds), *Mary on the Eve of the Second Vatican Council* (Notre Dame, IN: University of Notre Dame Press), 1–30

Cavanagh, Mary. 1959. 'Religion in Glasgow', *Tablet*, 9 May, 439–40

Cavendish, James C., Michael R. Welch, and David C. Leege. 1998. 'Social Network Theory and Predictors of Religiosity for Black and White Catholics: Evidence of a "Black Sacred Cosmos"?', *Journal for the Scientific Study of Religion* 37/3, 397–410

CBCEW. 2015. 'Crossing the Threshold': http://www.cbcew.org.uk/CBCEW-Home/Departments/Evangelisation-and-Catechesis/Crossing-the-Threshold-Non-Churchgoing-Catholics/8language9/eng-GB

Center for Applied Research in the Apostolate. 2008. 'The Impact of Religious Switching and Secularization on the Estimated Size of the U.S. Adult Catholic Population': http://cara.georgetown.edu/caraservices/FRStats/Winter2008.pdf

Central Intelligence Agency. 2016. 'The World Factbook: United Kingdom': https://www.cia.gov/library/publications/the-world-factbook/geos/uk.html#Geo

Champion Forest. 2017. 'Champions': http://www.championforest.org/about/cypresscreekcampus/

Charlesworth, Martin, and Natalie Williams. 2017. *A Church for the Poor: Transforming the Church to Reach the Poor in Britain Today* (Colorado Springs, CO: David C. Cook)

Chaves, Mark, and James C. Cavendish. 1994. 'More Evidence on U.S. Catholic Church Attendance', *Journal for the Scientific Study of Religion* 33/4, 376–81

Checkley, John. 1969. 'The Pope Sacks 30 Saints', *Daily Mirror*, 10 May, 1

Cherry, Stephen M. 2014. *Faith, Family, and Filipino American Community Life* (New Brunswick, NJ: Rutgers University Press)

Chesterton, G. K. 1926. *The Everlasting Man* (New York: Dodd, Mead, and Co.)

Chesterton, G. K. [1933] 1990. 'The Church and Agoraphobia', in *G. K. Chesterton: Collected Works, Vol. III* (San Francisco, CA: Ignatius Press), 451–3

Chinnici, Joseph P. 2004. 'The Catholic Community at Prayer, 1926–1976', in James O'Toole (ed.), *Habits of Devotion: Catholic Religious Practice in Twentieth-Century America* (Ithaca, NY: Cornell University Press), 9–87

Christakis, Nicholas A., and James H. Fowler. 2009. *Connected: The Surprising Power of Our Social Networks and How They Shape Our Lives* (New York: Little, Brown, and Co.)

Christopher, David P. 2015. *British Culture: An Introduction*, 3rd edn (London: Routledge)

Chupungco, Anscar J. 2016. 'The Vision of the Constitution on the Liturgy', in Alcuin Reid (ed.), *T&T Clark Companion to Liturgy* (London: T&T Clark), 261–78

Churchill, Rhona. 1968a. 'The Pope's Bitter Pill', *Daily Mail*, 30 July, 1

Churchill, Rhona. 1968b. 'Why We Shall Defy the Pope', *Daily Mail*, 30 July, 6

Cimino, Richard, and Christopher Smith. 2014. *Atheist Awakening: Secular Activism and Community in America* (New York: Oxford University Press)

Clancy, John G. 1963. *Apostle for Our Time: Paul VI* (New York: Kennedy and Sons)

Clapson, Mark. 1998. *Invincible Green Suburbs, Brave New Towns: Social Change and Urban Dispersal in Postwar England* (Manchester: Manchester University Press)

Clements, Ben. 2014. 'Research Note: Assessing the Determinants of the Contemporary Social Attitudes of Roman Catholics in Britain: Abortion and Homosexuality', *Journal of Contemporary Religion* 29/3, 491–501

Clements, Ben. 2017. 'Weekly Churchgoing amongst Roman Catholics in Britain: Long-term Trends and Contemporary Analysis', *Journal of Beliefs & Values* 38/1, 32–44

Clymer, Adam. 1987. 'Poll Finds Catholics Defecting from Church', *New York Times*, 10 September, B10

Coblentz, Jessica. 2009. 'To Share a Meal with Jesus', in Kate Dugan and Jennifer Owens (eds), *From the Pews in the Back: Young Women and Catholicism* (Collegeville, MN: Liturgical Press), 115–22

Coccopalmerio, Francesco. 2010. 'On *Omnium in Mentem*: The Basis of the Two Changes', *L'Osservatore Romano*, 31 March: http://www.ewtn.com/library/canonlaw/bas2changes.htm

Collins, Gail. 2009. *When Everything Changed: The Amazing Journey of American Women from 1960 to the Present* (New York: Back Bay)

Collins, Marie L. 2004. 'Breaking the Silence: The Victims', *Concilium* 2004/3, 13–19

Congar, Yves. 1963. *Report from Rome: On the First Session of the Vatican Council* (London: Geoffrey Chapman)

Corrin, Jay P. 2013. *Catholic Progressives in England after Vatican II* (South Bend, IN: University of Notre Dame Press)

Cragun, Ryan T., and Joseph H. Hammer. 2011. '"One Person's Apostate is Another Person's Convert": What Terminology Tells us about Pro-religious Hegemony in the Sociology of Religion', *Humanity & Society* 35, 149–75

Cressler, Matthew J. 2017. *Authentically Black and Truly Catholic: The Rise of Black Catholicism in the Great Migration* (New York: New York University Press)

Crockett, Alasdair, and David Voas. 2006. 'Generations of Decline: Religious Change in Twentieth-Century Britain', *Journal for the Scientific Study of Religion* 45/4, 567–84

Crossley, James. 2018. *Cults, Martyrs and Good Samaritans: Religion in Contemporary English Political Discourse* (London: Pluto Press)

Cuneo, Michael W. 1997. *The Smoke of Satan: Conservative and Traditionalist Dissent in Contemporary American Catholicism* (Oxford: Oxford University Press)

Curran, Charles E. 2006. *Loyal Dissent: Memoir of a Catholic Theologian* (Washington, DC: Georgetown University Press)

Curran, Charles E. 2008. *Catholic Moral Theology in the United States: A History* (Washington, DC: Georgetown University Press)

Cusic, Don. 2009. 'Retail and Contemporary Christian Music', in Don Cusic (ed.), *Encyclopedia of Contemporary Christian Music: Pop, Rock, and Worship* (Santa Barbara, CA: ABC-Clio), 385–90

Darwin, Charles. [1859] 1964. *On the Origin of Species: A Facsimile of the First Edition* (Cambridge, MA: Harvard University Press)

Davie, Grace. 2002. *Europe: The Exceptional Case: Parameters of Faith and Society in the Modern World* (London: Darton, Longman & Todd)

Davie, Grace. 2014. *Religion in Britain: A Persistent Paradox*, 2nd edn (Oxford: Wiley-Blackwell)

Davies, Michael. 1997a. *A Short History of the Roman Rite* (Charlotte, NC: TAN Books)

Davies, Michael. 1997b. *The Catholic Sanctuary and the Second Vatican Council* (Charlotte, NC: TAN Books)

Davies, Michael. 2003. *Liturgical Time Bombs in Vatican II: The Destruction of Catholic Faith Through Changes in Worship* (Charlotte, NC: TAN Books)

Davies, Michael. [1980] 2009. *Pope Paul's New Mass* (Kansas City, MO: Angelus Press)

Davis, Emory G. 1966. 'Bits and Pieces from an Irreverent Xmas Card', *Chicago Defender*, 31 December, 18

Dawkins, Richard. 2006. *The God Delusion* (London: Bantam Press)

Day, Abby. 2011. *Believing in Belonging: Belief and Social Identity in the Modern World* (Oxford: Oxford University Press)

Day, Abby, and Lois Lee. 2014. 'Making Sense of Surveys and Censuses: Issues in Religious Self-identification', *Religion* 44/3, 345–56

Day, Thomas. 1990. *Why Catholics Can't Sing: The Culture of Catholicism and the Triumph of Bad Taste* (New York: Crossroad)

Delaney, Enda. 2007. *The Irish in Post-War Britain* (Oxford: Oxford University Press)

Deloria, Vine. [1969] 1988. *Custer Died for Your Sins: An Indian Manifesto* (Norman, OK: University of Oklahoma Press)

Demerath, N. J. 2000. 'The Rise of "Cultural Religion" in European Christianity: Learning from Poland, Northern Ireland, and Sweden', *Social Compass* 47/1, 127–39

DeVille, Adam J. 2017. '*Orientalium Ecclesiarum*', in Matthew L. Lamb and Matthew J. Levering (eds), *The Reception of Vatican II* (New York: Oxford University Press), 324–46

Dillon, Michele. 1999. *Catholic Identity: Balancing Reason, Faith, and Power* (Cambridge: Cambridge University Press)

Dinges, William D. 1987. 'Ritual Conflict as Social Conflict: Liturgical Reform in the Roman Catholic Church', *Sociological Analysis* 48/2, 138–57

Dixon, R., S. Bond, K. Engebretson, R. Rymarz, B. Cussen, and K. Wright. 2007. *Research Project on Catholics Who Have Stopped Attending Mass: Final Report* (Melbourne: Australian Catholic Bishops Conference): https://www.catholic.org.au/all-downloads/organisations-1/pastoral-research-office-1/197-disconnected-catholics-report-april-2007-1/file

Dolan, Jay P. 2002. *In Search of an American Catholicism: A History of Religion and Culture in Tension* (New York: Oxford University Press)

Donnelly, Mark. 2005. *Sixties Britain: Culture, Society and Politics* (Harlow: Pearson Longman)

Doorly, Moyra. 2007. *No Place for God: The Denial of Transcendence in Modern Church Architecture* (San Francisco, CA: Ignatius Press)

Doty, Robert C. 1968. 'Pope Bars Birth Control By Any Artificial Means: Tone Forthright', *New York Times*, 30 July, 1

Dougherty, Kevin, and Andrew L. Whitehead. 2011. 'A Place to Belong: Small Group Involvement in Religious Congregations', *Sociology of Religion* 72/1, 91–111

Douglas, Mary. [1970] 1996. *Natural Symbols: Explorations in Cosmology* (London: Routledge)

Douthat, Ross. 2012. *Bad Religion: How We Became a Nation of Heretics* (New York: Free Press)

Douthat, Ross. 2018. *To Change the Church: Pope Francis and the Future of Catholicism* (New York: Simon & Schuster)

Dowd, Mark. 2017. *Queer and Catholic: A Life of Contradiction* (London: Darton, Longman & Todd)

Downey, Allen B. 2014. 'Religious Affiliation, Education, and Internet Use', *ArXiv*: https://arxiv.org/abs/1403.5534

Dreher, Rod. 2002. 'Sins of the Fathers', *National Review*, 11 February, 27–30

Dreher, Rod. 2006. 'Orthodoxy and Me': http://journeytoorthodoxy.com/2010/06/crunchy-cons-conversion-crisis/

Dreher, Rod. 2011. 'What's So Appealing About Orthodoxy?', *Washington Post*, 17 March: https://www.washingtonpost.com/guest-voices/post/whats-so-appealing-about-orthodoxy/2011/03/17/ABu3Z6l_blog.html?utm_term=.8de31a821654

Dreher, Rod. 2017. *The Benedict Option: A Strategy for Christians in a Post-Christian Nation* (New York: Sentinel)

Dreher, Rod. 2018. 'Uncle Ted and the Grand Inquisitor', *American Conservative*, 22 June: http://www.theamericanconservative.com/dreher/uncle-ted-mccarrick-and-the-grand-inquisitor/

Driscoll, Jeremy. 2005. *Theology at the Eucharistic Table: Master Themes in the Theological Tradition* (Leominster: Gracewing)

Driscoll, Jeremy. 2017. '*Sacrosanctum Concilium*', in Matthew L. Lamb and Matthew Levering (eds), *The Reception of Vatican II* (New York: Oxford University Press), 23–47

Duffy, Eamon. 2004. *Faith of Our Fathers: Reflections on Catholic Tradition* (London: Continuum)

Dugan, Kate, and Jennifer Owens (eds). 2009. *From the Pews in the Back: Young Women and Catholicism* (Collegeville, MN: Liturgical Press)

Eade, John. 2002. 'How Far Can You Go? English Catholic Elites and the Erosion of Ethnic Boundaries', in Cris Shore and Stephen Nugent (eds), *Elite Cultures: Anthropological Perspectives* (London: Routledge), 209–26

Eagleton, Terry. 2002. *The Gatekeeper: A Memoir* (London: Allen Lane)

Ebaugh, Helen Rose Fuchs. 1988. *Becoming an Ex: The Process of Role Exit* (Chicago, IL: University of Chicago Press)

Eberstadt, Mary. 2012. *Adam and Eve After the Pill: Paradoxes of the Sexual Revolution* (San Francisco, CA: Ignatius Press)

Edgell, P., J. Gerteis, and D. Hartmann. 2006. 'Atheists as "Other": Moral Boundaries and Cultural Membership in American Society', *American Sociological Review* 71/2, 211–34

Edmondson, Elizabeth A. 2002. 'Without Comment or Controversy: The G.I. Bill and Catholic Colleges', *Church History* 71/4, 820–47

Edwards, Gareth. 1966. 'Modern English in the Mass', *America*, 22 October, 483–4

Ellis, John Tracy. 1956. *American Catholics and the Intellectual Life* (Chicago, IL: Heritage Foundation)

Eppstein, John. 1971. *Has the Catholic Church Gone Mad?* (London: Tom Stacey)

Everton, Sean F. 2018. *Networks and Religion: Ties that Bind, Loose, Build-up, and Tear Down* (Cambridge: Cambridge University Press)

Faggioli, Massimo. 2012a. *Vatican II: The Battle for Meaning* (Mahwah, NJ: Paulist Press)

Faggioli, Massimo. 2012b. *True Reform: Liturgy and Ecclesiology in* Sacrosanctum Concilium (Collegeville, MN: Liturgical Press)

Faggioli, Massimo. 2012c. 'Vatican II: Text and Context: Its Impact is Just Beginning', *Conversations on Jesuit Higher Education* 42/7, 20–1

Faggioli, Massimo. 2014. *Sorting Out Catholicism: A Brief History of the New Ecclesial Movements* (Collegeville, MN: Liturgical Press)

Feeney, Leonard. 1934. *Fish on Friday* (New York: Sheed & Ward)

Fichter, Joseph H. 1953. 'The Marginal Catholic: An Institutional Approach', *Social Forces* 32/2, 167–73

Field, Clive D. 2015. *Britain's Last Religious Revival? Quantifying Belonging, Behaving, and Believing in the Long 1950s* (Basingstoke: Palgrave Macmillan)

Field, Clive D. 2017. *Secularization in the Long 1960s: Numerating Religion in Britain* (Oxford: Oxford University Press)

Finke, Roger, and Rodney Stark. 1992. *The Churching of America, 1776–1990: Winners and Losers in Our Religious Economy* (New Brunswick, NJ: Rutgers University Press)

Fisher, James T. 2007. *Communion of Immigrants: A History of Catholics in America*, rev. edn (New York: Oxford University Press)

Fiske, Edward B. 1966. 'Less Fasting for Catholics', *New York Times*, 20 February, E10

FitzGerald, Frances. 2017. *Evangelicals: The Struggle to Shape America* (New York: Simon & Shuster)

Flanagan, Kieran. 1987. 'Resacralising the Liturgy', *New Blackfriars* 68/802, 64–75

Fliteau, Jerry. 2012. 'Unusual study asks former Catholics why they left the church', *National Catholic Reporter*, 23 March: http://ncronline.org/news/faith-parish/unusual-study-asks-former-catholics-why-they-left-church

Florian, Amy. 2004. 'My Neighbor, the Evangelical Megachurch', *Liturgy* 19/4, 25–32

Fortescue, Adrian. 1922. *The Mass: A Study of the Roman Liturgy* (London: Longmans, Green, and Co.)

Fortin, Roger Antonio. 2002. *Faith and Action: A History of the Catholic Archdiocese of Cincinnati, 1821–1996* (Columbus, OH: Ohio State University Press)

Franchi, Leonardo. 2016. *Shared Mission: Religious Education in the Catholic Tradition* (London: Scepter)

Francis. 2013a. *Evangelii Gaudium*: http://w2.vatican.va/content/francesco/en/apost_exhortations/documents/papa-francesco_esortazione-ap_20131124_evangelii-gaudium.html

Francis. 2013b. *Lumen Fidei*: http://www.vatican.va/holy_father/francesco/encyclicals/documents/papa-francesco_20130629_enciclica-lumen-fidei_en.html

Francis. 2016. *Amoris Laetitia*: http://w2.vatican.va/content/dam/francesco/pdf/apost_exhortations/documents/papa-francesco_esortazione-ap_20160319_amoris-laetitia_it.pdf

Francis, Leslie J., and Philip J. Richter. 2007. *Gone for Good?: Church Leaving and Returning in the 21st Century* (London: Epworth Press)

Fried, Rebecca A. 2016. 'No Irish Need Deny: Evidence for the Historicity of NINA Restrictions in Advertisements and Signs', *Journal of Social History* 49/4, 829–54

Gallup. 2016. 'New Hampshire Now Least Religious State in U.S.', 4 February: http://www.gallup.com/poll/189038/new-hampshire-least-religious-state.aspx

Gamber, Klaus. [1981] 1993. *The Reform of the Roman Liturgy: Its Problems and Background*, trans. Klaus D. Grimm (San Juan Capistrano, CA: Una Voce Press)

Gandy, Michael (ed.). 1993. *Catholic Parishes in England, Wales, and Scotland: An Atlas* (London: Michael Gandy)

Gans, Herbert L. 1967. *The Levittowners: Ways of Life and Politics in a New Suburban Community* (London: Allen Lane)

Gardner, Dan. 2011. *Future Babble: Why Expert Predictions Are Next to Worthless, and You Can Do Better* (New York: Dutton)

Geiringer, David. 2016. 'The Pope and the Pill: Exploring the Sexual Experiences of Catholic Women in Post-War England', unpublished PhD thesis, University of Sussex, UK

Geiringer, David. 2018. '"At Some Point in the 1960s, Hell Disappeared": Hell, Gender and Catholicism in Post-War England', *Cultural and Social History* (online early publication)

Gibson Mikoś, Susan. 2012. *Poles in Wisconsin* (Milwaukee, WI: Wisconsin Historical Society Press)

Glancey, Jonathan. 2007. 'Mirage on the Mersey', *Guardian*, 25 January: http://www.theguardian.com/artanddesign/2007/jan/25/architecture

Godin, Henri, and Yvan Daniel. [1943] 1949. 'France A Missionary Land?', ed. and trans. Maisie Ward, in Maisie Ward, *France Pagan?* (London: Sheed & Ward), 65–191

Godin, Seth. 2008. *Tribes: We Need You to Lead Us* (New York: Portfolio)

Goode, H., H. McGee, and C. O'Boyle. 2003. *Time to Listen: Confronting Child Sexual Abuse by Catholic Clergy* (Dublin: Liffey Press)

Goodhew, David (ed.). 2012. *Church Growth in Britain: 1980 to the Present* (London: Routledge)

Gray, Mark M. 2014. 'Portrait of the American Catholic Convert: Strength in New Numbers': http://nineteensixty-four.blogspot.co.uk/2014/04/portrait-of-american-catholic-convert.html

Greeley, Andrew. 1961. *Strangers in the House: Catholic Youth in America* (New York: Sheed & Ward)

Greeley, Andrew. 1964. 'The New Breed', *America*, 23 May: https://www.americamagazine.org/issue/100/new-breed

Greeley, Andrew. 1970. 'Religious Intermarriage in a Denominational Society', *American Sociological Review* 75/6, 949–52

Greeley, Andrew. 1985. *American Catholics since the Council: An Unauthorized Report* (Chicago, IL: Thomas More Press)

Greeley, Andrew. 1990. *The Catholic Myth: The Behavior and Beliefs of American Catholics* (New York: Charles Scribner's Sons)

Greeley, Andrew. 1997. 'The "October count" of Mass Attendance is Misleading Indicator', *Religion News Service*, 1 January: https://religionnews.com/1997/01/01/commentary-theoctober-countof-mass-attendance-is-misleading-indicator/

Greeley, Andrew. 2004a. *The Catholic Revolution: New Wine, Old Wineskins, and the Second Vatican Council* (Berkeley, CA: University of California Press)

Greeley, Andrew. 2004b. *Religion in Europe at the End of the Second Millennium: A Sociological Profile* (New Brunswick, NJ: Transaction)

Greeley, Andrew, William C. McCready, and Kathleen McCourt. 1976. *Catholic Schools in a Declining Church* (Kansas City, MO: Sheed & Ward)

Gregg, Stephen E., and Lynne Scholefield. 2015. *Engaging with Living Religion: A Guide to Fieldwork in the Study of Religion* (Abingdon: Routledge)

Gribble, Richard. 2003. 'Anti-Communism, Patrick Peyton, CSC and the C.I.A.', *Journal of Church and State* 45/3, 535–58

Guardian. 1967. 'Last of Meatless Fridays – Except for the Irish', *Guardian*, 29 December, 3

Gullickson, Aaron. 2018. 'The Diverging Beliefs and Practices of the Religiously Affiliated and Unaffiliated in the United States', *Sociological Science* 5, 361–79

Hackett, Conrad. 2014. 'Seven Things to Consider When Measuring Religious Identity', *Religion* 44/3, 396–413

Hadaway, C. Kirk, Penny Long Marler, and Mark Chaves. 1993. 'What the Polls Don't Show: A Closer Look at U.S. Church Attendance', *American Sociological Review* 58/6, 741–52

Hagerty, James. 2013. 'The Conversion of England: John Carmel Heenan and the Catholic Missionary Society, 1947–1951', *Recusant History* 46/3, 461–81

Hagstrom, Aurelie A. 2010. *The Emerging Laity: Vocation, Mission, Spirituality* (Mahwah, NJ: Paulist Press)

Hardy, Philip R., Kelly L. Kandra, and Brian G. Patterson. 2014. *Joy and Grievance in an American Diocese: Results from Online Surveys of Active and Inactive Catholics in Central Illinois* (Lisle, IL: Benedictine University): http://www.dio.org/uploads/files/Communications/Press_Releases/2014/Joy-and-Grievance-PUBLIC-FINAL-sep-11-2014.pdf

Harris, Alana. 2013a. *Faith in the Family: A Lived Religious History of English Catholicism, 1945–82* (Manchester: Manchester University Press)

Harris, Alana. 2013b. ' "The People of God Dressed for Dinner and Dancing"? English Catholic Masculinity, Religious Sociability and the Catenian Association', in Lucy Delap and Sue Morgan (eds), *Men, Masculinities and Religious Change in Twentieth-Century Britain* (Basingstoke: Palgrave Macmillan), 54–89

Harris, Alana. 2015a. 'Astonishing Scenes at the Scottish Lourdes: Masculinity, the Miraculous, and Sectarian Strife at Carfin, 1922–1945', *Innes Review* 66/1, 102–29

Harris, Alana. 2015b. ' "The Writings of Querulous Women": Contraception, Conscience and Clerical Authority in 1960s Britain', *British Catholic History* 32/4, 557–85

Harris, Alana. 2018a. 'A Fresh Stripping of the Altars? Liturgical Language and the Legacy of the Reformation in England, 1964–1984', in Kathleen Sprows Cummings, Timothy Matovina, and Robert A. Orsi (eds), *Catholics in the Vatican II Era: Local Histories of a Global Event* (New York: Cambridge University Press), 245–74

Harris, Alana. 2018b. '"A Galileo-Crisis Not a Luther-Crisis"? English Catholics' Attitudes to Contraception', in Alana Harris (ed.), *The Schism of '68: Catholicism, Contraception and 'Humanae Vitae' in Europe, 1945–1975* (Basingstoke: Palgrave Macmillan), 73–96

Harris, Alana, and Martin Spence. 2007. '"Disturbing the Complacency of Religion"? The Evangelical Crusades of Dr Billy Graham and Father Patrick Peyton in Britain, 1951–54', *Twentieth Century British History* 18/4, 481–513

Harris, Sam. 2004. *The End of Faith: Religion, Terror and the Future of Reason* (New York: Norton)

Hattersley, Roy. 2017. *The Catholics: The Church and its People in Britain and Ireland, from the Reformation to the Present Day* (London: Chatto & Windus)

Hawaii Catholic Herald. 2014. 'The Francis Effect: Catholics Love the Pope, But for the Lapsed, Not Enough to Return to Church', *Hawaii Catholic Herald*, 14 March: http://www.hawaiicatholicherald.com/2014/03/14/the-francis-effect-catholics-like-the-pope-but-for-the-lapsed-not-enough-to-return-to-church/

Hebblethwaite, Peter. 1975. *The Runaway Church* (London: Collins)

Hebblethwaite, Peter. 2010. *John XXIII: Pope of the Century*, rev. edn (London: Bloomsbury)

Henrich, Joseph. 2009. 'The Evolution of Costly Displays, Cooperation and Religion: Credibility Enhancing Displays and their Implications for Cultural Evolution', *Evolution and Human Behaviour* 30, 11–28

Herguth, Robert. 2016. *Genuflections: Famous Folks Talk about Growing Up Catholic* (Chicago, IL: Eckhartz Press)

Hildebrand, Dietrich von. [1967] 1993. *Trojan Horse in the City of God: The Catholic Crisis Explained* (Bedford, NH: Sophia Institute Press)

Hinze, Christine Firer, and J. Patrick Hornbeck. 2014. 'Introduction', in Christine Firer Hinze and J. Patrick Hornbeck (eds), *More than a Monologue: Sexual Diversity and the Catholic Church, Volume I: Voices of Our Times* (New York: Fordham University Press), 1–14

Hirst, David. 1969. 'Patriarchal Champion of St. George', *Guardian*, 15 May, 3

Hitchens, Christopher. 2007. *God is Not Great: How Religion Poisons Everything* (New York: Twelve Books)

Hoge, D. R., with K. McGuire, B. F. Stratman, and A. A. Illig. 1981. *Converts, Dropouts, Returnees: A Study of Religious Change among Catholics* (Washington, DC: United States Conference of Catholic Bishops; New York: Pilgrim Press)

Horn, Gerd-Rainier. 2015. *The Spirit of Vatican II: Western European Progressive Catholicism in the Long Sixties* (Oxford: Oxford University Press)

Hornbeck, J. Patrick. 2011. 'Deconversion from Roman Catholicism: Mapping a Fertile Field', *American Catholic Studies* 122/2, 1–29

Hornbeck, J. Patrick. 2013. 'Deconversion and Disaffiliation in Contemporary US Roman Catholicism', *Horizons* 40/2, 262–74

Hornsby-Smith, Michael P. 1980. 'The Statistics of the Church', in John Cumming and Paul Burns (eds), *The Church Now: An Inquiry into the Present State of the Catholic Church in Britain and Ireland* (Dublin: Gill & Macmillan), 55–66

Hornsby-Smith, Michael P. 1987. *Roman Catholics in England: Studies in Social Structure since the Second World War* (Cambridge: Cambridge University Press)

Hornsby-Smith, Michael P. 1991. *Roman Catholic Beliefs in England: Customary Catholicism and the Transformation of Religious Authority* (Cambridge: Cambridge University Press)

Hornsby-Smith, Michael P. 2010. *Reflections on a Catholic Life: From the Depression Years and Second World War to Fears of Global Meltdown and Recession* (Peterborough: FastPrint)

Hornsby-Smith, Michael, Kathryn A. Turcan, and Lynda T. Rajan. 1987. 'Patterns of Religious Commitment, Intermarriage and Marital Breakdown among English Catholics', *Archives de Sciences Sociales des Religions* 64/1, 137–55

Hout, Michael. 2000. 'Angry and Alienated: Divorced and Remarried Catholics in the United States', *America*, 16 December: https://www.americamagazine.org/issue/392/article/angry-and-alienated

Hout, Michael. 2016. 'St Peter's Leaky Boat: Falling Intergenerational Persistence Among U.S.-Born Catholics since 1974', *Sociology of Religion* 77/1, 1–17

Hout, Michael. 2017. 'Religious Ambivalence, Liminality, and the Increase of No Religious Preference in the United States, 2006–2014', *Journal for the Scientific Study of Religion* 56/1, 52–63

Hout, Michael, and Claude S. Fischer. 2014. 'Explaining Why More Americans Have No Religious Preference: Political Backlash and Generational Succession', *Sociological Science* 1, 423–47

Hout, Michael, and Andrew M. Greeley. 1987. 'The Center Doesn't Hold: Church Attendance in the United States, 1940–1984', *American Sociological Review* 52/3, 325–45

Hunt, Anne. 2015. 'A Council for the Laity? The Vision of Vatican II in Empowering the Lay Faithful', in Nigel Zimmermann (ed.), *The Great Grace: Receiving Vatican II Today* (London: Bloomsbury T. & T. Clark), 37–56

Hunt, Larry L., and Matthew O. Hunt. 2001. 'Race, Region, and Religious Involvement: A Comparative Study of Whites and African Americans', *Social Forces* 80/2, 605–31

Independent Inquiry into Child Sexual Abuse. 2018. *Ampleforth and Down-side (English Benedictine Congregation Case Study): Investigation Report*: https://www.iicsa.org.uk/key-documents/6583/download/ampleforth-downside-investigation-report-august-2018.pdf

Independent Television. [1960] 2015. 'First Appearance: Ken Barlow – Coronation Street': https://www.youtube.com/watch?v=00-RjLtTWmc

Ingram, Ulrike Krampe. 2005. 'Geographic Analysis of Two Suburban Mega Church Congregations in Atlanta: A Distance and Demographic Study', unpublished MA thesis, Georgia State University, USA

Investigative Staff of the Boston Globe. 2002. 'Church Allowed Abuse by Priest for Years', *Boston Globe*, 6 January, 1

Investigative Staff of the Boston Globe. [2002] 2015. *Betrayal: The Crisis in the Catholic Church*, updated edn (London: Profile)

Jenkins, Philip. 2007. *God's Continent: Christianity, Islam, and Europe's Religious Crisis* (Oxford: Oxford University Press)

Jenkins, Richard. 2008. *Social Identity*, 3rd edn (London: Routledge)

John XXIII. 1961. *Humanae Salutis*, trans. Joseph A. Komonchak: https://jakomonchak.files.wordpress.com/2011/12/humanae-salutis.pdf

John XXIII. 1962. 'Opening Address to the Council', 11 October: https://www.catholicculture.org/culture/library/view.cfm?RecNum=3233

John Paul II. 1980. 'Messages of John Paul II for the Opening for the National Pastoral Congress in Liverpool': https://w2.vatican.va/content/john-paul-ii/en/messages/pont_messages/1980/documents/hf_jp-ii_mes_19800502_pastorale-liverpool.html

John Paul II. 1983. 'Discurso del Santo Padre Juan Pablo II a la Asamblea del CELAM', Port-au-Prince, Haiti, 9 March: https://w2.vatican.va/content/john-paul-ii/es/speeches/1983/march/documents/hf_jp-ii_spe_19830309_assemblea-celam.html

John Paul II. 1990. *Redemptoris Missio*: http://w2.vatican.va/content/john-paul-ii/en/encyclicals/documents/hf_jp-ii_enc_07121990_redemptoris-missio.html

Johnston, Richard J. H. 1957. 'Creativity Urged for Young Rebels', *New York Times*, 21 March, 63

Jones, Michael. 2000. 'Introduction', in Michael Jones (ed.), *The New Cambridge Medieval History: Volume 6, c.1300–c.1415* (Cambridge: Cambridge University Press), 3–16

Jones, Robert P. 2016. *The End of White Christian America* (New York: Simon & Schuster)

Jones, Robert P., and Daniel Cox. 2017. *America's Changing Religious Identity: Findings from the 2016 American Values Atlas* (Washington, DC: Public Religion Research Institute)

Jones, Robert P., Daniel Cox, and Juhem Navarro-Rivera. 2014. *A Shifting Landscape: A Decade of Change in American Attitudes about Same-Sex*

Marriage and LGBT Issues (Washington, DC: Public Religion Research Institute)

Kane, Paula M. 2004. 'Marian Devotion since 1940: Continuity or Collapse?', in James O'Toole (ed.), *Habits of Devotion: Catholic Religious Practice in Twentieth-Century America* (Ithaca, NY: Cornell University Press), 89–129

Keen, A. J. 2012. *Digital Vertigo: How Today's Online Social Revolution is Dividing, Diminishing, and Disorienting Us* (London: Constable & Robinson)

Keillor, Garrison. 1986. *Lake Wobegon Days* (London: Faber and Faber)

Kelley, Dean M. [1972] 1986. *Why Conservative Churches are Growing: A Study in the Sociology of Religion* (Macon, GA: Mercer University Press)

Kelly, Michael. 2014. 'Catholics of 2014: Marie Collins', *OSV Newsweekly*: https://www.osv.com/MyFaith/CatholicPlaces/Article/TabId/779/ArtMID/13717/ArticleID/16607/Catholics-of-2014-Marie-Collins.aspx

Kenyon, Nicholas. 1980. 'Worship', in John Cumming and Paul Burns (eds), *The Church Now: An Inquiry into the Present State of the Catholic Church in Britain and Ireland* (Dublin: Gill & Macmillan), 83–8

Kettell, Steven. 2013. 'Faithless: The Politics of New Atheism', *Secularism and Nonreligion* 2, 61–72

Killen, Patricia O'Connell, and Mark A. Shibley. 2004. 'Surveying the Religious Landscape: Historical Trends and Current Patterns in Oregon, Washington, and Alaska', in Patricia O'Connell Killen and Mark Silk (eds), *Religion and Public Life in the Pacific Northwest: The None Zone* (Walnut Creek, CA: Altamira Press), 25–49

King-Hele, Sarah A. 2010. 'The Dynamics of Religious Change: A Comparative Study of Five Western Countries', unpublished PhD thesis, Manchester University, UK

Kirwin, Anthony P. 1965. 'The Young Strangers: The Views and Attitudes of Some Catholic Teenagers', *Tablet*, 6 November, 1237–8

Komonchak, Joseph A. 2012. 'Interpreting the Council and Its Consequences: Concluding Reflections', in James L. Heft and John O'Malley (eds), *After Vatican II: Trajectories and Hermeneutics* (Grand Rapids, MI: Eerdmans), 164–72

Komonchak, Joseph A. 2018. 'Afterword: The Council and the Churches', in Kathleen Sprows Cummings, Timothy Matovina, and Robert A. Orsi (eds), *Catholics in the Vatican II Era: Local Histories of a Global Event* (New York: Cambridge University Press), 275–90

Kotre, John N. 1978. *The Best of Times, The Worst of Times: Andrew Greeley & American Catholicism, 1950–1975* (Chicago, IL: Nelson-Hall)

Kraybill, Donald B. 1994a. 'Introduction: The Struggle to be Separate', in Donald B. Kraybill and Marc A. Olshan (eds), *The Amish Struggle with Modernity* (Hanover, NH: University Press of New England), 1–17

Kraybill, Donald B. 1994b. 'Plotting Social Change Across Four Affiliations', in Donald B. Kraybill and Marc A. Olshan (eds), *The Amish Struggle with Modernity* (Hanover, NH: University Press of New England), 53–74

Küng, Hans. 1963. *That the World May Believe: Letters to Young People*, trans. Cecily Hastings (London: Sheed & Ward)

Kurlansky, Mark. 2004. *1968: The Year that Shook the World* (London: Jonathan Cape)

Kynaston, David. 2007. *Austerity Britain, 1945–51* (London: Bloomsbury)

Kynaston, David. 2014. *Modernity Britain: A Shake of the Dice, 1959–62* (London: Bloomsbury)

LaFrance, Adrienne. 2015. 'A Skeleton, a Catholic Relic, and a Mystery about American Origins', *The Atlantic*, 28 July: http://www.theatlantic.com/national/archive/2015/07/a-skeleton-a-catholic-relic-and-a-mystery-about-americas-origins/399743/

Lakeland, Paul. 2004. *The Liberation of the Laity: In Search of an Accountable Church* (New York: Continuum)

Lang, Uwe Michael. 2009. *Turning Towards the Lord: Orientation in Liturgical Prayer* (San Francisco, CA: Ignatius Press)

Langston, J., D. Speed, and T. J. Coleman. Forthcoming. 'Predicting Age of Atheism: Credibility Enhancing Displays and Religious Importance, Choice, and Conflict in Family Upbringing', *Religion, Brain & Behavior*

Lanman, Jonathan A. 2012. 'The Importance of Religious Displays for Belief Acquisition and Secularization', *Journal of Contemporary Religion* 27, 49–65

Lanman, Jonathan A., and Michael D. Buhrmester. 2017. 'Religious Actions Speak Louder than Words: Exposure to Credibility-Enhancing Displays Predicts Theism', *Religion, Brain & Behavior* 7/1, 3–16

Latin Mass Society. 2013. 'Newly released statistics show the decline of the Catholic Church in England and Wales in 1960s and 1970s': http://www.lms.org.uk/resources/statistics-from-the-catholic-directory

Laudate Dominum. 1957. *The Sunday Missal for all Sundays and the Principal Feasts of the Year according to the Latest Decrees with Benediction, Vespers, Compline and a Collection of Prayers* (London: Widdowson)

Lawler, Philip F. 2008. *The Faithful Departed: The Collapse of Boston's Catholic Culture* (New York: Encounter Books)

Lee, Lois. 2015. *Recognizing the Non-religious: Reimagining the Secular* (Oxford: Oxford University Press)

Leege, D. C., and J. Gremillion. 1984. 'The U.S. Parish Twenty Years after Vatican II: An Introduction to the Study', *Notre Dame Study of Catholic Parish Life* 1, 1–8

Lesley, Alison. 2015. 'How the "Pope Francis Effect" May Help Fill U.S. Pews', *World Religion News*, 6 April: https://www.worldreligionnews.com/religion-news/christianity/how-the-pope-francis-effect-may-help-fill-u-s-pews

Lim, C., C. A. MacGregor, and R. D. Putnam. 2010. 'Secular and Liminal: Discovering Heterogeneity among Religious Nones', *Journal for the Scientific Study of Religion* 49/4, 596–618

Linker, Damon. 2018. 'The Unbearable Ugliness of the Catholic Church', *The Week*, 29 August: https://theweek.com/articles/792775/unbearable-ugliness-catholic-church

Lipstadt, Deborah E. 2014. ' "And It Not Be Stilled": The Legacy of Debbie Friedman', in Michael A Meyer and David N. Myers (eds), *Between Jewish Tradition and Modernity: Rethinking an Old Opposition* (Detroit, MI: Wayne State University Press), 110–22

Lodge, David. 2015. *Quite a Good Time to be Born: A Memoir: 1935–1975* (London: Harvill Secker)

Longley, Clifford. 2000. *The Worlock Archive* (London: Geoffrey Chapman)

Loveland, Anne C., and Otis B. Wheeler. 2003. *From Meetinghouse to Megachurch: A Material and Cultural History* (Columbia, MO: University of Missouri Press)

Lüchau, Peter, and Peter B. Andersen. 2012. 'Socio-economic Factors behind Disaffiliation from the Danish National Church', *Nordic Journal of Religion and Society* 25/1, 27–45

Lydon, John, Keith Zimmerman, and Kent Zimmerman. 1994. *Rotten: No Irish, No Blacks, No Dogs* (New York: St Martin's Press)

McAndrew, Siobhan. 2016a. 'Youth Research Council Survey of Young People's Religion and Lifestyles, 1957: User Guide', UK Data Service SN: 7933: http://doc.ukdataservice.ac.uk/doc/7933/mrdoc/pdf/7933uguide.pdf

McAndrew, Siobhan. 2016b. 'Religiosity and Secularity in the 1957 Youth Research Council Survey': http://www.brin.ac.uk/2016/religion-in-the-1957-youth-research-council-survey/

McBrien, Richard P. 1978. 'The Ex-Catholic Syndrome – I', *Catholic Transcript*, 30 June, 5

McBrien, Richard P. 2003. 'Waning Devotions May Be Sign of Liturgical Health', *National Catholic Reporter*, 4 April: http://www.natcath.org/NCR_Online/archives2/2003b/040403/040403q.htm

McBrien, Richard P. 2009. 'Perpetual Eucharistic Adoration', *National Catholic Reporter*, 8 September: https://www.ncronline.org/blogs/essays-theology/perpetual-eucharistic-adoration

McBrien, Richard P. 2010. 'Popes of the 20th Century: Paul VI', *National Catholic Reporter*, 23 August: https://www.ncronline.org/blogs/essays-theology/popes-20th-century-paul-vi

McCallion, Michael J., and John Ligas. 2018. 'Sociology of the Liturgy in Post-Modernity: Ritual Attunement and Dis-Attunement at Sunday Mass', *Antiphon* 22, 138–74

McClendon, David, and Conrad Hackett. 2014. 'When People Shed Religious Identity in Ireland and Australia: The Evidence from Censuses', *Demographic Research* 31, 1297–310

McClure, Paul. 2016. 'Faith and Facebook in a Pluralistic Age: The Effects of Social Networking Sites on the Religious Beliefs of Emerging Adults', *Sociological Perspectives* 59/4, 818–34

McClure, Paul. 2017. 'Tinkering with Technology and Religion in the Digital Age: The Effects of Internet Use on Religious Belief, Behavior, and Belonging', *Journal for the Scientific Study of Religion* 56/3, 481–97

McDannell, Coleen. 1995. *Material Christianity: Religion and Popular Culture in America* (New Haven, CT: Yale University Press)

McDannell, Coleen. 2011. *The Spirit of Vatican II: A History of Catholic Reform in America* (New York: Basic Books)

McGinn, Bernard. 2005. *The Harvest of Mysticism in Medieval Germany, 1300–1500* (New York: Crossroad)

McGreevy, John T. 1996. *Parish Boundaries: The Catholic Encounter with Race in the Twentieth-Century Urban North* (Chicago, IL: University of Chicago Press)

McInerny, Ralph M. 1998. *What Went Wrong with Vatican II: The Catholic Crisis Explained* (Bedford, NH: Sophia Institute Press)

MacKaye, William R. 1966. 'Catholic Bishops End Friday Meat Ban', *Washington Post*, 19 November, A1

McLelland, Vincent J. 1980. 'The Church and Religious Education', in John Cumming and Paul Burns (eds), *The Church Now: An Inquiry into the Present State of the Catholic Church in Britain and Ireland* (Dublin: Gill & Macmillan), 109–20

McLeod, Hugh. 2007. *The Religious Crisis of the 1960s* (Oxford: Oxford University Press)

McManus, Frederick R. 1956. *The Rites of Holy Week: Ceremonies, Preparations, Music, Commentaries* (Paterson, NJ: Saint Anthony Guild Press)

MacMillan, Frank. 1955. 'How Catholic is Glasgow? A Survey of Religious Practice', *Tablet*, 4 June, 541–2

Maines, David R., and Michael J. McCallion. 2007. *Transforming Catholicism: Liturgical Change in the Vatican II Church* (Lanham, MD: Lexington Books)

Manalang, Aprilfaye. 2013. 'How Does Religion Shape Filipino Immigrants' Connection to the Public Sphere?: Imagining a Different Self-Understanding of Modernity', unpublished PhD thesis, Bowling Green State University, USA

Manalang, Aprilfaye. 2018. ' "Mostly Catholic" or Loose Organizational Affiliation and Intergenerational Immigrant Identity: A Case Study of the Philippine-American Ecumenical Church, United Church of Christ

(PAECUSA-UCC) in Detroit, Michigan', *Interdisciplinary Journal of Research on Religion* 14/6, 1–20

Margolick, David. 2011. *A Predator Priest* (Amazon: Kindle Single)

Marini, Piero. 2013. 'The Constitution *Sacrosanctum Concilium*: The Primacy of the Liturgy in the Life of the Church': https://fdlc.org/sites/default/files/files/MARINI_SC_INGLESE_ULTIMA_11-12-2013.pdf

Marquardt, Marie Friedmann. 2005. 'Structural and Cultural Hybrids: Religious Congregational Life and Public Participation of Mexicans in the New South', in K. I. Leonard, A. Stepick, M. A. Vasquez, and J. Holdaway (eds), *Immigrant Faiths: Transforming Religious Life in America* (Oxford: AltaMira Press), 189–218

Marshall, John. 1999. 'Catholic Family Life', in Michael Hornsby-Smith (ed.), *Catholics in England 1950–2000: Historical and Sociological Perspectives* (London: Cassell), 66–77

Martin, James. 2017. *Building a Bridge: How the Catholic Church and the LGBT Community Can Enter into a Relationship of Respect, Compassion, and Sensitivity* (San Francisco, CA: HarperOne)

Marty, Martin E. 1995. *A Short History of American Catholicism* (Allen, TX: Thomas More)

Marty, Martin E. 1996. *Modern American Religion. Volume 3: Under God, Indivisible, 1893–1919* (London and Chicago, IL: University of Chicago Press)

Marty, Martin E. 2006. 'Remembering the Sabbath', *Sightings*, 14 August: https://divinity.uchicago.edu/sightings/remembering-sabbath-%E2%80%94-martin-e-marty

Masci, David. 2018. '5 Facts about the Religious Lives of African Americans', 7 February: http://www.pewresearch.org/fact-tank/2018/02/07/5-facts-about-the-religious-lives-of-african-americans/

Massa, Mark S. 2010. *The American Catholic Revolution: How the Sixties Changed the Church Forever* (New York: Oxford University Press)

Matovina, Timothy. 2011. *Latino Catholicism: Transformation in America's Largest Church* (Princeton, NJ: Princeton University Press)

Metropolitan Cathedral. 2016. 'Lutyens' Dream': http://www.liverpoolmetrocathedral.org.uk/the-second-cathedral/

Middendorf Woodall, Lisa. 2016. 'Confessions of a Guitar-Mass Catholic', *America*, 4 August: https://www.americamagazine.org/faith/2016/08/04/confessions-guitar-mass-catholic

Mirror. 1969. 'A "Miracle" from the Demoted Saint', *Daily Mirror*, 12 May, 3

Monson, Paul G. 2014. 'Sacred Seeds: The French Jesuit Martyrs in American Catholic Historiography', *Logos* 17/4, 87–107

Montgomery, Paul M. 1964. 'First English Mass in U.S. Offered in St. Louis', *New York Times*, 25 August, 21

Moore, Andrew S. 2018. 'Black and Catholic in Atlanta: Challenge and Hope', in Kathleen Sprows Cummings, Timothy Matovina, and Robert A. Orsi (eds), *Catholics in the Vatican II Era: Local Histories of a Global Event* (New York: Cambridge University Press), 135–56

Morris, Charles. 1997. *American Catholic: The Saints and Sinners Who Built America's Most Powerful Church* (New York: Crown)

Morrow, Maria C. 2016. *Sin in the Sixties: Catholics and Confession 1955–1975* (Washington, DC: Catholic University of America Press)

Morrow, Maria C. 2018. 'From Praiseworthy to Blameworthy: The Sacrament of Confession in Mid-Twentieth Century America', *U.S. Catholic Historian* 36/1, 127–50

Mortimer, Ian. 2014. *Centuries of Change: Which Century Saw the Most Change?* (London: Bodley Head)

Murphy-O'Connor, Cormac. 2015. *An English Spring: Memoirs* (London: Bloomsbury)

Muttarak, Raya, and Maria Rita Testa. 2015. 'Trends, Patterns, and Determinants of Interreligious Partnerships in Austria (1971–2001)', in B. J. Grim, T. M. Johnson, V. Skirbekk, and G. A. Zurlo (eds), *International Yearbook of Religious Demography 2015* (Leiden: Brill), 117–35

NatCen Social Research. 2015. *British Social Attitudes 2015 User Guide* (London: NatCen Social Research): http://doc.ukdataservice.ac.uk/doc/8116/mrdoc/pdf/8116_bsa_user_guide_2015.pdf

National Conference of Catholic Bishops. 1966. 'National Statement on Penance and Abstinence': http://www.usccb.org/prayer-and-worship/litur gical-year/lent/us-bishops-pastoral-statement-on-penance-and-abstinence. cfm

National Review. 1957. 'Rock 'n' Roll 'n' All', *National Review*, 9 March, 222–3

Newman, David M. 2010. *Sociology: Exploring the Architecture of Everyday Life* (Thousand Oaks, CA: Pine Forge Press)

Newman, John Henry. [1859–61] 1969. *The Letters and Diaries of John Henry Newman, Vol. XIX: Consulting the Laity, January 1859 to June 1861*, ed. Charles Stephen Desain (London: Thomas Nelson)

Newport, Frank. 2012. *God is Alive and Well: The Future of Religion in America* (New York: Gallup Press)

News Dispatches. 1969. 'Church Demotes 200 Saints: St. Christopher Included', *Washington Post*, 10 May, A1

Nicolaides, Becky, and Andrew Wiese. 2017. 'Suburbanization in the United States after 1945', in John Butler (ed.), *The Oxford Research Encyclopedia of American History*: http://americanhistory.oxfordre.com/view/10.1093/acrefore/9780199329175.001.0001/acrefore-9780199329175-e-64?rskey=TwfRFi&result=46

Niemelä, Kati 2007. 'Alienated or Disappointed? Reasons for Leaving the Church in Finland', *Nordic Journal of Religion and Society* 20/2, 195–216

Nolt, Steven M. 2016. *The Amish: A Concise Introduction* (Baltimore, MD: Johns Hopkins University Press)

Norris, Pippa, and Ronald Inglehart. 2015. 'Are High Levels of Existential Security Conducive to Secularization? A Response to Our Critics', in Stanley D. Brun and Donna A. Gilbreath (eds), *The Changing World Religion Map: Sacred Places, Identities, Practices and Politics* (New York: Springer), 3389–408

O'Dea, Thomas F. 1968. *The Catholic Crisis* (Boston, MA: Beacon Press)

O'Donnell, Ellen. 1998. '"To Keep our Fathers' Faith . . . ": Lithuanian Immigrant Religious Aspirations and the Policy of West of Scotland Catholic Clergy, 1889–1914', *Innes Review* 49/2, 168–83

O'Malley, John W. 2006. 'Vatican II: Did Anything Happen?', *Theological Studies* 67, 3–33

O'Malley, Timothy P. 2014. *Liturgy and the New Evangelization: Practicing the Art of Self-Giving Love* (Collegeville, MN: Liturgical Press)

O'Malley, Timothy P. 2016. 'The Francis Effect Isn't About Numbers', *Church Life Journal*, 29 September: https://churchlife.nd.edu/2016/09/29/the-francis-effect-isnt-about-numbers/

O'Rourke, P. J. 2014. *The Baby Boom: How It Got That Way, And It Wasn't My Fault, And I'll Never Do It Again* (London: Grove Press)

O'Toole, James M. 2000. 'Hear No Evil', *Boston College Magazine*, Fall: http://bcm.bc.edu/issues/fall_2000/features.html

O'Toole, James M. 2008. *The Faithful: A History of Catholics in America* (Cambridge, MA: Harvard University Press)

Observer. 1969. 'MP Attacks Demise of St George', *The Observer*, 11 May, 2

Opdycke, Sandra. 2007. 'The Spaces People Share: The Changing Social Geography of American Life', in Mark C. Carnes (ed.), *The Columbia History of Post-World War II America* (New York: Columbia University Press), 11–35

Orsi, Robert A. 1996. *Thank You, St. Jude: Women's Devotion to the Patron Saint of Lost Causes* (New Haven, CT: Yale University Press)

Orsi, Robert A. 2017. 'What is Catholic about the Clergy Sexual Abuse Crisis?', in Kristin Norget, Valentina Napolitano, and Maya Mayblin (eds), *The Anthropology of Catholicism: A Reader* (Oakland, CA: University of California Press), 283–92

Otterman, Sharon, and Laurie Goodstein. 2018. 'Stirred by Sexual Abuse Report, States Take On Catholic Church', *New York Times*, 6 September: https://www.nytimes.com/2018/09/06/nyregion/catholic-sex-abuse.html

Paice, Lauren. 2008. 'Overspill Policy and the Glasgow Slum Clearance Project in the Twentieth Century: From One Nightmare to Another?',

Reinvention 1/1: http://www2.warwick.ac.uk/go/reinventionjournal/volume1issue1/paice

Pariser, Eli. 2011. *The Filter Bubble: What the Internet is Hiding from You* (London: Penguin)

Pasquale, Frank L. 2007. 'Unbelief and Irreligion, Empirical Study and Neglect of', in Tom Flynn (ed.), *The New Encyclopedia of Unbelief* (Amherst, NY: Prometheus), 760–6

Paul VI. 1966. *Paenitemini*: http://w2.vatican.va/content/paul-vi/en/apost_constitutions/documents/hf_p-vi_apc_19660217_paenitemini.html

Paul VI. 1968. *Humanae Vitae*: http://w2.vatican.va/content/paul-vi/en/encyclicals/documents/hf_p-vi_enc_25071968_humanae-vitae.html

Paul VI. 1969. *Mysterii Paschalis*: https://w2.vatican.va/content/paul-vi/en/motu_proprio/documents/hf_p-vi_motu-proprio_19690214_mysterii-paschalis.html

Paul VI. 1972. 'Omelia di Paolo VI', 29 June: http://w2.vatican.va/content/paul-vi/it/homilies/1972/documents/hf_p-vi_hom_19720629.html

Paul VI. 1975. *Evangelii Nuntiandi*: http://w2.vatican.va/content/paul-vi/en/apost_exhortations/documents/hf_p-vi_exh_19751208_evangelii-nuntiandi.html

Pecklers, Keith F. 1998. *The Unread Vision: The Liturgical Movement in the United States of America, 1926–1955* (Collegeville, MN: Liturgical Press)

Pennsylvania Grand Jury. 2018. 'Report I of the 41st Statewide Investigating Grand Jury', Office of the Attorney General, Commonwealth of Pennsylvania

Penny Catechism. [1958] 2004. *The Penny Catechism: 370 Fundamental Questions and Answers on the Catholic Faith* (Houston, TX: Magnificat Institute Press)

Perrin, Henri. 1947. *Priest-Workman in Germany*, trans. Rosemary Sheed (London: Sheed & Ward)

Pew Hispanic Center. 2012. *When Labels Don't Fit: Hispanics and their Views of Identity*: http://www.pewhispanic.org/files/2012/04/PHC-Hispanic-Identity.pdf

Pew Research Center. 2009. *Faith in Flux: Changes in Religious Affiliation in the U.S.*: http://www.pewforum.org/files/2009/04/fullreport.pdf

Pew Research Center. 2012a. *'Nones' on the Rise: One-in-Five Adults have no Religious Affiliation*: http://www.pewforum.org/files/2012/10/NonesOnTheRise-full.pdf

Pew Research Center. 2012b. *Asian Americans: A Mosaic of Faiths*: http://www.pewforum.org/files/2012/07/Asian-Americans-religion-full-report.pdf

Pew Research Center. 2014. *The Shifting Religious Identity of Latinos in the United States*: http://www.pewforum.org/files/2014/05/Latinos-Religion-07-22-full-report.pdf

Pew Research Center. 2015a. *America's Changing Religious Landscape*: http://
assets.pewresearch.org/wp-content/uploads/sites/11/2015/05/RLS-08-26-full-report.pdf

Pew Research Center. 2015b. *U.S. Public Becoming Less Religious*: http://
assets.pewresearch.org/wp-content/uploads/sites/11/2015/11/201.11.03_
RLS_II_full_report.pdf

Pittsburgh Catholic. 1969. 'Survey Reveals: Devotions and Novenas Losing
Popularity Here', *Pittsburgh Catholic*, 3 January, 1

Pittsburgh Catholic. 1970. 'Ask an End to Obligatory Sunday Mass', *Pittsburgh Catholic*, 3 January, 1

Pius X. 1903. *Tra le Sollecitudini*: http://w2.vatican.va/content/pius-x/la/
motu_proprio/documents/hf_p-x_motu-proprio_19031122_sollecitudini.
html

Pius X. 1905. *Sacra Tridentina*: https://www.ewtn.com/library/CURIA/
CDWFREQ.HTM

Pius XI. 1930. *Casti Connubii*: https://w2.vatican.va/content/pius-xi/en/
encyclicals/documents/hf_p-xi_enc_19301231_casti-connubii.html

Pius XII. 1947. *Mediator Dei*: http://w2.vatican.va/content/pius-xii/en/encyc
licals/documents/hf_p-xii_enc_20111947_mediator-dei.html

Polish Catholic Mission. 2005. *The Polish Catholic Mission in England and
Wales* (London: Polish Catholic Mission)

Pollard, John. 2008. *Catholicism in Modern Italy: Religion, Society and
Politics since 1861* (London: Routledge)

Pontifical Council for Legislative Texts. 2006. *Actus formalis defectionis ab
Ecclesia Catholica*, 13 March: http://www.vatican.va/roman_curia/
pontifical_councils/intrptxt/documents/rc_pc_intrptxt_doc_20060313_
actus-formalis_en.html

Portsmouth Catholic Diocese. 2017. 'Vicariate for Evangelisation': http://
www.portsmouthdiocese.org.uk/evangelisation/

Proctor, Robert. 2014. *Building the Modern Church: Roman Catholic Church
Architecture in Britain, 1955–1975* (London: Routledge)

Putnam, Robert D. 2000. *Bowling Alone: The Collapse and Revival of American
Community* (New York: Simon & Schuster)

Putnam, Robert D., and David E. Campbell. 2010. *American Grace: How
Religion Divides and Unites Us* (New York: Simon & Schuster)

Rahner, Karl. [1954] 1967. 'The Christian among Unbelieving Relations', in
Theological Investigations: Volume III, trans. Karl-H. and Boniface Kruger
(London: Darton, Longman & Todd), 355–72

Ratzinger, Joseph. 1958. 'Die Neuen Heiden und die Kirche', *Hochland* 51,
1–11

Ratzinger, Joseph. 2000. *The Spirit of the Liturgy*, trans. John Saward (San
Francisco, CA: Ignatius Press)

Ratzinger, Joseph. [1983] 2006. 'Handing on the Faith and the Sources of Faith', in Jean-Marie Lustiger and Albert Decourtray (eds), *Handing on the Faith in an Age of Disbelief*, trans. Matthew J. Miller (San Francisco, CA: Ignatius Press), 13–40

Ratzinger, Joseph. [1966] 2009. *Theological Highlights of Vatican II*, trans. H. Traub, G. C. Thormann, and W. Barzel (Mahwah, NJ: Paulist Press)

Regnerus, Mark D. 2007. *Forbidden Fruit: Sex and Religion in the Lives of American Teenagers* (New York: Oxford University Press)

Reid, Alcuin. 2005. *The Organic Development of the Liturgy: The Principles of Liturgical Reform and their Relation to the Twentieth-Century Liturgical Movement Prior to the Second Vatican Council*, 2nd edn (San Francisco, CA: Ignatius Press)

Research and Statistics. 2017. *Statistics for Mission 2016*: https://www.churchofengland.org/sites/default/files/2017-10/2016statisticsformission.pdf

Richter, Philip J., and Leslie J. Francis. 1998. *Gone but not Forgotten: Church Leaving and Returning* (London: Darton, Longman & Todd)

Roberts, W. N. T. 1964. 'Why Do Catholics Lapse? I. The Size of the Problem', *Tablet*, 9 May, 517–19

Robertson, Nan. 1960. 'C. Y. O.'s Annual Contest is Marked by Cheerful, Tearful Din', *New York Times*, 15 February, 29

Rock, John. 1963. *The Time Has Come: A Catholic Doctor's Proposals to End the Battle Over Birth Control* (New York: Alfred Knopf)

Rockett, June. 2001. *Held in Trust: Catholic Parishes in England and Wales, 1900–1950* (London: Saint Austin Press)

Rowland, Tracey. 2010. *Benedict XVI: A Guide for the Perplexed* (London: Continuum)

Russell, Cheryl. 2013. *The Master Trend: How the Baby Boom Generation is Remaking America* (New York: Springer)

Saad, Lydia. 2018. 'Catholics' Church Attendance Resumes Downward Slide', *Gallup*, 9 April: https://news.gallup.com/poll/232226/church-attendance-among-catholics-resumes-downward-slide.aspx

San Francisco Chronicle. 1964. 'Pope Hints at New View on Birth Control', *San Francisco Chronicle*, 24 June, 1

Sarah, Robert. 2017. 'How Catholics Can Welcome LGBT Believers', *Wall Street Journal*, 31 August: https://www.wsj.com/articles/how-catholics-can-welcome-lgbt-believers-1504221027

Satter, David A. 1968. 'Mass Accompanied by Jazz Band, Dance', *Washington Post*, 23 August, D15

Scanlon, Margaret. 2009. 'Why I Stay', in Kate Dugan and Jennifer Owens (eds), *From the Pews in the Back: Young Women and Catholicism* (Collegeville, MN: Liturgical Press), 92–5

Schnabel, Landon, and Sean Bock. 2017. 'The Persistent and Exceptional Intensity of American Religion: A Response to Recent Research', *Sociological Science* 4, 686–700

Schreck, Alan. 2017. *A Mighty Current of Grace: The Story of the Catholic Charismatic Renewal* (Frederick, MD: The Word Among Us Press)

Schultz, Thom, and Joani Schultz. 2014. *Why Nobody Wants to Go to Church Anymore: And How 4 Acts of Love Will Make Your Church Irresistible* (Loveland, CO: Group Publishing)

Scorer, Richard. 2014. *Betrayed: The English Catholic Church and the Sex Abuse Crisis* (London: Biteback)

Scott, George. 1967. *The R.C.s: A Report on Catholics in Britain Today* (London: Hutchinson)

Seitz, John C. 2011. *No Closure: Catholic Practice and Boston's Parish Shutdowns* (Boston, MA: Harvard University Press)

Sewell, Dennis. 2001. *Catholics: Britain's Largest Minority* (London: Viking)

Shaw, Russell. 2013. *American Church: The Remarkable Rise, Meteoric Fall, and Uncertain Future of Catholicism in America* (San Francisco, CA: Ignatius Press)

Sheed, Frank. 1968. *Is It the Same Church?* (London: Sheed & Ward)

Sherkat, Darren E. 2014. *Changing Faith: The Dynamics and Consequences of Americans' Shifting Religious Identities* (New York: New York University Press)

Simpson, Mark. 2014. *End of Gays?* (Amazon: Kindle Single)

Singer, Eleanor. 2006. 'Introduction: Nonresponse Bias in Household Surveys', *Public Opinion Quarterly* 70/5, 637–45

Singleton, Ronald. 1965. 'Jesuit Prelate Attacks Vatican on Pill', *Daily Mail*, 13 October, 8

Smith, K. Annabelle. 2013. 'The Fishy History of the McDonald's Filet-O-Fish Sandwich', *Smithsonian Magazine*, 1 March: http://www.smithsonianmag.com/arts-culture/the-fishy-history-of-the-mcdonalds-filet-o-fish-sandwich-2912/

Smith, Anthony Burke. 1997. 'Prime-Time Catholicism in 1950s America: Fulton J. Sheen and "Life Is Worth Living"', *U.S. Catholic Historian* 15/3, 57–74

Smith, C., K. Longest, J. Hill, and K. Christofferson. 2014. *Young Catholic America: Emerging Adults In, Out of, and Gone from the Church* (Oxford: Oxford University Press)

Smith, Christian. 2018. *Religion: What It Is, How It Works, and Why It Matters* (Princeton, NJ: Princeton University Press)

Smith, Christian, and Melina Lundquist Denton. 2005. *Soul Searching: The Religious and Spiritual Lives of American Teenagers* (New York: Oxford University Press)

Smith, Dave. 2017. 'The Epistles for All Christians', unpublished PhD thesis, St Mary's University, Twickenham

Smith, Janet E. 1991. *Humanae Vitae: A Generation Later* (Washington, DC: Catholic University of America Press)

Smith, Tom W., Peter V. Marsden, and Michael Hout. 2015. *General Social Surveys, 1972–2014: Cumulative Codebook* (Chicago: National Opinion Research Center)

Smith, William G. 2008. 'Does Gender Influence Online Survey Participation? A Record-Linkage Analysis of University Faculty Online Survey Response Behavior', *ERIC* (Institute of Education Services): http://files.eric.ed.gov/fulltext/ED501717.pdf

Sokolov, Ivan. 2013. *Sacrifice and Initiative in Chess: Seize the Moment to Get the Advantage* (Alkmaar: New In Chess)

Spencer, Anthony E. C. W. 1975. 'Demography of Catholicism', *Month* 236, 100–5

Spencer, Anthony E. C. W. 2008. 'The Suppression of a Research Report. Another Long, Slow Failure. Reflections on a Very Secret Disaster': https://www.prct.org.uk/component/edocman/the-suppression-of-a-research-report-text/download?Itemid

Spencer, Anthony E. C. W. [1960] 2012. *Arrangements for the Integration of Irish Immigrants in England and Wales*, ed. Mary E. Daly (Dublin: Irish Manuscripts Commission)

Spencer, Anthony E. C. W. 2014. 'An Assessment of the Catholic Statistics in the 2014 Edition of the Catholic Directory. Part II. Mass Attendance, Baptisms, Marriages & Receptions': https://www.prct.org.uk/blogs

Spielmann, Rudolf. [1935] 1995. *The Art of Sacrifice in Chess*, trans. J. du Mont (New York: Dover)

Spretnak, Charlene. 2004. *Missing Mary: The Queen of Heaven and Her Re-Emergence in the Modern Church* (New York: Palgrave Macmillan)

Stachura, Peter D. 1999. *Poland in the Twentieth Century* (Basingstoke: Palgrave Macmillan)

Stark, Rodney. 2015. *The Triumph of Faith: Why the World is More Religious Than Ever* (Wilmington, DE: ISI Books)

Stark, Rodney, and Charles Y. Glock. 1968. *American Piety: The Nature of Religious Commitment* (Berkeley, CA: University of California Press)

Steensland, B., J. Z. Park, M. D. Regnerus, L. D. Robinson, W. B. Wilcox, and R. D. Woodberry. 2000. 'The Measure of American Religion: Toward Improving the State of the Art', *Social Forces* 79/1, 291–318

Steinfels, Peter. 2003. *A People Adrift: The Crisis of the Roman Catholic Church in America* (New York: Simon & Schuster)

Storm, Ingrid, and David Voas. 2012. 'The Intergenerational Transmission of Religious Service Attendance', *Nordic Journal of Religion and Society* 25/2, 131–50

Streib, H., R. W. Hood, B. Keller, R.-M. Csöff, and C. F. Silver. 2009. *Deconversion: Qualitative and Quantitative Results from Cross-Cultural Research in Germany and the United States of America* (Göttingen: Vandenhoeck & Ruprecht)

Stump, Roger W. 1986. 'Patterns in the Survival of Catholic National Parishes, 1940–1980', *Journal of Cultural Geography* 7/1, 77–97

Summerfield, Penny, and Nicole Crockett. 1992. '"You Weren't Taught That with the Welding": Lessons in Sexuality in the Second World War', *Women's History Review* 1/3, 435–54

Tablet. 1962. 'The Central Commission and Sexual Morality', *Tablet*, 12 May, 459

Tablet. 1964a. 'Varying the Vernacular', *Tablet*, 14 November, 1310

Tablet. 1964b. 'From Our Notebook', *Tablet*, 5 December, 1382

Tablet. 1964c. 'The English Bishops on Schema 13', *Tablet*, 31 October, 1244–5

Tablet. 1967. 'Talking at Random', *Tablet*, 14 October, 1069

Taylor, Charles. 2007. *A Secular Age* (Cambridge, MA: Belknap Press)

Tentler, Leslie Woodcock. 1990. *Seasons of Grace: A History of the Catholic Archdiocese of Detroit* (Detroit, MI: Wayne State University Press)

Tentler, Leslie Woodcock. 2004. *Catholics and Contraception: An American History* (Ithaca, NY: Cornell University Press)

Tentler, Leslie Woodcock. 2018. 'Through the Prism of Race: The Archdiocese of Detroit', in Kathleen Sprows Cummings, Timothy Matovina, and Robert A. Orsi (eds), *Catholics in the Vatican II Era: Local Histories of a Global Event* (New York: Cambridge University Press), 89–109

Thompson, Damian. 2005. *Waiting for Antichrist: Charisma and Apocalypse in a Pentecostal Church* (New York: Oxford University Press)

Thompson, Damian. 2015. 'Memories of the Catholic Ghetto', *Catholic Herald*, 20 November, 44

Thompson, Damian. 2018. 'Five Years of Pope Francis: Five Things You Need to Know', *Spectator*, 14 March: https://blogs.spectator.co.uk/2018/03/five-years-of-pope-francis-five-things-you-need-to-know/

Thompson, John J. 2000. *Raised by Wolves: The Story of Christian Rock & Roll* (Toronto: ECW Press)

Thumma, Scott, and Warren Bird. 2015. *Recent Shifts in America's Largest Protestant Churches: Megachurches 2015 Report*: http://www.hartfordinstitute.org/megachurch/2015_Megachurches_Report.pdf

Time. 1949. 'Religion: Revival in England', *Time*, 9 May: http://content.time.com/time/magazine/article/0,9171,800246,00.html

Tocqueville, Alexis de. [1831] 1996. 'Tocqueville's Essay on Religion and Government in America', in George Wilson Pierson (ed.), *Tocqueville in America* (Baltimore, MD: Johns Hopkins University Press), 152–62

Topping, Alexandra. 2015. 'Stonewall Chief: "It's a Better Time to be Gay. But Not for All"', *Guardian*, 31 May: https://www.theguardian.com/

world/2015/may/31/with-gay-rights-in-law-but-bullying-rife-stonewall-redraws-battle-lines

Towey, Anthony. 2009. '*Dei Verbum*: Fit for Purpose?', *New Blackfriars* 90/1026, 206–18

Trzebiatowska, Marta, and Steve Bruce. 2012. *Why are Women More Religious than Men?* (Oxford: Oxford University Press)

Turnham, Margaret H. 2012. 'Roman Catholic Revivalism: A Study of the Area that Became the Diocese of Middlesbrough, 1779–1992', unpublished PhD thesis, University of Nottingham, UK

Turnham, Margaret H. 2015. *Catholic Faith and Practice in England, 1779–1992: The Role of Revivalism and Renewal* (Woodbridge: Boydell Press)

Turpin, Hugh. 2018. 'Failing God? A Cognitive Anthropological Examination of the Relationship Between Catholic Scandals and Irish Secularisation', unpublished PhD thesis, Queen's University Belfast, UK, and University of Aarhus, Denmark

Turpin, Hugh, Marc Andersen, and Jonathan A. Lanman. 2018. 'CREDs, CRUDs, and Catholic Scandals: Experimentally Examining the Effects of Religious Paragon Behavior on Co-religionist Belief', *Religion, Brain & Behavior* (online early publication)

Tushnet, Eve. 2014. *Gay and Catholic: Accepting My Sexuality, Finding Community, Living My Faith* (Notre Dame, IN: Ave Maria Press)

Üffing, Martin. 2013. 'Catholic Mission in Europe 1910–2010', in Stephen B. Bevans (ed.), *A Century of Catholic Mission: Roman Catholic Missiology 1910 to the Present* (Oxford: Regnum), 34–43

Untener, Ken. [1999] 2007. 'Is the Church in Decline? An Optimistic Bishop Says "No"', in Ken Untener, *The Practical Prophet: Pastoral Writings* (Mahwah, NJ: Paulist Press), 38–48

US Census Bureau. 2017. 'Income, Poverty and Health Insurance Coverage in the United States: 2016', 12 September: https://www.census.gov/newsroom/press-releases/2017/income-povery.html

Vatican II. 1963. *Sacrosanctum Concilium* ('Dogmatic Constitution on the Sacred Liturgy'): http://www.vatican.va/archive/hist_councils/ii_vatican_council/documents/vat-ii_const_19631204_sacrosanctum-concilium_en.html

Vatican II. 1964. *Lumen Gentium* ('Dogmatic Constitution on the Church'): http://www.vatican.va/archive/hist_councils/ii_vatican_council/documents/vat-ii_const_19641121_lumen-gentium_en.html

Vatican II. 1965a. *Gaudium et Spes* ('Pastoral Constitution on the Church in the World of Today'): http://www.vatican.va/archive/hist_councils/ii_vati can_council/documents/vat-ii_cons_19651207_gaudium-et-spes_en.html

Vatican II. 1965b. *Apostolicam Actuositatem* ('Decree on the Laity'): http://www.vatican.va/archive/hist_councils/ii_vatican_council/documents/vat-ii_decree_19651118_apostolicam-actuositatem_en.html

Vatican II. 1965c. *Dei Verbum* ('Dogmatic Constitution on Divine Revelation'): http://www.vatican.va/archive/hist_councils/ii_vatican_council/documents/vat-ii_const_19651118_dei-verbum_en.html

Vaughan-Spruce, Hannah. 2018. *A Handbook for Catechists* (London: Catholic Truth Society)

Vernon, Glenn M. 1968. 'The Religious "Nones": A Neglected Category', *Journal for the Scientific Study of Religion* 7/2, 219–29

Voas, David. 2003. 'Intermarriage and the Demography of Secularization', *British Journal of Sociology* 54/1, 83–108

Voas, David. 2009. 'The Rise and Fall of Fuzzy Fidelity in Europe', *European Sociological Review* 25/2, 155–68

Voas, David. 2015. 'The Mysteries of Religion and the Lifecourse', *CLS Working Papers* 2015/1: http://www.cls.ioe.ac.uk/shared/get-file.ashx?itemtype=document&id=1985

Voas, David, and Steve Bruce. 2004. 'Research Note: The 2001 Census and Christian Identification in Britain', *Journal of Contemporary Religion* 19/1, 23–8

Voas, David, and Mark Chaves. 2016. 'Is the United States a Counterexample to the Secularization Thesis?', *American Journal of Sociology* 121/5, 1517–52

Voas, David, and Siobhan McAndrew. 2012. 'Three Puzzles of Non-Religion in Britain', *Journal of Contemporary Religion* 27/1, 29–48

Walch, Timothy. 1989. *Catholicism in America: A Social History* (Malabar, FL: Krieger)

Walker, Paul D. 2002. 'Prophetic or Premature? The Metropolitan Cathedral of Christ the King, Liverpool', *Theology* 105/825, 185–93

Walser, Robert. 1992. 'The Polka Mass: Music of Postmodern Ethnicity', *American Music* 10/2, 183–202

Washington Post. 1966. 'Text of Statement Abolishing Meatless Fridays', *Washington Post*, 23 November, A16

Waxman, Chaim I. 2001. *Jewish Baby Boomers: A Communal Perspective* (Albany, NY: State University of New York Press)

Weber, Max. [1906] 2002. '"Churches" and "Sects" in North America: An Ecclesiastical and Sociopolitical Sketch', in *The Protestant Ethic and the "Spirit" of Capitalism and Other Writings*, ed. and trans. Peter Baehr and Gordon C. Wells (London: Penguin), 203–20

Webster, Wendy. 2013. '"Fit to Fight, Fit to Mix": Sexual Patriotism in Second World War Britain', *Women's History Review* 20/4, 607–24

Weddell, Sherry A. 2012. *Forming Intentional Disciples: The Path to Knowing and Following Jesus* (Huntington, IN: Our Sunday Visitor)

Weigel, George. 2005. *The Cube and the Cathedral: Europe, America, and Politics Without God* (New York: Basic Books)

Weil, Martin. 1968a. '200 Walk Out on Cardinal during Masses', *Washington Post*, 23 September, A1

Weil, Martin. 1968b. 'Birth Control is Debated at Mass', *Washington Post*, 9 September, A1

Welch, Michael R. 1993. 'Religious Participation and Commitment among Catholic Parishioners: The Relative Importance of Individual, Contextual, and Institutional Factors', in David A. Roozen and C. Kirk Hadaway (eds), *Church and Denominational Growth: What Does (and Does Not) Cause Growth or Decline* (Nashville, TN: Abingdon Press), 324–45

Welsh, Thomas G. 2012. *Closing Chapters: Urban Change, Religious Reform, and the Decline of Youngstown's Catholic Elementary Schools, 1960–2006* (Lanham, MD: Lexington Books)

Welton, Violet. 1961. 'Two Tables', in David L. Edwards (ed.), *Priests and Workers: An Anglo-French Discussion* (London: SCM Press), 11–23

Werner-Leggett, Aenne. 2012. *Being Mary? Irish Catholic Immigrant Women and Home and Community Building in Harold Hill Essex 1947–1970* (The Hague: Eleven International)

White, James Emery. 2014. *The Rise of the Nones: Understanding and Reaching the Religiously Unaffiliated* (Grand Rapids, MI: Baker Books)

White, James F. 2003. *Roman Catholic Worship: Trent to Today* (Collegeville, MN: Liturgical Press)

White, Joseph M. 2007. *Worthy of the Gospel of Christ: A History of the Catholic Diocese of Fort Wayne-South Bend* (Huntington, IN: Our Sunday Visitor)

Wilcox, W. B., A. J. Cherlin, J. E. Uecker, and M. Messel. 2012. 'No Money, No Honey, No Church: The Deinstitutionalization of Religious Life Among the White Working Class', in L. A. Keister, J. McCarthy, and R. Finke (eds), *Religion, Work, and Inequality* (Bingley: Emerald), 227–50

Wilde, Melissa J., and Sabrina Danielsen. 2014. 'Fewer and Better Children: Race, Class, Religion, and Birth Control Reform in America', *American Journal of Sociology*, 119/6, 1710–60

Willard, Aiyana K., Joseph Henrich, and Ara Norenzayan. 2016. 'Memory and Belief in the Transmission of Counterintuitive Content', *Human Nature* 27, 221–43

Willen, Patricia. 2012. 'A Lost Generation?: Fewer Young Women are Practicing their Faith: How the Church Can Woo Them Back', *America*, 20 February: https://www.americamagazine.org/issue/5129/article/lost-generation

Williams, Simon. 2016. 'The Euphoria of a Queen Sacrifice': https://www.chess.com/article/view/the-euphoria-of-a-queen-sacrifice

Williamson, Clifford. 2016. *The History of Catholic Intellectual Life in Scotland, 1918–1965* (Basingstoke: Palgrave Macmillan)

Wills, Garry. 1972. *Bare Ruined Choirs* (Garden City, NY: Doubleday)

Wolfe, Thomas. [1940] 2011. *You Can't Go Home Again* (New York: Scribner)

Woodhead, Linda. 2016. 'The Rise of "No Religion" in Britain: The Emergence of a New Cultural Majority', *Journal of the British Academy* 4, 245–61

Woodhead, Linda. 2017. 'The Rise of "No Religion": Towards an Explanation', *Sociology of Religion* 78/3, 247–62

Wright, B. R. E., D. Giovanelli, E. G. Dolan, and M. E. Edwards. 2011. 'Explaining Deconversion from Christianity: A Study of Online Narratives', *Journal of Religion & Society* 13, 1–17

Wuthnow, Robert. 1988. *The Restructuring of American Religion: Society and Faith since World War II* (Princeton, NJ: Princeton University Press)

Wuthnow, Robert. 2007. *After the Baby Boomers: How Twenty—and Thirty—Somethings Are Shaping the Future of American Religion* (Princeton, NJ: Princeton University Press)

Wuthnow, Robert. 2014. *Rough Country: How Texas Became America's Most Powerful Bible-Belt State* (Princeton, NJ: Princeton University Press)

Wuthnow, Robert. 2015. *Inventing American Religion: Polls, Surveys, and the Tenuous Quest for a Nation's Faith* (Oxford: Oxford University Press)

Yamane, David. 2014. *Becoming Catholic: Finding Rome in the American Religious Landscape* (Oxford: Oxford University Press)

Yates, Ivan. 1964. 'Mass in English Today', *The Observer*, 29 November, 4

Zuckerman, Phil. 2011. *Faith No More: Why People Reject Religion* (New York: Oxford University Press)

Index